The Windows® 98 Registry: A Survival Guide for Users

John Woram

MIS:Press
An imprint of IDG Books Worldwide, Inc.

Foster City, CA ■ Chicago, IL ■ Indianapolis, IN ■ New York, NY

The Windows® 98 Registry: A Survival Guide for Users

Published by
MIS:Press
An imprint of IDG Books Worldwide, Inc.
An International Data Group Company
919 E. Hillsdale Blvd., Suite 400
Foster City, CA 94404
www.idgbooks.com (IDG Books Worldwide Web site)

Library of Congress Catalog Card Number: 98-88722

ISBN: 1-55828-591-1

Printed in the United States of America

10 9 8 7 6 5 4 3

1P/SS/QS/ZZ/IN

Distributed in the United States by IDG Books Worldwide, Inc.

Distributed by Macmillan Canada for Canada; by Transworld Publishers Limited in the United Kingdom; by IDG Norge Books for Norway; by IDG Sweden Books for Sweden; by Woodslane Pty. Ltd. for Australia; by Woodslane (NZ) Ltd. for New Zealand; by Addison Wesley Longman Singapore Pte Ltd. for Singapore, Malaysia, Thailand, and Indonesia; by Norma Comunicaciones S.A. for Colombia; by Intersoft for South Africa; by International Thomson Publishing for Germany, Austria and Switzerland; by Distribuidora Cuspide for Argentina; by Livraria Cultura for Brazil; by Ediciencia S.A. for Ecuador; by Ediciones ZETA S.C.R. Ltda. for Peru; by WS Computer Publishing Corporation, Inc., for the Philippines; by Contemporanea de Ediciones for Venezuela; by Express Computer Distributors for the Caribbean and West Indies; by Micronesia Media Distributor, Inc. for Micronesia; by Grupo Editorial Norma S.A. for Guatemala; by Chips Computadoras S.A. de C.V. for Mexico; by Editorial Norma de Panama S.A. for Panama; by Wouters Import for Belgium; by American Bookshops for Finland. Authorized Sales Agent: Anthony Rudkin Associates for the Middle East and North Africa.

For general information on IDG Books Worldwide's books in the U.S., please call our Consumer Customer Service department at 800-762-2974. For reseller information, including discounts and premium sales, please call our Reseller Customer Service department at 800-434-3422.

For information on where to purchase IDG Books Worldwideís books outside the U.S., please contact our International Sales department at 317-596-5530 or fax 317-596-5692.

For consumer information on foreign language translations, please contact our Customer Service department at 800-434-3422, fax 317-596-5692, or e-mail rights@idgbooks.com.

For information on licensing foreign or domestic rights, please phone +1-650-655-3109.

For sales inquiries and special prices for bulk quantities, please contact our Sales department at 650-655-3200 or write to the address above.

For information on using IDG Books Worldwideís books in the classroom or for ordering examination copies, please contact our Educational Sales department at 800-434-2086 or fax 317-596-5499.

For press review copies, author interviews, or other publicity information, please contact our Public Relations department at 650-655-3000 or fax 650-655-3299.

For authorization to photocopy items for corporate, personal, or educational use, please contact Copyright Clearance Center, 222 Rosewood Drive, Danvers, MA 01923, or fax 978-750-4470.

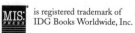

ABOUT IDG BOOKS WORLDWIDE

Welcome to the world of IDG Books Worldwide.

IDG Books Worldwide, Inc., is a subsidiary of International Data Group, the world's largest publisher of computer-related information and the leading global provider of information services on information technology. IDG was founded more than 30 years ago by Patrick J. McGovern and now employs more than 9,000 people worldwide. IDG publishes more than 290 computer publications in over 75 countries. More than 90 million people read one or more IDG publications each month.

Launched in 1990, IDG Books Worldwide is today the #1 publisher of best-selling computer books in the United States. We are proud to have received eight awards from the Computer Press Association in recognition of editorial excellence and three from Computer Currents' First Annual Readers' Choice Awards. Our best-selling ...For Dummies® series has more than 50 million copies in print with translations in 31 languages. IDG Books Worldwide, through a joint venture with IDG's Hi-Tech Beijing, became the first U.S. publisher to publish a computer book in the People's Republic of China. In record time, IDG Books Worldwide has become the first choice for millions of readers around the world who want to learn how to better manage their businesses.

Our mission is simple: Every one of our books is designed to bring extra value and skill-building instructions to the reader. Our books are written by experts who understand and care about our readers. The knowledge base of our editorial staff comes from years of experience in publishing, education, and journalism — experience we use to produce books to carry us into the new millennium. In short, we care about books, so we attract the best people. We devote special attention to details such as audience, interior design, use of icons, and illustrations. And because we use an efficient process of authoring, editing, and desktop publishing our books electronically, we can spend more time ensuring superior content and less time on the technicalities of making books.

You can count on our commitment to deliver high-quality books at competitive prices on topics you want to read about. At IDG Books Worldwide, we continue in the IDG tradition of delivering quality for more than 30 years. You'll find no better book on a subject than one from IDG Books Worldwide.

John Kilcullen
Chairman and CEO
IDG Books Worldwide, Inc.

Steven Berkowitz
President and Publisher
IDG Books Worldwide, Inc.

IDG is the world's leading IT media, research and exposition company. Founded, in 1964, IDG had 1997 revenues of $2.05 billion and has more than 9,000 employees worldwide. IDG offers the widest range of media options that reach IT buyers in 75 countries representing 95% of worldwide IT spending. IDG's diverse product and services portfolio spans six key areas including print publishing, online publishing, expositions and conferences, market research, education and training, and global marketing services. More than 90 million people read one or more of IDG's 290 magazines and newspapers, including IDG's leading global brands — Computerworld, PC World, Network World, Macworld and the Channel World family of publications. IDG Books Worldwide is one of the fastest-growing computer book publishers in the world, with more than 700 titles in 36 languages. The "...For Dummies®" series alone has more than 50 million copies in print. IDG offers online users the largest network of technology-specific Web sites around the world through IDG.net (http://www.idg.net), which comprises more than 225 targeted Web sites in 55 countries worldwide. International Data Corporation (IDC) is the world's largest provider of information technology data, analysis and consulting, with research centers in over 41 countries and more than 400 research analysts worldwide. IDG World Expo is a leading producer of more than 168 globally branded conferences and expositions in 35 countries including E3 (Electronic Entertainment Expo), Macworld Expo, ComNet, Windows World Expo, ICE (Internet Commerce Expo), Agenda, DEMO, and Spotlight. IDG's training subsidiary, ExecuTrain, is the world's largest computer training company, with more than 230 locations worldwide and 785 training courses. IDG Marketing Services helps industry-leading IT companies build international brand recognition by developing global integrated marketing programs via IDG's print, online and exposition products worldwide. Further information about the company can be found at www.idg.com.   10/8/98

Credits

Acquisitions Editor
Debra Williams Cauley

Development Editor
Matthew E. Lusher

Technical Editor
Serdar Yegulalp

Copy Editors
Nancy Crumpton
Michael D. Welch

Project Coordinator
Regina Snyder

Cover Coordinator
Andreas Schueller

Book Designer
Kurt Krames

Graphics and Page Layout
Lou Boudreau, Tyler Connor,
Angela F. Hunckler, Todd Klemme,
Brent Savage, Kathie S. Schutte,
Michael A. Sullivan

Proofreaders
Christine Berman, Kelli Botta
Rebecca Senninger, Rob Springer,
Janet M. Withers

Indexer
Sherry Massey

About the Author

John Woram is Consulting Editor at *Windows Magazine*, where he writes the monthly "Optimize Windows" column. He is the author of the extremely successful *PC Configuration Handbook*, which has sold over 250,000 copies and has been translated into six foreign languages. His previous book, *The Windows 95 Registry*, was a finalist for the 1996 Computer Press Association's "How-To Book" award.

*To Christina Marie,
still my one and only Hkey*

Preface

WARNING: Using Registry Editor incorrectly can cause serious problems that may require you to reinstall Windows 95. Microsoft cannot guarantee that problems resulting from the incorrect use of Registry Editor can be solved. Use Registry Editor at your own risk.

With minor variations, this cheery little greeting now appears in more than 300 Microsoft technical papers—an increase of some 200+ since *The Windows 95 Registry: A Survival Guide for Users* was published in late 1996. The message—complete with Windows 95 citation—even appears in some Windows 98 papers, although in others "Windows 95" has been updated to "the operating system." But whatever the words, one has the impression that Microsoft is still not overly enthusiastic about having its customers mess around with the Registry.

For those who insist, online help is available in Windows 95: Just click the Start menu's Help icon, look up "Registry," and you'll be invited to click a checkbox if you want your Registry restored, assuming of course that your network administrator has set up a backup agent on the server— assuming of course that you actually have a network, an administrator, a backup agent, and a server. Now then, what more could anyone possibly want to know about the Registry? It doesn't get much better in Windows 98, where a search for "Registry" turns up a handful of topics, most of which are little more than links to a Registry Checker applet.

In short, the Windows Registry is not entirely undocumented, but it comes close. Take away the restoration warnings, and it comes even closer. Hence this book, whose premise is that the Registry is right up there with death and taxes—unavoidable, rarely pleasant, but always something one wants to know a bit more about, if only to better cope with its mysteries. For like it or not, the Registry is about as inconsequential to the Windows system as the human brain is to the Windows user. Fortunately, further analysis of the relationship between Windows and brains is beyond the scope of the present treatment, which has quite enough to do explaining the basic mechanics of the Registry, how to tune it, and what to do when it breaks down.

Although one should never underestimate the power of the Registry to bring the system down, it is actually quite clever about curing itself whenever something, or someone, makes it sick. In the course of preparing this Windows 98 book and before that, its Windows 95 predecessor, various Registries were subjected to just about every indignity imaginable, often just to see what would happen if the Registry got kicked really hard here, and here, and there, too. Often enough, it would just bounce back without complaining, at least until even more elegant tortures were devised. But— and Microsoft's repeated warning notwithstanding— it was never necessary to execute the ultimate restoration technique, that of completely reinstalling Windows, to recover from a Registry indiscretion.

From the point of view of the typical user, it is often possible to edit the Registry by indirect means— that is, to make a configuration change via the Control Panel or the Tweak UI applet or by some other means, and just let Windows attend to the Registry on its own. So if you find yourself wondering "Wouldn't it be easier to just . . . ," the answer may very well be, "Yes". But this is a book about the Registry and how it handles the road, regardless of who's driving it. Sometimes, the easier path is mentioned; other times it's not. And at still other times, there is no easier path: Either you edit the Registry, or you do without. But regardless of who, or what, does the editing, it always helps to know a little something about how it all comes together. And in the Registry, it is sometimes a wonder that it comes together at all.

Structure of This Book

Describing the Registry is not unlike describing a bowl of spaghetti. Where do all the strands begin, and where do they end? No doubt there are beginnings and endings, but they're not always easy to find. Which brings us (or at least, me) to the first problem: how to unravel the Registry and lay it out for viewing and dissection. For better or worse, here's how it was done.

Although this opus is hardly symphonic, it is divided into four sections— some even slower than others. These are:

- Introduction and overview (Chapters 1–3)
- Editing and maintenance tools (Chapters 4 and 5)
- Customization techniques (Chapter 6)
- Troubleshooting (Chapters 7 and 8).

The first chapter offers a general introduction to the Registry and the Registry Editor utility, which is then used in Chapters 2 and 3 as a magnifying glass through which to view each of the Registry's six keys, one at a time. Because the user will no doubt spend a lot of time in the key known as *HKEY_CLASSES_ROOT*, all of Chapter 2 is devoted to its subkey structure, and then Chapter 3 covers the everything-else of the Registry key structure.

Given the internal relationships between one key and almost any other, a certain amount of back-and-forth work is required, so it may be best to quickly skim Chapters 2 and 3 and then go back for a closer read. Although a few keys are explained in detail out of proportion to their actual worth, these explanations can help you develop a basic understanding of similar key structures occurring elsewhere in the Registry.

The serious business begins in Chapter 4, where the Registry Editor is put to work as an editing tool. It doesn't take very long to discover a trio of qualities: it's fast, it's quiet, and it's dangerous. It protects itself against little accidents up to a point — it won't enable you to delete an entire HKEY, and it does offer an "Are you sure?" prompt when a subkey or Name entry is about to be erased. But once the entry is gone, it's gone forever. In the land of the Registry Editor, there's no such thing as an undo function. Or to put it another way, you can cut, but you can't paste. With that in mind, Chapter 5 on Registry maintenance deserves careful reading. Although Windows 98's self-restoring power is even greater than its predecessor, it's still not a bad idea to take out a bit of extra insurance before embarking on a serious editing trip. If you depend on Windows to do the job all by itself, it often will. But in fixing the edits you don't really want, it fixes the others, too, so take the time to save anything that's important. With luck you won't need it. But it'll be there if and when your luck runs out. You can think of Chapter 5 as techno-flossing: it's not that much fun, but it's good for you.

If you've done your homework and finished all your chores, it's time for a break. Chapter 6 covers various ways in which Registry edits can be used to customize anyone's Windows configuration. Because the Registry itself is so poorly documented (with the exception of what you're reading, of course), it may be unnecessary to point out that many of the edits described in this book are worse than poorly documented — they're not documented at all. Although the edits have been tested and retested under a variety of configurations, there's always a chance that under some other configuration the edit won't work as expected. So in case the unexpected does happen, it pays to remember that operators are *not* standing by. And that's why this chapter is followed by one that describes — if not all, then at least, some of — the things that can go wrong while wading through the previous chapters. The perceptive reader may detect a striking resemblance to the things that can go wrong while *not* wading through the previous chapters. So whenever bad things happen and the Registry is a prime suspect, you should start searching for evidence in Chapter 7. However, if a problem is polite enough to announce itself by displaying a message, then try Chapter 8, where such messages are lined up for inspection. Some messages are self-explanatory, while others border on the incomprehensible. If you encounter one of the latter, perhaps the explanation offered in this book will help. And if neither the message nor the explanation is enough to resolve the problem, then you'll find a reference to a section in the previous chapter, or to an earlier part of the book, where the required information can be found.

Conventions

And now, a few words about a question that has puzzled philosophers since August 24, 1995. When is a folder not a folder? To anyone who has already typed REGEDIT.EXE in the Run box, there's only one answer: when it's a Registry key. In fact, a Registry window can sometimes look quite like a Windows Explorer window, as shown here in Figure 1. Without looking at the Title and Menu bars, can you tell which is the Registry and which is not? Perhaps not, and even this minor oversight can be straightened out later on (in Chapter 6), but in the meantime, just remember that in the Registry, if it looks like a folder, and if it opens like a folder, it's a key.

This book contains many views of the Registry Editor window, not a few of which have been doctored a bit to present the most amount of useful information accompanied by the least amount of useless white space. In other words, many figures offer a composite view of several keys' worth of data, although the Registry itself divulges its contents only one subkey at a time. Figure 1-1 in Chapter 1 is as good an example as any. If this had been a real Registry window, only one of the open keys would be visible at a time. A line and arrow often lead from an open key to its contents, which is not really necessary in this one-line-per-key illustration but may be helpful elsewhere (in Figure 4-1, for example), when each of several keys leads to multiple lines of data. In other figures, a line runs from one location to another, serving as a visual aid in tracking the relationship between two or more Registry components. Needless to say, all these arrows and lines and composite views don't exist in real life — if one can consider the Registry as part of anyone's real life.

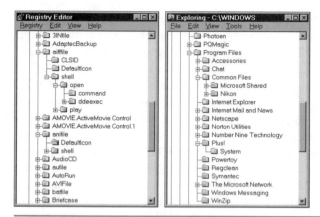

Figure 1 *At first glance, the Registry Editor window's Key pane bears a
close resemblance to a conventional Windows Explorer window.
Despite appearances, those icons on the left are keys, not folders.
Each one can be opened or closed, most can be renamed or
deleted, but none can be moved.*

In the interests of saving horizontal space, many lengthy key names and
Contents pane Data entries are broken into two lines, although the
Registry Editor itself does not offer a similar word-wrap feature. Here and
there, a figure inset shows an item related to — but not part of — the rest
of the illustration. Because many illustrations show Registry sections that
are actually at some distance from each other, a double tilde (≈) indicates a
point where intervening keys are omitted. A single tilde (~) terminates a
line leading to additional keys that are all omitted.

If the Registry Editor's Status bar is enabled, it displays the identity of
the currently open key, which leads to a potential problem in those illustrations that show more than one open key. Accordingly, an ellipsis (...) at the
end of any Status bar line indicates a line that has been edited to include only
that segment of the complete path that is common to all displayed keys.

Four PCs were used as Registry guinea pigs in preparing this book. The
PCs were configured as follows: Windows 98 with (as if there were a
choice) Internet Explorer 4 and Netscape Navigator 4.04, Windows 95
SR2.1 with Internet Explorer 4, Windows 95 SR2 with Internet 3,
Windows 95 original version with no Internet browser. All four systems
(plus two printers) were linked via the Windows 98/95 peer-to-peer networking software that comes with both versions of the operating system.
Additional free-standing Windows systems were tested from time to time,
just to make sure their behavior (or lack thereof) matched the test systems.

Wherever appropriate, significant variations are noted in the text. Although the described procedures worked on all systems tested, this is no guarantee that every suggestion found in here will work on every system found out there. Many Registry edits (especially in Chapter 6) are not yet supported by any known application — perhaps because they weren't intended for general use, or perhaps because they are to be introduced as "new" features in the future.

To end at the beginning, remember the warning: "Using Registry Editor incorrectly can cause serious problems. . . ." But using Registry Editor correctly can cause serious improvements, or if not that, then at least a few enhancements to the Windows operating system. Proceed with caution, make an extra backup, and all should be well.

And now, let the confusion begin.

Acknowledgments

This is the part that almost nobody ever reads where, under the guise of profuse thanks, the author publicly identifies those who can later be implicated for whatever is wrong with the manuscript.

Before there was a manuscript, however, there was a meeting. This was in the earliest days of Windows 95, and it led to my previous book about the same subject you see here. Paul Farrell — now associate publisher at IDG Books Worldwide — thought a book about the emerging Windows Registry might not be a bad idea, and I thought I knew at least a dozen people who might be coerced into actually buying a copy. Fortunately, we both underestimated, and that first book went through 11 printings and over 250,000 copies in its first two years. So I begin with thanks to Paul for having the nerve to support a book about such a formidable subject. I suppose he was correct in vetoing my recommendation to call this one *The Windows 98 Registry: A Field Guide to the Enchanted Forest.*

At IDG Books Worldwide, my acquisitions editor, Debra Williams Cauley, was a great help in guiding this book through the woods of the production process, and for tricking Matt Lusher into signing on as development editor. For reasons still unknown to me, Matt came up with the unusual concept of actually *reading* the manuscript before it went into print, and for pointing out at least a few spots where it was still a jungle in there. For help in hacking through the thornier trails, Matt enlisted Serdar Yegulalp, who, as technology editor and a colleague at *Windows Magazine,* should have known better than to serve as this book's technical editor.

Nevertheless, he did so, and his careful scrutiny was a great help in making a seemingly impenetrable subject much more accessible.

Getting ever closer to the printed page, copy editors Nancy Crumpton and Michael Welch did their best to turn the work into something that might pass for English. Just to make sure they'd feel needed, I inserted very few and very slight misteaks for them to find. Fortunately, they found them with remarkable speed. They may have found a few other problems, but I really don't have time to go into that just now.

In the production department, Regina Snyder served as project coordinator. Using methods that I would prefer not to know about, she made sure that all the pieces fit without the appearance of being hammered into place. Thanks also to the rest of the IDG Books team for its design, layout, and proofreading expertise.

Finally, my thanks again to Microsoft for continuing to make the Registry the heart, the soul, and, to a greater extent, the intestines of its operating system — and for leaving it to others to figure out how it works. Despite some evidence of design by a committee that didn't hold very many meetings, it remains such an inseparable part of Windows that a decent Registry guide book is an absolute requirement. I hope this is it.

Contents

Part IV: Troubleshooting 309

Part I

Structure

Chapter 1

Introduction to the Windows Registry

"The Registry simplifies the operating system by eliminating the need for AUTOEXEC.BAT, CONFIG.SYS, and INI files (except when legacy applications require them)."
  —*Microsoft Windows 95 Resource Kit*

"Microsoft discourages using INI files in favor of registry entries. . . ."
  —*Microsoft Windows 98 Resource Kit*

"The check is in the mail."
  —*American folklore*

If you believe the first two proverbs, you probably believe the last one too, and this book may therefore not be quite right for you. Actually, the first is not entirely false, because quite often the Registry does indeed make it possible to do away with CONFIG.SYS and AUTOEXEC.BAT files. As for the second, Windows 98 itself writes a DESKTOP.INI file into each of about 20 folders, and perhaps 30 or so other INI files are scattered about the hard drive, with more to follow as various applications are installed. So you may be sure that the INI file will be with us for a long time to come, even though much information formerly found in various INI files is now stored in the Registry. However, other information remains in its traditional INI file location for the benefit of those legacy applications that don't recognize the Registry. We therefore begin with a brief summary of its traditional use, in order to better understand its relationship with the Windows 95 and 98 Registries.

In the discussion that follows, some information is valid for all versions of Windows, while some applies only to certain versions. Therefore, the following distinctions are made:

Windows 3.*x*   Windows and Windows for Workgroups, versions 3.0 through 3.11 only

Windows 95   Windows 95 only

Windows 98   Windows 98 only

Windows   Windows 95 and 98, and occasionally all versions of Windows (as in the first sentence of the following section)

An INI File Overview

The ubiquitous Windows initialization file is recognizable to one and all by its distinctive INI extension, as in SYSTEM.INI, WIN.INI, and countless other WHATEVER.INI files. Most such files are written into the C:\Windows directory, though some may be found in other locations after this or that Windows application is installed. In any case, these INI files contain the configuration information that Windows needs in order to run both itself and the assortment of Windows applications and applets that are installed on the system.

INI file format and structure

With very few exceptions, such as the old WINWORD.INI (in Word for Windows, version 2), the INI file was — and still is — an ASCII file that can be edited via the DOS edit utility (C:\Windows\Command\ EDIT.COM), from the Windows Notepad applet, and from any word processor that can save a file in straight ASCII (text) format. The file is divided into sections, and information must be entered into the appropriate section in order to be recognized and implemented, as shown in these brief examples of typical INI file structure:

```
[SectionName]
item=filename.ext
driver=filename.drv
otheritem=C:\UTILITY\CUSTOM\whatever.ext

[AnotherSectionName]
Workgroup=ROCKVILLE
AutoLogon=Yes
```

```
EnableSharing=0
[YetAnotherName]
dma=1
irq=7
port=220
```

As these examples show, an INI file specifies many items that vary from one system to another and therefore cannot be "hard-coded" into Windows itself. Such items might include the following:

- Name of — and if necessary, path to — a specific file required by Windows
- A user-defined configuration (`AutoLogon=Yes, EnableSharing=0`)
- Hardware and/or software configuration (`dma=1, irq=7, port=220`)

In the final example, the DMA, IRQ, and port settings transmit information in one direction only; that is, the INI file informs Windows that a certain device requires the use of the indicated resources. If some other device requires one or more of the same resources, neither Windows itself nor its INI files can inform the device that the resource is unavailable and that it should therefore pick some other setting.

The SYSTEM.INI file

As its name implies, this system initialization file contains system-specific information that Windows requires in order to open successfully. The [boot] section was, and still is, especially critical in that it specifies various drivers that Windows needs. In Windows 95 and 98, the [386Enh] (Enhanced) section is typically much smaller than in Windows 3.*x*, because many of the virtual device drivers formerly listed here are now found in the C:\Windows\System\IOSUBSYS and \VMM32 folders. Because Windows automatically loads every VXD file it finds in these folders, a "device=" line for each one is no longer needed in the [386Enh] section of SYSTEM.INI.

Some other familiar sections are now conspicuous by their absence. For example, if Windows recognizes an installed sound card, the SYSTEM.INI section that formerly specified the card's resources (that is, IRQ, DMA, and I/O settings) may be completely deleted, with some resource settings stored in the Registry, while others are dynamically set each time Windows opens. If, however, Windows does *not* recognize the sound card, or some other hardware device, then that device's resource settings remain in SYSTEM.INI, as might occur with an old 8-bit sound card or similar device.

The WIN.INI file

In Windows 3.x, this file contained much of the data that the user might customize to suit personal preference, such as color schemes, some desktop items (pattern, wallpaper, icon spacing, and so on), port settings, fonts, and more. Windows stores much of this information in the Registry — in some cases actually deleting it from WIN.INI after making the necessary entries in the Registry.

In other cases, Windows maintains the same information in both WIN.INI and the Registry, and if for some reason the Registry data is missing, it refers to WIN.INI for the needed information. As typical examples, Windows removes font information from WIN.INI after it has been written into the Registry, but desktop pattern and wallpaper specifications are now found (and maintained) in both WIN.INI and the Registry. The Registry entries take precedence, and if the user writes conflicting information into WIN.INI, this data is removed and replaced by the Registry entries the next time Windows 95 or 98 opens.

Other INI files

Windows retains many other INI files and there isn't much consistency in how these are treated. In CONTROL.INI for example, the [drivers.desc] and [Patterns] sections remain, while the color scheme's [current] and [color schemes] sections are transplanted to the Registry. Therefore, if you discover that an old familiar INI file is only partially intact, it's quite likely that the missing information now resides in the Registry. As for what remains, some of it may be duplicated in the Registry, too.

The Rationale behind the Registry

In addition to the previously described INI files, Window 3.1 introduced the Registration Database, whose REG.DAT file contained information on how various applications would open and how some of them would print documents. The database excerpt in Figure 1-1 shows how this data would look if the Windows 3.1 REGEDIT.EXE utility was executed in its so-called *verbose mode*. The figure shows three registered applications (Pbrush, regedit, and wrifile), and under each one a *shell* branch leads to commands (*open* and *print,* in these examples) appropriate to the application. The figure also shows how the same information is now stored in the Windows 95 and 98 Registries.

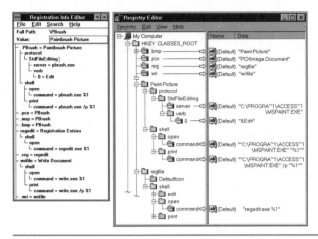

Figure 1-1 *This comparison of the Windows 3.1 Registration Info Editor and Windows 95 and 98 Registry Editor windows shows how the same information is displayed by each editor.*

A brief introduction to the Windows Registry Editor

Although using the Windows Registry Editor is not discussed in detail until Chapter 4, you'll need some familiarity with the applet in order to survive the rest of this chapter and the next two. Therefore, this section describes how to immediately access the Registry Editor, in order to better understand the definitions and description that follow. For the moment (that is, until Chapter 4), you'll use the Registry Editor *only* as a passive viewing device.

The Registry Editor utility (REGEDIT.EXE) is copied to the C:\Windows folder on the hard disk during the Windows setup procedure, but an icon is not made available as part of that procedure. For occasional use, simply select the Start menu's Run option, type **REGEDIT** in the Open: box, and either click OK or press Enter. For more extensive use, place a shortcut to the utility on the desktop or in any other convenient location. In either case, the Registry Editor window should appear on the Windows desktop when the REGEDIT.EXE file is executed. The Registry Editor's component parts are described later in this chapter.

MS Plus! and the Registry

The Microsoft Plus! Companion for Windows is a supplementary CD-ROM disc that adds additional features to Windows. In a few cases, a feature is already a part of Windows alone, and MS Plus! simply adds a section to the Registry to enable that feature. The same feature can be enabled without installing MS Plus! by editing the Registry as described in various sections of Chapter 5.

Even if MS Plus! itself is not installed, Windows 98 and some Service Release versions of Windows 95 add a Plus! subfolder beneath the Program Files folder, and this folder may in turn lead to additional sub-folders that may be viewed via the Explorer applet. Because of this, a Plus! subkey may be found in the Registry, and various Data columns (described later in this chapter in "The Contents Pane" section) may contain numerous references to Plus! folders, even though the complete MS Plus! is not installed on the system.

OEM versions of Windows 95

In the fourth quarter of 1996, Microsoft revised the version of Windows 95 supplied to various manufacturers for installation on computers sold to the general public. Among other things, the Registry in one of these OEM SR2 (Original Equipment Manufacturer, Service Release 2) versions of Windows may differ from that found on the software purchased separately from a retail outlet. In several places throughout this book, the term *SR 2 version* is used to specifically identify a Registry key or subkey that differs from the equivalent key in the conventional Windows 95 retail product. If necessary, a subversion number indicates an additional feature added still later.

In many cases, new features made available since the introduction of the original retail version of the Windows 95 CD-ROM disc may be downloaded from the Microsoft Web site (**www.microsoft.com**). Therefore, if a Registry component described here is not currently supported in your version of Windows 95, you may be able to find the necessary add-ons at the Web site. Presumably, a similar version identification scheme will be applied to Service Release updates of Windows 98 as they become available.

SR Version	Includes	Availability
1	Several updated DLL and VXD files	By download only
2	FAT32 support*	Bundled with new computers only
2.1	Adds USB support to SR2	Bundled with new computers only

* FAT32 support for Windows 95 is *not* available via download.

SR version check

To verify the SR version, open the My Computer icon's Context menu and select the Properties option. The General tab's System section lists the operating system and then a version number in the following format:

4.00.950	Windows 95 original retail version
4.00.950a	SR1 update (note no space before the lowercase *a*)
4.*xx.xxx* B	Any SR2 update (*xx.xxx* may vary, followed by a space and uppercase *B*)
4.10.1998	Windows 98 original retail version

As you might expect, some (but not all) of this version information is recorded in the Registry, as described in the "System Configuration Details" section of Chapter 6.

Definitions

This section offers a few definitions of terms unique to the Registry. There aren't that many, so they're listed here in the order in which they are likely to be encountered, rather than in the usual alphabetical sequence. Additional terms are defined in the chapter in which they are first used.

The Registry

Windows writes much of its configuration information into the hidden SYSTEM.DAT and USER.DAT files, which are found in the C:\Windows folder. If the system is configured for multiple users, a separate USER.DAT file is created for each user, and each such file is found in the user's own custom Profiles area, as described in more detail in the "USER.DAT [HKEY_USERS]" section of Chapter 4. These DAT files are referred to collectively as "The Registry."

Registry Editor

The Registry Editor is the Windows utility used to edit the Registry's SYSTEM.DAT and USER.DAT files. For routine configuration changes, the Registry is automatically edited whenever the user makes changes via the Control Panel, or from some other Windows applet or application. Alternatively, the Registry may be directly edited as described in Chapters 3 and 4.

In conventional INI file viewing, it is always clear which file is open because the user must load that file into an edit utility, where its name appears in the editor's title bar. By contrast, the Registry Editor loads data contained in the two DAT files, but does not identify either file by name. Instead, their contents are displayed as a single entity divided into six HKEY sections, as described in the sections that follow.

> **Note**
>
> Any change made via the Registry Editor takes place imme-diately, and the new information is written into SYSTEM.DAT or USER.DAT, as appropriate. The usual Save File operation is not required and, in fact, is not possible. In order to undo a change, the appropriate line must be re-edited. Registry edit-ing techniques are covered in Chapter 4.

HKEY

The Registry is divided into six sections, each identified as HKEY_*SectionName,* which immediately raises the question, what's an HKEY? In Microspeak, it is the programming "handle" to a "key" (hence, HKEY), in which configuration information is stored.

Key

A key is the Registry analog to the folder (formerly, directory) seen in the Windows Explorer. In fact, a folder icon appears next to each of the six HKEYs in the Registry.

Subkey

Again following the Explorer model, a boxed plus sign to the immediate left of any Registry key indicates one or more subkeys (analogous to sub-folders) are contained within the adjacent key. Each subkey may contain its own subkeys, and so on for several levels. Like the six HKEYs, each subkey is represented by a folder icon.

Key *versus* subkey

Because every HKEY and many subkeys lead to one or more additional subkeys, a tendency to describe the key, subkey, sub-subkey, sub-sub-sub-key, and so on must be avoided if at all possible. Accordingly, after any sub-key has been introduced, it may subsequently be referred to as a *key,* while a key immediately below it is referred to as a *subkey,* until such time as it becomes the focus of the discussion.

Subkey levels

Figure 1-2 shows how a subkey may be buried ten levels deep in the Registry, while in Figure 1-3 the same key name (*.Default;* note period at beginning of name) appears at three consecutive subkey levels. Refer to the section "A *.Default* subkey note" and to Figure 3-3 in Chapter 3 for another example of multiple *.Default* keys. Therefore, to prevent confusing two or more subkeys—especially if they share the same name—it is important to make a careful note of the path to the desired subkey. Space permitting, the complete path appears in the status bar, as shown here in Figure 1-3.

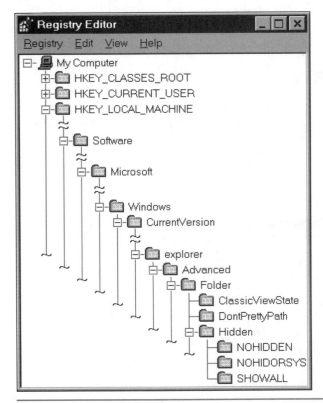

Figure 1-2 *This Registry Editor window shows a Windows 95 or 98 subkey that is buried ten levels deep.*

The Registry Editor Window

This section offers an overview of the Registry Editor window and its component parts. Like the Windows Explorer, this window is divided into two panes, as illustrated in Figure 1-4. Items common to most other Windows applications, and therefore already familiar to the user, are cited here for the sake of completeness, with descriptions kept to a minimum to save a few trees.

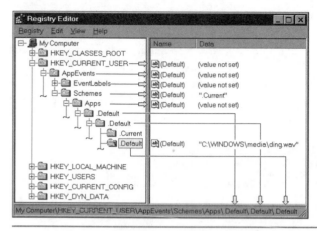

Figure 1-3 *Here the Contents pane shows three subkeys with the same name (.Default). The Status Bar at the bottom of the window reports the complete Registry path to the open (highlighted) key, which in this example is the final .Default subkey.*

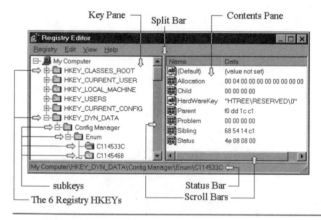

Figure 1-4 *The component parts of the Windows Registry Editor window*

Note

The phrases *Key pane* and *Contents pane* are introduced in Figure 1-4 and used throughout the book to distinguish one side of the Registry Editor window from the other. Both terms are the invention of the author and probably don't exist elsewhere than in these pages.

Title bar

The title bar at the top of the window contains the conventional Windows components: a Control menu icon, the title of the application, and the usual three buttons for minimize, restore, and close. No further explanation is offered here.

Menu bar

As with most Windows applets and applications, the menu bar appears directly under the title bar. As a central cross-reference guide, each menu and menu option is listed here, even if it is described elsewhere. In that case, a reference to the appropriate chapter and section is provided. The menus and menu options are listed in the sequence in which they appear, and Figure 1-5 shows the options that appear on each menu.

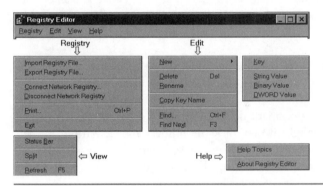

Figure 1-5 *The Registry Editor menus. The Edit menu's Copy Key Name option is available on Windows 95 OEM versions only and Windows 98.*

Control menu

Click the icon at the far left side of the title bar to access this menu. Its Move, Size, and other options are no different from those found on any other Control menu, and are not discussed here.

Registry menu

This menu is the Registry's equivalent to the File menu found on most other menu bars. Instead of using it to open, save, and close files, it's used to save or write Registry keys, or to open and close connections to remote Registries.

Import, Export Registry file These options are used to save (export) all or part of the Registry into a separate file, or to write (import) a previously-exported file back into the Registry, as described in detail in the "Registry Menu" section of Chapter 4.

Connect, Disconnect Network Registry These options are also described in the "Registry Menu" section of Chapter 4.

Print Use this option to print the Registry in whole or in part. Refer to the "Print" section in Chapter 4 for details about the Print option and a description of an alternative method of handling Registry print jobs.

Exit For those torn between the Control menu's Close option and the Exit button at the opposite end of the title bar, the Exit option does just what you think it does.

Edit menu Chapter 4 discusses Registry editing in detail, and all options on this menu are described in the "Edit Menu" section of that chapter.

View menu

This menu offers three options, described in the following sections, that are probably easier to perform via keyboard or mouse.

Status bar If a checkmark does not already appear to the left of this menu option, highlight it and click the primary mouse button (the left button, unless you've configured your mouse otherwise) to display the status bar at the bottom of the Registry Editor window. Better yet, press the Alt+V+B keys to toggle the status bar on and off as needed.

Split Select this option to place a double-arrow pointer on the vertical split bar that separates the Key and Contents panes. Drag the mouse horizontally to move the bar, then click either mouse button to conclude the operation. Or use the left- or right-arrow key to move the bar and then press the Enter key when you're done.

Refresh Select this option to refresh the Key and Contents panes, which is convenient if you've just edited an item in either pane. The Refresh option sorts the listed keys (if necessary) and removes highlighting from the Contents pane, if present. If a key is highlighted, the Refresh option does not remove that highlight. In any case, it's usually faster to press function key F5, which accomplishes the same task.

Help Menu

The Help menu provides only two options, as listed in the subsequent sections.

Help topics Select this option to access the Registry Editor's help system.

About Registry Editor Following the style of many other Windows About screens, this one is not about the Registry Editor at all. In case you need the reminder, it informs you of the Microsoft copyright and product license, and lists available memory and system resources.

The Key pane

Again, following the Windows Explorer example, the Key pane on the left side of the window shows the Registry "folders" that are referred to here as *keys*. The "My Computer" designation next to the computer icon at the top of the Key pane is embedded in the REGEDIT.EXE file. Therefore, and unlike the equivalent icon in Explorer, it does not change if the desktop icon of the same name is renamed. Refer to "'My Computer' Label in Registry Editor Window" in Chapter 6 if you really must change this to something else.

Although it is not possible to delete the six HKEY keys that appear directly beneath the My Computer icon, the subkeys beneath the first five HKEYs may be deleted or renamed, and additional subkeys may be added, as described in Chapter 4.

The Contents pane

The Contents pane on the right side of the window is divided into a series of rows and columns, as described in the following sections.

Value

Forget everything you learned about the English language: In Microspeak, each horizontal row in the Contents pane is referred to as a *value*. Thus, the information in the two columns is referred to elsewhere as the *Value Name* and the *Value Data*, even though the word *Value* does not appear in the Contents pane. Needless to say, data has some value (one hopes), and so no doubt does a name, but in this book these entries are referred to as the *Name column* and the *Data column*.

Data Type icon

In each row, the icon at the left side of the Name column indicates the format of the information in the Data column, as shown in the following list:

Icon text	Data format
	String (ASCII text)
	Binary or DWORD

Name

The Data Type icon is immediately followed by a descriptive name for the data that follows. The Registry Editor treats the icon and name as a single entity under the Name column.

> **Note**
>
> The first item in every key's Name column is always "(Default)", and the accompanying Data column is often – but not always – "(value not set)", as was shown in Figure 1-3.

Data

The information presented in this column is the data associated with the entry whose name appears in the Name column. Its format is indicated by the Data Type icon at the beginning of the row, and the data may take one of the following formats:

String data This describes any data in human-readable format, such as the following examples:

"0"	"1"
"apartment"	(value not set)
"C:\WINDOWS\SYSTEM \cool.dll,41"	"" (that is, two quotation marks with no space between)
"ROOT\PRINTER\0000"	"vxdfile"

Note that string data is always enclosed in quotation marks, with the exception of the (value not set) data and other parenthetical remarks that indicate an empty data block or null value.

Binary data In true Microspeak tradition, data defined as binary does not appear in binary format. Instead, it is given in hexadecimal format, as shown by these examples:

Name	Data
EditFlags	d8 07 00 00
Settings	60 00 00 00 00 01...04...ff ff ff...00

If a section of the Registry containing lines such as these were exported to a file (as described in Chapter 4), the same information would appear in the following format:

```
"EditFlags"=hex:d8,07,00,00
"Settings"=hex:60,00,00,00,00,01,...04,...ff,ff,ff,...00
```

Note that in this example the "hex:" label correctly identifies the data format. In any case, "binary" data displayed in the Registry can be recognized by the distinctive format *xx* space *yy* space *zz* space, where *xx*, *yy*, *zz* are hexadecimal numbers.

DWORD data As a final variation, hexadecimal data may be presented in *DWORD* (double-word) format; that is, as a four-byte sequence such as in the following two examples:

Name	Data
Height	0x00000240 (576)
Width	0x00000300 (768)

Although the DWORD format uses the same icon as the just-described binary data, it is easily recognized by 0x followed by an unspaced four-byte hexadecimal sequence, followed in turn by the decimal equivalent in parentheses. In an exported file, the same information would appear in the following format:

```
"Height"=dword:00000240
"Width"=dword:0000030
```

Data format comparisons

Don't waste a lot of time trying to make sense out of the various data formats. For example, the Registry Editor always displays true binary data—that is, a simple 0 or 1—in the String format, in which a single binary digit is enclosed in quotation marks. A decimal quantity in the Data column may also be designated as string data. As a rule of thumb, forget common sense and just realize that anything enclosed in quotes qualifies as string data. Any number *not* enclosed in quotes is Binary or DWORD data, even though it is never shown in binary format.

In case of format anxiety, double-click on any Contents pane icon: the Edit window's title bar will show one of the following legends, thus revealing the format of the data in that row:

Edit Binary value

Edit DWORD value

Edit String

If you decide to edit the data, just make sure the revision remains in the same format. The edit procedure itself is described in detail in Chapter 4.

Binary-DWORD conversion: As noted previously, the 0x00000300 DWORD has a decimal equivalent of 768, and it might logically follow that the same quantity might also be expressed as 00 00 03 00. However, it is conventional practice to enter these bytes in reverse sequence, and thus decimal 768 would be represented as 00 03 00 00, even though any calculator would convert a number written as hexadecimal 30000 (leading zeros omitted) into decimal 196,608. Therefore, to convert a sequence of hexadecimal bytes into its decimal equivalent, it is important to reverse the sequence of bytes first. Figure 4-14 in Chapter 4 provides an example, where an underlined four-byte sequence near the bottom of the illustration— 7C 02 00 00 —represents decimal 636, or hexadecimal 27C (*not* 7C02). Because the number represents a specific onscreen pixel location, its decimal value is important.

But elsewhere, the actual decimal equivalent of a four-byte sequence may have no significance because the bytes simply represent a series of binary "flags," as described in the "Registry Flags" section of Chapter 6. In this case, there is no need to reverse the byte sequence before interpreting it.

This information is presented here because some Windows applications may write the same Registry entry as a DWORD under one set of conditions and in binary format under other conditions, as also described in the "Registry Flags" section in Chapter 6.

Contents pane – INI file comparisons

To get an idea of the basic difference in how WIN.INI and the Registry handle the same data, the examples in the following table show font and desktop information as stored in WIN.INI, and as it now appears when viewed in the Registry Editor. Refer to the "INI Files and the Registry" section in Chapter 4 for details on how information may be moved from an INI file into the Registry.

Font data Every time Windows opens, the [fonts] section of WIN.INI is checked to see if any legacy application installed fonts there during the previous session. If it did, the lines are written into the Registry and removed from WIN.INI. In the case of TrueType fonts, the matching *filename*.FOT file is deleted because Windows doesn't need it.

The following examples show how a few TrueType fonts appear in WIN.INI and in the Registry:

WIN.INI File [fonts]	Windows Registry, Fonts Subkey Name	Data
Arial (TrueType)=ARIAL.FOT	Arial (TrueType)	"ARIAL.TTF"
Courier New (TrueType)=COUR.FOT	Courier New (TrueType)	"COUR.TTF"
Symbol (TrueType)=SYMBOL.FOT	Symbol (TrueType)	"SYMBOL.TTF"
Times New Roman (TrueType)=TIMES.FOT	Times New Roman (TrueType)	"TIMES.TTF"
Wingdings (TrueType)=WINGDING.FOT	WingDings (TrueType)	"WINGDING.TTF"

Note that the Registry Editor gives no indication of the actual source of the displayed data. In this case, the font data shown here is stored in SYSTEM.DAT, but the Registry Editor does not directly provide this information to the user. To determine the actual file location of any information displayed by the Registry Editor, refer to the "Registry Files" section in Chapter 4.

Desktop data This example shows how wallpaper was — and still is — specified in the WIN.INI file:

```
[Desktop]
Wallpaper=C:\WINDOWS\PLUS!.BMP
```

In the Registry, the [Desktop] section header becomes a desktop (usually lowercase *d* in Windows 95, uppercase *D* in Windows 98) subkey under the *HKEY_CURRENT_USER\Control Panel* subkey. If the subkey is highlighted, the Contents pane shows the following information:

Name	Data
Wallpaper	"C:\Windows\PLUS!.BMP"

For the sake of legacy applications that are not aware of the Registry, this and other wallpaper specifications remain in WIN.INI as well.

Split bar

The vertical bar separating the Key and Contents panes can be dragged horizontally in either direction. To do so, slowly move the mouse pointer toward the bar. When the pointer changes to a double-arrow, hold down the primary mouse button and drag the bar as desired. Or if you need to waste time, use the View menu's Split option, as previously described in the "View menu" section.

Scroll bars

As in any other window, a Registry Editor window pane may display scroll bars if the pane size is not sufficient to display all the information it contains.

Status bar

The Status Bar at the bottom of the Registry Editor window lists the full path to the highlighted subkey, whose contents are shown in the Contents pane on the right side of the split bar. The Status Bar is enabled or disabled via the View menu or by pressing the Ctrl+V+B keys, as previously described in the "View menu" section.

Chapter 2

The Registry Structure, Section I

An HKEY Overview

As noted in the previous chapter, there are six HKEYs in the Registry. For the purposes of this overview, two of these keys are defined as master HKEYs, and each derives its contents from its own hidden Registry file. Although these master HKEYs may contain data for several hardware configurations and for one or two users, only one of each such configuration can be enabled at a time. Therefore, the master HKEYs write the appropriate data into three other HKEYs every time Windows opens.

The choice of which hardware data to write into a derived key is decided as Windows detects the current hardware configuration as it opens. The configuration for the current user is determined as the user enters a name and password as part of the opening procedure. However, if the system is not set up to require a user name, or if the user presses the Escape key in response to the opening name and password prompts, then data for a *.Default* user is selected. In any case, data for unneeded hardware configurations, and for an alternate user, is ignored.

The contents of the sixth and final HKEY are dynamically derived from system RAM each time the system is powered on and are neither copied from, not written to, any other key.

Figure 2-1 illustrates the procedure just described. The shaded areas represent the two master HKEYs, both of which are shown open. Within each master HKEY, a line with an arrow leads from one of its subkeys to the HKEY that duplicates that subkey's contents. The two master HKEYs contain global data pertaining to various possible hardware and user configurations, while the three derived subkeys pertain only to the active hardware and current user configurations. An application does not need to deduce which configuration within a master HKEY is currently enabled. Instead, the application reads and writes data into the three derived keys. That data is immediately recorded in the appropriate subkey within one of the master HKEYs.

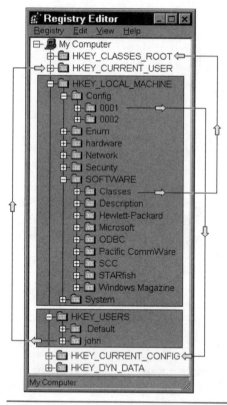

Figure 2-1 *The six Registry HKEYs. The contents of subkeys within the two shaded keys are duplicated by three of the other HKEYs, as indicated by the lines and arrows.*

For future reference, the HKEY headings in this and the next chapter begin with the abbreviation commonly used by Microsoft and others to identify the key whose full name immediately follows. This is followed by an [HKEY*subkey(s)*] in brackets to identify the master key source from which the HKEY is derived. Or in the case of a master key itself, a bracketed filename [SYSTEM.DAT *or* USER.DAT] indicates the Registry file in which the data is stored. Refer to the "Registry Files" section in Chapter 4 for detailed information about these files and about possible multiple copies of the USER.DAT file.

Because the HKEY_CLASSES_ROOT key alone requires about as much explanation as the other five keys combined, it is the only key described in this chapter. The other keys are all described in Chapter 3.

HKCR: HKEY_CLASSES_ROOT Key [HKLM\SOFTWARE\Classes]

As shown in Figure 2-2, the entire *HKCR* key structure is nothing more than a duplicate version of all subkeys found under the following key:

HKEY_LOCAL_MACHINE\SOFTWARE\Classes

Created every time Windows opens, its primary purpose is to provide backward compatibility with the Windows 3.1 registration database. But of more interest to the user, it provides convenient access to the *Classes* set of subkeys, which in their actual physical location are several levels below the *HKLM* key (described in the next chapter). In the present section, however, they are all immediately below the *HKCR* key, which makes it just that much easier to find and possibly edit them.

Both Windows Resource Kits place all these subkeys in two categories, *Filename-extension* subkeys and *Class-definition* keys, both of which are described as *sub*keys in this chapter. In addition, a third category (*Other HKCR Subkeys*) is added here, as a convenient place to describe a few sub keys that either don't fit comfortably under the *Filename-extension* and *Class-definition* categories or require a bit more explanation.

In any case, all such subkeys appear in alphabetical (ASCII code) order under the *HKCR* key and therefore also under HKLM\ SOFTWARE\Classes (see Chapter 3), and as long as any subkey format matches one of those descriptions, its contents should be quite similar to the examples given here.

Note

Remember that *HKCR* is used for the convenience of users and programmers, but its subkey contents are really stored under the HKLM\SOFTWARE\Classes section.

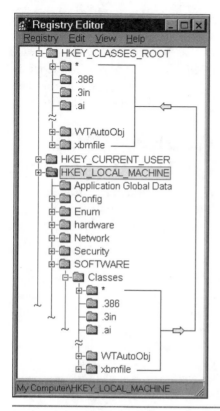

Figure 2-2 *This detail view shows how the entire contents of the* HKEY_LOCAL_MACHINE *key's* SOFTWARE\Classes *section is written into the* HKEY_CLASSES_ROOT *key.*

Filename-extension (.ext) subkeys

Most such subkeys are identified by a leading period, usually followed by the three characters of a conventional filename extension. Because there is no actual Registry subkey with an *.ext* name, this label is used here as a generic descriptor for all *Filename-extension* subkeys that begin with a leading period, such as *.386, .bmp, .doc, .txt,* and so on. A few applications add subkeys with one, two, or more than three characters, such as *.z, .ps, .ra, .html, .theme,* and so on. But whatever the extension, the information specified within each such key tells Windows what to do when an icon with that extension is double-clicked.

For example, a file named TESTFILE.TXT opens in the Notepad applet because the (Default) entry in the *.txt* subkey's Contents pane specifies the *FileType* subkey (described later) to be associated with any file with a TXT extension, as shown in Figure 2-3. This convention provides additional information about this file type under — in this case — a *txtfile* (text file) subkey located farther down the HKCR tree structure.

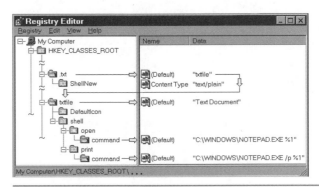

Figure 2-3 *This composite Registry Editor window illustrates the relationship between a Filename-extension key (.txt) and its associated FileType key (txtfile). The latter key's Shell key leads to subkeys for the Open and Print options that appear on any text file's Context menu.*

The (Default) entry in a few *.ext* keys shows "(value not set)" in the Data column, which indicates there is no associated *FileType* or *Class-definition* subkey. In this case, the *.ext* key itself may lead directly to a *shell\open\command* subkey set, and the latter subkey specifies the application that launches any file with the extension specified by the *.ext* subkey. In still other cases, the key leads instead to a *ShellNew* subkey, which is described in the "Shell, Shellex, ShellFolder, and ShellNew Key Structures" section.

MIME Contents pane modifications

Some Contents panes list a Content Type entry, as shown in Figure 2-3 for the *.txt* subkey. This additional information is the MIME (Multipurpose Internet Mail Extension) equivalent of the subkey file extension, and it may be written into the Registry by MS Plus! by most OEM versions of Windows 95, or by Windows 98. Table 2-1 lists some of the *Extension* subkeys in which a Content Type entry may be found.

Table 2-1 *MIME Data Added to Various HKCR\File-Extension Subkeys* *

HKCR Subkeys	Contents Pane (Default)	Content Type †	Explorer\View\Options, Registered File Types
.aif, .aifc, .aiff	AIFFFile	Audio/aiff	AIFF Format Sound
.aim	Aimfile	Application/x-aim	AOL Instant Messenger Launch
.art	Artfile	Image/x-jg	ART Image
.au	AIFFFile	Audio/basic	AU Format Sound
.avi	AVIFile	video/avi	Movie Clip (ActiveMovie)
.bmp	Paint.Picture	image/x-win-bitmap	Bitmap Image
.crt, .der	Certificatefile	application/x-x509-ca-cert	Internet Security Certificate
.dll	Dllfile	application/x-msdownload	Application Extension ‡
.exe	Application	application/x-msdownload	Application
.gif	Giffile	image/gif	GIF Image
.htm, .html	Htmfile	text/html	Internet Document (HTML)
.jpe, .jpeg, .jpg	Jpegfile	image/jpeg	JPEG Image
.mov	ActiveMovie	video/quicktime	Movie Clip (ActiveMovie)
.mpeg, .mpg	ActiveMovie	video/mpeg	Movie Clip (ActiveMovie)
.ra, .ram	Ramfile	audio/x-pn-realaudio	RealAudio
.snd	Aufile	audio/basic	AU Format Sound
.tif, .tiff	TIFImage.Document	image/tiff	TIF Image Document
.txt	txtfile	text/plainText	Document
.wav	SoundRec	audio/wav	Wave Sound
.xbm	xbmfile	image/x-xbitmap	XBM Image

* MIME data not present in original retail version of Windows 95.
† Indicated MIME data also appears as "Content Type (MIME)" on File Types tab.
‡ Edit flag excludes item from Registered file types list by default; see Table 6-1.

The Content Type information may be viewed one item at a time via Explorer's View menu: Select Options (Folder Options if IE4 is installed) and click on the File Types tab to display the Options (or Folder Options) sheet shown in Figure 2-4. The "Content Type (MIME)" line displays the "text/plain" entry from the *.txt* subkey's Contents Pane.

Refer to "A Property Sheet Handler for a Dialog Box" in the "PropertySheetHandlers" section later in this chapter for an explanation of how this specific Property Sheet Handler is written into the Registry. See also the "MIME and DataBase" subkey description in the "Other HKCR Subkeys" section near the end of this chapter.

A few special purpose .ext subkeys

Two subkeys that do not begin with a leading period — *Asterisk* (*) and *Unknown* — yet can be placed within the *Filename-extension* category, are also described in this section, as is a Windows 98 entry that looks like a filename extension (.mydocs), but isn't.

Asterisk (*)

This subkey is the first to appear under the *HKCR* key, and as elsewhere in the operating system, an asterisk signifies a wildcard. It might be better thought of as a ".*" subkey, because the information found under it is applied to all files regardless of their extension. As shown by the composite illustration in Figure 2-5, the *Asterisk* key leads to a *shellex* subkey, which in turn leads to *ContextMenuHandlers* and *PropertySheetHandlers* subkeys. For future reference, the specific relationship between the *Asterisk* key and these subkeys is discussed in the following sections. If any of the details in these sections describe subkeys that are unfamiliar, you may prefer to skim this section now, then return later after reading the rest of the chapter.

Shellex* and *ContextMenuHandlers If the *ContextMenuHandlers* subkey is not currently present, you can install the Briefcase applet in order to display it (it can be uninstalled later on if you don't need it). To do so, open Control Panel's Add/Remove Programs applet, select the Windows Setup tab, and highlight Accessories. Click the Details button, put a check next to Briefcase, click the OK and Apply buttons, and then exit Control Panel. A My Briefcase icon should appear on the desktop, and the *ContextMenuHandlers* and *BriefcaseMenu* Registry keys are now displayed.

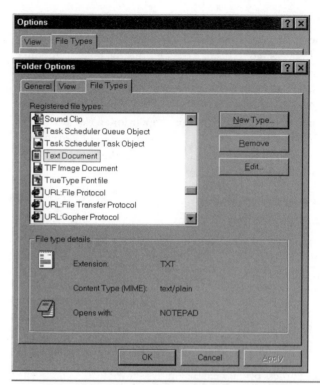

Figure 2-4 *In the Windows 98 Folder Options sheet, the File Types tab lists Registered file types, with details about the highlighted file type appearing below the list. The "Content Type (MIME):" line is inserted by MS Plus! and SR2 versions of Windows 95, and appears by default in Windows 98. The top of the illus-tration shows the equivalent Windows 95 title bar and tabs.*

If the *ContextMenuHandlers* key is already present but the *BriefcaseMenu* key is not, then some other subkey is beneath the *ContextMenuHandler* key. In the Contents pane for any such subkey, the (Default) line's Data column displays the name of a *CLSID* key, which is immediately recognizable as a lengthy hexadecimal string enclosed in curly braces. When such information appears under the *Asterisk* key, the features supported by the cited *CLSID* key are applied to all files regardless of their extension. In the specific *BriefcaseMenu* example, if any file is moved into the Briefcase, the key places an *Update* option on that file's Context menu. The same option does not appear on the Context menu of the file in its original location.

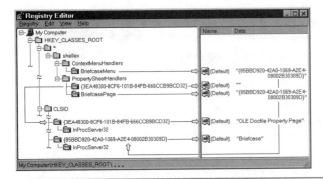

Figure 2-5 *This composite Registry Editor window shows the* Asterisk *key's subkey structure and illustrates how various subkeys under the* ContextMenuHandlers *and* PropertySheetHandlers *keys refer to the* CLSID *keys associated with the Windows Briefcase and a property sheet handler for OLE documents.*

Shellex* and *PropertySheetHandlers Unlike the *BriefcaseMenu* key, whose name reveals its purpose, the first subkey to appear under the *PropertySheetHandlers* key usually bears the unhelpful name of `{3EA48300-8CF6-101B-84FB-666CCB9BCD32}`, and its Content pane is empty. To discover its purpose, open the *CLSID* key found farther down in the HKCR section and then find the subkey whose name is the same hexadecimal string (both also shown in Figure 2-5). You can search on the name of the string if looking for all those numbers gives you a headache. That key's own Contents pane identifies it as an "OLE Docfile Property Page." Note that in this case, the customary definition of "* = all files" might be better interpreted as "* = all *OLE* document files." (Like the Windows Registry itself, this book makes no attempt to replace the term *OLE* with the more-recent *ActiveX* terminology.)

If the Context menu for any OLE document is open and its Properties option selected, the Properties sheet shows three tabs labeled "General," "Summary," and "Statistics." The latter two tabs are handled via the previously mentioned *CLSID* key. Because OLE documents can have a variety of extensions (Word DOC file, Excel XLS file, and so on), the presence of a subkey with this number under the *Asterisk* key makes these Properties sheet tabs available to any OLE document, regardless of its extension. Note that the *{3EA48300...* subkey here under the *Asterisk* key is simply a pointer to the subkey with the same name under the *HKCR\CLSID* key. At that location, the *InProcServer32* subkey indicates the file (DOCPROP.DLL) that actually handles the Summary and Statistics tabs. If that file were missing, these tabs would be missing, too.

> ## Comparison: Asterisk and Folder Subkeys
>
> Just as the *Asterisk* key pertains to all files without regard to their extensions, a *Folder* key performs similar functions for all folders. Refer to "Folder" in the "Other HKCR Subkeys" section later in this chapter for further details.

PropertySheetHandlers* and *BriefcasePage Similar in concept to the *BriefcaseMenu* subkey described previously, the *BriefcasePage* subkey supports the Update Status tab that appears on the Properties sheet of any file located in a Briefcase. This tab does not appear if the Properties option for the equivalent file outside the Briefcase is selected, because this particular property is appropriate only to a file located in the Briefcase.

.desklink

On Windows 98 Context menus, the cascading Send To menu's Desktop as Shortcut option is supported via this subkey. Refer to the "Context Menu" section of Chapter 6 for more details.

.mydocs

This Windows 98 special-purpose file extension is reserved for the My Documents object whose icon appears on the Desktop as a sheet of paper protruding from an open folder. The icon's Context menu Properties option displays a Target tab that reveals this "folder" is no folder at all, but rather a shortcut to the actual C:\My Documents folder. Like any other shortcut, it can be renamed without affecting the name of the target folder. But unlike any other shortcut, the Context menu's usual Delete option has been replaced by a Remove from Desktop option. If this option is selected, the icon is deleted and the *.mydocs* key acquires a *ShellNew* subkey that places a My Documents Folder on Desktop option at the bottom of the cascading New menu. To view this menu, open the Desktop's own Context menu and select the New option. If this option is selected, the My Documents icon returns to the Desktop, the *ShellNew* key is deleted, and the option disappears from the cascading New menu, thus preventing the user from placing a second such folder on the Desktop. Refer to "ShellNew Key" in the "Shell, Shellex, ShellFolder, and ShellNew Key Structure" section and to Figure 2-12, later in this chapter, for more details about this menu.

Unknown

If the Registry does not contain a *Filename-extension* key for a file with a certain extension (*.xyz*, for example), then Windows has no idea what actions are appropriate to the file and therefore refers to this *Unknown* subkey for instructions. Specifically, an unknown file's Context menu displays an "Open with ..." option. If selected, an Open With dialog prompts the user to choose the program that should be used to open the file. Refer to "openas" in the "Shell Key" section of "Shell, Shellex, ShellFolder, and ShellNew Key Structures" later in this chapter for details.

CLSID (class identifier)

Briefly stated, a CLSID number is a class identifier (or GUID — Globally Unique Identifier) key that identifies a Windows object for OLE automation purposes, and there is a subkey here for every such device registered on the system. Every CLSID label takes the following form:

```
{aa bb cc dd—ee ff—gg hh—ii jj—kk ll mm nn oo pp}
```

Each double-letter pair is a one-byte hexadecimal number, and there are always 16 such numbers (bytes) in a 4-2-2-2-6 sequence enclosed by braces. A long hexadecimal string that conforms to this format is randomly generated by a software supplier for every Windows application, and the chance that any two CLSID numbers would be identical is unlikely, to say the least. (Refer to the "CLSID Generator Utility" section in Chapter 6 for information on how to generate a unique CLSID number.)

If almost any *CLSID* subkey is opened, the Contents pane's (Default) entry identifies the object associated with that CLSID number, as shown by a few examples:

CLSID Subkey Name	Data Column
{21EC2020-3AEA-1069-A2DD-08002B30309D}	"Control Panel"
{645FF040-5081-101B-9F08-00AA002F954D}	"Recycle Bin"
{73FDDC80-AEA9-101A-98A7-00AA00374959}	"WordPad Document"
{00028BA1-0000-0000-C000-000000000046}	(value not set)

There are a few subkeys in which the Data column does not identify the object, as shown by the last example above. In a case such as this, a search for another subkey with the same name may help. In this specific example, the subkey shows up beneath a *ContextMenuHandlers* key, which in turn is a subkey for another *CLSID* key. That key's Contents pane identifies it as

"The Microsoft Network," so we may conclude that this "(value not set)" subkey is likewise part of the Microsoft Network.

In still other cases, there may be a *ProgID* (described later) subkey below the *CLSID* key, and that key's Contents pane may identify the object.

CLSID

Although no subkey under the *CLSID* key is actually so labeled, this generic designation is used here and elsewhere in this book in any discussion that refers to all subkeys under the *CLSID* key. If such a subkey requires specific identification, then the first four bytes are given, followed by an ellipsis — *{21EC2020...*, for example. If necessary, the 16-byte hexadecimal character string is given in full.

Refer to the "Start Menu" section in Chapter 6 for information on using a CLSID to place a new item on the Start menu.

Note

If a *CLSID* subkey is found elsewhere in the Registry, it usually serves as a pointer to a key with the same number found in the *HKCR\CLSID* section.

Server and *handler* subkeys

One or more of the following subkeys can be found under each *CLSID* key in this section of the Registry:

InprocHandler, InprocHandler32	in-process handler
InprocServer, InprocServer32	in-process server
LocalServer, LocalServer32	local server

The "32" suffix indicates a 32-bit device. Although not described in detail here, each key's Contents pane gives the path and filename for the server file that supports the function specified by the *CLSID* key. In most cases, if that file is damaged or missing, an error message is displayed when the function is accessed. For example, the C:\Windows\System\Viewer\SCCVIEW.DLL file supports the Context menu's Quick View option. If the file is missing, a "There is no viewer . . ." message appears if that option is selected.

In contrast, a key in the list at the beginning of this section may cite a file that does not exist. In this case, the function is for the moment supported by other means, but may be handled by this subkey if some application installs a file with the specified name in the future. See *"{D3B1DE00..."* in the "Shellex and PropertySheetHandlers" section later in the chapter for a specific example.

ProgID (programmatic identifier)

This subkey is found under many, but not all, *CLSID* keys, and its Contents pane Data column identifies a *FileType* key that, in most cases, matches the *FileType* seen in the *CLSID* key's own Data column. Occasionally though, the *ProgID* key cites a different key name, and that key refers back to the name found in the *CLSID* key, as shown by the two examples in Figure 2-6. The two *DefaultIcon* keys seen in the lower part of the figure are described in the "DefaultIcon precedence" section later in this chapter.

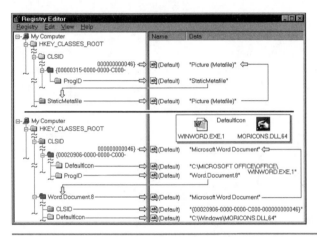

Figure 2-6 *This composite Registry Editor window shows the relationship between a* CLSID *key's* ProgID *subkey and a* FileType *key. The* ProgID *subkey specifies the* FileType *key, where a* CLSID *subkey points back to the* CLSID *key. In the lower section of the figure, the* DefaultIcon *specified under the* CLSID *key* (WINWORD.EXE, 1) *is superseded by the icon specified below the* Word.Document.8 *key* (MORICONS.DLL, 64). *Therefore, all Word document files display the latter icon.*

FileType

The names of many subkeys that follow the final *Filename-extension* sub-key describe various file types, such as *AVIFile, batfile, htmlfile, txtfile,* and so on. Each such key is described here as a *FileType* subkey because it provides additional information about a file type whose filename extension appeared as one of the *Filename-extension* subkeys described earlier in this chapter.

The Filename-extension/FileType key relationship

If the user double-clicks an object named, say, *filename.txt*, Windows looks up the *.txt* key, which refers it to the associated *txtfile* key, which in turn leads to a *Shell* subkey and then to two Action subkeys (or *verbs* in Microspeak). Each one (in this example, *open* and *print*) has its own *command* subkey, whose Contents pane lists the command line that launches the appropriate application (in the present example, NOTEPAD.EXE) and opens (or prints) the *filename.ext* file.

This little two-step subkey routine may seem like a bit of extra work, because the Action keys could have been placed directly under the *.txt* key to spare Windows the bother of looking up the *txtfile* key in order to complete the desired action. However, this convention makes it easy to quickly reassign a file association. For example, Figure 2-7 shows a few *HKCR* keys in a system with two browsers installed. If IE4 is currently the default browser, the *.htm* and *.html* keys both refer to the Microsoft *FileType* key named *htmlfile*, and that key of course contains all the Action subkeys required by IE4. The figure shows that Netscape's own *FileType* key — *NetscapeMarkup* — is also present, so when the user designates Netscape Navigator as the default browser, a single line in the *.htm* and *.html* key's Contents pane changes from *htmlfile* to *NetscapeMarkup*. Thus, a double-click on any .htm or .html file will now open Netscape Navigator instead of Internet Explorer.

Refer to "CurVer" in the "Other HKCR Subkeys" section later in this chapter for yet another variation in this system.

FileType subkeys

Because most of these subkeys are common to both *FileType* and other keys, they too are separately described later in this section. If the subkey appears under a *Shell, Shellex* or *ShellNew* key, refer to the "Shell, Shellex, ShellFolder, and ShellNew Key Structures" section that follows. Otherwise, consult the "Other HKCR Subkeys" section for further details.

Shell, Shellex, ShellFolder, and ShellNew Key Structures

Many *HKCR* keys lead to one or more subkeys that specify various shell functions, each of which is described in this section. But first, what is a shell?

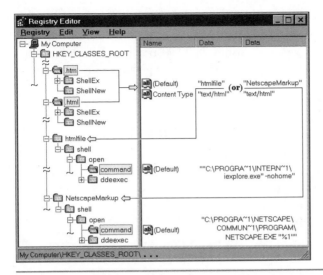

Figure 2-7 *The .htm and .html keys' Contents pane Data column cites the*
FileType *key for the current default browser, which in this*
example is either htmlfile *or* NetscapeMarkup. *In either case,*
Windows follows the appropriate route to find the correct
browser to open.

The Shell defined

As anyone who has shucked an oyster knows, a shell is that hard calcium-
like structure that tries to protect its owner (in this case, the oyster) from
the outside world (usually, a hungry diner). In technical jargon, the word is
a general descriptor of any program that protects — or *tries* to protect —
the operating system from the user, and vice versa. The general idea is that
the user communicates with the shell, and the shell communicates with the
operating system. Acting as an interface between these parties, the shell
translates the needs of one into the requirements of the other. By so doing,
the shell enables the user to communicate with the operating system in
something that approaches human, rather than machine, language.

The concept of the computer shell originated in the hoary days of
UNIX. In DOS (which was strongly influenced by UNIX), the shell was
the well-known COMMAND.COM program, which accepted a command such as FORMAT C: /s from the user and translated it into something the machine could understand. The Windows GUI (graphical user
interface) is an improved shell (according to current wisdom) that further
shields the user from the complexities of the operating system.

From time to time, the basic Windows shell needs some unique enhancements to accommodate a specific task, and these are handled by various shell subkey structures within the Registry. In each case, the information contained under one of these subkeys pertains only to the item below which the subkey appears. Typical examples of some of these keys are given in this section.

Overview of Shell, Shellex, ShellFolder, and ShellNew keys

This section begins with a brief summary of these keys, with details provided in subsequent sections.

Key Name	Contains
Shell	Action keys such as *Edit, Open, Play, Print,* and so on
Shellex	Handler routines for Context menus and Property sheets
ShellFolder	Attribute flags to enable/disable specific Context menu options
ShellNew	Instructions for documents listed on the cascading New menu

Although the Registry itself is inconsistent in its use of upper- and lowercase letters to label these keys, this book follows the style shown here in all text explanations. However, the figures show whatever style the programmer-du-jour used when that key was written. Thus, you may discover *Shell, shell, ShellEx, Shellex, shellex,* and two exceptions to the rule: there are no variations on the *ShellFolder* or the *ShellNew* keys.

A subkey under the *Shell* key may sometimes be referred to as an Action key because the key and its own subkeys support a specific action supported by the application or file type under which the key appears. The most common Registry action keys are described in the next section, but other such keys may be installed by various software applications. In most cases, the key functions in a manner similar to those described later.

The Shell key

Each action subkey under the *Shell* key contains instructions that pertain only to the item under which the *Shell* key appears. If a *Shell* key appears under a *FileType* key (described above), then the names of Action subkeys beneath the *Shell* key appear as options on the Context menu, when a file matching that *FileType* is selected. The first letter (usually) of the menu option is underlined — for example, <u>O</u>pen and <u>P</u>rint.

If a *Shell* subkey appears under a *Filename-extension* key, then refer to the associated *FileType* key for information about that file's Action subkeys and Context menu options. Refer to the "Change Context Menu Options" section in Chapter 6 for instructions on how to change an option name as it appears on the Context menu or select a different letter to be underlined.

The Action keys listed here are usually followed by a *command* subkey, which specifies the executable file that performs the specified operation on the file whose Context menu is open.

Note

The name of any Action key has no special significance, other than serving as a convenient Context menu indicator of the action that occurs if that menu option is selected. In most (but not all) cases, the name of the key is the name that appears on the Context menu. However, that name may be changed as desired, without affecting the operation of the key itself. Refer to the "Change Context Menu Options" section in Chapter 6 for information on how to edit the name of an Action key on the Context menu.

The descriptions given in this chapter pertain only to actions initiated via the Context menu and have no effect on the way an open application handles the same task. Thus, if the *Open* subkey under, say, the *txtfile* key were missing, that action would not appear on the Context menu for any text file. However, if the Notepad applet itself were opened, its own File menu's Open option would continue to function in the normal manner.

Config

The *config*(uration) subkey appears as a *Shell* subkey under the *scrfile* (screen saver) key. Its *command* subkey displays only "%1" in the Contents pane Data column, which signifies that the selected filename should be executed. In the specific case of a screen saver file — DANGER~1.SCR, for example — simply typing the filename on a command line is sufficient to configure the system to use that screen saver.

cplopen

This key appears under the *cplfile* key's *Shell* subkey and might just as well have been labeled "open" instead of "cplopen." If any file with a CPL extension is selected, its Context menu displays a default "Open with Control Panel" option at the top of the menu, because that phrase appears in the *cplopen* subkey's (Default) Data column. If selected, the Control Panel applet whose filename is highlighted will open, thereby bypassing the intermediate step of opening Control Panel itself. To open two or more such applets simultaneously, highlight the appropriate *filename*.CPL files and then select the "Open with Control Panel" option.

Edit

This subkey is found under the *Shell* key in the *batfile*, *regfile*, and *txtfile* tree structures. In each case, its *command* subkey specifies that the selected BAT, REG, or TXT file be loaded into the Notepad applet for editing.

Explore

This subkey is found under the *CLSID\Shell* key for the *Folder*, *Inbox*, and *Microsoft Network* subkeys. In each case it opens the selected object in the two-paned Explorer view, in which the left pane shows the Desktop and the right is the Contents pane for the selected folder. The *Open* subkey on the same Context menu displays the Contents pane only.

Find

This subkey is located under the *CLSID* keys for *My Computer* and *Network Neighborhood* and is also under the *Directory* and *Drive* keys, and in each case a *command* subkey launches EXPLORER.EXE. A *ddeexec* (dynamic data exchange/execute) subkey specifies a subroutine embedded within EXPLORER.EXE that is to be executed (which in this case is *FindFolder*). Refer to "ddeexec (dynamic data exchange/execute)" in the "Other HKCR Subkeys" section later in this chapter, for more information about the *ddeexec* subkey.

A *Find* subkey under the *CLSID* key for the Microsoft Network executes a separate MSNFIND.EXE file.

install

This special-purpose subkey appears under the *inffile* (INF file) and *scrfile* (screen saver) keys. If a Context menu for either file type is opened, the Install option runs the executable file that installs the selected file. In either case, a *command* subkey specifies the appropriate command line, and a "%1" parameter at the end of that line indicates that the specific file selected is the one to be installed.

Open

As its name suggests, this key leads to a *command* subkey that specifies the executable program that opens the selected file.

openas

This special-purpose key appears under the *Unknown* key's *Shell* subkey (see the preceding "Unknown" section). This key structure is used when Windows is not sure which executable program is appropriate to open or print the selected file, in which case the Context menu lists an Open with ... option. If selected, the *openas* key's *command* subkey displays an Open With dialog box, in which the user is prompted to specify the program to open the file.

The dialog box includes an "Always use this program to open this file" checkbox, which really means "Use the selected program to open any file with the same extension as this one." If the box is checked, then the next time a file with the same extension is selected, the Context menu will display an Open option instead of the Open With option. However, other options appropriate to the same program may not appear on the menu. Refer to the section "Change Context Menu Options" in Chapter 6 for further details and instructions on how to edit the Registry so that all appropriate options are displayed on the Context menu.

Play

The *AudioCD, AVIFile,* and other audio/video keys contain this subkey, and in each case, a *command* subkey specifies the executable program (CDPLAYER.EXE, MPLAYER.EXE, and so on) that loads and plays the selected file. If a /close switch appears on the executable's command line, you can delete it if you would prefer to keep the player applet open at the end of a playback, as described in the "Command-Line Edits" section of Chapter 6.

Print

Common to most document subkeys, the *Print* key's *command* subkey opens the appropriate executable program, loads and prints the selected file, then closes the executable program.

Printto

If present, the *Printto* key's *command* subkey specifies the executable file with command-line switches and/or parameters to be used if a file is dragged to a printer icon. For example, if you drag a document file to a printer icon and drop it there, the application cited in the *command* subkey opens, prints the document, and then closes.

If the *Shell* subkey under a *FileType* key lacks the *Printto* and *Printto\command* subkeys, then drag-and-drop printing is handled by the

Print subkey (described in the previous section). Refer to the "Drag-and Drop Print Editing" section in Chapter 6 for suggestions on changing the application used to print a document file.

The Shellex key

The Shellex (shell extension) key usually contains one or more *Handler* subkeys such as those whose contents are described in this section. In each of the following examples, the keys provide some additional feature or features not otherwise available — hence, the shell extension terminology. As with the Action subkeys under the *Shell* key described previously, the presence of these handler subkeys under a specific *Shellex* subkey makes sure the features do not appear where they are neither required nor usable.

ContextMenuHandlers

In addition to options placed on a Context menu by the *Shell* key's action subkeys (described previously), other options may be placed there via a subkey under the *Shellex\ContextMenuHandlers* key, as shown by the examples in Table 2-2. Figure 2-8 shows default Context menus for shortcut and Microsoft Network objects and also indicates how each menu would appear if its *ContextMenuHandlers* subkey were missing.

Table 2-2 *Context Menu Options for Various Windows Objects*

Object	Context Menu Option	HKCR Subkey Location *
Briefcase	Update All	Folder\...\BriefcaseMenu
Drive (removable)	Copy Disk	Drive\...\{59099400-
Explorer File menu (IE4)	New option	Directory\Background\...\New
File in Briefcase	Update	*\...\BriefcaseMenu
Folder, folder shortcut	Sharing ...	Folder\...\SharingMenu
Folder in Briefcase	Update	Folder\...\BriefcaseMenu
ICM file	Install in Place	icmfile\...\{DBCE2480-
	Install to Color Directory	icmfile\...\{DBCE2480-
Microsoft Network	Connection Settings, Delete	CLSID\{00028B00- \...\{00028BA1-
My Computer	Map/Disconnect Network Drive	Integral part of SHELL32.DLL file, not controlled via shellex key
My Documents (Win98)	Remove from Desktop	CLSID\{450D8FBA- \...\{450D8FBA-

Object	Context Menu Option	HKCR Subkey Location *
Network Neighborhood	Map/Disconnect Network Drive	Integral part of SHELL32.DLL file, not controlled via shellex key
Printer	Sharing ...	Printers\...\SharingMenu
Recycle Bin	Empty Recycle Bin	CLSID\{645FF040-\...\ {645FF040-
Shortcut, application	Open	lnkfile\...\ {00021401-
Shortcut, folder	Open, Explore, Find	lnkfile\...\ {00021401-

* Each "\...\" represents omitted \shellex\ContextMenuHandlers\ key structure.

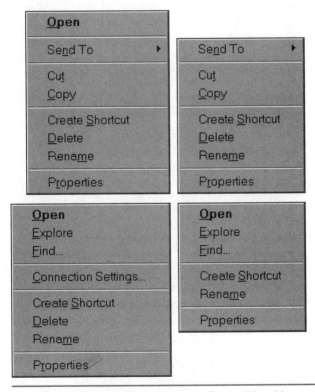

Figure 2-8 *If the* HKCR\lnkfile *key's* ContextMenuHandlers *subkey is missing, the Open option on a shortcut icon's Context menu is no longer seen, as shown in the upper menu examples. The lower examples show the effect of a missing* ContextMenuHandlers *subkey beneath the Microsoft Network's* CLSID *key.*

SharingMenu This subkey under *ContextMenuHandlers* in the *Folder* and the *Printers* keys places a Sharing option on the appropriate Context menu, but only if the following conditions are in effect:

Object	Required Condition
Folder	File sharing is enabled.
Printers	Printer sharing is enabled, and a printer is installed on a local (not network) port.

To enable file and/or printer sharing, open Control Panel's Network applet and click the File and Print Sharing button. (If the button is disabled, complete the numbered steps below and then resume reading here.) Click the Add button and then check the box next to either or both of the following options:

- "I want to be able to give others access to my files." (that is, to share folder contents)

- "I want to be able to allow others to print to my printer(s)." (the long way to specify "Enable Printer Sharing")

If the previously mentioned Sharing button is disabled (that is, grayed out), perform the following steps to enable it:

1. Click the Add button.
2. Highlight Service and click the Add button.
3. Highlight Microsoft.
4. Highlight File and Printer Sharing for Microsoft Networks.
5. Click the OK button and follow any prompts that are displayed.

IconHandler

This *Shellex* subkey is found under the *lnkfile, piffile,* and a few other keys, where it does just about what you would expect it to do. To demonstrate this, use Explorer to search the C:\Windows folder and its subdirectories for *.LNK or *.PIF files. Open the Context menu for any such file, and its icon should appear near the top of the General tab, placed there by the *IconHandler*, whose Contents pane Data column points to the *{00021401...* key. If the *IconHandler* subkey were missing, a generic document shortcut icon would be displayed there instead.

PropertySheetHandlers

The subkey beneath any key with this name serves as a pointer to a *CLSID* key. There are two subkey formats that may be used, and each is briefly reviewed in the following sections. In each case, the parenthetical reference is to the subkey(s) used here to illustrate the format under discussion:

Single property sheet (AVIFile and batfile) In Figure 2-9, both examples of the *PropertySheetHandlers* key support a single properties sheet. For the AVI file, the key's Contents pane shows "AviPage" in its Data column. A subkey with that name appears immediately below, and that key's own Contents pane points to the *{00022613... CLSID* key associated with the AVI file. That key's *InProcServer32* subkey's Contents pane contains the following information:

    (Default)   "C:\WINDOWS\SYSTEM\mmsys.cpl"

This indicates that the MMSYS.CPL file contains the Properties sheet information required by AVI files. If that file is missing, then the Details and Preview tabs on an AVI file's Properties sheet will also be missing.

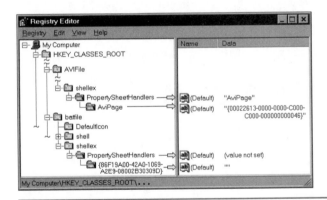

Figure 2-9: *The* AVIFile *key's* PropertySheetHandlers *subkey points to an* AVIPage *subkey, which in turn points to the* CLSID *key associated with AVI files. By contrast, the* batfile *key's* PropertySheetHandlers *subkey leads directly to a* CLSID *pointer.*

The *batfile* key's *PropertySheetHandlers* subkey in the same figure contains no information in its own Contents pane. The name of the subkey beneath it directly identifies the *CLSID* key that supports the associated Properties sheet.

Multiple property sheets (Asterisk) The *PropertySheetHandlers* sub-key under the *Asterisk* key (described previously in this chapter) must support two property sheet handlers. Therefore, the *PropertySheetHandlers* key's own Contents pane remains empty, and each subkey beneath it supports its own properties sheet. As shown earlier in Figure 2-5, one of two formats may be employed. In the case of the *{3EA48300...* subkey, the key name itself is the pointer to the associated *CLSID* key. In the *BriefcasePage* subkey also seen in the Figure 2-5, the *CLSID* pointer is in the Contents pane's Data column.

As in the preceding AVIPage example, the specified *CLSID* key contains the path and filename for the file that contains the appropriate Properties sheet data.

A property sheet handler for a dialog box Strictly speaking, a dialog box—such as the one shown earlier in Figure 2-4—might not be thought of as a properties sheet because it is not accessed via some Context menu's Properties option. Nevertheless, its various components may be modified via a subkey that resembles the just-described *PropertySheetHandlers* key. In Figure 2-10, the bottom of the Contents pane for *FileTypesPropertySheetHook* refers to a *CLSID* key. This key contains an *InProcServer32* subkey that specifies the URL.DLL file that inserts the "Contents Type (MIME):" line in the Options dialog box.

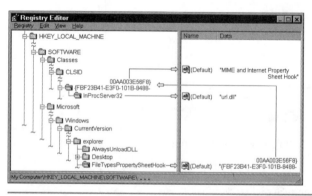

Figure 2-10 The Microsoft *key's* FileTypesPropertySheetHook *subkey points to the* CLSID *key in the* CLSID *section. To better illustrate the relationship, the* {FBF23B41... *key is shown under the* HKEY_LOCAL_MACHINE *key because that's where the Microsoft key also resides. The former key only is also located in the "HKCR: HKEY_CLASSES_ROOT" key's* CLSID *section described in this chapter.*

Third-party handler keys

Under the *Shellex* key, various . . . *Handlers* keys often lead to one or more subkeys (see Figure 2-11) inserted by third-party applications. Note that a *Norton Shell Extensions* subkey is under both the *ContextMenuHandlers* and *PropertySheet Handlers* keys, and both of them cite the same *CLSID* key. This means the key handles both Context menu and Property sheet functions. In this specific example, the Context menu handler places a System Information option on every drive's Context menu, while the property sheet handler places a Norton tab on every drive's Properties sheet.

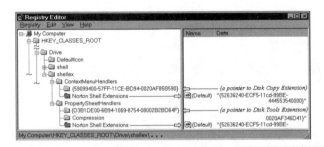

Figure 2-11 *Both* Norton Shell Extensions *subkeys point to a common* CLSID *key that supports the Context menu and Property sheet options installed by Norton Utilities, version 3.0.*

The ShellFolder Key

This key's Contents pane contains an Attributes entry, written in either of the following formats:

Name	Data	Comment
Attributes	0x00000050 (80)	(DWORD format)
Attributes	50 00 00 00	(Binary format)

In either case, the value in the Data column determines the options displayed on the Context menu for the item under which the ShellFolder key is displayed. Refer to the "Attribute Flags [Attributes]" section of Chapter 6 for information on editing these flags.

The ShellNew key

If the New option is selected on either the desktop Context menu or Windows Explorer File menu, a cascading menu displays a list such as that shown in Figure 2-12. For each menu option, a *ShellNew* key can be found under the *Filename-extension* subkey associated with that document type. For example, Figure 2-13 shows the .bmp and .doc *Filename-extension* subkeys, whose Contents panes point to a *FileType* subkey (described earlier), which in Figure 2-13 are *Paint.Picture* and *Word.Document.8*, respectively. The Contents pane for each of these keys lists the text that appears on the cascading New menu, and the *Shell\open\command* subkey specifies the executable file that will be launched to create the appropriate new document on the desktop.

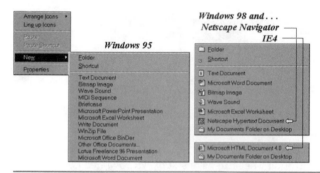

Figure 2-12 *On the desktop menu, the New option leads to a cascading menu of available new document types. Icons are displayed on the menu if IE4 is installed, and the "My Documents" option is supported in Windows 98 only.*

The role of the *ShellNew* key itself varies depending on the information in its Contents pane. To illustrate this, open the *ShellNew* subkey under any *Filename-extension* key, note the word that appears on the second line of the Name column (*Command, Data, Filename,* or *Nullfile*), and then find that word in the sections that follow. In each of these examples, the contents of the Data column determine the action taken, as described in the following sections. If Internet Explorer is the only installed browser on your system, refer to "HTML Document" in the "Desktop New Menu" section of Chapter 6 for information on adding this option to the New menu list.

Notes:

1. The examples of the ShellNew subkey entries included in the following sections are representative of those seen on several typical

Windows systems. However, variations have been noted between one system and another, and these may be due to the influence of various third-party applications.

2. Assuming the *Filename-extension* key contains a *ShellNew* subkey (not all do), then if a new file of that type is placed on the desktop via the Context menu's New menu, the filename takes the following format:

    `New <FileType>.<ext>`

    where *FileType* is the text string found in the associated *FileType* subkey's Data column. Thus for a new bitmap image, a title of *New Bitmap Image.bmp* would appear under the icon on the desktop.

3. In the four examples provided in the following sections, only *Command* actually runs an executable program at the time the appropriate option is selected on the Context menu's cascading New menu. The other entries simply place a new document file on the desktop, without actually running the executable program associated with that file format.

Command

The Data column specifies a command line that is executed if the associated option on the New menu is selected. The command line includes the path, filename, and command-line parameters required to create the specified new item. Although various applications may write a *Command* entry in their associated *.ext* key (the *.mdb* key in Microsoft Access, for example), Windows itself uses *Command* only in the *ShellNew* key's Contents pane for the following two subkeys.

Briefcase (.bfc subkey) A New Briefcase icon is placed on the desktop the first time this option is selected. If it is selected again, a New Briefcase (2) icon is displayed, and so on.

Shortcut (.lnk subkey) If this option is selected, Windows of course has no idea which application requires a new shortcut. Therefore, a Create Shortcut dialog box prompts the user to enter the desired command line or to browse for the desired application.

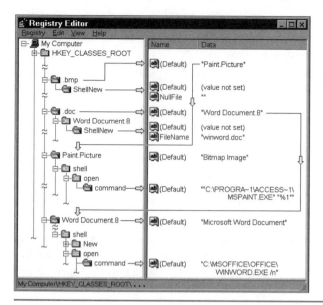

Figure 2-13 *In this composite Registry Editor window, the .bmp key's
ShellNew subkey shows a NullFile entry in its Contents pane.
Therefore, if a new Bitmap Image is selected from the New
menu shown in Figure 2-12, the MS Paint applet opens, but a
template file is not loaded. By contrast, the .doc key's
ShellNew subkey shows a FileName entry whose Data
column specifies winword.doc, a template document found in
the C:\Windows\ShellNew folder. If Microsoft Word
Document is selected from the New menu, this file is loaded
into Microsoft Word.*

Data

If the word *Data* appears in the Name column, then the binary data string
in the Data column is written into a new file of the appropriate format. For
example, a multimedia application may write a Data entry into the
Contents pane in the *.mid* (MIDI file) and/or *.wav* (Wave file) key's
ShellNew subkey, such as the 18-byte hexadecimal sequence shown in
Figure 2-14. This is the standard header that appears at the beginning of
any MIDI file, which is shown by the shaded area in the Debug window in
Figure 2-14. If this sequence is present in the Data column, then the application that wrote the Data entry supports MIDI recording, and therefore
the New MIDI Sequence.mid file in the C:\Windows\Desktop folder
should be 18 bytes long.

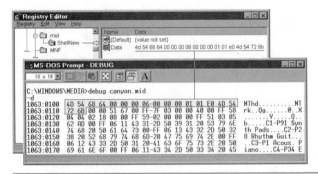

Figure 2-14 *If the MIDI sequence option on the New menu (shown in Figure 2.12) is selected, the .mid file's ShellNew subkey opens a new MIDI file. The 18-byte hexadecimal string seen in the Contents pane's Data entry is the header that appears at the beginning of any MIDI file. In the MS-DOS prompt - DEBUG window, the shaded area shows that header as it appears in the CANYON.MID (or any other) MIDI file.*

If the *.mid* subkey does not contain a *ShellNew* key, then of course no MIDI sequence option is displayed on the desktop Context menu's cascading New menu. Refer to "Add Menu Option" in the "Desktop New Menu" section of Chapter 6 for information on how to add a MIDI sequence or other option to that menu.

Note

If a *Data* line is followed by a *NullFile* line (described later), then the latter takes precedence, and the *Data* line is ignored.

FileName

When *FileName* appears in the Name column, the Data column specifies a new document file that is placed on the desktop, not unlike the binary header described in the previous section. However, the binary header is written as a new file, while a new document file is actually a copy of a blank document file presently located in the C:\Windows\ ShellNew folder. This blank file may be quite a bit larger than the 18-byte MIDI header described previously, because it contains all the basic data required for any new file created under the same format.

If the new document file's icon is double-clicked, the executable file that loads the file is the one specified under the *FileType* subkey associated with the *Filename-extension* key. To locate it, open the *Filename-extension* key itself and note the *FileType* listed in its Contents pane. Then locate the subkey with that name and open its *Shell\open\command* subkey. The path and filename for the executable file are located in the (Default) row's Data column, as shown by the Word.Document.8 example in Figure 2-13.

Notes:

1. The *New* subkey that also happens to appear under the same *Shell* subkey is not part of the desktop Context menu's cascading New menu. It is instead one of the Action subkeys described in the "Shell Key" section earlier in this chapter.

2. The retail version of Windows 95 wrote a 56-byte entry in the *.wav* subkey's Contents pane, which consisted of a waveform file header, using the procedure described in the "Data" section earlier. In Windows 98, this *Data* entry is replaced by a *FileName* entry that cites a SNDREC.WAV file now found in the C:\Windows\ ShellNew folder. Although two bytes longer, this too is simply the required header for a waveform file. Refer to the "Desktop Object Opens, Then Closes" section in Chapter 7 to troubleshoot a new wave sound icon that does not perform as expected.

NullFile

The Data column shows an empty pair of quotation marks. As with the *Filename* description earlier, the command to open the associated file type is found under the *FileType* subkey associated with the *Filename-extension* key. In this case, a null file (of zero-byte length) is created on the desktop. A *Nullfile* entry is found under the *.bmp* and other subkeys, because the specific format of the file you want to create is of course unknown, and therefore Windows cannot predict the correct file header to write into the new file. Presumably, you will open the null file, add something to it, and then save it in whatever format you prefer, at which time the correct header will be written into the file.

Other HKCR Subkeys

This section covers a few important *HKCR* subkeys that may need a bit of explanation. Their descriptions were put off until now because a passing acquaintance with the *Shell* and *Shellex* key structures (described previously) may make it a bit easier to wade through the information in this section.

In a few cases, a heading appears for a subkey that one might expect to find, even though that subkey does not in fact exist. In each such case, there is a brief explanation of how the associated item is supported in the absence of a subkey. The characteristics of several *DefaultIcon* subkeys are briefly described (as in the "AudioCD" section that follows). For more details about the *DefaultIcon* key itself, refer to the section of that name that follows.

Figure 2-15 summarizes the relationship between many of the subkeys described in this section.

AudioCD

This subkey is linked to the *Drive* and the *Folder* subkeys, both of which are described later in this chapter. The purpose of the *AudioCD* subkey is to specify a File type icon and to support the Play option required by audio compact discs. Refer to the "AutoRun" section later in this chapter for information pertaining to CD-ROM (data) discs.

DefaultIcon

The icon specified here appears only on the list of Registered file types on the File Type tab, where it is identified as "AudioCD."

Shell

Although each option listed here appears on the Context menu for any audio compact disc, only the play option is directly supported by a subkey in this section.

explore This option is placed on any CD audio disc's Context menu by the *Shell\explore* subkey found under the *Folder* key.

find This option is placed on the Context menu by the *find* subkey under the *Drive* key.

open Similar to the *explore* subkey described previously, this option is displayed on the Context menu through the *Shell\open* subkey under the *Folder* key.

play This is the only CD audio option supported by a subkey under the *CDAudio* key. Its *command* subkey specifies that the CDPlayer applet will be used to play the audio compact disc.

Note

Autoplay: If the *Shell* key's own Contents pane Name and Data columns show (Default) and "play," respectively, then the executable file (CDPLAYER.EXE, or similar) listed in the *play* key's *command* subkey plays an audio compact disc as soon as it is inserted in the CD-ROM drive. Refer to the "AutoRun" section later in this chapter and the "Drive Media Icons" section of Chapter 6 for information about customizing this feature.

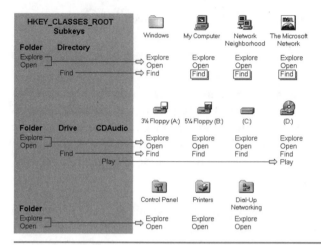

Figure 2-15 *A few Context menu options are shown under various Desktop and Explorer icons. The horizontal lines and arrows indicate the various* HKEY_CLASSES_ROOT *subkeys where each option originates. The three boxed Find options are supported separately by a* Shell\find\command *subkey under the* CLSID *key associated with each object.*

Shellex

This key is conspicuous by its absence under the *AudioCD* key, so of course there are no *ContextMenuHandlers* or *Property-SheetHandlers* subkeys either. The functions usually supported by these subkeys are handled via the *Drive* key's *Shellex* subkey structure, as described in the "Drive" section later in this chapter.

AutoRun

This subkey is written into the Registry if both of the following conditions are met:

- The Auto insert notification box is checked (open Device Manager, highlight the specific CD-ROM drive, click the Properties button, and select the Settings tab).

- A CD-ROM disc containing an AUTORUN.INF file is inserted in the CD-ROM drive *after* Windows has opened (refer to the "Hard Drive Icon" section of Chapter 6 for a method of adding an AUTORUN.INF file to a hard drive and the reason for doing that).

If these conditions are met, an executable program (usually, AUTORUN.EXE) specified in the CD-ROM disc's AUTORUN.INF file is executed when the disc is inserted in the drive. If the disc is subsequently removed, its *AutoRun* subkey remains in place, but it is rewritten if another CD-ROM disc is inserted in the drive, provided that disc contains an AUTORUN.INF file in its root directory. In any case, the contents of that file are written into the *AutoRun* subkeys, as shown in the following table and in Figure 2-16.

AUTORUN.INF File Contents	Subkey*	Contents Pane Data Column
`[autorun]`		
`OPEN=AUTORUN\AUTORUN.EXE`	*Command*	E:\AUTORUN\AUTORUN.EXE
`ICON=AUTORUN\WIN95CD.ICO`	*DefaultIcon*	E:\AUTORUN\WIN95CD.ICO

* The full paths are HKCR\AutoRun\4\Shell\AutoRun\command and AutoRun\4\DefaultIcon.

The numbered subkey immediately below the *AutoRun* key indicates the drive letter (3 = D, 4 = E, 5 = F, and so on). Under default conditions, the *AutoRun* key leads to a numbered subkey for the CD-ROM drive only, which is drive E (*4*) in Figure 2-16. The entire *AutoRun* structure is erased from the Registry every time Windows closes and does not appear again until the next time the preceding two conditions are met. However, if a valid AUTORUN.INF file is on any hard drive partition (as described in Chapter 6), then the *AutoRun* key and the subkey(s) referring to the hard drive remain in place, and only the CD-ROM subkey is erased.

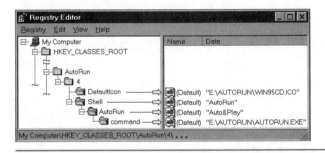

Figure 2-16 *In this typical* AutoRun *key example, the* 4 *subkey signifies drive 4 – that is, drive E. Fresh Contents pane data – such as that shown in this figure – is written into the Registry whenever a CD-ROM disc with an AUTORUN.INF file is inserted in the CD-ROM drive.*

Note

The *AutoRun* key described in this section refers to CD-ROM (data) discs only. Refer to the "AudioCD" section earlier in this chapter, for details on playing audio compact discs in a CD-ROM drive.

CurVer (current version)

The typical relationship between a *Filename-extension* key and its associated *FileType* key was described in the "*Filename-extension* (.ext) subkeys" section earlier in this chapter and was illustrated in Figure 2-3. In that example, the subkeys beneath the *FileType* key (*txtfile*) contained all the information required to support documents with a TXT extension. But in other cases, a *FileType* key may lead to only two subkeys; *CLSID* and *CurVer*. The former specifies the CLSID for the current version of the application, and the latter points to yet another *FileType* key that contains additional subkeys for that version. If the application is subsequently upgraded, the following Registry edits may be made as part of its setup procedure:

1. The *Filename-extension* key's Contents pane is modified to point to a new *FileType* key.

2. The original *FileType* key remains. Its *CLSID* key is also retained, but other subkeys may be modified or deleted. In addition, a new *CurVer* subkey points to the new *FileType* key described in Step 1.

3. The new *FileType* key leads to a complete set of subkeys that now support the latest version of the application.

To illustrate this convention, Figure 2-17 shows some of the keys written into the Registry when the old Microsoft Word version 6 is installed. Note that the *.doc* key points directly to the *Word.Document.6* key, and the *Word.Document* key above it is apparently not required. However, if some other filename extension were associated with the *Word.Document* key, its *CurVer* subkey would refer files with that extension to the current version — that is, to the *Word.Document.6* key.

Figure 2-18, however, shows what happens when Microsoft Word 97 is installed as an upgrade over Word 6. Both the *.doc* key and the *Word.Document* key's *CurVer* subkey are rewritten to point to a new *Word.Document.8* key, and the subkeys beneath it support this new version. Although the former *Word.Document.6* key remains, it now contains a *CurVer* key that wasn't there before. In addition, its *Shell* key has been removed, and other changes have also been made. You can check these changes by comparing the *Word.Document.6* key structures in Figures 2-17 and 2-18.

A search for *CurVer* keys turns up countless other key structures written in the same manner, thus adding considerable bloat to the Registry. Nevertheless, this convention is recommended (and heavily used) by Microsoft, and even some third-party application designers are now following the practice.

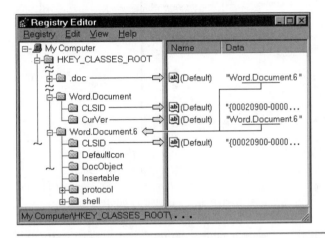

Figure 2-17 *A few keys written into the Registry when Microsoft Word version 6 is installed. Word version 7 makes no changes to this arrangement.*

ddeexec (dynamic data exchange/execute)

If this subkey appears under a *Shell* key's Action subkey, its Data column specifies a subroutine embedded within an executable program. The name of this executable program may be found by opening the *command* subkey that appears above the *ddeexec* subkey, as shown by these examples:

HKCR Subkeys	Command Subkey Shows:	ddeexec Subkey Shows:
Drive\shell\find	Explorer.exe	"[FindFolder("%l",%l)]"
Folder\shell\explore	Explorer.exe /e /idlist, %l, %L	"[ExploreFolder("%l",%l,%S)]"
Folder\shell\open	Explorer.exe /idlist, %l, %L	"[ViewFolder("%l",%l,%S)]"

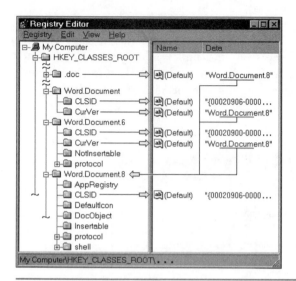

Figure 2-18 *If* Word 97 *is installed as an upgrade, the* .doc *key and* Word.Document.6 *key's* CurVer *key are rewritten and the former* Word.Document.6 *structure is revised. Compare this version with that shown in the previous figure.*

In each line of the preceding table, column 1 lists a subkey structure under the *HKCR* key. If the final key in that column is opened, its *command* and *ddeexec* subkeys show the executable program and its subroutine, as listed in columns 2 and 3 of the table.

The information in the subkeys under the *ddeexec* key may of course be viewed by sequentially opening each key and noting the Contents pane's Data entry. The same information may be seen more conveniently by opening Explorer's View menu. For example, Figure 2-19 shows a Microsoft Word Document entry in the Registry and as it appears by completing the following steps:

1. Open Explorer's View menu, select Options, and click the File Types tab.

2. Highlight "Microsoft Word Document" in the list of Registered file types.

3. Click the Edit button.

4. Highlight "print" in the Actions box.

5. Click the Edit button.

The various Registry entries in the Contents pane Data column at the top of the figure appear on the Editing action sheet also shown in

Figure 2-19. If the checkmark in the Use DDE box is cleared, all entries below it are cleared from the sheet and deleted from the Registry. For information about any listed item, click the ? button in the upper-right corner of the Editing actions sheet and then point to any entry on the sheet.

DefaultIcon

As its name suggests, this subkey specifies the icon that is displayed next to any object associated with the key under which it appears. If Options on the Explorer's View menu is selected, the File Types tab shows the same icon next to the associated registered file type.

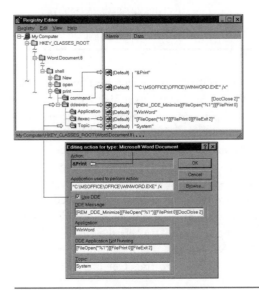

Figure 2-19 *The Registry Editor window at the top shows various Contents pane entries for the open subkeys under the Word.Document.8 key's Shell subkey. The bottom part of the figure shows how this information is presented to the user. To view this data, open the Explorer's View menu, select Options, click the File Types tab, and highlight Microsoft Word Document. Then click the Edit button, highlight Print, and click the next Edit button. Similar data should be seen with any other Windows word processor. Note that the quotes enclosing each Data entry in the Registry do not appear below. The DDE Message box is horizontally extended to display the entire line.*

The *DefaultIcon's* Contents pane contains a (Default) entry, whose Data column specifies the icon to be used, as shown by these examples:

Subkey	Contents Pane Shows:	
	Name	**Data**
Exefile	(Default)	"%1"
Paint.Picture	(Default)	"C:\Progra ~ 1\Access ~ 1\MSPAINT.EXE,1"
{645FF040...	(Default)	"C:\WINDOWS\SYSTEM\shell32.dll,32"
	empty	"C:\WINDOWS\SYSTEM\shell32.dll,31"
	full	"C:\WINDOWS\SYSTEM\shell32.dll,32"
{00020906-...	(Default)	"C:\MSOFFICE\OFFICE\WINWORD.EXE,1"
Word.Document.8	(Default)	"C:\Windows\MORICONS.DLL,64"

The "%1" in the first example specifies that the icon for any *exefile* (*filename.exe*) is to be taken from the executable file itself. If that file does not contain an icon, then Windows displays one of its own generic icons. Note that if the "%1" parameter were replaced with the path and filename for a specific icon source (as in the *Paint.Picture* example), then *all* files with an EXE extension would display that icon, instead of their own icon.

The *{645FF040...* example is a special case that handles the Recycle Bin icon. If the Bin is empty, the empty wastebasket icon specified on the *empty* line is displayed. However, when any file is deleted (actually, moved to the Recycle Bin), the icon changes to a full wastebasket, as specified on the *full* line. In either case, as the Recycle Bin is emptied and then refilled, the appropriate icon specification is copied to the (Default) line and displayed on the desktop.

DefaultIcon precedence

The *{00020906...* and *Word.Document.8* subkeys demonstrate another unique case in which a specified default icon is superseded by another default icon located elsewhere in the Registry. For example, Figure 2-6 showed the *CLSID* and *FileType* keys for a Microsoft Word Document, and both of these keys contain a *DefaultIcon* subkey. If both subkeys were absent, Windows would create a Word document file icon consisting of a dog-eared blank page with a miniature version of the WINWORD.EXE icon superimposed on it. If only the *DefaultIcon* subkey under the *CLSID* key is present, the icon specified there appears next to every Word file. However, if the *DefaultIcon* subkey under *Word.Document.8* is also present, then the icon specified there takes precedence over the one under the *CLSID* key. The icons specified by these two *DefaultIcon* keys are both shown in the inset in Figure 2-6, and in this example the MORI-CONS.DLL file's icon is the one that is seen next to every DOC file.

The same comments apply to any other case in which a *DefaultIcon* subkey appears under a *CLSID* key and also under a *FileType* key—the *FileType* key being the one specified under the *CLSID* key's *ProgID* subkey. Refer to the "DefaultIcon Subkey" section of Chapter 6 if you would like to change the icon associated with an executable program or a document file.

DefaultIcon precedence and Internet Explorer 4 As yet another variation on the default icon, the following new key structure is added to the Registry by Internet Explorer 4:

HKCU\Software\Classes\CLSID

If a *DefaultIcon* subkey is found under any *CLSID* key within this section, the icon specified there takes precedence. Refer to "Classes and CLSID" in the "Software Configuration Keys" section in Chapter 3 for more information, and to the "Desktop Icons" section in Chapter 6 for details on changing this icon.

Other DefaultIcon variations In all cases, the icon specified by a *DefaultIcon* key is displayed next to the associated file type on Explorer's File Types tab, and also next to all files of the same type when viewed in an Explorer window. In a few cases the *DefaultIcon* subkey specifies the icon on the File Types tab list but has no effect on a nonfile object viewed in an Explorer window. Although each of the objects listed in the following table uses the same icon as shown on the File Types tab, its presence in an Explorer window is independent of the *DefaultIcon* subkey.

HKCR Subkey	Registered File Types
AudioCD	AudioCD
Directory	File Folder
Drive	Drive
Folder	Folder
My Briefcase	Briefcase

Column 1 lists the subkey under which the *DefaultIcon* subkey appears, and column 2 specifies the name shown in the Registered file types list, which is viewed by opening the Explorer's View menu, selecting Options (Folder Options in IE4), and then clicking the File Types tab.

Directory

Within the Registry, a *Directory* is a folder that contains nothing but files and possibly some file subdirectories — in other words, just what a directory was in the days before Windows 95. Refer to the "Folder" section later in this chapter for additional information on the distinction between a Registry directory (or file folder) and a folder.

DefaultIcon

The icon specified here appears only on the list of Registered file types on the File Type tab, where it is identified as "File Folder" (open Explorer's View menu, select Options, and click File Type tab).

Shell

The *Shell* key leads to the single action key described in the following section.

find   This subkey places the Find option on a Folder's Context menu, but only if that folder meets the *Directory* conditions described above.

Drive

As its name suggests, this key supports the system's diskette, CD-ROM, and hard drives, and a few functions unique to this key are described here. Because the *{CLSID}* keys described as follows do not directly identify the functions they support, a parenthetical reference has been added to the section head to indicate the purpose of the key.

DefaultIcon

This icon is the one seen next to *Drive* in the Registered file types list on the File Types tab (to view the list, open Explorer's View menu, select Options, and then the File Types tab). It has no effect on the various drive icons used to identify diskette and hard drives in an Explorer window. These icons are not directly specified in the Registry but may nevertheless by changed as described in "Hard Drive" in the "Drive Icons" section of Chapter 6.

Shell

Although three actions appear on any drive's Context menu, only one is supported by one of the following subkeys in the *Drive* section.

find This is the only subkey found under the *Drive* key's *Shell* subkey. If any drive Context menu is opened, this key supports the menu's Find option.

explore and open Although both options appear on any drive's Context menu, they are placed there via the *Shell\explore* and *Shell\Open* subkeys found under the *Folder* key and consequently do not appear under the Drive\Shell key described here.

Shellex and ContextMenuHandlers

Although these keys were previously described in the "Shellex" section, a few of the options that appear on a drive's Context menu are briefly reviewed in the sections that follow. Note that only one of these options is directly supported by a *ContextMenuHandlers* subkey under the *Drive* key.

{59099400-57FF-11CE-BD94-0020AF85B590} (Copy Disk option)

The *Copy Disk* option on the Context menu is supported by the *{59099400...* subkey here, which is simply a pointer to a subkey of the same name under the *CLSID* section. That key's *InProcServer32* subkey supports the Copy Disk option that appears on the Context menu for diskette drives only.

Eject Although this option appears on the Context menu for CD-ROM and other removable-media (except diskette) drives, there doesn't seem to be a subkey associated with it, even though it is supported via the SHELL32.DLL file. For the moment then, it appears to be hard-coded into the operating system.

Format Because the Format option is unique to diskette and hard drive Context menus, you might reasonably expect to find a *ContextMenuHandlers* subkey that supports this function. However, such a key does not exist, and the Format function also appears to be hard-coded into the system via the SHELL32.DLL file.

Sharing This Context menu option is supported by a subkey under the *Folder* key's *Shellex* subkey. Refer to the discussion (in the "Shellex Key" section earlier in this chapter) of that key's *ContextMenuHandlers and SharingMenu* subkeys for additional details.

Shellex and PropertySheetHandlers

These keys are also described in the "Shellex Key" section, with the following subkeys unique to the *Drive* key briefly described in the sections that follow.

{D3B1DE00-6B94-1069-8754-08002B2BD64F} (Tools tab) and Disk Tools

On some systems, only the *{D3B1DE00...* subkey is present, and its Contents pane is empty. On others, the Contents pane points to a *Disk Tools* subkey, and that key's Contents pane cites the *{D3B1DE00...* subkey. In either case, in the HKCR\CLSID section, the *{D3B1DE00...* key's own Contents pane describes it as "Disk Tools Extension," and its InProcServer32 subkey cites a C:\Windows\System\disktool.dll file, which does not exist on most systems. On some OEM versions of Windows 95, the *{D3B1DE00...* key may be cited as shown in the title of this section, yet the key itself is missing from the CLSID section described earlier.

When present, "Disk Tools Extension" and/or the subkey named *Disk Tools* would certainly suggest that this subkey structure has something to do with the Tools tab on any drive's Properties sheet. However, the absence of the DISKTOOL.DLL file and the missing *{D3B1DE00...* subkey indicate that this entire key structure does nothing at the present time, and in fact, the presence and function of the Tools tab is unaffected if part or all of it is deleted.

This subkey is cited here as a specific example of a structure that seems to be nothing more than a place holder for a file that, if installed in the future, will support the indicated function. However, in the absence of that file, the function is supported internally by other means. No modification to the above description has been noted in Windows 98.

Compression If present, this subkey's Contents pane points to a *{7C7E55A0...* subkey whose *InProcServer32* subkey supports a Compression tab on the selected drive's Properties sheet.

Sharing The Sharing tab on a drive's Properties sheet is supported via the *MSSharing* subkey under the *Folder\shellex\PropertySheetHandlers* key.

Folder

There seem to be two Microspeak definitions for a folder: Outside the Registry, the term usually defines what used to be known as a directory or subdirectory. Within the Registry, a folder is *any* object that can be opened to reveal other objects. Thus, each of the items in the following list is classified as a folder:

Briefcase	Diskette drive	My Computer
CD-ROM drive	Explorer folder (any)	Network Neighborhood
Control Panel	Hard drive	Printers
Dial-Up Networking	Microsoft Network	RecycleBin

DefaultIcon

The icon specified here appears only on the list of Registered file types on the File Type tab, where it is identified as "Folder" (open Explorer's View menu, select Options, and click the File Type tab).

Shell

The subkeys found under this key support options that appear on every folder's Context menu. In addition to the conventional file folder formerly known as a *directory*, other folders include My Computer, Network Neighborhood, all drives, and the Control Panel, Printers, and Dial-Up Networking folders.

Explore This subkey supports the Explore option, in which the Explorer opens a window with two panes — Folders and Contents.

Find Because the *Folder\Shell* key does not lead to a subkey with this name, the Find option on any Context menu is supported by a *Find* subkey located elsewhere, such as under the *Directory* or the *Drive* keys described earlier in this section. For other objects (My Computer, Network Neighborhood, Microsoft Network, and so on), a *Shell\Find* subkey is located under the *CLSID* key associated with that object. Still other folders (Control Panel, Printers, Dial-Up Networking) do not require a Find option on their Context menu.

Open Similar to the Explore option, this subkey supports the Open option on every folder's Context menu, in which the Explorer opens a single-pane Contents window.

Shellex and ContextMenuHandlers

This key combination leads to the two subkeys described in the following sections.

BriefcaseMenu If the Context menu for a Briefcase folder is opened, the subkey supports the appearance of the Update option on the Context menu. If the Context menu for the equivalent folder outside the Briefcase is selected, the Update option does not appear, because this option is appropriate only to objects located in the Briefcase.

SharingMenu Although the name may imply the existence of a Sharing menu, this subkey actually supports the Sharing option on the Context menu.

Shellex and PropertySheetHandlers

The subkeys described in the following sections support various tabs that appear on the Properties sheet for any folder whose Context menu supports a Properties option. Note that this menu option is disabled for the Control Panel, Printers, and Dial-Up Networking folders.

BriefcasePage If the Context menu for a folder in any Briefcase is opened and its Properties option selected, this subkey supports the Update Status and Update Info tabs.

MSSharing Under the conditions previously described for *BriefcasePage*, this subkey supports the Sharing tab seen on a folder's Properties sheet.

MIME and Database

This two-subkey structure is inserted below the *HKCR* key if MS Plus! is installed over the original Windows 95 retail version, and is also present in most subsequent versions and in Windows 98. The latter key leads to one or more database subkeys such as *Content Type* that is described in the following sections. Each such key leads to additional subkeys containing information that helps an Internet-based application handle various characteristics of file types.

Content Type

As the key name suggests, this is a database of MIME content types.

In the Contents pane for each of subkeys beneath it, an Extension entry specifies the extension associated with that content type. Thus, if an audio waveform file is transmitted, an accompanying header identifies it as "audio/wav," and the subkey of that name indicates it should be treated as a file type whose extension is WAV, as shown by the first two lines in the following table:

HKCR Subkey	Name	Data
MIME\Database\Content Type\audio/wav	Extension	".wav"
.wav	Content Type	"audio/wav"
MIME\Database\Content Type\text/plain	Extension	".txt"
.txt	Content Type	"text/plain"

QuickView

Each subkey under this key lists a file extension recognized by the QuickView applet. If the applet has not been installed, these *File-extension* subkeys may still be present on some systems, and each one's Contents pane gives a description, as in the following examples:

Key	Contents pane Data column
.asc	"ASCII File"
.bmp	"Windows Bitmap Graphics File"
.dll	"Dynamic Link Libraries"
.doc	"ANY of a number of word processing file formats"
.ini	"configuration files"

If QuickView is installed (via Control Panel's Add/Remove Programs applet, Accessories component), then a subkey is added beneath every *File-extension* key. Each one has the same name and contents, as shown here:

Subkey Name	Contents Pane Data Column
{F0F08735-0C36-101B-B086-0020AFF07DD04F}	"SCC Quick Viewer"

After the final *File-extension* subkey, a *Shell\open\command* subkey specifies the executable file. As elsewhere in the Registry, the previously cited *{F0F08735...* subkey in the *CLSID* section specifies the file (SCCVIEW.DLL) that supports QuickView.

Chapter 3

The Registry Structure, Section II

This chapter continues the discussion of the Registry Editor's HKEY structure that began in Chapter 2. Fortunately, the five HKEYs described here require little more space than that devoted to the single HKEY_CLASSES_ROOT key of the previous chapter.

HKCU: HKEY_CURRENT_USER Key [HKU*UserName* or HKU\.Default]

The information contained within the seven subkeys of *HKCU* pertains to the user who is currently logged on, hence the "Current User" designation. As with the *HKCR* key described in Chapter 2, a new *HKCU* key is created as Windows opens. Its contents come from the current user's profile, which is stored under a *username* subkey beneath the *HKU* (HKEY_USERS) key described in the "HKU: HKEY_USERS [USER.DAT]" section later in this chapter, and shown in Figure 3-1. If the system is not configured for multiple users, or if the user bypasses the password prompt by pressing the Escape key, then *HKCU* takes its data from the *.Default* subkey (note the leading period) found under *HKU*.

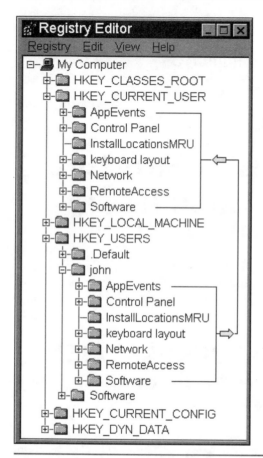

Figure 3-1 *If two subkeys appear under the* HKEY_USERS *key, one is labeled* .Default *and the other is the name of the current user. As shown here, the contents of the latter key also appear under the* HKEY_CURRENT_USER *key. On a single-user system, the contents of the* .Default *key appear instead. In Windows 98, a Software key also appears under the* HKEY_USERS *key, but its contents are not copied into the* HKEY_CURRENT_USER *key.*

The seven *HKCU* subkeys are listed in Table 3-1, with additional details offered here.

Table 3-1 *HKEY_USERS\.Default Subkeys*

Subkey(s)	Contents
AppEvents	
EventLabels	Labels that appear in the Sound applet's Events: box
Schemes	Subkeys with path and filename for waveform files specified in the Sound applet's Events: box
Control Panel	See Table 3-2
InstallLocationsMRU	The locations from which applications were recently installed (MRU = Most-Recently Used)
keyboard layout	Two or more subkeys with data about keyboard layout, language, and so on
Network	*Persistent* and *Recent* network connections subkeys
RemoteAccess	*Address* and *Profile* subkeys for Microsoft Network or other (if installed; otherwise, subkeys are empty)
RunMRU †	(*Windows 95 Resource Kit erroneously reports location here.*)
Software	Data on Windows software
StreamMRU †	(*Windows 95 Resource Kit erroneously reports location here.*)

† Actual location is HKEY_USERS\.Default\Software\Microsoft\Windows\ CurrentVersion\Explorer.

AppEvents

Within the context of Windows, an "event" is just about any action whose occurrence can be celebrated in sound, if not quite in song. Such events range from the trivial to the profound; that is, from a menu popup to a general protect fault. Subkeys under the *AppEvents* key structure provide the necessary support, as described in the following sections.

EventLabels

For each subkey in this section, the Contents Pane's (Default) entry lists a label for a single sound event, which may be viewed via the Control Panel Sounds applet. The Events window on that applet's Properties sheet displays a list of these event labels, each read from one of the subkeys under the *EventLabels* key.

Note that each *EventLabels* subkey is responsible for the label only; the associated sound is specified via the *Schemes* subkey described in a section that follows. Table 3-2 lists the subkeys installed by Windows, and Figure 3-2 further illustrates the relationship between the *EventLabels* subkey, the Sounds tab, and the *Schemes* subkey.

Table 3-2 *Control Panel Sounds Tab Events and Equivalent EventLabels Subkey*

Sound †	Subkey Name ‡	Sound †	Subkey Name ‡
Windows			
Asterisk	*SystemAsterisk*	Minimize	*Minimize*
Close Program	*Close* §	New Mail Notification	
Critical Stop	*SystemHand*		*MailBeep*
Default sound	*.Default*	Open program	*Open* §
Exclamation	*SystemExclamation*	Program error	*AppGPFault*
Exit Windows	*SystemExit*	Question	*SystemQuestion*
Maximize	*Maximize*	Restore Down	*RestoreDown*
Menu command	*MenuCommand*	Restore Up	*RestoreUp*
Menu popup	*MenuPopup*	Start Windows	*SystemStart*
Windows Explorer			
Empty Recycle Bin	*EmptyRecycleBin*		
Sound Recorder	**Media Player**		
Close program	*Close* §	Close program	*Close* §
Open program	*Open* §	Open Program	*Open* §

† Indicated event name appears on Sounds tab on Control Panel's Sounds Properties sheet.

‡ Full subkey path is HKU*username*\\AppEvents\\EventLabels*Subkey name*.

§ Same subkey label shared by *Windows, Sound Recorder* and *Media Player* sections in the Sound applet's Events list.

Schemes

This key leads to two subkeys that define sounds associated with various Windows applications.

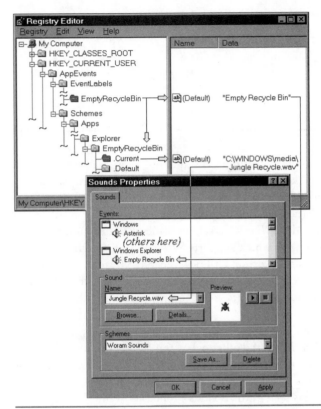

Figure 3-2 *The Control Panel Sounds applet's Properties tab derives its information from the HKCU keys shown here.*

Apps The *Apps* (applets) key leads to subkeys for each subdivision of the Events list on the Sounds tab. A few examples follow, along with the subkey associated with each one:

Sound Applet Events List	Apps Subkey
in Windows 95 and 98:	HKCU\AppEvents\Schemes\Apps\...
Windows	.Default
Windows Explorer	Explorer
Media Player	Mplayer
Sound Recorder	SndRec32

Continued

Sound Applet Events List	Apps Subkey
Typical Windows Applications	
Norton Navigator	*NortonNavigator*
Winword	*WinWord*
Microsoft Office	*Office97*

If a Windows application supports sound events, it may either add its own section and subkey to these lists or install its sound events within the Windows section of the Sounds tab, in which case the events will be listed under the *.Default* (note leading period) subkey. Microsoft's pre-Office 97 versions of Word added a *WinWord* subkey, while the later Office 97 suite adds an *Office97* subkey, which supports Word and other Office application sounds. Likewise, Norton Utilities version 3.0 adds the separate Norton Navigator section shown in the preceding list, while Ipswitch SW_FTP Pro Explorer adds its sound events to the regular Windows section.

Note that Figure 3-2 shows two *EmptyRecycleBin* keys; one directly below the *EventLabels* key, the other below the *Schemes\Apps\Explorer* key. The *.Current* (again, note leading period) subkey's Data entry specifies the specific sound that is heard when the Recycle Bin is flushed, and the filename written there is seen in the Sounds Properties' Name: box, as shown in the figure. Other subkeys specify the sounds available within each available scheme.

A *.Default* subkey note   Perhaps the Microspeak Dictionary ran out of words because, as Figure 3-3 shows, the same name (*.Default*) has different meanings within the *AppEvents* key structure. Note that just below the *Schemes\Apps* key, a *.Default* subkey leads immediately to yet another *.Default* subkey. The first contains nothing more than the word "Windows," which appears at the head of the Events list on the Sounds tab, as shown in Figure 3-2. The next leads to the subkeys that specify the sounds available for the event associated with the other *.Default* subkey seen above, under the *AppEvents\EventLabels* key. That is of course, the "Default sound" event, and the *.Current* subkey at the bottom of the figure specifies the path and filename for the sound associated with that event. Needless to say, there is no relationship between the use of *.Default* as a subkey name and the (Default) entry in every Contents pane's Name column.

Names There is a subkey under the *Names* key for each sound scheme listed on the drop-down list that appears in the Schemes box near the bottom of the Sounds tab, as shown by the partial list in Figure 3-3. Because the "Jungle Sound Scheme" is currently enabled on this system, the *Jungle0* key name appears in the *Schemes* key's Contents pane, as also seen in the figure.

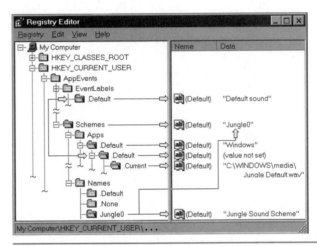

Figure 3-3 *The first* .Default *key refers to the event of that name, while the third* .Default *key leads to the subkeys that list various sounds that may be applied to that event (only the* .Current *sound is displayed here). The other* .Default *key specifies the name ("Windows") that appears at the head of the Events list.*

Control Panel

The subkeys beneath this key support Desktop characteristics that may be configured via various Control Panel applets (Accessibility Options, Display, Mouse, Regional Settings, and so on). Table 3-3 is a cross-reference guide between the *Control Panel* subkeys and associated applets.

Note

Status Indicator. Informal tests suggest that the *Accessibility* key's *Status Indicator* subkey is not fully operational. The Contents pane's *Docked* entry shows 0x00000001 (1) in the Data column, even on an undocked laptop computer. In fact, the key seems to be among the missing in OEM versions of Windows 95 and in Windows 98.

Table 3-3 *Cross-Reference Guide: HKCU\Control Panel Subkeys and Control Panel Applets*

HKCU\Control Panel Key and Subkey	Control Panel Applet and Tab	Check Box, Other
Accessibility	Accessibility Options	
HighContrast	Display	Use High Contrast
KeyboardResponse	Keyboard	various
MouseKeys	Mouse	Use MouseKeys
SerialKeys	General	Support Serial Key Devices
ShowSounds	Sound	Use ShowSounds
SoundSentry	Sound	Use SoundSentry
Status Indicator †		
Stickykeys	Keyboard	Use StickyKeys
TimeOut	General	Automatic Reset
ToggleKeys	Keyboard	Use ToggleKeys
Appearance	Display	
Schemes	Appearance	Scheme box
Colors	**Appearance**	Color boxes
Cursors	**Mouse**	
Schemes	Pointers	Scheme box
Desktop	Display	
	Screen Saver	
	Background	Wallpaper
	Plus! (if installed)	Visual settings
ResourceLocale	*Not accessible via Control Panel*	
WindowMetrics	Appearance	Item and Font boxes
International	**Regional Settings**	
	Regional Settings	Drop-down menu ‡
	Time	
Mouse	**Mouse**	
PowerCfg		

† This (empty) subkey is written the first time *Stickykeys* is enabled. Contents Pane entries written when *Stickykeys* is disabled.

‡ Indicated region is read from KERNEL32.DLL file, not from Registry.

InstallLocationsMRU

The Contents pane of this subkey simply lists the last five locations from which software has been installed. A typical list might look something like this:

Name (Default)	Data (value not set)
a	"A:\"
b	"c:\windows\options"
c	"M:\ADMIN\NETTOOLS\REMOTEREG\"
d	"e:\
e	"e:\win98\"
MRUList	"cbaed"

The MRUList (Most-Recently-Used List) entry indicates the sequence in which the listed sources were used.

keyboard layout

Subkeys beneath this key indicate keyboard language layout and configuration details, most of which are installed and configured via the Language tab in Control Panel's Keyboard applet.

preload

This key leads to a series of numbered subkeys — one for each installed language. In each case, the Contents pane lists the eight-digit number that identifies the language — 00000409 = English (United States), for example — and subkey *1* specifies the default language.

substitutes

If a keyboard language specified above is configured with a nondefault keyboard layout, a subkey with that language number appears here, and its Contents pane specifies the number of the new keyboard layout. For example, if the English (United States) language keyboard were configured for a Dvorak layout, the *substitutes* key would lead to a subkey named *00000409* (see the preceding section), and its Contents pane would show the string value 00020409, which identifies the Dvorak keyboard layout.

toggle

The string value in the Contents pane indicates the key combination that toggles between keyboard languages, as follows:

Data	Toggle Key Combination
1	Left Alt+Shift
2	Ctrl+Shift
3	None

Network

On a network system, if a network drive or folder is mapped to a local drive letter, a record of that connection appears under one or both of the two subkeys shown in Figure 3-4 and described in the following sections.

Persistent

If a checkmark is placed in the Reconnect at logon box when the network drive or folder is mapped to a local drive letter, then this key leads to a subkey whose label is that drive letter. The Contents pane specifies the network provider, path to the remote source, and the name of the local user who mapped the drive. If the Reconnect at logon box is subsequently cleared, the Contents pane entries are deleted.

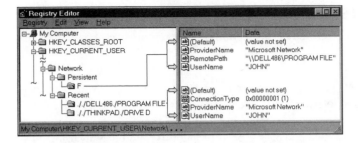

Figure 3-4 *The* Network *key's* Persistent *and* Recent *subkeys specify various network connections.*

Note

Various messages may be seen as Windows opens and closes, depending on the contents of the *Persistent* key and the actual system status. Refer to Chapter 8 for information about such messages.

Recent

The same information is also stored under this subkey, but the format is slightly different, as shown in the following table and in Figure 3-4.

Subkey(s)	Mapped Drive Identified As	Comment
Persistent	\\DELL486\PROGRAM FILE	Data column in Contents pane
Recent	././DELL486./PROGRAM FILE	Subkey label

In this example, the C:\Program Files folder on a network computer (Dell486) has been mapped to drive F on the local computer, and the Reconnect at logon box was checked when the drive was mapped. Note that the Contents pane in the *Persistent* subkey uses backslashes, while the subkey names beneath the *Recent* key use a period followed by a forward slash, because the backslash itself is an illegal character within a Registry key name.

The *Recent* key also shows a recent connection to a network drive on another computer (drive D on a ThinkPad). Note also that despite its long filename capabilities, both Windows 95 and 98 continue to use only the first 12 characters of the mapped device name, and these are forced into uppercase.

RemoteAccess

The subkeys described in this section provide remote-access information.

Addresses

The Contents pane lists the current user's remote-access providers, such as the Microsoft Network, with additional details under the *Profile* subkey, which is described in the following section. On a system not set up for remote access, the name of the local computer is found here instead.

Profile

This key leads to one or more subkeys, each named for one of the access providers listed in the *Addresses* key cited above. In each case, the Contents pane provides additional details about that provider, along with the current user's account name. Password information is not given here.

Software

Most subkeys found under this critical key bear the name of a software company. However, one or more other subkeys may appear here, too — especially if Windows 98 and/or Internet Explorer 4 are installed — and for purposes of this discussion these additional keys are designated here as *Software Configuration* keys. Needless to say, the number of keys in each category varies considerably from one system to another, depending on specific software configuration details. As elsewhere in the Registry, the key names are listed alphabetically, so there is no way to tell one type from the other, except for the obvious clue of a recognizable company name. The format in which data is stored also varies because no standards prescribe how such entries should be written into the Registry. Refer to "Data Format Comparisons" in Chapter 1 for a few examples of such differences.

Note

The subkey information found beneath this *Software* key pertains to software configuration for the current user only. Thus, if the system is set up for multiple users, the names and the content of the *Company Name* and *Software Configuration* subkeys will vary according to the current user's preferences.

Company Name

A subkey under each key with a company name leads to one or more additional subkeys — one for each of that manufacturer's installed applications. Each such key leads in turn to subkeys specific to that application.

It probably won't come as a surprise to discover a key with the name *Microsoft* on every Windows system. As with any other *Company Name* key, it leads to one or more (or in this case, *many* more) subkeys — one for each installed applet, application, or other Microsoft-installed component. To better illustrate the differences between the *HKCU\Software* and *HKLM\SOFTWARE* keys in general, and the *Microsoft* subkeys in particular, refer to the "Microsoft Software and SOFTWARE Subkeys" section which appears after the "HKLM: HKEY_LOCAL_MACHINE Key [SYSTEM.DAT]" section later in this chapter.

Software Configuration keys

Those subkeys under the *Software* key that do not bear a company name are used to describe various general software configuration details. A few typical examples are given in the following sections.

Software versus *SOFTWARE*

User-independent data for each software application is stored under the *HKLM\SOFTWARE* key (described below), and such data applies to all users. To help distinguish one key from another, note that the Windows 95 key name is *Software* here and *SOFTWARE* under the *HKLM* key. Unfortunately this distinction was removed in Windows 98, where both keys are a lowercase *software*. To further confuse the issue within the "HKLM: HKEY_LOCAL_MACHINE key [SYSTEM.DAT]" section, the subkey immediately below it is rendered as *Classes* in Windows 95 and *CLASSES* in Windows 98. Thus, the same key structure may appear in either of the following formats:

Windows 95	HKEY_LOCAL_MACHINE\SOFTWARE\ Classes
Windows 98	HKEY_LOCAL_MACHINE\Software\ CLASSES

Further commentary on Microsoft style (or lack thereof) is fortunately beyond the scope of this text, which sticks with *HKCU\Software* and *HKLM\SOFTWARE* to preserve the distinction between the same subkey structure in these two locations – at least while reading about them in this book. After that, you're on your own.

Classes and CLSID The *Classes* key is written into the Registry if Internet Explorer 4 is installed and leads directly to a *CLSID* subkey, which in turn leads to one or more subkeys, each with a distinctive CLSID name. In the Contents pane for each such key, the (Default) line may or may not list the name of the object associated with the CLSID number. A few such numbers and object names are included in the following list to help identify some of the *CLSID* subkeys that may appear in this section.

CLSID	Object Name
{208D2C60-3AEA-1069-A2D7-08002B30309D}	Network Neighborhood
{20D04FE0-3AEA-1069-A2D8-08002B30309D}	My Computer
{21EC2020-3AEA-1069-A2DD-08002B30309D}	Control Panel
{450D8FBA-AD25-11D0-98A8-0800361B1103}	My Documents
{645FF040-5081-101B-9F08-00AA002F954E}	Recycle Bin
{88667D10-10F0-11D0-8150-00AA00BF8457}	Microsoft Network

If no object name is in the Contents pane, the name for that object is probably listed instead under the *CLSID* key with the same name in the *HKCR\CLSID* section of the Registry. The purpose of the subkeys at that location was described in the "CLSID (Class Identifier)" section of Chapter 2. When a key with the same Class Identifier number is found here too, then the information under it supersedes that in the *HKCR\CLSID* section.

DefaultIcon If MS Plus! 98 or Internet Explorer 4 is installed, this subkey may appear under some of the *CLSID* keys listed previously. Refer to "The *DefaultIcon* Subkey" in the "Desktop Icons" section of Chapter 6 for information about how changes are made here, either automatically or by the user.

WORDPAD.INI A key with this name has been observed in several Windows 95 SR2 configurations. Although its six subkeys correspond with the six tabs on WordPad's Options dialog box (open the View menu, select Options) and with corresponding sections in a C:\Windows\ WORDPAD.INI file, neither this Registry structure nor the INI file seems to do anything. Instead, all WordPad configuration changes are written into subkeys with the same names found under the following key:

HKCU\Software\Microsoft\Windows\CurrentVersion\Applets
\WordPad

The *WORDPAD.INI* key structure under discussion has been deleted on several systems with no apparent effect on the applet and is mentioned here simply as an example of a Registry structure that either doesn't really belong here or is awaiting future implementation.

HKLM: HKEY_LOCAL_MACHINE Key [SYSTEM.DAT]

The information contained within this key is stored in the hidden SYSTEM.DAT file in the C:\Windows folder, and by default the key contains the seven subkeys described in this section. In addition, other subkeys may be inserted by third-party applications. If so, the identity of the application is probably listed in the Data column of the Contents Pane's (Default) entry.

Two *HKLM* subkey structures (*Config\0001* and *SOFTWARE\ Classes*) are sources for the *HKCC* key (discussed later in this chapter) and the *HKCR* key, which was described in the previous chapter.

Config and 000x

The *Config* key contains one or more subkeys labeled *000x,* where *x* = 1, 2, 3, and so on. Each such subkey contains a hardware configuration profile available to the local machine. For example, a laptop might have a *0001* subkey for its docked configuration and a *0002* subkey for its undocked configuration. Or a desktop system might have one configuration that takes some external device into account, and another for when that device is not physically present. Either computer might have one or more additional hardware configuration profiles, in which case that many additional subkeys would be found here, too.

To view the available configurations, open Control Panel's System applet and select the Hardware Profiles tab. The available hardware profiles are listed alphabetically. The first profile is contained in subkey *0001*, the second in *0002*, and so on. In most cases, Windows determines which configuration is required as it opens and exports the appropriate *Config* subkey into the *HKCC* key described later in this chapter. Refer to the discussion of that key for a description of the subkeys found under the *0001* key, and to the "Hardware Profile Editing" section of Chapter 6 for assistance in creating, editing, or removing a hardware profile.

Enum

This enumerator key contains a subkey for each hardware device type connected to the system since Windows was installed. As you might suspect by now, each key leads to one or more subkeys, each of which names a single physical device. Each of these has its own subkey(s), which again vary from one system to another, depending on the manufacturer of the installed devices. For each such subkey, the Contents pane lists Name and Data information such as that shown in the following examples:

Name	Data (for an external modem)	Data (for a network card)
Class	Modem	Net
DeviceDesc	DeskPorte 28.8	Intel EtherExpress PRO10 (PnP Enabled)
FriendlyName	Microcom DeskPorte FAST Plug & Play	*(None; perhaps the above is friendly enough)*
HardwareID	SERENUM\MNP0336	INT 1030, ISAPNP\INT 1030
Mfg	Microcom, Inc.	Intel
PnP Rev	0.99	–
HWRevision	–	1.0.00

The Contents pane for these and other devices also lists other data, as appropriate to the device. Once Windows writes a key or subkey into this section, that key remains in place even if the cited device or device type is physically removed from the system. However, a specific device key is removed if that device is removed via a Windows uninstall procedure. If Windows itself is unable to remove the device, then its key(s) can be deleted by editing the Registry, as described in Chapter 4.

The location of a specific subkey may vary from one system to another. For example, the *PNP0100* subkey identifies the system timer, which is present on any system regardless of its type. However, the subkey may be found under the *BIOS* or *Root* keys, depending on the specific system type. In the case of a hard drive, its subkey will be found under the key that describes its type (*ESDI, SCSI,* for example).

The following sections briefly summarize some of the subkeys that may be found under the *Enum* key, with additional details provided in Table 3-4. A parenthetical phrase describes a key whose identity may not be immediately clear from its name. It's not a bad idea to skim each of these sections, even if the subkeys they describe do not exist on your system because many of these subkey examples may exist under a different key, as for example, in the case of a hard drive. In any case, the data found in the Contents pane should be much the same, regardless of where the key itself is actually placed in the *Enum* key structure. Needless to say, not every subkey listed here will appear on every system. In case of doubt, refer to the "Registry Search Indicators" section of Chapter 4 for suggestions on how to search the *Enum* key section for a specific device.

Table 3-4 *Cross-Reference Guide: Device Manager and HKLM\Enum Subkeys* *

Device Manager Tab Shows Device Type, Description †	ENUM Subkey	Additional Subkey ‡
CDROM		
NEC CD-ROM DRIVE 501	*SCSI*	*NEC_ \ROOT&*
Disk drives		
DEC DSP3107LS	*SCSI*	*DEC_ \ROOT&*
GENERIC NEC FLOPPY DISK	*FLOP*	*GENERIC\ROOT&*
GENERIC NEC FLOPPY DISK	*FLOP*	*GENERIC\ROOT&*
Display adapters		
ATI Graphics Ultra Pro (mach32)	*PCI*	*VEN_ \BUS_*
Floppy disk controllers		
Standard Floppy Disk Controller	*Root*	**PNP0700\0000*
Keyboard		
Standard 101/102-Key or Microsoft Natural Keyboard	*Root*	**PNP0303\0000*
Modem		
DeskPorte 28.8	*SERENUM*	*MNP0336\ROOT&*

Continued

Table 3-4 *Continued*

Device Manager Tab Shows Device Type, Description †	ENUM Subkey	Additional Subkey ‡
Monitor		
MAG Innovision MX17F/S	*Monitor*	*Default_Monitor\0001*
Mouse		
Standard PS/2 Port Mouse	*Root*	**PNP0F0E\0000*
Network adapters		
Dial-Up Adapter	*Root*	*Net\0000*
Intel EtherExpress PRO/10	*ISAPNP*	*INT 1030\00A3478A*
Other devices		
APC BACK-UPS PRO	*SERENUM*	*APC1065\ROOT&*
Ports (COM & LPT)		
Communications Port (COM1)	*Root*	**PNP0500\0000*
Communications Port (COM2)	*Root*	**PNP0500\0001*
Printer Port (LPT1)	*Root*	*Ports\0000*
Printers §		
HP Laser Jet 4	*Root*	*printer\0000*
HP DeskJet 1200C/PS		
SCSI controllers	*Root*	*printer\0001*
Adaptec AHA-174X EISA Host	*Root*	**ADP1740\0000*
PCI NCR C810 SCSI Host	*PCI*	*VEN_ \BUS_*
System devices		
Direct Memory access controller	*Root*	**PNP0200\0000*
Intel Mercury Pentium(r) Processor to PCI bridge	*PCI*	*VEN_ \BUS_*
Intel PCI to EISA bridge	*PCI*	*VEN_ \BUS_*
I/O read data port for ISA Plug and Play enumerator	*ISAPNP*	*READDATAPORT\0*
ISA Plug and Play bus	*EISA*	**PNP0A00*
Numeric data processor	*Root*	**PNP0C04\0000*

Device Manager Tab Shows Device Type, Description †	ENUM Subkey	Additional Subkey ‡
PCI bus	*Root*	*PNP0A03\0000*
Programmable interrupt controller	*Root*	*PNP000\0000*
System board	*Root*	*PNP0C01\0000*
System CMOS/read time clock	*Root*	*PNP0B00\0000*
System speaker	*Root*	*PNP0800\0000*
System timer	*Root*	*PNP0100\0000*

* Shows devices installed on typical Pentium system. Key names vary from one system to another.

† Device description is stored in last subkey listed in table.

§ Printers do not appear on Device Manager tab.

‡ Some subkey names abbreviated here.

BIOS

This key appears on systems with plug-and-play BIOS and contains many of the devices that would otherwise be found under the *Root* key (described later in this chapter).

EISA

On an EISA system, each installed EISA device is represented by its own subkey. At minimum, there should be a *PNP0A00* key, whose device description is "ISA Plug and Play bus."

ESDI

If this key is present, an ESDI device, probably a hard drive, is installed in the system. Among other items in each drive subkey's Contents pane, a CurrentDriveLetterAssignment entry in the Name column is accompanied by the drive letter in the Data column. If the physical drive is partitioned into logical drives, the Data column lists each letter — for example, "CDE" for a drive with three partitions.

FLOP

There is one subkey immediately below this key for each installed diskette drive. As in the hard drive subkey described previously, in each subkey's Contents pane, a CurrentDriveLetterAssignment in the Name column is accompanied by the drive letter in the Data column.

HTREE (Hardware Tree)

This undocumented key contains a *RESERVED* subkey, under which there is a *0* subkey. The latter key may be empty, or it may contain a binary ForcedConfig or ConfigFlags entry. Taking a hint from the key name, this structure may be reserved for future use.

INFRARED

On Windows 98 systems, a *KnownDevices* subkey lists infrared hardware devices, even if the PC itself contains none of these devices. The list is simply copied from the [Generic_AddReg] section of the C:\Windows\INFRARED.INF file, and if an actual infrared device is subsequently installed, additional Registry information may be written, as required by that device.

ISAPNP (ISA Plug-and-Play)

This key appears on an ISA or EISA system, and its subkeys specify installed ISA devices. For example, an *INT1030* subkey specifies an Intel EtherExpress PRO/10 plug-and-play network card. This and other data pertaining to the card's configuration can be found in subkeys beneath this key.

Even if no such devices are installed, a subkey under a *READDATAPORT* key should specify the ISA plug-and-play enumerator.

LPTENUM (LPT Enumerator)

A subkey appears under this key only if a plug-and-play printer is configured for a parallel port. In other words, neither a conventional (non-PnP) printer nor a PnP network printer will be specified here.

MF (multifunction devices)

This key appears if a multifunction device is installed, with *CHILDxxxx* subkeys beneath it leading to subkeys for each of the device's multiple functions. Thus, if a dual IDE controller and a combination modem/network card are both installed, the *CHILD0000* and *CHILD0001* keys shown in Figure 3-5 would be displayed. Each lengthy subkey name (some are truncated in the figure) identifies the specific device, with additional hardware configuration information in the Contents pane. Because the modem/network card in this example is a PC-card device, it is listed again under the *PCMCIA* key.

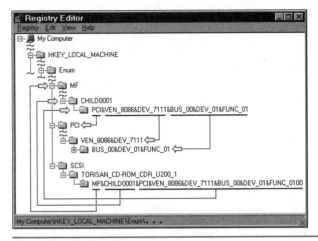

Figure 3-5 *The* MF *(multifunction) key leads to two or more* CHILDxxxx *subkeys, which in turn lead to subkeys for each function of a multifunction device. The* Default_Monitor *key leads to subkeys defining the characteristics of various installed monitors. In this example, subkey* 0001 *specifies an external monitor used by a laptop computer in its docked mode, while* 0002 *is the laptop's built-in display panel. The* VSC4151 *subkey identifies an external monitor connected to a built-in video port on a different laptop. Finally, the* PCMCIA *key leads to subkeys for various PC card devices. See the text for additional details.*

MONITOR and DEFAULT_MONITOR subkeys

The *Default_Monitor* subkey contains a subkey (*0001, 0002,* and so on) for each hardware profile. As shown later in Figure 3-6, the Contents pane for each such key identifies the monitor used for that configuration. On a desktop system, the information in each *000x* subkey is usually identical because the same monitor is used for each configuration. By contrast, if a laptop computer uses its own screen when undocked and an external monitor when docked, then the identity of each monitor is indicated in its own *000x* subkey.

Note, however, that although these *000x* subkeys appear beneath a key labeled *Default_Monitor,* this subsection of the *HKLM* key does not reveal which monitor is currently in use. That information is instead contained in one of the subkeys under the *HKDD\Config Manager\Enum* key. Refer to the "Default Monitor Subkey" section later in this chapter for further details.

In addition to the *Default_Monitor* key and its subkey(s), one or more additional subkeys may appear under the *Monitor* key, such as the *VSC4151* subkey also seen in Figure 3-6. In this case, the key name identifies a monitor connected to a laptop computer's video output port. As elsewhere in the *Enum* key structure, the key remains in the Registry even if the external monitor is no longer connected.

Network

Unlike the other subkeys under the *Enum* key, the *Network* key's subkeys specify various network parameters (such as clients, services, protocols) but not the network hardware itself.

PCI

PCI bus hardware is listed here, including PCI SCSI host adapters, and a PCI-to-EISA bridge (if present). Each subkey name takes the form of VEN_*xxxx*&DEV_*yyyy*, where *xxxx* is a vendor identification number and *yyyy* is that vendor's device number for the cited device. Typical examples are the following:

Subkey Name	Vendor	Device
VEN_1000&DEV_0001	NCR	PCI C810 SCSI Host Adapter
VEN_1002&DEV_4158	ATI Technologies	Graphics Ultra Pro (mach32)
VEN_8086&DEV_0482	Intel	PCI to EISA bridge
VEN_8086&DEV_04A3	Intel	Pentium(r) Processor to PCI bridge

The vendor and device identification is usually found in a subkey beneath the key in the preceding list. If a PCI device appears elsewhere in the *Enum* section, its subkey name may serve as a cross-reference from one location to another, as shown in Figure 3-6.

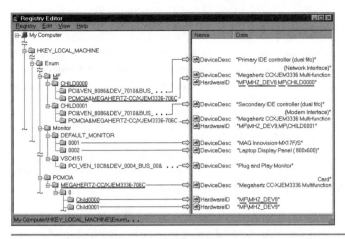

Figure 3-6 *In this* Enum *key structure detail view, the lengthy subkey name at the bottom cross-references an* MF *key structure, and the lowest subkey under the* MF *key points to a set of keys within the* PCI *key structure. In each key name, the underlined component identifies another key, as indicated by the lines and arrows.*

PCMCIA (Personal Computer Memory Card International Association)

According to at least a few industry watchers, the abbreviation really means *People Can't Memorize Computer-Industry Abbreviations.* The more user-friendly term *PC Card* has gained recent popularity, although the abbreviation is still used within the Registry. Just remember that *PCMCIA* and *PC Card* may be used interchangeably, and that on a system that supports PCMCIA/PC card hardware, there should be a subkey here for every PC card device that has been installed on the system, even if that device is not currently present. A multifunction PC card device, such as the modem/network card previously described in the "MF (multifunction devices)" section may also be listed here, as shown at the bottom of Figure 3-6. Again there are two *CHILD...* subkeys, one for each function. Note that various key name and Contents pane entries agree with similar data found under the *MF* key, as indicated by the underlined segments in both locations.

Root

Although both Windows Resource Kits state this section is for legacy devices, it may in fact contain a mixed bag of both legacy and Windows devices, as described in the following sections.

Legacy devices In most cases, there are at least a few subkeys whose name is **PNPxxxx* (note leading asterisk) or *PNPxxxx* (no asterisk), where *xxxx* is a hexadecimal number. The asterisk denotes an item on the system board, such as a DMA or programmable interrupt controller, numeric data processor, and so on. If the asterisk is omitted, the cited item is probably part of a plug-in adapter card.

Depending on specific system configuration, a separate *Ports* subkey may list the printer port(s), or these may be listed under a **PNP0400* key, either in this *Root* key area or else under the *BIOS* key. In addition, a *Printer* key leads to separate subkeys for each installed printer, other than those listed under the *LPTENUM* key described previously.

Windows devices The Windows Direct Cable Connection applet installs subkeys here for each COM and LPT port that supports this feature, and there may be additional subkeys for *Net* and other installed hardware, as shown by the following examples:

Key	Subkey	Contents
MDMGEN	*COM1*	Microcom DeskPorte FAST
Net	*0000*	Dial-Up Adapter
PNPC031	*COM1*	Serial cable on COM1
	COM2	Serial cable on COM2
PNPC032	*LPT1*	Parallel cable on LPT1

Figure 3-7 shows a partial list of the many device subkeys found under the *Root* key. For comparison purposes, Figure 3-8 shows how some of these are listed by the Windows Device Manager tab in Control Panel's System applet. A checkmark (which does not appear in the actual screen display) indicates a device type listed under the *Root* subkey in Figure 3-7. Some of the checked items may appear instead under the *BIOS* key described previously, if that key is present.

SCSI (Small Computer System Interface)

As its name suggests, the subkeys found here define installed SCSI devices. However, a PCI SCSI host adapter is listed under the PCI subkey, and not under this *SCSI* subkey.

SERENUM (Serial Enumerator)

The subkeys in this section specify devices installed on a serial port, as for example, a serial modem, uninterruptible power supply with serial port notification, and so on. A serial mouse, however, is not listed here.

TAPECONTROLLER

On Windows 98 systems, this key is added if the Backup applet in the System Tools group is installed (via the Windows Setup tab in Control Panel's Add/Remove Programs applet). A *TAPEDETECTION* subkey structure appears below this key even if tape backup hardware is not installed. If a tape drive is installed, then numbered subkeys specify configuration and driver details.

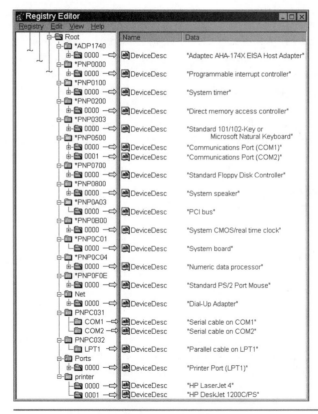

Figure 3-7 *The* HKEY_LOCAL_MACHINE *key's* Enum\Root *key may lead to a collection of subkeys. Under each subkey, one or more additional subkeys specify various hardware components.*

USB (Universal Serial Bus)

If USB is supported by your version of Windows (Windows 98 and Windows 95 SR 2.1) and a USB hardware device is present, this key leads to a *ROOT_HUB* key structure that contains a subkey identifying the USB host controller. In addition, another subkey structure exists under the *USB* key for each installed USB device.

hardware

This section appears to be awaiting full implementation. According to both versions of the Windows Resource Kit, it contains "information about serial ports and modems used with the HyperTerminal program." Its *Description* and *devicemap* key structures are described in the following sections.

DESCRIPTION (Description, in Windows 98)

This section contains a brief description of various hardware components, with a single *System* key beneath it leading to one or more of the subkeys listed here. Under each one, each numbered subkey (*0, 1,* and so on) indicates the presence of one of the cited items.

CentralProcessor This subkey is not present on the original retail version of Windows 95, although with luck, its namesake is. In Windows 95 SR versions and in Windows 98, the key's Contents pane contains vendor identification data that appears on the "My Computer" Properties sheet General tab. Refer to "Computer" in the "System Configuration Details" section of Chapter 6 for details on temporarily displaying additional information on this tab.

FloatingPointProcessor This key, and a *0* subkey beneath it, indicate the presence of a floating-point processor, although the key structure itself may contain no additional information.

MultifunctionAdapter Here, each numbered subkey contains limited configuration information about a multifunction adapter (if that adapter is not found under the *Enum* key's *MF* subkey described earlier). In addition, an Identifier entry specifies the device type ("ISA," for example).

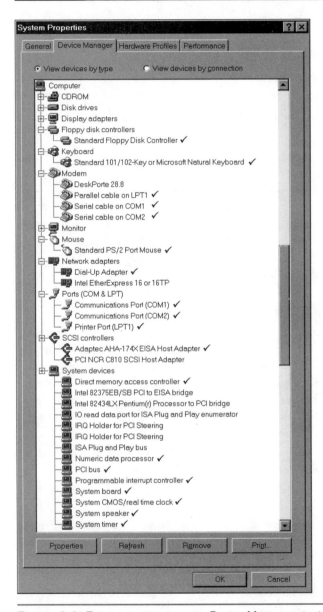

Figure 3-8 *This expanded view of a Device Manager tab shows many of the devices installed on the system. A checkmark identifies a device specified under the* Root *subkey shown in Figure 3-7. Depending on specific system configuration, some of these devices may be specified under some other* HKLM\Enum *subkey.*

devicemap

This key leads to a *serialcomm* subkey, which contains nothing but the following:

Name	Data
(Default)	(value not set)
COM1	"COM1"
COM2	"COM2"

No modem information is given here, and if HyperTerminal is set to use a COM port other than COM1 or COM2, that information is also not present here. Furthermore, if the system contains only one COM port, the COM1 and COM2 listings are still found here.

Network and Logon

If the system is set up for Dial-Up Networking or other network configurations, the *Logon* subkey gives the current user's username and other configuration details. The contents—but not the name—of this subkey changes on startup to specify the appropriate configuration for the current user. However, if the current user logged on by pressing the Escape key at the name/password prompt, then this subkey shows the name of the last person who logged on and entered a valid username.

Refer to the "System and CurrentControlSet" section later in this chapter for additional details about the current user.

Security

The following subkeys may be found on a system configured for remote network administration.

Access

This leads to an *Admin\Remote* subkey, which contains the name of the network administration computer.

Provider

This subkey's Contents pane may contain one or more lines such as those briefly described in the following table:

Name Column	Data Column	Comment
Address_Book	"msab32.dll"	Network address book translator
Address_Server	"*(server name)*"	
Container	"*(server name)*"	
Platform_Type	00 00 00 00	Share-level access control
	01 00 00 00	User-level access control

Software (SOFTWARE in Windows 95)

The subkeys under this key contain installed-software data that applies to all users, regardless of their personal configuration preferences. Thus, a Windows-aware software application places a *Company Name* subkey here, as described later in this section. A subkey with the same name may also appear under the *HKCU\Software* key if the software supports individual user configurations.

CLASSES (Classes in Windows 95)

The subkeys under this key are "buried" several levels below the master HKEY in which they are stored. For example, the following lines show how the same subkey (*.bmp*) may be accessed here in the *HKLM* section and also in the *HKCR* section.

Level	Key and Subkeys	Key and Subkey
1	*HKEY_LOCAL_MACHINE*	*HKEY_CLASSES_ROOT*
2	*SOFTWARE*	*.bmp*
3	*Classes*	
4	*.bmp*	

The *HKCR* key structure makes access to the same information more convenient, because it bypasses the intermediate *SOFTWARE\ Classes* subkeys at levels 2 and 3 in the *HKLM* section. Therefore, this set of subkeys was described in detail in the "HKCR: HKEY_CLASSES_ROOT key [HKLM\SOFTWARE\ Classes]" section of Chapter 2. Remember however, that if a change occurs within an *HKCR* subkey, that change simultaneously takes place here, too. In fact, it is here in *HKLM* that the information is actually stored.

Clients

Despite the ambiguous name and the location outside the *Microsoft* key structure, this key is actually part of the Microsoft Outlook or Outlook Express applet.

Description

Judging by the *Microsoft* and *Rpc* subkeys that follow, this is a description of the Microsoft RPC (remote procedure call) system. Although far beyond the scope of this book, the *uuid* (universally unique identifier) subkeys contain network address and other data needed when an application on one system needs to make a function call to a remote system.

The (*Company Name*) subkey

No doubt several *SOFTWARE* subkeys in this section bear the name of a software manufacturer. Under each such key is one subkey for each of that manufacturer's Windows-compatible software products that are installed on the system. Although the specific *Company Name* subkey structure of course varies from one system to another, there's very little doubt that every system will have a *Microsoft* subkey under its *HKLM\SOFTWARE* key. Because there's no escaping this key and its multiple subkeys, it is explained separately at the end of the present "HKLM: HKEY_LOCAL_MACHINE Key [SYSTEM.DAT]" section. Refer to the "Microsoft Software and SOFTWARE Subkeys" section later in this chapter for all the gory details, which should generally apply to other *Company Name* subkeys as well.

System and CurrentControlSet

As the key names may suggest, the *System* and *CurrentControlSet* keys lead to data that controls how the system (that is, Windows 95 or 98) configures itself as it opens. This data is found under the two subkeys described in the following sections.

control

On a network system, this key's Contents pane usually shows a CurrentUser entry, whose Data column lists the name of the current user, which is read from the *HKLM\Network\Logon* key (described above). The information in that key was written when Windows opened and prompted the user to enter a name and password. However, if the name/password prompt is disabled, then the current user name is that which was entered immediately after Windows was installed. If the prompt is enabled, but bypassed by pressing the Escape key at the name/password prompt, then there is no *CurrentUser* entry here. Nor does this entry appear on a non-networked single-user system.

Figure 3-9 illustrates the sequence on a network system when the user enters a valid user name and password. To verify this, type in a valid name in any distinctive mix of uppercase and lowercase letters and note its appearance in the *Logon* and *control* subkeys, as illustrated in Figure 3-9. Then restart Windows and note that the User name prompt shows the user name just as it was typed at the beginning of the previous session. Now press the Escape key to open in the default user mode. The Registry's *Logon* key continues to show the previous user name, while the *control* key does not. Also note there is no stylistic consistency between the opening prompt ("User name"), the *Logon* key entry ("username"), and the *control* key entry ("Current User").

A few of the subkeys that appear under the *control* key are briefly described in the following sections.

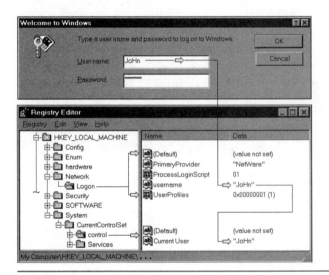

Figure 3-9 *If a user logs on with a valid password, the user name is written into the Registry's* Logon *and* control *keys. If the next user bypasses the user/password prompt by pressing the Escape key, the* Logon *key retains the previous user's name, but the* control *key does not.*

ComputerName With luck, you don't need to be told what this key contains.

IDConfigDB No doubt the key name means (in reverse English) "Database of Configuration Identification(s)," and its Contents pane displays entries such as those shown here:

Name	Data (laptop)	Data (desktop)
CurrentConfig	"0002"	"0001"
FriendlyName0001	"Docked"	"Original Configuration"
FriendlyName0002	"Undocked"	(*other configuration(s), if any*)

The CurrentConfig entry specifies which of the listed configurations is currently enabled. On some laptop systems, the CurrentConfig number may not change unless the computer is powered off and back on again as part of the docking/undocking procedure.

SessionManager From its name, one might deduce that the key has something to do with the management of a Windows session, although Microsoft documentation has little or nothing to say about a Session Manager. Nevertheless, the subkeys found here contain much information that may be helpful to the advanced user looking for troubleshooting clues, as briefly summarized here.

AppPatches Each subkey under the *AppPatches* key lists a specific application, and additional subkeys contain the patch(es) required if that application is run under Windows.

    CheckBadApps: The applications listed here may have problems running correctly under Windows.

    CheckBadApps400: The applications listed here may have problems running correctly under Windows if Microsoft Internet Explorer 4 is installed. (The fact that this key exists at all is unsettling.)

    CheckVerDLLs: A Windows application is supposed to check the version number of a DLL file listed here, before installing its own DLL, which may be an earlier version. Some do, some don't. Refer to the "DLL File Check" section of Chapter 7 for information about troubleshooting DLL-related files.

    HackIniFiles: This key's Contents pane Data column cites a single line in each of three INI files, and this line is written into the cited INI file when Windows 95 or 98 is installed, to optimize that INI file for operation under Windows 95 or 98. If the cited line is subsequently erased from the INI file, the deletion is permanent; that is, the *HackIniFiles* key does not rewrite it the next time Windows opens.

Known16DLLs: Windows searches various folders for 16-bit DLL files in the "Default Search Order" shown in the following table. However, if a DLL file is listed in the *Known16DLLs* key's Contents pane, then the search order for that file is as shown in the "Revised Search Order" column.

Default Search Order	Revised Search Order
1. Current folder	C:\Windows\System
2. C:\Windows	C:\Windows
3. C:\Windows\system	Current folder
4. Executable file folder	Executable file folder
5. Folders specified by PATH	Folders specified by PATH

KnownDLLs: This key's Contents pane specifies the DLL files that are loaded into memory when Windows starts, even if no application requires them.

Update: Although the Windows Resource Kits simply state that the (unidentified) value here indicates ". . . whether Windows was installed over an earlier version of Windows," the Contents pane in fact lists more detailed information relevant to future upgrades. Refer to the "Windows Update Policies" section of Chapter 6 for information about revising this key. Also see the "Unable to update configuration . . ." error message in Chapter 8.

WarnVerDLLs: Added by Internet Explorer 4, the key lists DLL files that may cause conflicts.

VMM32Files: Each subkey in this section is the name of a former virtual device driver file that is now part of the VMM32.VXD file in the C:\Windows\System folder.

Services

This key leads to a long series of subkeys that may specify various drivers, provide descriptions of installed hardware, or furnish other information pertaining to system configuration. A few examples are briefly described in the following sections.

Arbitrators The four subkeys under the *Arbitrator* key specify the resources that Windows has allocated, as shown in Figure 3-10 and described here.

AddrArb: The address arbitrator lists memory addresses that Windows has assigned to hardware devices. Figure 3-10 shows how Device Manager's View Resources tab reports the same information. In this specific example, a legacy sound card occupies the 000E0000–000E7FFF memory range, and of course the system ROM BIOS is at 000F0000–00FFFFFF. Although the View Resources tab shows both blocks as "Unavailable for use by devices," neither is listed in the *AddrArb* key's Contents pane.

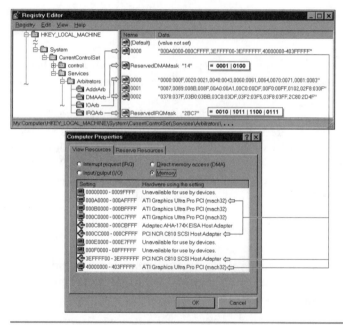

Figure 3-10 *The* Services\Arbitrators *key leads to subkeys for arbitration of various resources. The Computer Properties window at the bottom of the illustration shows how address resources are display on the Device Manager's View Resources tab.*

DMAArb: The Direct Memory Address Arbitrator uses a bit mask format to specify the reserved DMA configuration. In the example shown in Figure 3-10, the bit mask is hexadecimal 14, whose binary equivalent specifies DMA 4 and 2, as indicated by the underlined decimal numbers below the binary value.

```
Hex                 - binary -
14            =     0   0   0   1       0   1   0   0
bit position        7   6   5   4       3   2   1   0
```

IOArb: Here, each numbered entry in the Name column specifies some of the I/O (input/output) ports used by known hardware devices. About eight such ports are listed in each row, and the list proceeds sequentially from I/O port 0000 to the highest port used by a known device. The port assignments are separated by commas, and a port range is indicated by a colon between the starting and ending port number, as follows:

```
0087, 0089:008B, 008F, 00A0:00A1, 00C0:00DF
```

The first two entries would appear as 0087–0087 and 0089–008B in the Device Manager's Input/output (I/O) list. If that list shows a port as "In use by unknown device," that port does not appear on the list in the *IOArb* key's Contents pane.

IRQArb: The Interrupt Request Arbitrator subkey follows the style of the *DMAArb* subkey described previously. Thus, the ReservedIRQMask shown in Figure 3-10 specifies the IRQs indicated here by the underlined numbers under the binary value:

```
Hex                 - binary -
2BC7          =  0  0  1  0    1  0  1  1    1  1  0  0    0  1  1  1
bit position    15 14 13 12   11 10  9  8    7  6  5  4    3  2  1  0
```

Class There is a subkey here for every supported class of hardware device, with a numbered subkey (*0000, 0001, 0002*, and so on) beneath it for each device or device configuration in that class that is (or was) installed.

Display: This key leads to one or more numbered (*0000, 0001,* and so on) subkeys — one for each configuration. Each in turn leads to *DEFAULT, INFO* (Windows 98 only), and *MODES* subkeys, as shown in Figure 3-11.

The *DEFAULT* subkey specifies the display driver and its default mode, as follows:

Name	Data	Default color depth	Default resolution
Mode	"8,640,480"	$8 = 2^8 = 256$ colors	$640,480 = 640 \times 480$

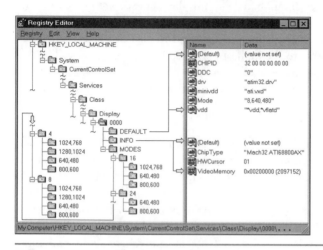

Figure 3-11 *The* DEFAULT *key's Contents pane specifies the current video drivers, while the* MODES *subkeys list the various color depths and resolutions supported by the installed driver.*

The mode specified here is not necessarily the currently enabled color mode, which is specified beneath yet another *Display* key, as described at the beginning of the "HKCC: HKEY_CURRENT_CONFIG key [HKLM\Config\000*x*]" section later in this chapter, and illustrated in Figure 3-20 in that section.

In Windows 98, the *INFO* key displays information about the chip type, hardware cursor, video memory, and other data — not all of which is shown in Figure 3-11.

Subkeys under the *MODES* key list each available color depth, and another level of subkeys specifies the screen resolutions available at each color depth. Both key sets are sorted alphabetically by name, which accounts for the *16, 24, 4, 8* sequence, and likewise the order of the screen resolution subkeys. The Contents pane for each of these keys is empty.

Modem: The Contents pane of each numbered subkey lists details about a modem or other installed communications device, as shown in Figure 3-12. Beneath each such key, additional subkeys specify commands appropriate to that device, such as the modem AT commands shown in the figure. If the Windows Direct Cable Connection has been installed and enabled, a separate subkey appears for each available cable connection, even if a DCC cable is not physically attached.

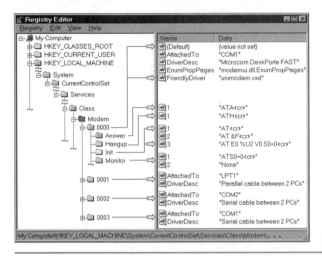

Figure 3-12 *The* Modem *key leads to one or more numbered subkeys, once for each communications device. In this example, the modem itself is specified by the 0000 key, whose subkeys list various AT commands. The other three subkeys (0001–0003) specify DCC (Direct Cable Connection) devices. For each device, the Contents pane seen here shows a partial listing of its actual parameters.*

Monitor: Each DriverDesc entry in the Contents pane of the numbered subkey(s) beneath this key identifies a monitor, either by name and model number (MAG Innovision MX17F/S, for example) or by type (Laptop Display Panel 800 × 600). The MaxResolution specifies the maximum resolution supported by the monitor. Compare this key with the *Display* key described previously and with the *HKCC\Display\Settings* key described later in the chapter.

VxD: A subkey is listed here for every installed virtual device driver.

The Microsoft Software and SOFTWARE Subkeys

As previously noted, *Microsoft* subkeys appear beneath the *HKCU\Software* and *HKLM\SOFTWARE* keys, and subkeys under each one identify various Microsoft components, as shown in Figure 3-13. Because both key structures are found on every Windows system, a comparison is provided here to give a better idea of the differences between subkeys with the same name. Although these details apply only to the specific subkeys described, similar comparisons can be made between most other *Company Name* subkey systems that appear under the *HKCU\Software* and *HKLM\SOFTWARE* keys.

In the comparisons that follow, remember that subkeys under *HKCU\Software* pertain to the current user only, and therefore change if a different user logs onto the system. By contrast, those under *HKLM\SOFTWARE* pertain to the basic software installation on the local machine, without regard to a specific user's personal configuration. Each *HKCU* subkey description is followed by a description of the equivalent subkey under the *HKLM* key. If a *Company Name* or application subkey appears under *HKLM\SOFTWARE* only, then it may be inferred that either the cited software is not separately configurable for multiple users, or the current user has not installed that software.

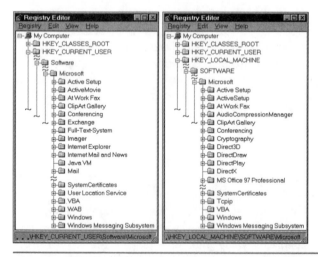

Figure 3-13 *This partial list of software subkeys under the* Microsoft *key at two Registry locations shows that not all subkey names are common to both locations. In the HKLM example, note the two subkeys with the same name (almost) at the top of the list.*

The HKCU\Software\Microsoft\Windows subkey

Several keys in this section are briefly described for comparison with the similar key structure found in the following "HKLM\SOFTWARE \Microsoft\Windows" section.

CurrentVersion

The Contents pane of this key is empty, and the key itself functions solely as a repository of the subkeys that follow, some of which are described in the following sections.

Applets This key leads to multiple subkeys for various Windows applets. In each case, the subkey describes parameters that pertain to the current user. Only a few of these applets are listed in the following sections.

CdPlayer: The *Settings* subkey's Contents pane lists the various settings that determine the appearance and playing characteristics of the CDPlayer applet. These settings are refreshed when the applet closes and then used to set up the applet the next time it opens. If artist, title, and track list information is saved via the applet's Edit Play List option, this data is written into a CDPLAYER.INI file and not stored in the Registry.

FreeCell: The Contents pane lists games won and lost and other critical information that should not fall into enemy hands. A similar key for Solitaire does not exist, so feel free to lie about your amazing skill without fear of being caught.

Regedit: The FindFlags entry stores the current Find parameters of the Registry Editor in DWORD format, as shown by this default entry:

Name	Data
FindFlags	0x00000003 (3)
View	*(60 byte hexadecimal string)*

The legal values are set by the four least-significant bits of the DWORD, as shown here:

0	0	0	0		0	0	0	0		0	0	0	0		1	1	1	1
15	14	13	12		11	10	9	8		7	6	5	4		3	2	1	0

Bit	Decimal Value	Signifies
0	1	Match whole string only
1	2	Keys
2	4	Values
3	8	Data

Thus, a decimal value of 3 in the Data column indicates the Keys and Match whole string boxes (bits 2 and 1) are checked. A decimal value of 15 (8 + 4 + 2 + 1) signifies all boxes are checked, and so on.

The View entry simply describes the size and position of the Registry Editor window. Refer to "Variations in the Registry Structure"and to Figure 4-14 in Chapter 4 for details on how to interpret this data.

WordPad: The user's custom configuration of the WordPad applet is written into the subkeys found here, despite the presence on some systems of the *WORDPAD.INI* key, previously mentioned in the "Software Configuration Keys" section.

Explorer The subkeys found here define various details pertaining to the current user's Explorer configuration.

ExpView: The Contents pane of this "Explorer View" key has a single Settings entry, in which the hexadecimal string in the Data column specifies the current size and position of the Explorer window, as well as the state of the Toolbar and Status Bar options. The Settings entry is similar in concept to the View entry mentioned in the discussion of the *RegEdit* key in the previous section.

RecentDocs: The Contents pane of this key lists the most-recently used (that is, opened) documents, and this list appears onscreen if the Start menu's Documents option is selected. Figure 3-14 shows that the list is stored in the Registry in binary format, and the Edit Binary Value window inset shows the contents of one of these strings. Note that the filename seen in the window (README.TXT) is followed by a shortcut filename (Readme.txt.lnk), and this shortcut file is stored in the C:\Windows\Recent folder.

The MRUList (Most-Recently Used) entry in the Contents pane indicates the sequence in which these documents were opened.

RunMRU: This key's Contents pane lists the most-recently used (that is, run) items that were accessed via the Start menu's Run option. The list may be viewed by clicking on the down arrow in the Run dialog box. As with the *RecentDocs* key described previously, an MRUList specifies the order in which these items were run. But unlike the *RecentDocs* key, here the Contents pane lists each item in string (ASCII text) format, which is also shown in Figure 3-14.

Shell Folders: Here, the Contents pane lists the paths to various Windows folders.

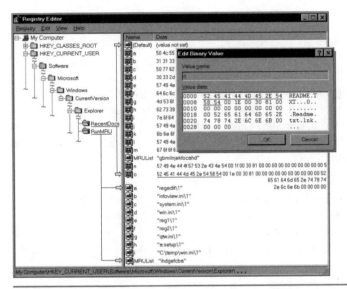

Figure 3-14 *The contents of the Start menu's cascading Documents option are written into the* RecentDocs *key in binary format. In contrast, the contents of the Run option's drop-down menu are stored in the* RunMRU *key in text string format.*

Policies If the System Policy Editor has been used to impose certain restrictions on the current user, these restrictions are listed here. Refer to the "System Policy Editor" section of Chapter 4, for details about using this utility.

Explorer: The Contents pane lists various restrictions that are in place, as shown here by a few examples:

Name	Data	Comments
NoFind	0x00000001 (1)	Disables Find option
NoRun	0x00000001 (1)	Disables Run option
NoSetFolders	0x00000001 (1)	Disables Folders on Settings option

Network: In similar fashion, the Contents pane describes restrictions imposed on network operations.

Note

Policies: Keep in mind that any restrictions found under either of these subkeys can be easily disabled by the knowledgeable user, either by editing the appropriate line to change the DWORD from "1" to "0" or by simply erasing the line.

Run This key lists applets to be executed each time the current user logs on. For example, the Contents pane displays the following line if the user checks the "Show settings icon on task bar" box. This box can be found on the Display Properties' Settings tab in Windows 95 and on the General tab in Windows 98. Click the Advanced button on the Settings tab to access the General tab.

Name	Data
Taskbar Display Controls	"RunDLL desktop16.dll,QUICKRES_RUNDLLENTRY"

Applets executed for all users are listed under the subkey with the same name in the *HKLM\Software\Microsoft\Windows* section, as described in the following sections.

Telephony A Windows 98 addition to the Registry, the *Cards* subkey leads to a list of *Cardxx* subkeys, one for each available telephone calling card account. Information appropriate to each card is given, and the user's PIN code (if any) is given in an encrypted format. A *Locations* key leads to *LocationX* subkeys, one for each location that has been configured via Control Panel's *Telephony* applet. Refer to the discussion of the *Telephony* subkey and to Figure 3-17 in the next section for additional details and an illustration of the relationships between these two key structures.

The HKLM\SOFTWARE\Microsoft\ Windows subkey

As an aid to help distinguish this key structure from its counterpart under the *HKCU* key (previously described), the Windows 95 Registry set the word "SOFTWARE" in all uppercase letters. Although Windows 98 abandons this style, it is preserved in this book to help maintain the distinction between these two sections, which are otherwise quite similar in appearance.

CurrentVersion

In contrast to its empty *HKCU\Software* counterpart, the Contents pane of this *CurrentVersion* key contains much information about the Windows installation, including product ID number and name, as well as the identity of the registered user (RegisteredOwner) and organization (RegisteredOrganization). Some of this information is displayed on the General tab when the "My Computer" object's Properties option is selected. A few of the many subkeys beneath this key are briefly described here.

Applets Again there's quite a difference between this key and its *HKLU\Software\...* equivalent, but it's in the opposite direction because this key has comparatively few subkeys beneath it. In fact, it doesn't appear at all until one of the Windows System Tools is run for the first time. Depending on which tools have been used, one or more of the following subkeys will appear. The same information is also written into another subkey under the following key:

> HKLM\SOFTWARE\Microsoft\CurrentVersion\Explorer\...

In each case, the name of that subkey is given here in parentheses. Refer to that key name in the text that follows for further details.

Backup (LastBackup): This subkey is written into the Registry the first time the Windows Backup utility is used. Its Contents pane describes the available backup configurations, and a Tape-DriveDetected entry indicates the presence (1) or absence (0) of a tape drive.

Check Drive (LastCheck): This key is written by the Windows ScanDisk utility, and the subkeys beneath it contain an entry for every drive letter that has been tested by the utility. The subkeys are listed here:

Subkey name	Test type	Components checked
LastCheck	Standard	Files and folders
LastSurfaceAnalysis	Thorough	Same, plus disk surface check

Defrag (LastOptimize): The *Defrag* key at this location is a recent addition — not used in Windows 95, it is written into the Registry by Windows 98 the first time the utility is executed, and its two subkeys are as follows:

Subkey Name	Name	Data (typical examples)
AppStartParams	Exclude Files	SYSTEM.DAT\USER.DAT\SYSTEM.INI\WIN.INI
AppStartRegions	C	<u>03 00 00 00</u> <u>4C 39 00 00</u>

The *AppStartParams* key lists files that will be excluded from the defrag procedure. A backslash separates the filenames, and additional files can be added to the list. In the *AppStartRegions* key Contents pane, the eight bytes comprise two DWORDs (shown underlined) that specify the first and last cluster of the region reserved for program start optimization. In the example given previously, Clusters 03 through 394C on drive C make up that region.

Explorer The subkeys found here define various details pertaining to the configuration of the local machine, regardless of which user is currently logged on.

Desktop, MyComputer, and NameSpace subkeys: The Contents panes of the *Desktop* and *MyComputer* keys are both empty, but both keys lead to a *NameSpace* subkey, which brings up the question: What's a *NameSpace?* It appears to be nothing more than the space on the desktop itself, or within an open My Computer window. A number of object icons at both locations are specified under these two *NameSpace* subkeys. The following table contains a few examples:

Desktop\NameSpace Subkeys	Contents Pane Data Column
{00020D75-0000-0000-C000-000000000046}	Inbox
{00028B00-0000-0000-C000-000000000046}	The Microsoft Network (1.3)

Desktop\NameSpace Subkeys	Contents Pane Data Column
`{450D8FBA-AD25-11D0-98A8-0800361B1103}`	My Documents
`{645FF040-5081-101B-9F08-00AA002F954E}`	Recycle Bin
`{88667D10-10F0-11D0-8150-00AA00BF8457}`	The Microsoft Network (2.5)
`{FBF23B42-E3F0-101B-8488-00AA003E56F8}`	The Internet
My Computer\Name Space	**Subkey**
`{992CFFA0-F557-101A-88EC-00DD010CCC48}`	Dial-Up Networking
`{D6277990-4C6A-11CF-8D87-00AA0060F5BF}`	Scheduled Tasks

In each case, the subkey name serves as a pointer to the *CLSID* subkey beneath the *HKCR* key described in Chapter 2, and the Contents pane reveals that key's identity. If one of the subkeys listed previously is not present under the *NameSpace* key, then that object does not appear in the indicated NameSpace. Other subkeys may be added by third-party applications.

FindExtensions: The *Find* option on the Windows Start menu opens a cascading menu that lists two or more search areas, such as Files or Folders, Computer, People, and so on. A *FindExtensions* subkey points to the *CLSID* key that supports each listed option, as shown in Figure 3-15. Refer to "Find" in the "Start Menu" section of Chapter 6 for information about customizing this menu list.

LastBackup, LastCheck, LastOptimize: If one or more of these keys are present, its Contents pane Name column shows a listing for each drive letter, and the Data column specifies the number of days elapsed since the indicated function was last performed. The information contained here may be viewed via the Tools tab on the Properties sheet for any drive, as follows:

Tools Tab	Subkey Name
Error-checking status	*LastCheck*
Backup status	*LastBackup*
Defragmentation status	*LastOptimize*

Figure 3-16 illustrates the relationship between the *Applets* subkeys described earlier and the *Explorer* subkeys listed here. Note that the date of the most-recent ScanDisk surface check is written into the *LastCheck* sub-keys at both locations. Windows refers to the data in the *Explorer\LastCheck* key's Contents pane to calculate the number of days since the last operation, as reported on the Tools tab.

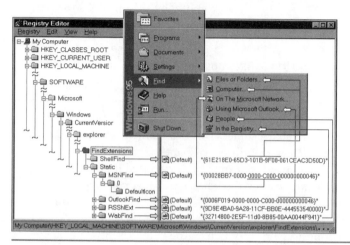

Figure 3-15 *Subkeys under the* FindExtensions *key point to the CLSID keys that support various options found on the cascading Find menu. In each case, an* InprocServer32 *subkey under that CLSID key specifies the appropriate DLL file.*

Shell Icons: This subkey appears under the *Explorer* key if the Windows 95 version of MS Plus! is installed, and its Contents pane may specify icons that supersede various default icons formerly taken from the SHELL32.DLL file. For details on how to add or edit this subkey, refer to "The Shell Icons Key" section of Chapter 6. If MS Plus! 98 is installed, *DefaultIcon* subkeys are written under various *CLSID* keys in the following location instead:

HKEY_CURRENT_USER\Software\Classes\CLSID

Refer to "Classes and CLSID" at the end of the "HKCU: HKEY_CURRENT_USER Key [HKU\UserName or HKU\. Default]," section earlier in this chapter for details about this key structure, and to the "Desktop Icons" section of Chapter 6 for additional information about how changes are made here.

Setup The Contents pane of this key, which has no *HKCU* equivalent, contains a list of paths to various Windows components, and one or more of the following subkeys.

OptionalComponents: Here, the Contents pane lists most (but not all) of the subkeys found beneath this key. Each such subkey identifies a specific Windows component (Accessibility, CD Player, Character Map, and so on), and the following information appears in the Contents pane:

Name	Data	Comments
INF	"*filename*.inf"	The INF file that installs this component
Installed	"0" *or* "1"	0 = not installed, 1 = installed
Section	"*section name*"	The section of the INF file cited above

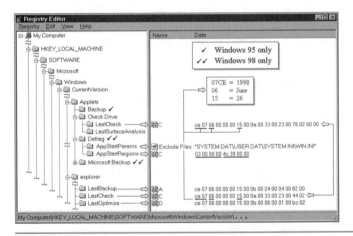

Figure 3-16 *The date of Scandisk's last surface check is written into two* LastCheck *subkeys. The* Defrag *key (Windows 98 only) lists files that are not to be checked by the utility, along with other configuration details.*

Updates: If this key is present, the subkeys under it are sequentially numbered (*UPD001, UPD002, . . .*), and in the Contents pane for each one, the Name column's (Default) entry describes a Windows update. Each subsequent Name entry lists the path and filename for the update, and the Data column specifies the version number of the updated file.

WinbootDir: One of the few unmysterious Registry keys, this one contains just what you would expect from its name: the path to the Windows startup, or boot, files, which by default is C:\Windows.

Telephony In the *Locations* subkey Contents pane, a CurrentID entry specifies the identification number of the current dialing location, and that same number is repeated in the Contents pane of a *LocationX* subkey located immediately below, as shown at the bottom of Figure 3-17. At the equivalent *LocationX* (*Location1,* in this example) subkey under the *HKCU\...\Locations* key, a CallingCard entry identifies the telephone calling card used at this location. Because this example shows that number to be 7, the *Card7* subkey specifies the configuration setup for this card on this PC.

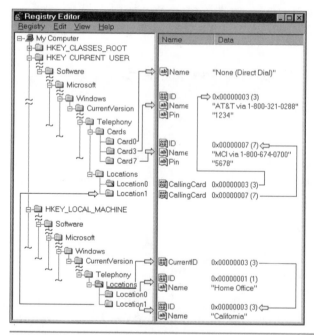

Figure 3-17 *Beginning near the bottom of the figure, the* Locations *key specifies a current ID number, and the subkey below with that number matches a subkey with the same name under the* Telephony *key (located in the middle of the figure). That key points to the Calling Card, which in this example is the* Card7 *key.*

A *Country List* key at this location (not shown in Figure 3-17) leads to multiple numbered subkeys, one for each country. Windows reads this list from the C:\Windows\System\TAPISRV.EXE file and rewrites it into the Registry every time Control Panel's Telephony applet is opened, so the list may be updated via a new version of this file. A *Providers* subkey (also not shown) duplicates some of the data found in the C:\Windows\TELEPHON.INI file.

HKU: HKEY_USERS [USER.DAT]

According to Microsoft Windows 95 documentation, this key contains "the *.Default* subkey plus all previously loaded user profiles for users who have logged on." Windows 98 adds the clarification ". . . who have logged on in the past." Neither statement is correct. There is indeed a *.Default* subkey, which, as its name implies, specifies the default user configuration for anyone who logs on without a user profile. Thus, if no password prompt appears as Windows opens, or if it does appear but the user simply presses the Escape key instead of entering a User name and password, then data contained within the *.Default* key is used to configure the session, and no other subkey is seen beneath the *HKEY_USERS* key.

When a new user logs on for the first time, a custom USER.DAT file is created for that user in a new C:\WINDOWS\Profiles*username* folder. Initially, the file contains two versions of the C:\Windows\USER.DAT file, the first of which is an exact replica. This is followed by a revised version, in which all references to *.Default* are changed to *username,* along with other changes appropriate to the new *username* configuration. As this user tailors the configuration to suit personal preference, these changes are made only within the *username* section of this custom USER.DAT file. The *.Default* section remains an untouched "carbon copy" of the original C:\Windows\USER.DAT file.

When the Registry Editor is subsequently opened, the *HKEY_USERS* key shows two subkeys, one named *.Default* and the other labeled with the *username* under which the user logged on. Figure 3-18 shows such a key, with its *.Default* and *username* (*john,* in this example) keys expanded to show their subkeys. In this case, the *.Default* set is ignored, and the *username* set is replicated under the *HKEY_CURRENT_USER* key, which is also shown in Figure 3-18. Note that the *.Default* key's *Software* subkey shows only four manufacturer's subkeys, while the same subkey under the *username* key shows six, and these are of course also seen under the *HKCU* key. This indicates that when the present user logged on for the first time, only four software applications had been installed and that the present user subsequently installed two more applications.

If nothing else, the simple expedient of showing only a *.Default* and a current *username* subkey prevents one user with busy fingers from "fixing" some other user's configuration.

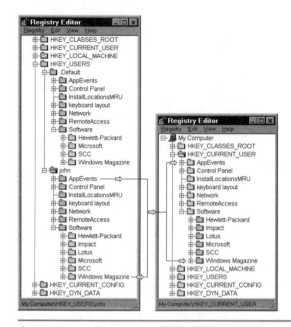

Figure 3-18 *At the left of the illustration, the current user's Software list includes a few items not available to a .Default user, and as in Figure 3-1, this list is part of the current user's configuration that is written into the* HKEY_CURRENT_USER *key shown at the right.*

To summarize, if the *HKU* key shows a *.Default* subkey only, then that key is replicated under the *HKCU* key, but if a second (*username*) key is present, then that key is replicated instead. In either case, the subkeys themselves are described in the "HKCU: HKEY_CURRENT_USER Key [HKU*UserName or* HKU\.Default]" section earlier in this chapter.

Software

Windows 98 adds yet another *Software* key to the Registry, which is reproduced here in its entirety, along with the Contents pane of the final subkey:

HKCU\Software\Microsoft\Windows\CurrentVersion\Telephony \HandoffPriorities

Name	Data
(Default)	(value not set)
RequestMakeCall	"DIALER.EXE"

The same information is duplicated in the TELEPHON.INI file as shown here:

```
[HandoffPriorities]
RequestMakeCall=DIALER.EXE
```

Additional information from the INI file is found under the *Providers* subkey in the *HKLM\...\Telephony* structure briefly mentioned earlier in this chapter.

HKCC: HKEY_CURRENT_CONFIG Key [HKLM\Config\000x]

As shown earlier in Figure 2-1, and in greater detail in Figure 3-19, the data seen here is derived from the *HKLM\Config\000x* subkey, where *000x* is the subkey for the current hardware configuration. If there is only one such configuration (as on most desktop systems), then the information is taken from *HKLM\Config\0001*, which is the only subkey under the *Config* key.

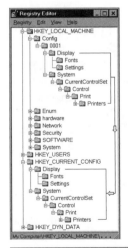

Figure 3-19 *Hardware configuration information in the* HKEY_LOCAL_
MACHINE\Config\0001 *key is written into the* HKEY_
CURRENT_CONFIG *key. A laptop computer would have two
numbered Config subkeys, one each for docked and
undocked modes. In either case, the appropriate one is
written into the* HKCC *key when the system is powered on.*

Assuming two or more *000x* subkeys are under *HKLM\Config* (as on many laptops that support a docked and an undocked configuration), then each one contains the subkeys described in this section. However, only the specific subkey set found here in *HKCC* is currently enabled.

Note that *HKCC* does not reveal the identity of the specific *HKLM\Config\000x* key from which it is derived.

Display

This key leads to the *Fonts* and *Settings* subkeys described in the following sections. In Figure 3-20, the composite Contents pane illustrates typical entries within both subkeys.

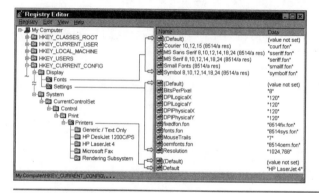

Figure 3-20 *The* Fonts *key specifies screen fonts formerly listed in the [fonts] section of WIN.INI, while the* Settings *key specifies system fonts from the [boot] section of SYSTEM.INI, where the same font listings are still retained. The* Printers *key simply lists the current default printer, while other installed printers are identified by empty subkeys below it.*

Fonts

This subkey specifies the screen fonts that were formerly listed in the [fonts] section of WIN.INI.

Settings

This subkey defines color depth (BitsPerPixel) and other screen characteristics and specifies the system fonts that were formerly loaded via the [boot] section of SYSTEM.INI. These fonts are still listed there, however, for the benefit of applications that don't recognize the Windows 95 and 98 Registry.

The Resolution entry specifies the current horizontal and vertical resolution, in pixels (1024,768, for example).

Enum

If present, this key may contain various subkeys (*BIOS, PCI, Root, SCSI,* and so on), which in turn specify plug-and-play BIOS or other elements. Note however that an element found here represents a formerly available device that has been removed from the system configuration. Because the structure of this key varies as edits are made from within the Device Manager, refer to the discussion of the *Enum* key in the "HKLM: HKEY_LOCAL_MACHINE Key [SYSTEM.DAT]" section earlier in this chapter for more details about the keys that appear in, and disappear from, this area.

Software

As if there weren't enough Registry keys with this name, this one is written into the Registry if IE4 is installed, and it leads to the subkey structure and Contents pane entries shown here:

Microsoft\Windows\CurrentVersion\InternetSettings

Name	Data	Connection Tab Settings
EnableAutodial	01 00 00 00	Connect to the Internet using a modem
	00 00 00 00	Connect to the Internet using a local area network
ProxyEnable	01 00 00 00	Access the Internet using a proxy server
ProxyServer	*www.xx.yy.zz:pp*	*(address:port, if entered)*

Note

Other Connection tab settings are written into the Contents pane at a different location: HKCU\Software\Microsoft\ Windows\CurrentVersion\Internet Settings.

System

This key leads in turn to a series of empty (value not set) subkeys and finally to the *Printers* subkey, which specifies the current default printer, which is also shown in Figure 3-20. If more than one printer is installed, an additional subkey is displayed beneath the Printers key for each one. These subkey labels serve as a simple list of available printers, but the keys contain no further information.

HKDD: HKEY_DYN_DATA Key [system RAM]

The dynamic data displayed under this HKEY is created fresh every time Windows opens. The data is written into RAM and continuously updated as required, and it is displayed here under the *Configuration Manager* and *PerfStats* subkeys. In addition, other keys may be written here as the result of an installed hardware device, as described in the "Third-Party Hardware Key" section at the end of this section.

Configuration Manager

This key is also known as the *Hardware Tree* because its contents define the current hardware configuration of the system. The root of this hardware tree is the *Enum* subkey described in the next section.

Enum

This hardware enumerator key leads in turn to an extensive series of subkey branches, each labeled with an eight-character hexadecimal number (*C111326C, C113CBB4,* for example). In the Contents pane for each of these subkeys, a HardWareKey data entry serves as a pointer to a subkey series that may be found within the *HKLM\Enum* key section described earlier.

Table 3-5 lists Contents-pane entries taken from some of the many *C . . .* subkeys found under the *Enum* subkey on a typical personal computer. In each case, the actual *C . . .* key name is not given, because this varies from one configuration to another. The first two columns list a subkey sequence found under the *HKLM\Enum* key described earlier. The final column shows the information displayed in the DeviceDesc row, which would be seen if the final subkey in the indicated area were opened.

Table 3-5 *Contents of Typical HKEY_DYN_DATA Key's Enum Subkey* *

In the Contents pane, HardWareKey Entry Points to this HKLM\Enum Subkey †		DeviceDesc(ription), Taken from the Indicated HKLM\Enum Subkey
EISA\	*PNP0A00\0	ISA Plug and Play bus
FLOP\	GENERIC_NEC_FLOPPY_DISK_	GENERIC NEC FLOPPY DISK (A)
FLOP\	GENERIC_NEC_FLOPPY_DISK_	GENERIC NEC FLOPPY DISK (B)
HTREE\	RESERVED\0	(empty)
HTREE\	ROOT\0	(A nonexistent key)
ISAPNP\	INT1030\00A3478A	Intel EtherExpress PRO/10 (PnP Enabled)

In the Contents pane, HardWareKey Entry Points to this HKLM\Enum Subkey †		DeviceDesc(ription), Taken from the Indicated HKLM\Enum Subkey
ISAPNP\	READDATAPORT\0	IO read data port for ISA PnP enumerator
MONITOR\	DEFAULT_MONITOR\0001	MAG Innovision MX17F/S
NETWORK\	JADM\0000	HP JetAdmin
NETWORK\	JADM\0002	HP JetAdmin
NETWORK\	MSTCP\0000	TCP/IP
NETWORK\	NETBEUI\0000	NetBEUI
NETWORK\	NETBEUI\0002	NetBEUI
NETWORK\	NWLINK\0000	IPX/SPX-compatible Protocol
NETWORK\	NWLINK\0002	IPX/SPX-compatible Protocol
NETWORK\	VREDIR\0000	Client for Microsoft Networks
NETWORK\	VREDIR\0001	Client for Microsoft Networks
NETWORK\	VREDIR\0004	Client for Microsoft Networks
NETWORK\	VREDIR\0005	Client for Microsoft Networks
NETWORK\	VSERVER\0000	File and printer sharing for Microsoft Networks
NETWORK\	VSERVER\0001	File and printer sharing for Microsoft Networks
NETWORK\	VSERVER\0002	File and printer sharing for Microsoft Networks
NETWORK\	VSERVER\0003	File and printer sharing for Microsoft Networks
NETWORK\	VSERVER\0008	File and printer sharing for Microsoft Networks
NETWORK\	VSERVER\0009	File and printer sharing for Microsoft Networks
NETWORK\	VSERVER\0010	File and printer sharing for Microsoft Networks
NETWORK\	VSERVER\0011	File and printer sharing for Microsoft Networks
PCI\	VEN_1000&DEV_0001\...	PCI NCR C810 SCSI Host Adapter
PCI\	VEN_1002&DEV_4158\...	ATI Graphics Ultra Pro (mach32)
PCI\	VEN_8086&DEV_0482\...	Intel PCI to EISA bridge
PCI\	VEN_8086&DEV_04A3\...	Intel Mercury Pentium Processor to PCI bridge

Continued

Table 3-5 *Continued*

In the Contents pane, HardWareKey Entry Points to this HKLM\Enum Subkey †		DeviceDesc(ription), Taken from the Indicated HKLM\Enum Subkey
ROOT\	*ADP1740\0000	Adaptec AHA-174X EISA Host Adapter
ROOT\	*PNP0000\0000	Programmable interrupt controller
ROOT\	*PNP0100\0000	System timer
ROOT\	*PNP0200\0000	Direct memory access controller
ROOT\	*PNP0303\0000	Standard 101/102-Key or Microsoft Natural Keyboard
ROOT\	*PNP0500\0000	Communications Port (COM1)
ROOT\	*PNP0500\0001	Communications Port (COM2)
ROOT\	*PNP0700\0000	Standard Floppy Disk Controller
ROOT\	*PNP0800\0000	System speaker
ROOT\	*PNP0A03\0000	PCI bus
ROOT\	*PNP0B00\0000	System CMOS/real time clock
ROOT\	*PNP0C01\0000	System board
ROOT\	*PNP0C04\0000	Numeric data processor
ROOT\	*PNP0F0E\0000	Standard PS/2 Port Mouse
ROOT\	NET\0000	Dial-Up Adapter
ROOT\	PNPC031\COM1	Serial cable on COM1
ROOT\	PNPC031\COM2	Serial cable on COM2
ROOT\	PNPC032\LPT1	Parallel cable on LPT1
ROOT\	PORTS\0000	Printer Port (LPT1)
ROOT\	PRINTER\0000	HP LaserJet4
ROOT\	PRINTER\0001	Generic / Text Only
ROOT\	PRINTER\0002	HP DeskJet 1200C/PS
SCSI\	DEC_____DSP3107LS_____4	DEC DSP3107LS (hard disk)
SCSI\	NEC_____CD-ROM_DRIVE:5012	NEC CD-ROM DRIVE:501
SERENUM\	APC1065\...	APC BACK-UP UPS PRO S/N: xxxx
SERENUM\	MNP0336\...	DeskPorte 28.8 (modem)

* *Enum* key leads to multiple subkeys, each labeled with an eight-character hexadecimal number (not shown here). Hex subkey labels vary from one configuration to another.

† Actual *HardwareKey* Data column entry has no space after backslash (added here for clarity).

Although the previously described *HKLM\Enum* subkey lists every device ever installed on the computer, only those devices currently in use will appear under the *Enum* subkey here in the *HKDD\ConfigManager* section. The information shown in these keys is continuously updated and is therefore valid whenever it is displayed.

Default Monitor subkey Figure 3-21 shows a typical example of the relationship between a subkey here in the *HKDD\ ConfigManager\Enum* section and the associated subkey in the *HKLM\Enum* section. In this example, the *C1151CF0* subkey's Contents pane shows the following information:

Name	Data
HardWareKey	"MONITOR\DEFAULT_MONITOR\0001"

The Data column specifies the subkey in which the monitor is actually identified. To locate that key, add *HKEY_LOCAL_MACHINE\Enum* to this entry. The complete key name is therefore:

HKEY_LOCAL_MACHINE\Enum\Monitor\Default_Monitor\0001

In Figure 3-21, the DeviceDesc entry in that key's Contents pane identifies the current monitor as a MAG Innovision MX17F/S.

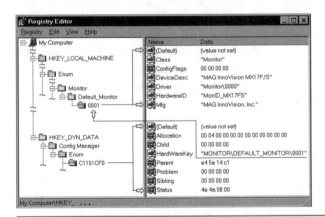

Figure 3-21 *In the open C1151CF0 key in this HKEY_DYN_DATA section, the Contents pane's HardWareKey listing specifies a subkey in the HKEY_LOCAL_MACHINE section where the default monitor is identified. In a similar manner each such subkey has a HardwareKey listing that points to some other hardware component.*

Note

If an external monitor is connected to a laptop computer, it is usually possible to toggle between that monitor, the laptop's own screen, or both – typically, by holding down the Fn key and pressing a Function key labeled CRT/LCD (or similar). This action, however, has no effect on the information displayed in the subkeys just described.

PerfStats (performance statistics)

This section provides the dynamic links to performance statistics that may be monitored onscreen via the System Monitor applet. Its size in Windows 95 is enormous, as may be demonstrated by highlighting the key and exporting it to a PERFSTAT.REG file, whose file size will be 4,827,877 bytes, most of which is due to the lengthy hexadecimal strings written into the *StartStat* and *StopStat* keys. Of course, this is an ASCII translation of RAM-resident PerfStats data and would not otherwise be found in a file because neither SYSTEM.DAT nor USER.DAT maintain a record of this subkey. Nevertheless, the file size and content may help users to better understand the amount of data contained here. In Windows 98, these entries are limited to four bytes per line, so a *PerfStats* export is typically less that 10 Kbytes.

If you do export this subkey, make sure you erase the file after examining it — it wastes a lot of space and can't be reimported anyway. Refer to Chapter 4 for more information about Registry import/export operations.

In Figure 3-22, the *StatData* subkey under the *PerfStats* key is opened, and its Contents pane shows the items currently available to the System Monitor. The various Name entries seen here are derived from other subkeys found under the *PerfStats* key in the HKLM section, as illustrated by the *KERNEL* and *VFAT* key examples shown in Figure 3-22, where information in the Data column (not shown) is derived and constantly refreshed, as necessary, from system RAM.

To illustrate how this works, open the System Monitor's Edit menu, select the Add Item option, and then select Memory Manager. Next, scroll down the Item list and select Swapfile size and Swapfile in use. The System Monitor window should now look like the one shown at the top of Figure 3-23. Highlight either graph, and the status bar at the bottom of the window displays the graph name, followed by the last (that is, the current) value and the peak value, both expressed in decimal notation. The figure shows how the status bar report changes, depending on which graph is selected.

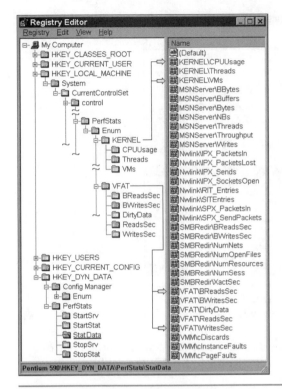

Figure 3-22 *In this* HKEY_DYN_DATA *key sample, the Contents pane shows a partial listing of items in the underlined* StatData *subkey's Contents pane. Each item in the Name column is read from the indicated section under the* HKEY_LOCAL_ MACHINE\...\PerfStats *key. The Data column entries (not shown) are dynamically read into the key and continuously refreshed during the course of any Windows session.*

Now open the following Registry key:
HKEY_DYN_DATA\Config Manager\PerfStats\StatData

and scroll to the bottom of the Contents pane. The Swapfile and SwapfileInUse entries show the current values for these two items, and the hexadecimal data should agree with the decimal value reported as Last value in the System Monitor's status bar. Remember that the Data column shows the hexadecimal value in reverse sequence. To convert from one format to the other, reverse the order of the hexadecimal characters and then convert to decimal format. If the resultant value does not agree with that reported by the System Monitor's status bar, open the Registry Editor's View menu, select the Refresh option, and try again.

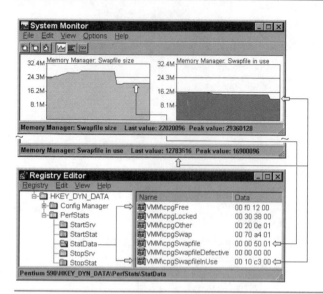

Figure 3-23 *Data shown in the* StatData *key's Contents pane can be read via the System Monitor applet. Four-byte binary data in the Contents pane is converted to a decimal value displayed in the System Monitor's Status bar and is displayed by the graph. As the binary data changes in the* HKEY_DYN_DATA *key, so does the graph.*

The following list summarizes the hexadecimal and decimal values shown in Figure 3-23 for Swapfile and SwapfileInUse:

Name in Contents Pane	Data	Inverted Data	Decimal Value
VMM\cpgSwapfile	00 00 50 01	01 50 00 00	22,020,096
VMM\cpgSwapfileinUse	00 10 c3 00	00 c3 10 00	12,783,616

In the previous discussion of the *HKDD\Config Manager* key's *Enum* subkey, it was pointed out that information in a Data column pointed to a key under *HKLM*'s own *Enum* subkey, as illustrated in Figure 3-21. The *PerfStats* key described in the present section follows the same general procedure, except that here the pointer is the information in the Name column rather than in the Data column (this was shown in Figure 3-22). Figure 3-23 shows how this information may be viewed by the user. At the bottom of the illustration, the *HKDD* key leads to the *PerfStats\StatData* subkey, whose partial contents are shown at the bottom of the Contents pane.

Here, the Name column shows a list of subkeys, each of which points to a subkey that resides under the following *HKLM* key:

HKLM\System\CurrentControlSet\control\PerfStats\Enum\VMM

This key is further illustrated in Figure 3-24, where dynamic data is again shown within the *HKDD* section and an accompanying pointer indicates the associated *HKLM* location. In this example, *HKLM*'s *cpgSwapfile* subkey offers the following information in its Contents pane:

Name Column	Data Column	To Display Data
Description	"Size of swap file in bytes."	Open System Monitor, highlight Swapfile size, click Explain button.
Name	"Swapfile size"	Open System Monitor, highlight Swapfile size, click Explain button. Also appears in Item box.
Differentiate	"FALSE"	(*Not part of data display*)

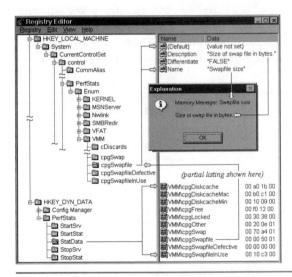

Figure 3-24 *In the Contents pane listing at the bottom of the illustration, the VMM\cpgSwapfile entry in the Name column is derived from the HKLM subkey of that name (cpgSwapfile). That key pane contains the information shown by the Contents pane at the top of the illustration, and this information is displayed to the user via the Explanation window shown in the inset.*

The Explanation box inset in Figure 3-24 shows how the Data column entries are displayed to the user. In much the same manner, dynamic data for any System Monitor item is found under the *PerfStats* subkey, and the Contents Pane's Name column points the way to Static data stored in another subkey under *HKLM*, as shown in the previous example.

Note

If you search the Registry for *DiskCacheMac*, you'll find it appears several times. It should of course be *DiskCacheMax*, but no harm is done because the item is simply a pointer from one location to another, perhaps programmed by someone with Mac Envy.

Third-party hardware key

A subkey other than *Config Manager* and *PerfStats* directly under the *HKDD* key was probably placed there by an accessory hardware device. If neither the key name itself nor its subkey contents are sufficient to identify the device, look for another subkey with the same name under the *Enum* key above. In that key's Contents pane, a HardWareKey entry specifies a key structure under the *HKEY_LOCAL_ MACHINE\Enum* key, as shown in Figure 3-25. Open the lowest subkey in that structure (which is *00020176* in this example), and the DeviceDesc entry reveals the identity of the device.

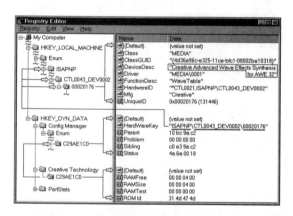

Figure 3-25 *To verify the hardware source of an extra subkey under the HKDD key, such as the* Creative Technology *key seen here, note the name of its subkey and then search the* Enum *key structure for a subkey with the same name. That key's HardWareKey entry is a pointer to a key structure beneath the HKLM\Enum structure, and a DeviceDesc entry there identifies the installed hardware device.*

Part II

Editing and Maintenance Tools

Chapter 4

Registry Editing Utilities

In the previous chapters, the Registry Editor was used simply as a passive device to view the structure of the Registry. The present chapter begins by reintroducing the Editor, this time in its primary role as an editing utility used in Windows. Then this chapter describes its use in real mode; that is, from a DOS (!) command prompt prior to launching the Windows GUI (graphical user interface). This is followed by a description of how to use the Windows INF file as a Registry-editing tool, and then it's on to the System Policy Editor, which is, in effect, a special-purpose Registry editor. The final section describes various methods to print selected sections of the Registry.

An HKEY Review

Figure 2-1 in Chapter 2 illustrates the relationship between five of the six HKEYs in the Registry Editor's Key pane. As shown in that figure, the sources of three HKEYs are subkeys within two of the other HKEYs that, for identification purposes, were described as the master HKEYs. For reference purposes, the six HKEYs are listed in the following table, along with the source for each key. The files that are the source of the two master HKEYs are then described in some detail in the "Registry Files" section which follows. Again for future reference, the name of the HKEY contained within each file is given in brackets.

HKEY Name	Source HKEY (or filename)	Subkey in Source HKEY
HKEY_CLASSES_ROOT	*HKEY_LOCAL_MACHINE*	*SOFTWARE\Classes*
HKEY_CURRENT_USER	*HKEY_USERS*	*.Default (or UserName)*
HKEY_CURRENT_CONFIG	*HKEY_LOCAL_MACHINE*	*Config\000x*
HKEY_LOCAL_MACHINE	SYSTEM.DAT	–
HKEY_USERS	USER.DAT	–
HKEY_DYN_DATA	(*Dynamically derived from system RAM*)	

The Registry files

The files described in this section are known collectively as "The Registry," and their attributes are read-only and hidden. In Windows 95 only, the system attribute is also set. Except as noted, the files are written into the C:\Windows folder, not the C:\Windows\System folder as stated in some Microsoft documentation. Table 4-1 lists the files described here, as well as other files associated with the Registry.

Table 4-1 *Windows Registry Editor Files*

Filename	Location	Purpose
REGEDIT.EXE	C:\Windows	The executable Registry Editor file
REGEDIT.HLP	C:\Windows\Help	Help file
REGEDIT.CNT	C:\Windows\Help	Help topics listed on Contents tab
REGEDIT.LNK	(*as specified by user*)	Shortcut to REGEDIT.EXE (optional)
SYSTEM.DAT †	C:\Windows	System-specific data
SYSTEM.DAO †	C:\Windows	Backup copy, Windows 95 only
USER.DAT †	C:\Windows	User-specific data for default user
USER.DAT †	C:\Windows\Profiles\UserName	User-specific data for specified user (UserName) only
USER.DAO †	C:\Windows	Backup copy, Windows 95 only
USER.DAO †	C:\Windows\Profiles\UserName	Windows 95 backup copy, for specified user (UserName) only
filename.REG	(*as specified by user*)	ASCII text file(s) created by user, via Export option on File menu (optional)
CFGBACK.EXE ‡	Windows 95 CD-ROM	To back up Registry
CFGBACK.HLP ‡	Windows 95 CD-ROM	Help file

Filename	Location	Purpose
HKLMBACK	On backup set (temporary file)	To restore SYSTEM.DAT file
HKUBACK	On backup set (temporary file)	To restore USER.DAT file
REGBACK.INI ‡	C:\WINDOWS	CFGBACK.EXE initialization file

† File attributes are system, hidden, read-only.
‡ Refer to Chapter 5 for details (also +s +h +r attributes).

SYSTEM.DAT [HKEY_LOCAL_MACHINE]

As explained in Chapter 3, the *HKLM* key contains the basic hardware and software configuration data that applies to the computer, without regard to the current user. Its *Config* subkey leads to one or more numbered subkeys, one for each available hardware configuration (*0001* = docked, *0002* = undocked, and so on). All of this data is written into a single hidden SYSTEM.DAT file in the C:\Windows folder.

USER.DAT [HKEY_USERS]

The *HKU* key contains one or two subkeys, the first of which is always labeled *.Default*. This key contains configuration data that pertains to the default user — that is, to any user who logs on and bypasses the password prompt by pressing the Escape key. If the system is set for single-user operation (with or without a password), then only the *.Default* subkey is found under the *HKU* key, and its contents are read from, and written to, the USER.DAT file in the C:\Windows folder. Windows 98 adds a *Software* subkey under the *HKU* key, as briefly described in the previous chapter. This key is not copied into the *HKCU* key structure.

If the following conditions are met, a C:\Windows\Profiles folder is created, and that folder contains one or more *UserName* folders, as shown in Figure 4-1:

1. The system is configured for a *UserName* and password prompt.

2. On the Passwords Properties sheet's User Profiles tab, the following radio button is enabled:

   Users can customize their preferences and desktop settings. Windows switches to your personal settings . . .

   whenever you log in   (Windows 95)

   when you log on   (Windows 98)

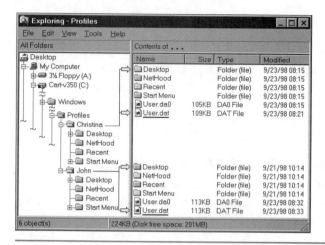

Figure 4-1 *If Windows 95 is configured for multiple users, a C:\Windows\Profile folder holds a separate folder for each user. Each such* UserName *folder contains the user's own USER.DAT file and a USER.DA0 backup copy. Subfolders (for example, the Desktop folder) hold the user's customized configuration information. Windows 98 does not create a USER.DA0 file, as explained in the next chapter.*

If these conditions are met, then a new \UserName folder is created in the C:\Windows\Profiles folder when a new user logs in (or even, on) for the first time. The \UserName folder holds the user's own USER.DAT file, which initially contains two copies of the C:\Windows\USER.DAT file. One is an exact duplicate, while in the other all *.Default* keys are rewritten as *UserName*, as follows:

Duplicate version of C:\Windows\USER.DAT

```
[HKEY_USERS\.Default]
[HKEY_USERS\.Default\Control Panel]
[HKEY_USERS\.Default\Control Panel\Appearance]
```
(and so on ...)

Revised version to specify UserName

```
[HKEY_USERS\john]
[HKEY_USERS\john\Control Panel]
[HKEY_USERS\john\Control Panel\Appearance]
```
(and so on ...)

The Registry Editor now shows two subkeys under the *HKU* key, one labeled *.Default* and the other *UserName*. In this case, the latter subkey is written into the *HKCU* key, as was illustrated in Figure 2-1. As the user makes configuration changes, these are written into the *UserName* section of the USER.DAT file in that user's folder, while the *.Default* section remains unchanged.

As Windows opens, it reads the C:\Windows\USER.DAT file, on the assumption that no user name will be specified. However, if the user logs on as John (or whoever), then the C:\Windows\Profiles\John\USER.DAT file is read, and its settings supersede those of C:\Windows\USER.DAT. You can note this by observing the opening wallpaper, which is specified in C:\Windows\USER.DAT. After the logon prompt, this changes to the wallpaper specified in the user's personal USER.DAT file, located in the folder just described.

If some other user logs on later, that user's USER.DAT file is read, and again the *HKU* key shows a *.Default* and a *UserName* subkey — the latter now labeled for the current user. Some Microsoft documentation states that the *HKU* key contains a subkey for *every* user, but in fact it shows at most only two subkeys, regardless of how many users have logged on to the computer in the past.

Registry Editor menu details

Chapter 1 presented a brief overview of all Registry Editor menus (see Figure 1-4), and additional details are given here for those menu options frequently used during an editing session. In the descriptions that follow, these options are listed alphabetically under each menu.

Registry menu

As noted in Chapter 1, the Registry menu shown in Figure 4-2 is equivalent to the File menu found on most other menu bars.

Connect Network Registry In theory, this option allows the user to connect to a Registry on a network computer. The fact that the option is enabled suggests this might indeed be possible, if only one could penetrate the Microsoft documentation to learn the means to do so. However, a careful reading between the lines reveals the following disconnected facts:

- Remote Registry Service does not work with share-level security. In other words, it requires user-level security.
- User-level security requires a user database.
- Neither Windows 95 nor Windows 98 supports a user database.

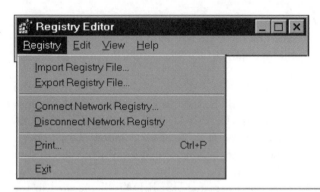

Figure 4-2 *The Registry Editor's Registry menu*

Therefore, neither version alone supports the Remote Registry Service that is required to use this option. Apparently, a Windows NT or NetWare server is required to enable this feature.

Disconnect Network Registry Given the preceding explanation of the Connect Network Registry option, it should come as no surprise that Disconnect Network Registry is disabled (even though the figure shows it enabled for readability).

Export Registry File Use this option to export all or part of the current Registry to a script file that may be subsequently imported back into the Registry, as described in the "Export operations" section later in this chapter.

Import Registry File Assuming a previous version of a Registry key (or of the entire Registry) has been saved to a script file via the Export Registry File option previously described, this option imports (*merges* would be a better description) the contents of that file back into the Registry. Refer to the "Import Operations" section later in this chapter, for details.

Print To print all or part of the Registry, highlight the desired key or subkey and then select this option. A Print dialog box, such as the one shown in Figure 4-3, is displayed with the Selected branch radio button in the Print range area enabled. To print the entire Registry, either highlight My Computer in the Registry Editor window, or click the All radio button. But before doing so, refer to the "Registry Print Jobs" section at the end of this chapter, for details about printing the Registry.

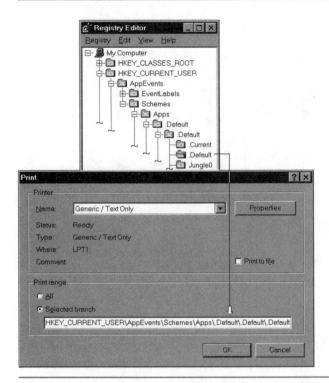

Figure 4-3 *In this Registry Editor Print dialog box, the enabled radio button next to Selected branch indicates the specified key will be printed. Put a check in the Print to file checkbox to print an ASCII text copy of the selected key to a file instead of to the printer.*

Edit menu

The options on the Registry Editor's Edit menu are shown in Figure 4-4 and summarized in the following sections.

Copy Key Name This option is not part of the original retail version of Windows 95 but was added to later SR versions and is also available in Windows 98. If it's part of your Edit menu, simply highlight any key (or any Contents pane entry), and then select the option to copy that key's full Registry path to the Clipboard, where the information is stored in Text and OEM Text formats only. Because the Registry Editor's Edit menu does not offer a Paste option, press the Ctrl+V keys to paste the copied key name into any other Registry location. You can also paste into the Find window's Find what box (described subsequently) or into any document whose Paste option supports Text and OEM Text formats. Because the

Copy Key Name option does not save a graphics image to the Clipboard, the copied key name cannot be pasted into the Paint applet or other applications that require this format.

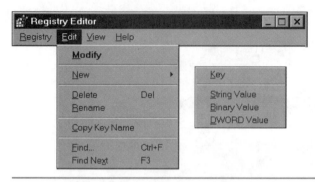

Figure 4-4 *The Registry Editor's Edit menu. Select the* New *option to open the cascading menu.*

Delete Simply highlight the desired key or Contents pane entry, then use this option to delete it. Because the deleted item cannot be undeleted, you may want to export the key in which it appears, just in case you decide later on that the item should not have been deleted.

If one of the six HKEYs is highlighted, the Delete option is disabled. If any Contents pane's (Default) entry is highlighted, the option is not disabled even though that item cannot be deleted. If you attempt to do so anyway, an "Unable to delete all specified values" message is displayed, and the delete action is ignored.

To delete multiple entries, hold down the Ctrl key while highlighting the entries to be deleted. Or hold down the Shift key and select the first and last entries to be deleted. Then choose the Delete option (or press the Delete key) to delete all selected entries. Both techniques function in the Contents pane but not the Key pane.

Find Select this option (or press Ctrl+F) to open the Find dialog box shown in Figure 4-5. Enter the text you wish to find into the Find what textbox, check one or more of the checkboxes below it, and then press the Find Next button to begin the search. Refer to the "Search techniques" section later in the chapter, for suggestions on using this option.

Find Next This menu option finds the next occurrence of the selected text string, but it's much faster to simply press function key F3 to perform this operation.

New To add a new entry to the Registry, first highlight the appropriate existing key in the Key pane and then select this option to open the cascading New menu whose options are described in this section. Note that if My Computer is highlighted, all New menu options are disabled because it is not possible to add a new HKEY, nor to add an entry to the My Computer Contents pane.

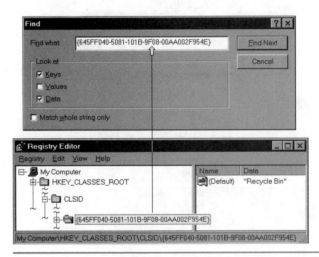

Figure 4-5 *Use the Edit menu's* Copy Key Name *option (if available, see Figure 4-4) to copy a lengthy* CLSID *key name to the Clipboard and then paste the key name into the Find dialog box's Find what area. This procedure is more reliable than entering such data at the keyboard.*

Key: If this option is selected, a new subkey is added at the bottom of the existing subkey structure below the currently opened key. As shown in Figure 4-6, an open key appears with a boxed "New Key #1" legend. If you do not rename the key and select the Key option again, a "New Key #2" key is added, and so on.

To add a subkey beneath either key, highlight the new key and again select the Key option. Repeat as desired to create the required key structure. Rename each new key as it is created or later on, as desired. When you are done, open the View menu and select the Refresh option to sort the new keys. Or don't bother — they'll be sorted for you the next time you open the Registry Editor.

String, Binary, or DWORD Value: To add an entry to the Contents pane of any key, highlight that key and then select the appropriate format from the cascading New menu. In each case, a boxed "New Value #*x*" entry will appear in the Name column of the Contents pane, and the Data column will show an empty value in the appropriate format. For example, if a new entry is created in sequence in each of the three available formats, the Contents pane would show the following entries:

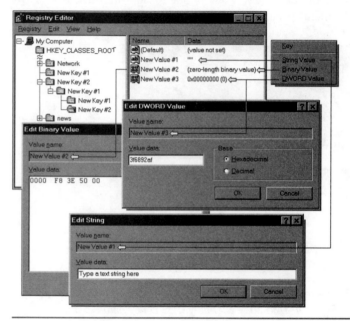

Figure 4-6 *If a small icon or the adjacent Name entry in the Contents pane is double-clicked, an Edit Value dialog box opens in whatever format is appropriate for the data on that line. In each Edit dialog box, the information seen here in the Value Data area is transferred to the appropriate New Value #x line in the Contents pane when the OK button is clicked.*

Name	Data	Format (on New Menu)
New Value #1	""	String Value
New Value #2	(zero-length binary value)	Binary Value
New Value #3	0x00000000 (0)	DWORD Value

Double-click any entry in the Name column to open one of the Edit dialog boxes shown in Figure 4-6. Then enter the desired data into the Value data box in the format appropriate for that data. In Figure 4-6, the

Contents pane shows the initial null entries, and each dialog box shows a typical Value data entry, which replaces the null data when the OK button is clicked.

> **Note**
>
> The Registry Editor automatically encloses every Data column text string in quotes. Therefore, do not type quotes in the Value data box when editing a string, unless an additional set is required.

Rename Highlight any key, Contents pane icon, or Name entry and then select this option to rename the selected item. If the Rename option is disabled, it is not possible to rename that item, as for example, the (Default) entry on the first line of every Contents pane.

View and Help menus

All options on these menus were described in the "View Menu" and "Help Menu" sections of Chapter 1.

Context menus in the Registry Editor

Figure 4-7 shows the Context menu for any key in the Registry Editor's Key pane. The Delete and Rename options are disabled if an HKEY's Context menu is opened. Figure 4-7 also shows the Context menus for entries in the Contents pane Name column or elsewhere within the pane.

With the exception of the options described in the following sections, the others on these menus (Delete, Find, Rename, and Copy Key Name) are the same as the options on the Edit menu described previously.

Collapse A minus sign to the left of any key indicates that subkeys beneath it are displayed, in which case the Collapse option appears at the top of the menu. If selected, the subkey structure collapses (disappears), and a plus sign appears next to the key.

Expand If a plus sign appears to the left of any key, the Expand option appears at the top of the menu, and if selected, the key structure expands to show the subkeys beneath it. If no sign appears next to a key, then the Expand option is visible but disabled, indicating that no further action is possible at this subkey level.

There's not much point however in using the Collapse and Expand options because you can accomplish the same tasks much faster by alternately clicking the plus/minus box next to each key.

Modify Selecting this Contents pane option simply opens whatever Edit window (see Figure 4-6) is appropriate to the data format of the highlighted item in the Name column. Or just press the Enter key to do the same thing.

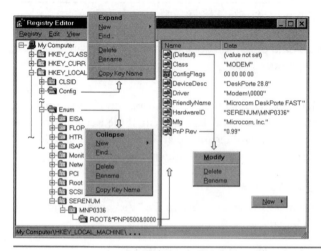

Figure 4-7 *If a Registry key's Context menu is opened, the first option is either Expand or Collapse, depending on the current status of the selected key. In the Contents pane, three Context menu options are displayed if any item in the Name column is selected. Otherwise, only the cascading New option is available.*

New This option appears on the View menu and on Registry Editor Context menus and is the only option on that menu if the mouse is right-clicked over an empty space in the Contents pane — that is, over any space other than a listing in the Name column. It may be initially puzzling to see it pop up if the mouse is clicked over a Data column item, but in this context the entire Data column is unrecognized and therefore treated as if it were empty space.

Registry Editing Techniques

Don't even *think* about editing the Registry until you've made a complete backup copy of the hidden SYSTEM.DAT and USER.DAT files mentioned earlier in this chapter. The next chapter reviews various backup procedures that you may use. In most cases, Windows is clever enough to protect itself against Registry mishaps, but it never hurts to buy a little extra insurance—at least until you're comfortable enough with the Registry to patch it up if it gets hurt by accident.

Back up a Contents pane entry

Keep in mind that the Registry Editor does not support an Undo option, which means that all edits are final. Also, if you edit any key that appears at two locations, the edit occurs simultaneously at both those locations (*HKCR\.bat* and *HKLM\SOFTWARE\Classes\.bat*, for example). Therefore, in addition to the overall backups described in Chapter 5, and the Registry export procedures described later in this chapter, it's not a bad idea to make a copy of a Contents pane entry prior to editing it, especially if the original data is lengthy and/or complex, as shown in this example:

C:\Windows\rundll.exe   setupx.dll,InstallHinfSection   DefaultInstall 132 %1

If you edit a line such as this and then decide to restore the original, you may have trouble doing so unless your memory is excellent—or you have a backup available.

Use the following procedure to make a single-line backup of any Contents pane entry.

1. Double-click the Name entry to be copied.

2. Press Ctrl+C to copy the highlighted Value data line, and then click the OK button.

3. Create a new entry called *whatever*bak (where *whatever* is the name of the entry in the Name column).

4. Double-click its Name entry icon.

5. Press Ctrl+V to paste the copied data into the Value data box.

Now you can edit the original entry as desired, and if it doesn't work, delete the edited line and then delete the "bak" segment to restore the original data. Windows itself ignores your *whatever*bak entries, so this technique may prove convenient if you edit several Contents pane entries and then want to selectively restore some, but not all, to their original state.

Illegal edits

In most cases, a disabled (grayed) option on the Edit menu indicates it is not possible to use that option on the highlighted Registry key. For example, if My Computer is highlighted, the Delete, Rename, and Copy Key Name (if available) options are disabled. Or if an HKEY is highlighted, Delete and Rename are disabled.

In other cases, an Edit menu option may appear to be available, even if it is not. To illustrate, highlight the (Default) item in any Contents pane and then select the Delete option. After the "Are you sure?" message is displayed, you'll get an "Unable to delete all specified devices" message, which indicates this item cannot be removed.

Although the Registry Editor thus protects its contents from certain disastrous accidents, it nevertheless permits the user to make many potentially life-threatening operations without comment. Therefore, reread everything you can find about backup procedures before making any serious moves.

INI files and the Registry

As noted in Chapter 1 (see the "Contents Pane — INI File Comparisons" section), a certain amount of interaction occurs between the Registry and various INI files. While some INI data is transplanted to the Registry, Windows may also add or revise INI file data every time Windows starts, so that it contains information appropriate to the current user. So, if you see something in an INI file immediately after installing a new application, and whatever it is has disappeared the next time you look, it has probably been relocated to a Registry subkey. Likewise, if the remaining INI file content changes from one session to another, it's a sure sign that the Registry is at work in the background.

Here's one more example of what can happen: When you change wallpaper from within Windows, WIN.INI retains the old wallpaper specifications for the moment, even though the new wallpaper appears onscreen. But the next time Windows opens, it checks the Registry and then rewrites WIN.INI as required to bring it into conformity with the Registry.

As a result of these file interactions, you may want to keep an eye on your INI files — especially WIN.INI — until you become familiar with the Registry's mode of operation. Windows 98 makes a backup copy of WIN.INI (and SYSTEM.INI, too) each time it backs up the Registry files, which is described in greater detail in the next chapter.

Registry navigation keys

Table 4-2 lists various keystroke combinations that may be useful during a Registry-editing session. Note especially that if a key structure is visible in the Key pane, pressing any key combination jumps to the first subkey that begins with those characters. Thus, if the *HKCU\AppEvents\Schemes\Apps\ .Default\.Default\.Current* subkey is displayed, and the *HKEY_CUR- RENT_USER* key is currently highlighted, quickly press .C to jump to the *.Current* subkey. If a slight pause occurs between pressing the period (.) and

C keys, the highlight jumps to the first .*Default* subkey (because it begins with a period) and then moves on to the first available subkey that begins with *C* (probably, the *CCSelect* subkey).

Table 4-2 *Registry Editor Navigation Keys* *

Keyboard Key	Primary Action	Secondary Action †
↓	Opens next lowest key on same level	
↑	Opens next highest key on same level	
→	Expands open key	Opens next lowest key
←	Opens next highest key	Collapses its subkeys
Alt+Home	Opens My Computer icon	
Alt+Home+←	Opens My Computer icon and collapses HKEYs	
Tab	Toggles between Key and Contents panes	
F1	Accesses help	
F2	Renames open key	
F3	Accesses Find and/or Find Next	
Alt+F4	Exits Registry Editor	
F5	Refreshes the screen	
F6	Toggles between Key and Contents panes	
F10	Highlights Registry menu	
Shift+F10	Opens Context menu	Closes Context menu
Any character	Opens next visible key whose name begins with that character	

* List does not include Alt keys for menus and menu options. Refer to underlined letters on Menu bar and in menu options.

† If listed, action occurs on alternate key presses.

Search techniques

In order to edit a Registry key or Contents pane entry, first you must find it. If you already know the location, then the fastest way to access it is usually to successively click the plus signs next to the appropriate HKEY and its subkeys until the desired key is found and opened. However, if you're not sure where the key or Contents pane entry is located, then use the Edit menu's Find option to search for it.

It's usually possible to hasten the search action by checking only one box in the Look at area of the Find dialog box. To verify this, time a search for *StopStat* (an *HKDD* subkey) with all three boxes checked, and again with only the Keys box checked. The latter search may take about half the time of the former.

Obviously, every Registry key exists in the Key pane, so there's no point wasting time searching the other two areas. However, a reference to the *name* of a key may be found in either column in the Contents pane, as was shown in Figures 3-21 through 3-24 in the previous chapter. Most filename citations are found in the Data column, although a few filename lists are in the Name column of the *InstalledFiles* and *VMM32Files* subkeys under the *HKLM\System\CurrentControlSet\control* key.

Given a bit of experience, it should be possible to predict the location of an item with some degree of certainty and, by then checking only the appropriate box, find it in a lot less time than it would take to search the whole works.

Registry search indicators

The customary "busy" mouse pointer does not appear during a Registry search. Instead, the Find box shown in Figure 4-8 remains onscreen until the search has concluded. If the search is successful, then the found item is highlighted. If the search is unsuccessful, the Registry editor does not display a "not found" message. However, a "Finished searching" message is displayed, which is also shown in Figure 4-8. If function key F3 is pressed repeatedly to find all occurrences of the search item, the same message appears when F3 is again pressed after the final successful search.

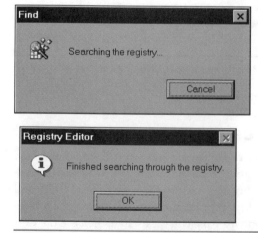

Figure 4-8 *The Find box is displayed during a Registry search operation, but the usual "busy" mouse pointer does not appear. When no more search items are found, a Registry Editor window shows a "Finished searching" message.*

Binary and DWORD searches

The Find option is unable to find binary or DWORD data stored in the Contents pane's Data column. If you need to find specific data in either format and know the general area where it should be, export only the appropriate key structure and then use your word processor's Find option, as shown in these examples:

Format	Data Column Shows	Search For
Binary	45 3a 8d ac d4	45,3a,8d,ac,d4
DWORD	0x00087439 (554041)	dword:00087439

Binary and DWORD data are written into a Registry script file as shown in the "Search for" column in the preceding table and also in Figure 4-9. Therefore, search for binary data by entering the hexadecimal byte characters separated by commas. In a DWORD search, the leading "0x" and the parenthetical decimal equivalent are not written into the script file, but the "dword:" prefix is. Depending on context, it may be helpful to begin the search with that prefix, to avoid finding *CLSID* entries that contain the same character string.

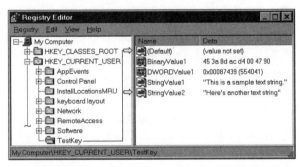

TestKey saved via the Export option

TestKey saved to a PRN file

REGEDIT4

```
[HKEY_CURRENT_USER\TestKey]
"StringValue1"="This is a sample text string."
"BinaryValue1"=hex:45,3a,8d,ac,d4,00,47,90
"DWORDValue1"=dword:00087439
"StringValue2"="Here's another text string"
```

```
[HKEY_CURRENT_USER\TestKey]
StringValue1=This is a sample text string.
BinaryValue1=45,3a,8d,ac,d4,00,47,90
DWORDValue1=39,74,08,00
StringValue2=Here's another text string
```

Figure 4-9 *This "do nothing" key's Contents pane shows examples of binary, DWORD, and string data. For comparison purposes, the text examples below the window show how this data is exported into a Registry script file (left) and printed to a file (right). Note the differences in the use of quotes, format of DWORD data, and so on.*

Copy/Paste search techniques

For most Find operations, it's sufficient to type the desired data into the Find what box and then search for it. However, if you've just encountered a complex key name or Data column entry and now want to find other occurrences of that item, you may prefer to copy the highlighted data to the Clipboard, and then paste it into the Find what box. Although the Registry Editor's Edit menu does not support a Copy option, and the familiar Ctrl+C key press does not always work, one of the following techniques permit you to copy any item in the Registry Editor window.

Key name Use the Edit menu's Copy Key Name option (described previously) to copy a lengthy key name, such as the *CLSID* number shown at the bottom of Figure 4-5. Paste that string into the Find what box, cut the *HKEY_CLASSES_ROOT\CLSID* at the head of the string, and then search for other occurrences of that unique string.

If the Copy Key Name option is not available, use the Data column procedure described in a later section.

Name column A Name entry cannot be copied to the Clipboard by highlighting it and pressing the Ctrl+C keys. Instead, open its Context menu and select the Rename option. The boxed name can now be copied via the Ctrl+C keys.

Data column Double-click the small icon to the left of the Name entry and then press Ctrl+C to copy the highlighted Value data box.

Device searches

Sometimes the identity of a device may be obvious from the name that appears to the right of its key. For example, if a key name is *NEC___CD-ROM_DRIVE:5012*, it should be reasonably clear that the key refers to a CD-ROM drive manufactured by NEC. Other keys are not quite so obvious though, as shown by the *SERENUM* (Serial Enumerator) and *MNP0336* subkeys in Figure 4-10. If either subkey is highlighted, the Contents pane simply shows (Default) and (value not set), neither of which is very informative. To track down the necessary information for this specific example, open the *HKLM\ Enum* key that appears immediately below the last *000x* key and look for a *SERENUM* subkey. Note that this *Enum* key is at a different level than the subkeys of the same name that may appear under one or more of the *000x* keys just above it. Its own subkeys specify various serial devices, one of which is *MNP0336*. Open the *ROOT&...* subkey immediately below it to display a list of its contents, which includes sufficient information to identify the device hiding behind the *MNP0336* key. If necessary, use the same general technique to find information about other devices listed under any *000x* key's *Enum* subkey. Or in any other location where an ambiguous key name is discovered, search the Registry for other occurrences of that name, one of which may lead to a clue (or another subkey) that identifies the device.

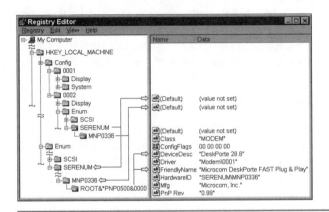

Figure 4-10 *If the Contents pane data is ambiguous for a key name, a search for another key of the same name often leads to data sufficient to identify the device.*

General hardware search As another hardware device-search technique, highlight the *HKLM\Enum* key and search the subkey Data columns for a likely device description (system timer, HP DeskJet, SyQuest SyJet, and so on). To find all system drives (diskette, CD-ROM, hard drive), search the Name column for CurrentDriveLetterAssignment to find drive A. Then press function key F3 repeatedly to find each successive drive letter. Once the desired item is found, note the key and subkey in which that device is specified.

Default monitor search In Figure 3-21 in the previous chapter, the DeviceDesc entry in the *Enum\Monitor\Default_Monitor\0001* subkey's Contents pane identifies the current monitor as a MAG Innovision MX17F/S. To identify the current default monitor if more than one *000x* subkey appears in this section, search the Data column entries in the *HKDD\ConfigManager\Enum* section for MONITOR\ DEFAULT_ MONITOR\, which will appear in the HardwareKey entry's Data column. Note the actual *000x* subkey name at the end of that line and then find that subkey under the *HKLM\Enum\ Monitor\Default_Monitor* key above. As in the example shown in Figure 3-21, the DeviceDesc entry indicates the monitor name and model number.

Import/export operations

In becoming familiar with these actions, remember that Microspeak definitions rarely follow conventional English usage. For example, neither the Import nor the Export operation actually *moves* something between two locations, as is usually the case when these terms are used. Instead, the Import option *merges* a copy of a saved (that is, exported) Registry file back into the Registry. Export *saves* a copy of the selected key(s), while leaving the original in place.

Import operations

To import a saved Registry file back into the current Registry, select Import Registry File on the Registry menu, highlight the desired file, and click on the Open button. Notwithstanding its ambiguous name, the button actually merges the selected file into the Registry. In Windows 98 only, the following message appears if an Import operation is attempted from a location other than the Registry Editor's own Import Registry File dialog box:

Are you sure you want to add the information in *path\filename*.REG to the registry?

In either case, the following message is displayed at the conclusion of the Import action:

Information in *path\filename*.REG has been successfully entered into the registry.

Remember to keep in mind the following unique characteristics of the Import action:

- An imported Contents pane entry overwrites a current Registry entry of the same name and does so without warning.

- An imported key and/or Contents-pane entry is *added* to the current Registry if that entry does not already exist there.

- An existing entry in the current Registry is left undisturbed if the imported file does not contain a replacement for it.

- If the imported subkey is to appear beneath a key (or key structure) that does not already exist, the Import action writes that key/key structure into the Registry.

These characteristics apply to every key, subkey, and Contents pane entry in the current Registry. For example, Figure 4-11 shows a hypothetical *NewKey* Registry structure before and after importing the NEWKEY.REG file seen at the bottom of the figure. Note that the Import action has revised the key structure according to the guidelines cited previously. That is, it updated the *SubKey A* Contents pane, left *SubKey B* untouched, added a line to *SubKey C,* and added a new *SubKey D.* If the untouched *SubKey B* is no longer wanted, it will have to be deleted as a separate operation.

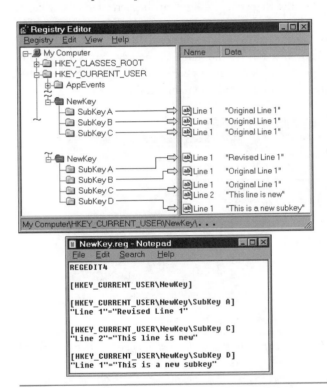

Figure 4-11 *This composite Registry window shows a* NewKey *and its subkey structure before and after importing the* NEWKEY.REG *file seen at the bottom of the illustration.*

If it is important that an existing key/subkey structure be completely replaced by a new version, then use the following procedure:

1. Export the existing key, as *AnyName*BAK.REG (just in case — you can always erase it later).

2. Delete that key in the current Registry.

3. Import the new *AnyName.Reg* file into the Registry.

Or, refer to the "Example of using the INF File as a Registry Editor" section later in this chapter, for an alternative method of handling a Registry import, which may be convenient if the same information must be imported into several Registries.

Export operations

To save all or part of the Registry, highlight any branch (that is, any key or subkey) and then select the Export option to open the Export Registry File dialog box shown in Figure 4-12. The Selected Branch textbox near the bottom of the dialog box verifies the name of the key that is about to be exported. Both that key, and all subkeys beneath it, will be saved to a file, whose name must be entered in the File name textbox.

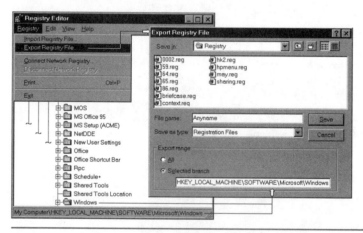

Figure 4-12 *When the Export Registry File option is selected, the name of the open Registry key appears in the Selected branch textbox in the Export Registry File dialog box. Click on the All radio button if you would rather export the contents of the entire Registry.*

There is no export status message. The mouse pointer may change to the busy-mode hourglass (or a similar) icon while data is being exported, but no message is displayed at the conclusion of the operation. The mouse pointer simply returns to its normal-mode appearance.

Import/export tips

If you plan to use the Registry Editor's Import/Export options frequently, you might want to consider the following suggestions.

Set up a Registry folder   Create a dedicated C:\Registry (or similar) folder for Registry files and also a Registry shortcut on the desktop. Open the shortcut's Context menu, select Properties, and click the Shortcut tab. Type **C:\Registry** in the Start in textbox, click the Apply button, and then click the OK button. The next time you select the Import or Export option, the contents of the C:\Registry folder are displayed in the dialog box.

Disable automatic Registry imports   By default, any file exported via the Export Registry File option is saved with an extension of REG, and — again, by default — when you double-click a file with that extension, it is immediately imported back into the Registry. This is quite convenient if it's what you really want to do, but if you make a practice of regularly editing the Registry, it's all too easy to make a mess of things by accidentally double-clicking the wrong file. After you've done this a few times, consider one of the following alternatives.

Revise the Registration association: Open Explorer's View menu, select Options (Folder Options if IE4 is installed), and then click on the File Types tab. In the list of Registered file types, select Registration Entries and click the Edit button to open the Edit File Type dialog box whose Actions box shows Edit, **Merge** (in boldface type), and print. Highlight the Edit action and click the Set Default button to make Edit, rather than Merge, the default (boldface) action. The next time you double-click (accidentally or on purpose) a file with the REG extension, the file will open in Notepad for editing, which may be preferable to an accidental Registry merge. When you really *do* want to merge a file into the Registry, then do so via its Context menu.

The action described here does not affect a double-click from within the Import Registry File dialog box, but if you've gone to the trouble to open that box, then presumably you really do want to merge something into the Registry. As mentioned earlier, Windows 98 adds the extra step of an "Are you sure . . . ?" prompt if an Import is attempted from another location.

Use some other extension: As an alternative to the previous suggestion, use an extension other than REG for potentially hazardous Registry files. Assuming you've created a dedicated C:\Registry folder, the presence of say, a few *.re_* files in addition to the usual *.reg* files should be no cause for confusion. If you double-click a *filename.re_* file, Windows has no idea what to do with it, so it won't get imported into the Registry by accident. When you are ready to import it, use the Registry Editor's Import option. Or refer to the "Add Context Menu Options" section in Chapter 6 for additional suggestions about setting up a permanent *.re_* (or similar) key in the Registry.

Creating a Registry script file for importing

Some sources warn against editing the Registry directly and recommend instead that a Registry script file be created and then imported into the Registry. In most cases, however, this may be more trouble that it's worth. Although the file is in straight ASCII text format, the proliferation of slashes, double-slashes, and commas turns file creation into a tedious procedure at best, and it may be even easier to misedit the file than to misedit the Registry itself.

Even if duplicate information must be entered into several Registries, it's usually easier and faster to edit one Registry directly and then export the appropriate section(s) to a script file that may be subsequently imported into other Registries. Nevertheless, here are a few guidelines for creating a Registry script file for those occasions when you feel the urge to do so.

The REGEDIT4 file header Whenever the Export option (described above) is used, a 12-byte header is written into the file, consisting of the word *REGEDIT4,* followed by two sets of linefeed/carriage-return bytes, as shown by the first underlined segment of this Debug script excerpt:

```
D:\registry>debug network.reg
-d
146B:0100   52 45 47 45 44 49 54 34-0D 0A 0D 0A 5B 48 4B 45   REGEDIT4....[HKE
146B:0110   59 5F 43 55 52 52 45 4E-54 5F 55 53 45 52 5C 4E   Y_CURRENT_USER\N
146B:0120   65 74 77 6F 72 6B 5D 0D-0A 22 52 65 73 74 6F 72   etwork].."Restor
...
146B:01A0   45 5D 0D 0A 22 52 65 6D-6F 74 65 50 61 74 68 22   E].."RemotePath"
146B:01B0   3D 22 5C 5C 5C 5C 44 45-4C 4C 34 38 36 5C 5C 43   ="\\\\DELL486\\C
146B:01C0   22 0D 0A 22 55 73 65 72-4E 61 6D 65 22 3D 22 4A   ".."UserName"="J
-
```

If this header is slightly altered (REGEDIT, or REGEDIT3, for example), no error message is displayed when the Import option is selected, even though the file will not in fact be imported into the Registry.

Use of backslash and quotes in Registry script file Figure 4-13 shows a Registry Editor window in which the Contents pane displays some network-related data. Note in particular the RemotePath entry's underlined Data column (also underlined in the preceding script excerpt) and compare that entry against the way the same data appears in the Registry script file, where it is also underlined. The comparison shows that each backslash in the Contents pane is written as a double backslash in the script file. In addition, the script file uses single backslashes within the Key\subkey structure, but of course these separators do not appear in the Registry Editor's Contents pane. As a final comparison, note the use of quotes in the script file and compare each line with its equivalent in the Registry Editor's Contents pane.

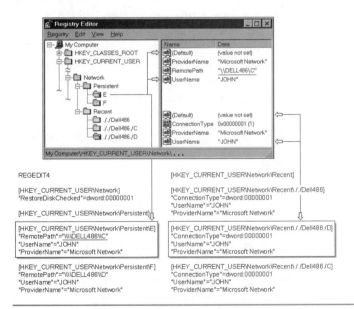

Figure 4-13 *This Registry Editor window displays the contents of a few network-related keys, while the boxed portions of the Registry script file excerpt beneath it show how that information is exported into the file. Compare the underlined RemotePath entry in both locations.*

The point of these tedious comparisons is to draw attention to the distinctive style that must be followed when editing a Registry script file. After making a few minor editing errors, you too may agree that it's usually far simpler to just edit the Registry directly, and never mind the safety-first aspects of script file editing.

Variations in the Registry Structure

In any examination of the Registry, it's important to keep in mind that there is no "standard" way to store data here. For example, a DWORD was described in Chapter 1 as a four-byte sequence. It might therefore seem that the DWORD format would be used whenever data is stored within four bytes. But, search the Registry for EditFlags (check the Values box only) and you'll find that many four-byte sequences are expressed as binary values rather than as DWORDs. There doesn't seem to be any consistent pattern to the choice between these formats, other than perhaps the personal preference of the programmer du jour.

To demonstrate how similar information may be written in more than one format, the Registry example in Figure 4-14 shows how the same information is stored by various Windows applications. To create the illustration, the following three application windows were opened:

Manufacturer	Application	Subkey with Size, Position Data
Hewlett-Packard	JetAdmin	*Position*
Windows Magazine	Wintune98	*Settings*
Microsoft	Registry Editor	*Regedit*

Each application window was adjusted so its dimensions and onscreen position were the same as the others. With the Registry Editor window placed on top, each application's size-and-position subkey was opened so that its Contents pane could be examined. Because only one Registry key can be opened at a time, Figure 4-14 is a cut-and-paste composite view, edited to show all three subkeys in a single Contents pane. Also, the illustration shows only those items pertaining to the size and position of each application window.

Note that Hewlett-Packard's *Position* subkey reports the height and width of the window, followed by the x, y coordinates of its upper-left corner. In this example, the window's height and width are 544 and 803 pixels, and the upper-left corner is at $x = 158$ and $y = 92$ pixels, measured from the left side and the top of the screen.

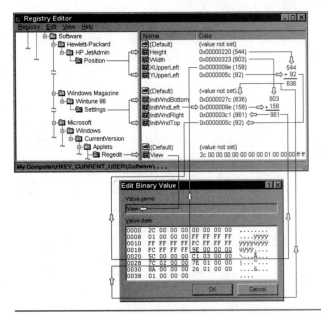

Figure 4-14 *This composite view of a Registry Editor window shows how different software applications present the same basic information in their Contents panes. The addition examples on the right side of the Contents pane show how to "do the math," to verify that each data set creates a window of the same size and position.*

The specified window height and top (544 + 92) mean that the bottom is at pixel 636. Therefore, the window width and left side (803 + 158) would place its right side at pixel 961. And that's just the way the *Windows Magazine* Wintune 98 utility reports the same information, in its *Settings* subkey. Note that both utilities require four data entries to report the windows size and placement but use different names for their subkeys and within the Contents pane's Name column. The applications do however use the same DWORD data format to report their values.

In contrast, the subkey for Microsoft's own Registry Editor window is tucked five levels down, in the *Regedit* subkey, and its Contents pane does not even vaguely resemble the previous two examples. In this specific example, the equivalent information is written into a 60-byte binary Data entry named View. Because the Data column entry extends well beyond the window border, the Edit Binary Value window inset in Figure 4-14 shows the complete data string. Note that the *0x0000009e* DWORD for the upper-left corner in the other two applets is stored here at bytes 1C-1F, where it is written in reverse format as *9E 00 00 00*. It is followed in turn

by the other three DWORDs found in the *Windows Magazine Settin*
subkey. Note also that the same hexadecimal letters appear as lowerca
a-f in the Contents pane's Data column, but as uppercase *A-F* in the Ec
window.

A series of lines from one applet's Data column entry to another's m
help show how that data is displayed in each location. For general inform
tion, the final four DWORDs in the Edit Binary Value window define tl
Registry Editor's split bar position (*7E 01 00 00*), the width of the Nar
(*8A 00 00 00*) and Data (*26 01 00 00*) columns, and finally, the condition
the Status Bar at the bottom of the Registry Editor window (*01 00 00 0C*
enabled).

Some Microsoft applets and applications specify their window size
just described, and some don't. For example, Word version 7.0's *Data* su
key has a single entry named Settings, whose Data column contains a
Kbyte binary sequence that includes the window specifications and mu
else, including a list of recently opened document files. (So does Word'
but recent filenames are stored in Unicode format, and the key size is abc
three times larger.) In contrast, the Internet Explorer's *Document Windo*
subkey defines its own window by specifying its height, width, *x*, anc
data. But they're not DWORDs. Instead, the Explorer writes the data
binary values — that is, as separate four-byte entries, each written in t
reverse hexadecimal format found within the Registry Editor's View ent

The point of this little review is to illustrate how different formats n
be used to record the same information. And the point to remember is
you've seen one subkey, you definitely haven't seem them all.

The Registry Editor in Real Mode

The *Windows 95 Resource Kit* refers to "the Windows-based version
Registry Editor or the real-mode version on the Windows 95 emerge
startup disk," and the *Windows 98 Resource Kit* refers to "the MS-DC
based version of the Registry Editor." Although both statements may s
gest there are two utilities with the same name, there is in fact only o
The REGEDIT.EXE file on the emergency startup diskette is simp
copy of the same file in the C:\Windows folder, and either may be used
real-mode editing of the Registry.

If a Registry problem prevents Windows from opening in its graph
mode, then there is no alternative, and the real mode is the only way to
Just remember that in its real mode, the Registry Editor is quite fast —
very dangerous. While the right command sequence can save the day,
wrong one can ruin it — and perhaps the next few days as well.

To use the Registry Editor in real mode, either reboot the system to the command prompt, or select the "Restart the computer in MS-DOS mode" radio button on the Shut Down dialog box. Then type **REGEDIT** at the command prompt, followed by the appropriate command-line switch(es), which are listed in the following sections.

REGEDIT command-line switches

To review the Registry Editor's list of command-line switches, type **REGEDIT** at the command prompt to display a list similar to that shown in Figure 4-15. Unlike other applications executed from a command-line prompt, it is not necessary to append a forward slash-question mark (/?) at the end of the line to display this list. (If REGEDIT is typed from a DOS box within Windows, the Windows Registry Editor window opens.)

```
Imports and exports registry files to and from the registry.

REGEDIT [/L:system] [/R:user] filename1
REGEDIT [/L:system] [/R:user] /C filename2
REGEDIT [/L:system] [/R:user] /E filename3 [regpath1]
REGEDIT [/L:system] [/R:user] /D regpath2

/L:system     Specifies the location of the SYSTEM.DAT file.
/R:user       Specifies the location of the USER.DAT file.
filename1     Specifies the file(s) to import into the registry.
/C filename2  Specifies the file to create the registry from.
/E filename3  Specifies the file to export the registry to.
regpath1      Specifies the starting registry key to export from.
              (Defaults to exporting the entire registry).
/D regpath2   Specifies the registry key to delete.
```

Figure 4-15 *Exit Windows and type **REGEDIT** at the command prompt to display a list of switches that may be used with the Registry Editor in real mode. The /D switch was not available in the early retail version of Windows 95.*

For future reference, the switches are reviewed in alphabetical order. In each example, type **REGEDIT** and a space, and then replace the italicized *filename* or *HKEY* with the actual filename and/or HKEY and subkey that you want to process. Replace *filename*.REG with the complete path and filename, as appropriate. Note that the undocumented /S switch (not seen in Figure 4-15) is not supported in real mode.

filename.REG   If no switch precedes *filename*.REG, that file is imported into the Registry without affecting any other part of the Registry.

/C *filename*.REG

Copy. Use with extreme caution. The /C switch replaces the entire existing Registry with the *filename*.REG file. If that file is not a full version of a valid Registry backup, then the accidental use of this switch can make subsequent repair work even more difficult. The Registry Editor does not check *filename*.REG for validity, and no warning message appears if the new Registry is invalid.

/D HKEY\subkey

Delete. This switch was not supported in the early retail version of Windows 95 but is available in SR versions and in Windows 98, where it can be quite helpful in removing a troublesome Registry subkey. Refer to the "Alternate Real-Mode Recovery" section in Chapter 7 for an example of its use.

/E *filename*.REG

Export. There's no danger here. The /E switch simply exports the entire existing Registry into a file named *filename*.REG, typically about 20–25 percent larger than the sum of the SYSTEM.DAT and USER.DAT files.

/E *filename*.REG HKEY (or HKEY\subkey)

Export. In this example, only the structure within the specified HKEY, or HKEY\subkey, is exported.

/L:C:\<*path*>\SYSTEM.DAT

Location. Specifies the location of the SYSTEM.DAT file, but only if it is not in the C:\Windows directory.

/R:C:\<*path*>\USER.DAT

USER.DAT location. Specifies the location of the USER.DAT file, but only if it is not in the C:\Windows directory.

/S

Silent (undocumented, not supported in real mode). The Registry edit specified on the command line takes place "in silence." That is, no advisory message indicates the success (or failure) of the action.

Real-mode export notes

If the Registry Editor attempts to export a Registry HKEY while operating in real mode, the results will be as described in the following sections. A "Cannot export . . ." message is displayed if the specified export operation is not possible.

HKEY_CLASSES_ROOT

Although this key does not actually exist in either DAT file, the real-mode export operation is nevertheless able to create it by extracting the *HKEY_LOCAL_MACHINE* key's *SOFTWARE\Classes* key structure on the fly.

HKEY_CURRENT_USER

If this key is exported from the C:\Windows\USER.DAT file, the real-mode export operation changes each occurrence of *HKEY_USERS\. default* to *HKEY_CURRENT_USER*. If exported from a USER.DAT file in a C:\Windows\Profiles*UserName* folder, each occurrence of *HKEY_USERS\ UserName* likewise becomes *HKEY_CURRENT_USER*.

HKEY_LOCAL_MACHINE

This key holds the contents of the SYSTEM.DAT file and can be exported in real mode.

HKEY_USERS

This key holds the contents of the USER.DAT file and can also be exported in real mode.

HKEY_CURRENT_CONFIG

This key is created as the Windows GUI opens by reading one of the *HKEY_LOCAL_MACHINE\Config\000x* key structures. No current configuration exists in real mode, so the key does not yet exist and therefore cannot be exported. To export one of the configurations that may become the *HKEY_CURRENT_CONFIG* key structure once the Windows GUI opens, type the following command line instead:

    REGEDIT filename.REG /E HKEY_LOCAL_MACHINE\
    Config\000x

where *x* is the number of the desired configuration.

HKEY_DYN_DATA

The information contained within this key structure is not written into the Registry until the Windows GUI opens and therefore cannot be exported in real mode.

Use of command-line switches within Windows

Because the previously described switches are so closely associated with real-mode operation, it's often overlooked that a few of them can also be used in Windows, even if not within the usual Registry Editor window. Many Registry operations can be conducted by selecting the Start menu's Run option, and then typing **REGEDIT** followed by the appropriate switches, as described previously. Generally, there's little point in doing so because it's surely easier to work within a Registry Editor window than via this command-line option.

However, the command-line switches may be useful in performing pre-defined operations, either as required or automatically every time Windows opens. In this case, the undocumented /S switch is especially useful, because it does away with a pause at the conclusion of the operation. Refer to the "Registry Edits at Startup" section of Chapter 6 for information on the use of command-line switches from within Windows.

The INF File as a Registry Editor

Although the Windows INF file was probably not thought of as a stand-in for the Registry script file, it does offer an alternative way to edit the Registry that some users may prefer to the methods described previously. According to both Windows Resource Kits, these "Device information files provide information used by Windows to install software that supports a given hardware device." While the statement is certainly true, it describes only one function of an INF file, which can support both hardware *and* software installations. In fact, the INF file is actually a *Setup* Information file, and is correctly identified as such in the list of Registered file types. With a little practice, it can be used as an alternate Registry editing device.

If an INF file's Context menu is opened and its *Install* option selected, the file contents are read, and significant changes may be made to the Registry, as prescribed by sections of that file, which superficially resemble the familiar INI file format. A few of these sections are reviewed here, to show how they affect the Registry, and how they can be used to edit it, even if a new hardware or software device is not being installed.

Not all INF file sections, nor all lines within a section, are included in this chapter's review. In most cases, information to the left of the equal sign should be entered as written here, while that to the right may vary as desired. However, a subsequent section name must of course agree with whatever was specified in a previous section. Spaces added here for clarity may or may not be found in actual INF files and do not affect operation.

A few INF file sections

Although a complete description of the INF file structure is beyond the scope of this chapter, a nodding acquaintance with the few details offered here may help in troubleshooting some Registry problems. For additional details, refer to Appendix C, "Windows 9*x* INF Files," in either Windows Resource Kit. But read with care, for its pages contain many errors, a few of which are pointed out in this chapter. In general, the CD-ROM version is more accurate than the printed version.

[Version]

The standard opening section for all INF files is as follows:

```
[Version]
Signature = "$Chicago$"    Identifies a Windows 95 or 98 INF
                           file by the original Windows 95 beta
                           name
```

The Signature line must be written as "$Chicago$" and not "$Windows 95$" as indicated in the print version of the *Windows 95 Resource Kit*. (The *Windows 98 Resource Kit* corrects the error.)

[DefaultInstall]

This section specifies additional sections of the INF file, in which various Registry edit sections may be specified, as shown by the examples given here:

```
[DefaultInstall]
AddReg    = AddRegKey       Name  of  the  INF  file
                            section in which new Registry
                            entries are specified.

DelReg    = DeleteRegKey    Name  of  section  in  which
                            Registry entries to be deleted
                            are specified.
```

Although both Resource Kits cite only an [Install] section, only items listed in the [DefaultInstall] section are executed when an INF file's Install option is selected. To find examples, search the INF files in the C:\Windows\Inf folder for those that contain this section header (SHELL.INF, for example).

[AddRegKey] and [DelRegKey]

These sections are cited on the AddReg and DelReg lines in the preceding [DefaultInstall] section. Although programmers delight in giving obscure names to sections such as these, there seems to be no performance advantage in doing so. Consequently, each section described here is given a simple name that describes what it actually does. *Real* programmers may of course change these names to help assure minimum comprehension. The text in italics illustrates the format in which a line should be entered, and sample lines are provided to illustrate actual Registry modifications.

[AddRegKey]

HKEY,	Subkey(s),	Name,	Flag,	Data (typical example)
HKCR,	.abc,	TestLineA,	0,	"Any ASCII Text String"
HKCR,	.abc,	TestLineB,	1,	3E, A2, 7D, FF
HKCR,	.abc,	TestLineC,	2,	"Any ASCII Text String"
HKCR,	.abc,	TestLineD,	3,	5A, 33, F6, B9
HKCR,	.abc,	TestLineE,	0x10001,	80, 3A, FF, 00

The entries in this section are added to the Registry, and each column heading in the preceding table is briefly described here:

HKEY	This is of course the HKEY under which the entry is to appear. For reasons best left unexplained, the Resource Kit refers to this HKEY entry as *reg-root-string*.
Subkey(s)	This is the complete subkey structure that appears under the specified HKEY. If the structure were more complex than the simple example shown here, it would be *subkeyName/sub-subkeyName/sub-sub-subkeyName*, and so on.
Name	The entry written here appears in the final subkey's Contents pane Name column.
Flag	A number here specifies the format of the data, as follows:

Flag	Data Format	Data Entry Comments
0 (or none)	Text string	To preserve spaces in text, enclose the line in quotes.
1	Binary	Enter hexadecimal numbers separated by commas.
2	Text string	Same as 0, but ignored if *Name* entry already exists.
3	Binary	Same as 1, but ignored if *Name* entry already exists.
0x10001	DWORD	Four data bytes written as reverse notation DWORD. Thus, 80, 3A, FF, 00 becomes 0x00ff3a80 (16726656).

Data	This entry appears in the Contents pane's Data column. Make sure to follow the format specified by the *Flag* entry.

Flag and Data Entry Notes:

1. If the flag is omitted, binary data will be entered as an ASCII string.

2. If a valid binary flag (1 or 3) is present, but an invalid hexadecimal number is entered (AR instead of A5, for example), that line — and all lines following it — will be ignored.

3. Note distinctive flag format (0x10001) required to specify DWORD entry.

[DelRegKey]

HKEY,	Subkey(s),	Name,	Flag,	Data
HKCR,	.abc,	(none)	(none)	(none)
HKCU,	Testkey,	StringValue1	(none)	(none)

As you might expect, this section specifies a subkey structure that is to be removed. The permissible entries are as described in the preceding [AddRegKey] section, except that there are no *Flag* or *Data* entries.

If the *Name* entry is omitted, then the entire specified subkey structure is deleted. Otherwise, only the cited *Name* entry and its associated Data column entry are removed. Thus, the two lines in the preceding [DelRegKey] section remove the entire *HKCR\.abc* subkey structure, but only the StringValue1 entry in the *HKCU\Testkey*. Other *TestKey* entries and subkeys are left undisturbed.

In addition to the DelReg=DelRegKey and the [DelRegKey] section described previously, an undocumented flag in the section specified by the AddReg= line can be used to delete a single Name and Data entry, as shown here:

```
[DefaultInstall]
AddReg=AddRegKey


[AddRegKey]
HKCR, .abc, TestEntry1, 4,
```

Assuming an entry whose name is TestEntry1 is in the *HKCR\.abc* key, the "4" flag removes that entry from the Contents pane, regardless of its Data format and its apparently contradictory inclusion within a section that is supposed to add data to the Registry.

Example of using the INF file as a Registry Editor

As an example of how an INF file can be used to perform certain routine Registry editing chores, this section shows how to remove the various recent history lists viewed via the Start menu's Documents, Find, and Run options. These lists are maintained in the Registry in the following subkeys and are shown in Figure 4-16.

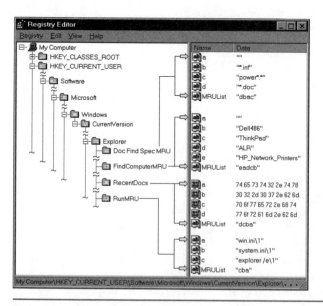

Figure 4-16 *In this composite view, the four open subkeys contain the history lists that are displayed when various Start menu options are selected.*

HKEY_CURRENT_USER\Software\Microsoft\Windows
\CurrentVersion\Explorer\...

Subkey	Start Menu Option	Find Menu Option
Doc Find Spec MRU	Find (cascading menu)	Files or Folders . . .
FindComputerMRU	Find (cascading menu)	Computer . . .
RecentDocs	Documents	
RunMRU	Run	

To remove one or more of the Start menu lists specified in columns 2 and 3, create a KillList.INF (or similar) file such as the following, but without the parenthetical comments. Note that quotes are required around any key name that includes one or more spaces.

```
[version]
signature=$Chicago$


[DefaultInstall]
AddReg=AddRegKey          (optional)
DelReg=DelRegKey


[AddRegKey]                        (this key and its contents are optional)
HKCU, Software\Microsoft\Windows\CurrentVersion\Explorer\"Doc Find Spec MRU"
HKCU, Software\Microsoft\Windows\CurrentVersion\Explorer\FindComputerMRU
HKCU, Software\Microsoft\Windows\CurrentVersion\Explorer\RecentDocs
HKCU, Software\Microsoft\Windows\CurrentVersion\Explorer\RunMRU


[DelRegKey]                        (note comma at end of each line)
HKCU, Software\Microsoft\Windows\CurrentVersion\Explorer\"Doc Find Spec MRU",
HKCU, Software\Microsoft\Windows\CurrentVersion\Explorer\FindComputerMRU,
HKCU, Software\Microsoft\Windows\CurrentVersion\Explorer\RecentDocs,
HKCU, Software\Microsoft\Windows\CurrentVersion\Explorer\RunMRU,
```

Each line in the [DelRegKey] section deletes the contents of the subkey cited at the end of the line, after which each line in the [AddRegKey] section writes a new (and empty) replacement key to take its place. Include one or more of these lines in each section, depending on which lists you want to delete. To verify that KillList.INF deletes the desired lists, open its

Context menu, select the Install option, and then check the specified Registry subkey(s), which should now be empty. With the exception of the Documents list, the associated Start menu list should also be empty. An additional step is required to delete this list, as described in the section that follows.

Automated list removal

Because a conventional INF file is usually run only once, the Context menu's Install option offers the appropriate means to do that. You could of course change the INF file's default action from Open to Install, but this would mean that if anyone double-clicked *any* INF file, it would be installed without so much as an "Are you sure?" warning. Therefore, if a custom INF file is to be used as a Registry editing tool, it may be more convenient to execute it from a desktop shortcut or a batch file. To do so, begin with these four preliminary steps:

1. Open the *HKCR\inffile\shell\install\command* subkey.

2. Double-click the (Default) entry in the Name column.

3. Press the Ctrl+C keys to copy the highlighted Value data entry to the Clipboard (which is easier than typing it in at the keyboard).

4. Click the OK or Cancel button, exit the Registry Editor, and follow either of the following procedures.

To create a Desktop shortcut:

1. Open the Desktop's Context menu and then the cascading New menu.

2. Select the Shortcut option.

3. Press Ctrl+V to paste the Value data line into the Command line textbox.

4. Replace the "%1" at the end of the line with the path and name of the INF file you created. The line should now look like this:

```
C:\Windows\RUNDLL.EXE SETUPX.DLL,InstallHinfSection
DefaultInstall 132 C:\<path>\KILLLIST.INF
```

This rather lengthy command string must be entered as a single continuous line. Filenames are shown as all caps but need not be written that way.

5. Click the Next button, type an appropriate name for the shortcut, and press the Finish button to conclude the operation.

If you prefer to delete all the lists specified in KillList.INF every time Windows starts, simply move the shortcut into the C:\Windows\Start Menu\Programs\StartUp folder.

To create a batch file:

1. Open Notepad and press Ctrl+V to paste the Value data line into it.

2. Replace the "%1" at the end of the line with the path and name of the INF file you created. Refer to Step 4 in the previous procedure for details.

3. If your INF file contains a line in the [DelRegKey] to delete the Documents list, then add the following line to this batch file:

```
erase C:\Windows\Recent\*.LNK
```

4. Save the file as KillList.BAT (or give it a similar name).

The erase line specified in Step 3 erases the shortcut files in the indicated folder, and this in turn deletes the Documents list whenever the batch file is run. As with the Shortcut procedure previously described, you can move the batch file into the C:\Windows\Start Menu\ Programs\StartUp folder to delete all lists specified in KillList.INF every time Windows starts. Or put the batch file in some other convenient location and drag a shortcut icon onto the desktop so the lists can be deleted whenever it's necessary (or politically correct) to do so.

Warning

Because the INF file is a very efficient Registry editing tool, its potential for harm should never be underestimated. Before installing any software received from a dubious source, you might want to read the contents of its INF file to see what it will do to your Registry, *before* letting it do it. If you discover any Registry-wrecking content, erase the entire file set and think about getting your software from other sources. If the INF file appears to be in order, but you're not entirely sure about it, heed all the warnings about backing up the Registry before proceeding.

Using the INF file as a troubleshooting tool

Refer to the "Restriction Recovery Procedure" section of Chapter 7 for suggestions on using the INF file during a Registry troubleshooting session.

The System Policy Editor

The System Policy Editor applet can be used to write data into the Registry to restrict access to a variety of Windows features. By default, the applet (POLEDIT.EXE) is not installed as part of the Windows setup procedure, but it is available in one of the following locations on your Windows CD:

Windows 95 \admin\apptools\poledit folder

Windows 98 \tools\reskit\Netadmin\poledit folder

You may prefer to leave it uninstalled and just access it from the disc as needed. If the disc itself is not readily available to others, this may keep busy little fingers from "fixing" policies when no one's around to maintain order. But if you do decide to install it, follow this procedure:

Open Control Panel's Add/Remove programs applet, select the Windows Setup tab, click the Have Disk button and then the Browse button. Select the appropriate folder (see the preceding list), highlight the POLEDIT.INF file, and then follow the prompts to complete the installation, which adds a System Policy Editor option to the cascading System Tools menu. Select that option, open the System Policy Editor's File menu, and select the Open Registry option to display Local User and Local Computer icons, as seen in Figures 4-17 (Windows 95) and 4-18 (Windows 98).

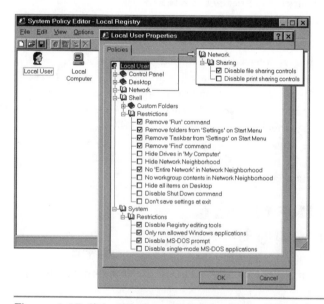

Figure 4-17 *If the Windows 95 System Policy Editor's Local User icon is selected, various restrictions can be imposed by checking the appropriate checkboxes.*

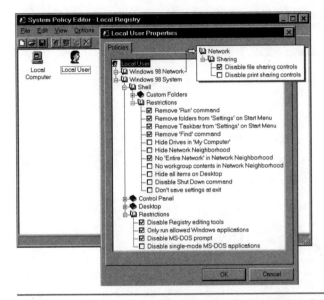

Figure 4-18 *Although the Windows 98 System Policy Editor swaps the Local User and Local Computer icon sequence and rearranges the Policies tab list, it offers the same options available in Windows 95.*

Double-click the Local User icon to open the Local User Properties window and the Policies tab seen in both Figures 4-17 and 4-18. Despite differences in physical layout, the same items are found on both menus, with the notable exception of the Help button that is missing in the Windows 98 Local User Properties window. It might just as well have been missing in the Windows 95 version, too, because it didn't do anything. Next, click one of the book icons shown opened in the figures to access various restriction checkboxes; place a checkmark in a checkbox, and that feature will be disabled. If the Control Panel book is selected, five additional books are displayed, as shown in Figure 4-19. Put a check in the checkbox under a book to display a Settings list at the bottom of the window. Then check one or more of those boxes as required.

As a result of the checkboxes that were checked in Figures 4-17 and 4-18, DWORD entries are written into the Contents pane for the subkeys shown in Figure 4-20. For future reference, Tables 4-3 and 4-4 list the restrictions shown in Figures 4-17 through 4-19 and identify each subkey entry written into the Registry.

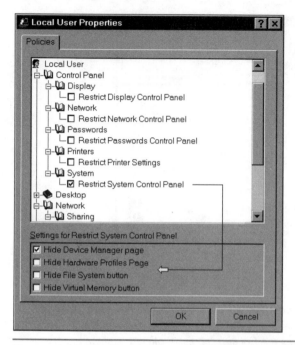

Figure 4-19 *The Control Panel book icon leads to five additional books, each of which contains a single checkbox. When a checked box is highlighted, the Settings area at the bottom of the window lists additional restrictions that may be imposed.*

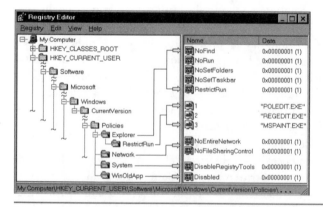

Figure 4-20 *The boxes checked in Figures 4-17 and 4-18 write these entries into the* Policies *subkeys. Refer to Table 4-3 for a list of these and other restrictions.*

Table 4-3 *Cross-Reference Guide:*
*Local User Policies and Registry Subkeys, Part I ***

Policies Control Panel Book, Checkbox, Settings	Registry Subkey and Entry
Display, Restrict Display Control Panel	*System*
Disable Display Control Panel	NoDispCPL
Hide Background page	NoDispBackgroundPage
Hide Screen Saver page	NoDispScrSavPage
Hide Appearance page	NoDispAppearancePage
Hide Settings page	NoDispSettingsPage
Network, Restrict Network Control Panel	*Network*
Disable Network Control Panel	NoNetSetup
Hide Identification Page	NoNetSetupIDPage
Hide Access Control Page	NoNetSetupSecurityPage
Passwords, Restrict Passwords Control Panel	*System*
Disable Passwords Control Panel	NoSecCPL
Hide Change Passwords page	NoPwdPage
Hide Remote Administration page	NoAdminPage
Hide User Profiles page	NoProfilePage
Printers, Restrict Printer Settings	*Explorer*
Hide General and Details page	NoPrinterTabs
Disable Deletion of Printers	NoDeletePrinter
Disable Addition of Printers	NoAddPrinter
System, Restrict System Control Panel	*System*
Hide Device Manager page	NoDevMgrPage
Hide Hardware Profiles page	NoConfigPage
Hide File System button	NoFileSysPage
Hide Virtual Memory button	NoVirtMemPage

* Settings (shown indented in the table) appear at the bottom of the Policies tab if the
checkbox under the indicated book is checked (see Figure 4-19).

Table 4-4 *Cross-Reference Guide:*
Local User Policies and Registry Subkeys, Part II

Policies Book and Checkbox	Registry Subkey and Entry
Network, Sharing	***Network***
Disable file sharing controls	NoFileSharingControl
Disable print sharing controls	NoPrintSharingControl
Shell, Restrictions	***Explorer*** *
Remove Run command	NoRun [1]
Remove folders from 'Settings' on Start Menu	NoSetFolders [2]
Remove Taskbar from 'Settings' on Start Menu	NoSetTaskbar [2]
Remove 'Find' command	NoFind [3]
Hide Drives in 'My Computer'	NoDrives [4]
Hide Network Neighborhood	NoNetHood
No 'Entire Network' in Net Neighborhood	NoEntireNetwork [5]
No workgroup contents in Net Neighborhood	NoNetworkGroupContents [5]
Hide all items on Desktop	NoDesktop
Disable Shut Down command	NoClose [1]
Don't save settings at exit	NoSaveSettings
System, Restrictions	***Explorer*** *
Disable Registry editing tools	DisableRegistryTools [6]
Only run allowed Windows applications	RestrictRun
Disable MS-DOS prompt	Disabled [7]
Disable single-mode MS-DOS applications	NoRealMode [7]

* Unless otherwise noted, entries are in *Explorer* subkey's Contents pane.

[1] Removes option from Start menu (after reboot).

[2] Removes option from Start menu only if *both* NoSet restrictions are set.

[3] Removes option from Start menu (after reboot). F3 still functions though.

[4] Previously shared drives still viewable in Network Neighborhood.

[5] In Network subkey

[6] In System subkey

[7] In WinOldApp subkey

Shell, Restrictions

A few of the items in the Shell, Restrictions book are briefly reviewed here.

Disable Shut Down command

If some other policy has disabled the Registry Editor, and the System Policy Editor is also unavailable, then think twice before enabling this restriction. Otherwise, there will be no way to exit Windows other than via the reset button or power switch. While both remain effective, neither comes highly recommended.

Hide all items on Desktop

This option takes effect the next time Windows opens and does just what you think it does, with one important exception: Because shortcuts in the StartUp folder are executed, a customized desktop can be set up by selecting this restriction and then creating one or more shortcuts in the StartUp folder to display only those desktop items that you want to see. Refer to the "Customizing the Desktop" section of Chapter 6 for details.

Hide drives in My Computer

If any drive is currently shared, the contents of that drive can still be accessed via Network Neighborhood.

System, Restrictions

The consequences of checking two of the restrictions in this section are briefly reviewed here.

Disable Registry Editing tools

This disables the Registry Editor while leaving other Windows applications enabled. A subsequent attempt to open the Editor displays an error message. Note however that this restriction has no effect on third-party utilities, such as the Norton Registry Editor.

Only run allowed Windows applications

If this box is checked, a Show button appears and leads to a list of allowed applications (not shown in Figure 4-17 or 4-18). Enter the applications that should *not* be restricted, and those applications will be listed in the *RestrictRun* subkey seen in Figure 4-19. Note that this subkey does the opposite of what its name implies: Access to applications listed in its Contents pane will *not* be restricted, while all other applications will no longer run. Therefore, you might want to make sure the list begins with POLEDIT.EXE and/or REGEDIT.EXE. If these applications are not specified here, they too will not run, and that makes it difficult to further revise the list, or to ever use the Registry Editor again.

Note

If this policy restriction is cleared, the list of applications in the *RestrictRun* subkey's Contents pane is deleted. Therefore, if the restriction is subsequently re-enabled, don't forget to re-enter the list of applications that you want to be able to run.

System policy restriction WARNING

After setting the desired restrictions, if you open the File menu and select the Save option, the new policies take effect immediately. So before experimenting, review the notes given here, because some restrictions may lead to problems. Or refer to the "Restriction Recovery Procedures" section of Chapter 7 if you discover such problems the hard way.

Restricting the default user

The System Policy Editor can offer at least some protection against the casual or unauthorized user. If the computer is configured for a user name and password prompt as Windows opens, then bypass the prompt by pressing the Escape key to log on as a default user. Then use the System Policy Editor to set restrictions that will be enabled for all users who subsequently bypass the user name and password prompt. These policies are not be enabled if an authorized user enters a valid name and password. (Refer to the "HKU: HKEY_USERS" section and the discussion of the USER.DAT file, in Chapter 3 for more information about the default user.)

If such protection against system meddlers is necessary, you may want to save the REGEDIT.EXE utility to diskette and then erase it from the C:\Windows folder. Put the diskette, and the Windows CD-ROM containing POLEDIT.EXE, in a busybody-free location. Note however that doing this is *not* the ultimate security system and can be defeated by a knowledgeable user with relatively little effort. If security problems persist, other measures will be required. Corporate downsizing comes to mind.

Registry Print Jobs

The following section describes various ways to handle a Registry print job from within the Windows Registry Editor utility described at the beginning of this chapter. But before printing anything, remember that a full printout can run to 1,000 or more pages, and that includes only the *HKEY_LOCAL_MACHINE* and *HKEY_USERS* keys. As described in

Chapters 2 and 3, three of the other keys are derived from these two keys as Windows opens, and therefore they are neither printed nor saved, unless specifically selected as described subsequently. The dynamically created *HKEY_DYN_DATA* key structure is also not printed, which is probably a good thing because it would add about another 1,000 pages to a Windows 95 print job. The key size is considerably smaller in Windows 98 though, due to a revision in the way data is written. See the "PerfStats (Performance Statistics)" section of Chapter 3 for more details.

Print (Registry menu option)

Use this option only to send a small subsection of the Registry to the printer. Otherwise, consider the Print to File option described in the next section or the Export/Print procedure, which is described in the section that follows.

Print to File

Most Print dialog boxes support a Print to File option, such as that shown in Figure 4-3 earlier in the chapter. By default, this action usually saves a file in a format that can later be sent directly to the printer. While this can be helpful if the printer is located elsewhere, it may be more convenient to reconfigure the option to save a straight ASCII text version of the desired Registry section to a file, and then print that file. Follow the procedure described here to do so. But first, review the "Export/Print procedure" section which follows, for an alternative way to print that may be more convenient.

1. Open the Start menu, highlight the Settings option, and select the Printers folder. Or select it via the My Computer window.

2. Double-click the Add Printer icon in the Printers window.

3. When the Add Printer Wizard window appears, click the Next button.

4. Select Local printer and again click the Next button.

5. Scroll down the Manufacturers list, highlight "Generic," and click the Next button.

6. In the Available ports list, highlight "LPT1:", and click the Next button (or select some other port, as desired).

7. Click the No radio button underneath "Do you want your Windows-based programs to use this printer as the default printer?"

8. Click the No button underneath "Would you like to print a test page?" and click the Finish button.

9. If prompted to do so, insert the Windows CD-ROM disc in the drive so that the necessary drivers can be installed.

At the conclusion of this operation, a Generic / Text Only icon should be displayed in the Printers window, as shown in Figure 4-21. Open its Context menu, select the Properties option, select the Paper tab, and change the Paper source to "Continuous - No Page Break" as is also shown in the figure. This prevents the generic printer driver from introducing its own page breaks into the text file, which — if the file is to be read and printed from a word processor — would simply get in the way of those inserted by the word processor.

Now select the Print option and, when the Print dialog box appears, use the down arrow in the Name box to select the Generic / Text Only printer. Click the Print to File checkbox, give the file a suitable name, and click the OK button to create it. The file can be subsequently viewed in any word processor or ASCII text editor, where it can be edited before printing.

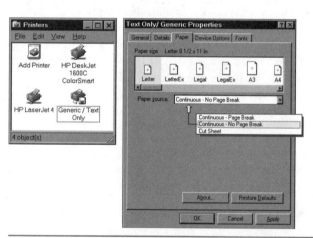

Figure 4-21 *If a generic printer is installed and configured to print to a file, its printer icon in the Printers window displays a diskette overlay. Make sure the paper source is "Continuous - No Page Break" so that the driver does not insert its own page breaks into the file.*

Export/Print procedure

Remember that the Registry menu's Export option saves an ASCII text file version of the selected Registry key or keys, which can be conveniently reviewed by any word processor and then printed in whole or in part. This is by far the easiest way to handle any print job, because the exported section can be reviewed before committing the whole works to the printer. It's also a convenient means to export and print those sections of the Registry that are not included in a full print job. For example, to print just the HKEY_CLASSES_ROOT section, select that key, export it, review it in a word processor, and then print it. Note the page count though, for even this "small" section of the Registry can be a paper-eater.

Print versus Export/Print

For reference purposes, Table 4-5 lists the page count and file size for typical HKEYs exported to a Registry REG file and also saved to a PRN file. Note that in the exported file versions, the size of the full copy is 12 bytes less than the sum of the *HKEY_LOCAL_MACHINE* and *HKEY_USERS* keys, thus reconfirming that these are the only two keys saved in a full Registry export.

Table 4-5 *File Size of Typical Exported HKEYs*

HKEY Name	Saved to PRN File		Exported to REG File	
	Page Count	File Size	Page Count	File Size
Windows 95				
HKEY_CLASSES_ROOT	741	1,365,332	658	1,188,126
HKEY_CURRENT_CONFIG	2	1,709	1	1,524
HKEY_CURRENT_USER	178	500,054	159	455,699
HKEY_DYN_DATA	1,256	5,307,703	1,072	4,852,050
HKEY_LOCAL_MACHINE	1,216	2,573,911	1,155	2,282,566
HKEY_USERS	180	503,248	160	458,159
Full copy †	1,395	3,077,181	1,314	2,740,713
Windows 98				
HKEY_CLASSES_ROOT	868	1,631,562	769	1,424,835
HKEY_CURRENT_CONFIG	2	2,367	2	2,153
HKEY_CURRENT_USER	171	505,927	153	460,730
HKEY_DYN_DATA	16	31,313	15	29,900
HKEY_LOCAL_MACHINE	1,435	3,025,882	1,361	2,680,194
HKEY_USERS	172	508,643	154	463,033
Full copy †	1,614	3,534,522	1,515	3,143,215

† A full exported REG file is the sum of the *HKLM* and *HKU* keys, less 12 bytes.

The reason for the size discrepancy is that each exported Registry file contains the following header:

```
REGEDIT4¶
¶
```

Each EOL (End Of Line) character (¶) signifies two bytes (linefeed and carriage return), which therefore adds four bytes to the eight-byte text string and accounts for the header total of 12 bytes. Because a full Registry export has only one such header, its file size should agree with the sum of the two HKEYs cited previously, less one 12-byte header. If it does not, it's because some *MRU* entries in the Registry changed during the export operations. But if these keys are exported in real mode (as described earlier), then the math always works out as expected.

Note that for each key, the PRN-format file size is larger than the exported REG file. The reason why may be demonstrated by exporting any convenient single key, such as the sample *TestKey* shown earlier in Figure 4-9. Next, print the same key to a generic text file and then review both files in a word processor, as follows:

Exported as *TESTKEY.REG*	Characters	EOL
REGEDIT4	8	2
	0	2
[HKEY_CURRENT_USER\TestKey]	27	2
"StringValue1"="This is a sample text string."	46	2
"BinaryValue1"=hex:45,3a,8d,ac,d4,00,47,90	42	2
"DWORDValue1"=dword:00087439	28	2
"StringValue2"="Here's another text string."	44	2
	0	2
	195	16 = 211 bytes
Printed to file as TESTKEY.PRN	**Characters**	**EOL**
······[HKEY_CURRENT_USER\TestKey]	34	2
······StringValue1=This is a sample text string.	49	2
······BinaryValue1=45,3a,8d,ac,d4,00,47,90	43	2
······DWORDValue1=39,74,08,00	30	2
······StringValue2=Here's another text string.	47	2
	203	14 = 217 bytes

Note that each line in the TESTKEY.PRN file is slightly longer than the same line in the TESTKEY.REG file, which accounts for why a PRN file is larger than the equivalent REG file. The file comparison also reveals the following points about each file type:

Exported key (*TESTKEY.REG*)

- Name entries and Data column strings enclosed in quotes
- Binary data prefaced by "hex:" or "dword:"
- Binary data written in same sequence as that shown in Contents pane

Key saved to file (*TESTKEY.PRN*)

- Each line is padded with seven leading spaces
- No entries enclosed in quotes
- DWORD entry is written in reverse sequence, with the numbers separated by commas

In both files, entries are written in the order in which they were entered or edited in the Registry, which is not necessarily the order in which they currently appear in the Contents pane, where they are sorted alphabetically.

Chapter 5

Registry Maintenance

Quite a few methods can be used to back up the Registry files and then restore them later. In order to present a reasonably concise (and consecutive) overview of available options, backup procedures are described first, followed by a companion section in which associated restore procedures are described. In both sections, these procedures apply to the Registry *only*. It's a good idea to back up everything else from time to time, but this is no place to discuss that issue.

In a few cases a section may visit, or revisit, information found in other chapters. However, the present coverage reviews only those aspects relevant to Registry backup and restore procedures. The chapter continues with a description of various techniques that can be used to compare any two Registry files and concludes with a discussion of several cleanup procedures.

Registry Backup Procedures

Keep in mind that even the finest Registry backup is only as good as the day on which it was made. It's therefore more than worth the bother to make a complete Registry backup by whatever means is most convenient immediately before doing anything serious to the Registry.

Windows 95 backups

These procedures apply to Windows 95 only, and keep in mind that any backup files created under this version of Windows cannot be restored to a system after it has been upgraded to Windows 98. For future reference, Table 5-1 lists the files associated with some of the backup utilities described in this section.

Table 5-1 *Name and Location of Windows 95 Registry Backup Utility Files*

Application and File	Location *	Purpose
Registry Editor		
REGEDIT.EXE	C:\Windows	Executable file
SYSTEM.DAO †	C:\Windows	SYSTEM.DAT backup
USER.DAO †	C:\Windows	USER.DAT backup
Configuration Backup Utility		
CFGBACK.EXE	*x*:\other\Misc\Cfgback	Executable file
REGBACKx.RBK	C:\Windows	Full Registry backup ‡
REGBACK.INI	C:\Windows	Backup file record
Emergency Recovery Utility		
ERU.EXE	x:\other\Misc\Eru	Executable file
SYSTEM.D_T	A: or C:\ERD	SYSTEM.DAT backup
USER.D_T	A: or C:\ERD	USER.DAT backup

* *x*:\ = CD-ROM drive letter, followed here by path on the Windows 95 disc (all versions).

† Created as part of normal Windows 95 startup (not by REGEDIT.EXE).

‡ Compressed file contains complete SYSTEM.DAT and USER.DAT.

Automatic backups

Every time Windows 95 opens successfully, it saves a single version of each of the following two backup files.

SYSTEM.DA0 A copy of SYSTEM.DAT is written into a hidden SYSTEM.DA0 file, which is also in the C:\Windows folder. By definition, this file is known to be valid, because a new version is created only if Windows 95 opens successfully. Consequently, Windows may use the DA0 backup file as a recovery device if it detects a Registry problem on a subsequent session startup. In that case, the SYSTEM.DA0 file is copied to SYSTEM.DAT, and Windows 95 should open in its last valid configuration.

USER.DA0 A backup copy of USER.DAT is written into a hidden USER.DA0 file in the C:\Windows folder. Also, if the user enters a valid username and password, a copy of that user's USER.DAT file is likewise copied as USER.DA0, both of which are in the C:\Windows\Profiles*UserName* folder.

Once Windows 95 has opened, no USER.DA0 file is updated if a new user logs on via the Start menu Shut Down option's "Close all programs and log on as a different user" radio button.

Configuration Backup utility

A Registry backup and restore utility is located in the following folder on the Windows 95 CD-ROM disc:

Folder	File
Other\Misc\Cfgback	CFGBACK.EXE
	CFGBACK.HLP

Double-click on the executable file to open the Microsoft Configuration Backup window shown in Figure 5-1 and then click on the Continue button to read each of three informational screens. (The Close button in the upper right corner had no effect on these screens and was in fact removed from SR versions of Windows 95.) Figure 5-2 shows the Configuration Backup dialog box, which appears next (the Close button is now enabled). Give the proposed backup a distinctive name and click the Backup button to begin the process. Just to make sure you're really serious about all this, the confirmation box, shown in the figure inset, is displayed. Click the Yes button to begin the backup. The Working and Configuration Backup windows shown in Figure 5-3 report the status of the procedure.

The Configuration Backup utility creates a single C:\ Windows\ REGBACK*x*.RBK file, where *x* is the number of the backup. The file contains a complete compressed copy of the current SYSTEM.DAT and USER.DAT files. In addition, a C:\Windows\ REGBACK.INI file records the following information for up to nine backup files (and at the same time, proves that, yes, Windows 95 *does* use INI files):

REGBACK.INI	Comments
[File1]	
FileDescription=Backup-1	Selected Backup Name (Figure 5-2)
Date=9/22/98	Date of first backup
[File2]	
FileDescription=Backup-2	
Date=9/25/98	Date of second backup

Continued

REGBACK.INI	Comments
. . and so on, through	
[File9]	
[StartWizard]	
Show=1	1 = display opening windows (Figure 5-1)

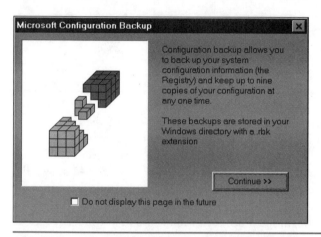

Figure 5-1 One of several informational windows that introduce the Microsoft Configuration Backup utility. If the "Do not display" checkbox is checked, a Show=0 line in the [StartWizard] section of REGBACK.INI disables these windows.

Emergency Recovery utility

As its name implies, this utility is primarily intended for use in restoring your system configuration should it become necessary to do so, and it is also found on the Windows 95 CD-ROM disc, in the following location:

Folder	File	Comments
Other\Misc\eru	ERU.EXE	Actually, this is the emergency *backup* utility
	ERD.E_E	*This* is the recovery disk utility
	ERU.INF	Setup file, to accompany ERD
	ERU.TXT	A ReadMe text file

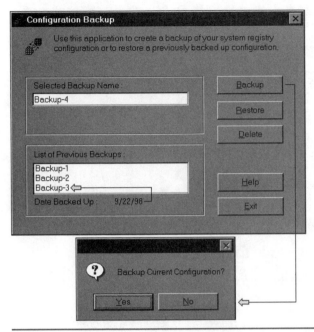

Figure 5-2 *The Configuration Backup dialog box is used to back up and
restore the Registry. Enter an appropriate name in the Selected
Backup Name textbox and click the Backup button to display
the confirmation dialog box seen in the inset. The Restore and
Delete buttons are enabled if a backup listed at the bottom of
the screen is highlighted. An erroneous checkbox (not seen here)
may be displayed next to the backup date. If so, just ignore it.*

The accompanying ERU.TXT file states that ". . . the recommended
[backup] location is a bootable floppy in drive A" but does not point out
that no diskette can possibly store all the files that must be saved. For
example, Figure 5-4 shows a typical list of files to be saved, and you may
notice that the critical SYSTEM.DAT file is missing. Click the Custom
button to find out why. As shown in Figure 5-5, the diskette doesn't have
enough room to store all the files, and therefore SYSTEM.DAT has been
omitted from the checklist. In most cases in fact, SYSTEM.DAT won't fit
on a single disk even if all the other files were omitted, and you may therefore prefer to back up all the files to a C:\ERD folder on the hard drive
instead of to diskette. Or if SYSTEM.DAT is small enough to fit on a single diskette, back up everything else to one diskette, then rerun the applet,
and back up only SYSTEM.DAT to another one.

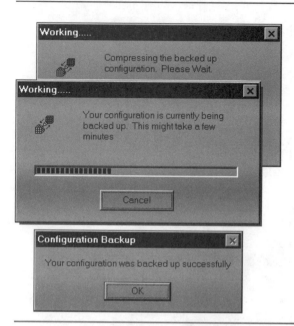

Figure 5-3 *These two Working dialog boxes report the progress of the backup procedure. The Configuration Backup window is displayed when the backup concludes successfully.*

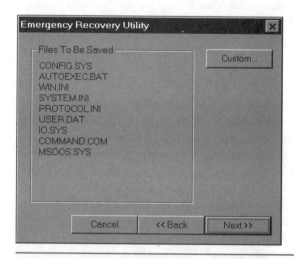

Figure 5-4 *If the Emergency Recovery Utility is used to create a recovery diskette, the list of saved files probably does not include the SYSTEM.DAT file, due to space limitations on the diskette.*

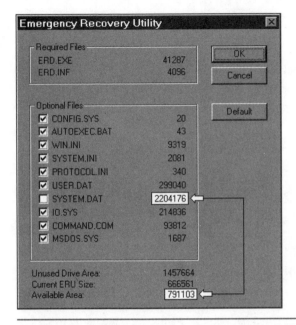

Figure 5-5 *Under default conditions, the Optional Files checklist usually precludes the inclusion of SYSTEM.DAT because its file size exceeds the diskette's available space.*

In any case, one of the messages shown in Figure 5-6 is displayed at the conclusion of the procedure. If the files were saved to the hard disk, the message concludes with "It is not advisable to run the recovery while in Windows." Not only that, it's impossible. If you try to do so, a message directs you to "re-boot computer and execute the program from a command-line prompt." Note also that if the backup utility can't find a CONFIG.SYS or AUTOEXEC.BAT file on the boot partition (presumably, C:\), it looks in the root directory of other drives, and if it finds these files, copies them to a diskette without comment. Only if the file(s) can't be found elsewhere does a warning message state that a "... file is not present and will not be backed up."

Figure 5-7 shows a typical directory listing if an incomplete file set is saved to a diskette in drive A. Refer to the "Emergency Recovery Utility" section later in this chapter, for information about restoring the Registry files from the recovery diskette or hard drive folder.

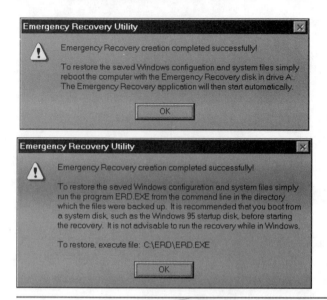

Figure 5-6 *Messages seen at the successful completion of a recovery diskette, or when backing up to a folder on the hard drive.*

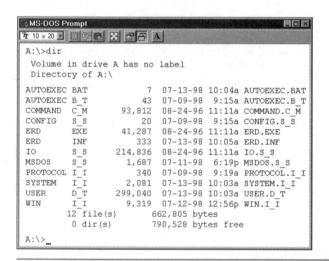

Figure 5-7 *A typical directory listing from an emergency recovery diskette.*

Windows 98 backups

Unlike Windows 95, Windows 98 does not save backup copies of the Registry files in the same directory as the Registry itself, but instead maintains *five* compressed backup sets in the C:\Windows\Sysbckup folder. The backup operation occurs only once a day, immediately after the system is powered on for the first time. The operation is not repeated if the PC is subsequently turned off and back on again, nor if system power remains on for several consecutive days. The backup files are given consecutive alphanumeric filenames, as shown in Figure 5-8 by the five RB00*x*.CAB files. The figure inset shows that each CAB file contains a compressed copy of the SYSTEM.DAT and USER.DAT Registry files, plus copies of the most-recent SYSTEM.INI and WIN.INI files.

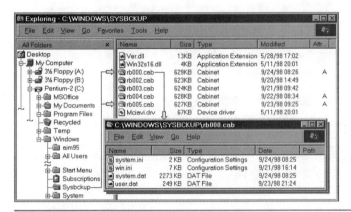

Figure 5-8 *Windows 98 makes a daily backup of SYSTEM.INI, WIN.INI, and the two Registry files once a day when the system is powered on. The backups are maintained in the C:\Windows\ Sysbckup folder in five compressed RB00x.CAB files.*

As each backup is created, it takes the name of the file that was erased on the previous day. Next, the current oldest file is deleted, and that filename is used the next time a backup is made. Therefore, the filename sequence always lacks one number in the range between RB000 and RB005, as shown in Table 5-2.

Table 5-2 *Windows 98 Backup Filename Sequence* *

Today's Date	Fifth	Sixth	Seventh	Eighth	Ninth	Tenth	Eleventh	Twelfth
Filename								
RB000.CAB	†	**6**	6	6	6	6	†	**12**
RB001.CAB	1	†	**7**	7	7	7	7	†
RB002.CAB	2	2	†	**8**	8	8	8	8
RB003.CAB	3	3	3	†	**9**	9	9	9
RB004.CAB	4	4	4	4	†	**10**	10	10
RB005.CAB	5	5	5	5	5	†	**11**	11

* For each filename, the numbers in the adjacent columns indicate the date on which it was created. The bold number identifies the newest backup filename.

† The backup filename in this row was erased today.

The user may force an extra backup set to be created at any time and may also specify other files to be included.

Force extra Registry backup

The Windows 98 Registry Checker may be used at any time to create an extra Registry backup set. To do so, open the Start menu, select the Programs, System Tools, and System Information menu options to open the Microsoft System Information window shown in Figure 5-9. Now open the Tools menu and select the Registry Checker option. This runs the Registry Checker utility, which in turn offers to create another backup set, as shown by the figure insets. You can also run the utility by simply typing **SCANREGW** or **SCANREG** in the Start menu's Run box. However, refer to the SCANREG.INI File section which follows before letting the Registry Checker proceed.

The SCANREG.INI file

As continuing evidence that the INI file lives on, Windows 98's SCAN-REG.INI may be edited to change the default location for the RB00*x*.CAB files described previously and to add files to the backup set. To do so, edit the file to include one or more lines such as the following:

Add This Line	Comments
`BackupDirectory=C:\REGISTRY\BACKUPS`	Change as desired to specify any new location
`Files=10, filename.ext, filename.ext`	10 = C:\Windows
`Files=11, filename.ext, filename.ext`	11 = C:\Windows\System
`Files=30, filename.ext, filename.ext`	30 = C:\
`Files=31, filename.ext, filename.ext`	31 = C:\

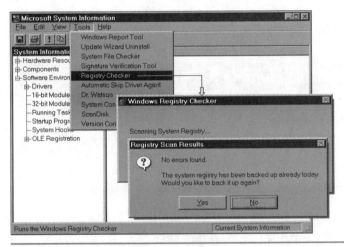

Figure 5-9 *The System Information Tools menu provides a Registry Checker option to scan the current Registry and, if desired, make a new backup set.*

The first line above changes the backup location from the default C:\Windows\Sysbckup folder to the location specified by the path following the equal sign. Each Files=*xx* line adds the specified files to the backup set, where *xx* identifies the source location for the files on that line, as indicated in the "Comments" column above. For further details, open the existing SCANREG.INI and read the comments at the beginning of the file.

If you need an occasional extra backup set, you may wish to create a custom INI file that specifies an alternate location. Then temporarily rename the default file as SCANREG.OLD and your custom file as SCANREG.INI. After creating the backup set, rename the files again so that your custom backup set won't interfere with the normal Windows 98 backup procedure.

Backup of corrupted Registry file

If Windows 98 detects a corrupted Registry file during startup, it nevertheless creates a backup anyway and erases the oldest file set, as previously described. But instead of applying the usual RB00*x*.CAB filename (where *x* is the number of yesterday's erased CAB file), the defective backup set is named RBBAD.CAB and there will therefore be a temporary (one-day) gap of two numbers within the 0–5 range. On succeeding days, the RBBAD.CAB file is ignored, and the numbering system reverts to the normal 0–5 range described previously. The defective RBBAD.CAB file remains in the C:\Windows\ Sysbckup folder indefinitely, or until it is replaced by a new RBBAD.CAB file if a subsequent problem arises. In any case, it can be deleted by the user if not needed for after-the-fact problem solving purposes.

Corrupted File Format

Unlike the compressed file format in which Windows 98 stores valid Registry backups, the four files in an RBBAD.CAB file are written into that file in uncompressed format. Therefore, the typical RBBAD.CAB file is slightly larger than the sum of the four files it contains, and many times larger than the valid backup file sets.

The SYSTEM.1ST Registry backup file

This hidden file is written into the root directory immediately after the Windows 95 or 98 setup procedure concludes successfully. Although described in some Microsoft documentation as a "copy of the Registry," it is in fact a copy only of the initial *HKLM* key configuration. Because Windows never upgrades this file, it soon becomes out of date as Windows itself is configured and reconfigured. Nevertheless, it may be better than nothing if all other attempts to recover the Registry fail. Refer to the "SYSTEM.1ST File" section in Chapter 7 for additional troubleshooting details. There is no equivalent USER.1ST file.

Real-Mode Registry backups

The Registry Editor can be used in real mode for routine Registry backups. For example, exit Windows and type one of the following lines at the MS-DOS prompt to back up all or part of the Registry to a file named *filename*.REG:

REGEDIT /E *filename*.   REG

REGEDIT /E *filename*.   REG HKEY_CLASSES_ROOT

REGEDIT /E *filename*.   REG HKEY_CLASSES_ROOT\   batfile

If the export (/E) switch is followed by a filename, but no HKEY is specified — as on the first line above — then the entire contents of the Registry are exported into the *filename*.REG file. Otherwise, the specified key and all its subkeys are exported to the *filename*.REG file. In either case, the exported file serves as a valid backup of the entire Registry or of the key structure listed on the command line.

Registry backups from within Windows

This is perhaps the simplest of all backup procedures. Just highlight any element in the Registry Editor's Key pane, open the Registry menu, select the Export Registry File option, give the file a name, and click on the Save button to complete the backup. For example, highlight one of the following Key pane items to back up the indicated section of the Registry:

Highlight:	To back up:
My Computer	Entire Registry
HKEY_CLASSES_ROOT	*HKEY_CLASSES_ROOT* and its subkeys only
HKEY_USERS\.Default\AppEvents	The *AppEvents* subkey and its subkeys only

Don't forget to use this convenient backup medium to save a copy of any key structure before editing it.

Third-party backup utilities

In case of doubt, check the user's guide (if any) for specific information about how the utility handles Registry backup issues. Since there are about as many variations in this procedure as there are software packages, this aspect of Registry backups is not covered in this book. In most cases though, one of the backup procedures that is described should do the job if the third-party utility doesn't.

Print (hard-copy) backups

A paper copy of a Registry key structure is often handy for reference purposes, but remember that the size of a complete HKEY printout may exceed 1,000 pages(!). You may therefore prefer to print only that portion of the Registry that contains the key structure you want to examine. In any case, refer to the "Registry Print Jobs" section and to Tables 4-3 and 4-4 in Chapter 4 before hitting the Print button. For comparison purposes, Table 5-3 shows the format of a Registry subkey printed to a PRN file and also exported to a Registry (REG) file.

Table 5-3 *Comparison of Registry Editor and Registry Files* *

TestKey in Registry Editor Window

Name Column	Data Column
(Default) †	(value not set)
NumericData 1	34 45 62 23 21 57 40
NumericData 2	0x0045da9f (4577951)
SampleText	"This is a sample."
SampleWithNumbers	"3.14 + 2"

TestKey printed to TESTKEY.PRN file

```
[HKEY_USERS\TestKey]] ‡
SampleText=This is a sample.
NumericData 1=34,45,62,23,21,57,40
SampleWithNumbers=3.14 + 2
NumericData 2=9f,da,45,00 §
```

TestKey exported to TESTKEY.REG file

```
REGEDIT4
[HKEY+USERS\TestKey] ‡
"SampleText"="This is a sample."
"NumericData 1"=hex:34,45,62,23,57,40
"SampleWithNumbers"="3.14 + 2"
"NumericData 2"=dword:0045da9f
```

* See also Figure 4-9 for another comparison.
† Lines following (Default) listed alphabetically.
‡ Line sequence indicates order in which entries were made.
§ Note reverse order of hexadecimal number sequence.

Registry Restore Procedures

After using any of the previously described backup procedures, refer to the appropriate procedure in this section for information about restoring the backed-up data.

Windows 95 recovery procedures

Make sure to ignore this section if you have upgraded to Windows 98. But first, destroy any Registry backups made under Windows 95 (unless you want to find out what *real* troubleshooting is all about). However, if you are still using Windows 95, then keep on reading.

The Backup .DA0 Registry files

In most cases, there is no reason for the user to access the hidden SYS-TEM.DA0 and USER.DA0 files in the C:\Windows folder. That's because these files are reserved for use by Windows 95 itself in case it becomes necessary to perform an automatic Registry restore operation as part of system startup. Because both files are rewritten every time Windows 95 successfully opens, they represent the last configuration known to be good.

If something unfortunate happens during the current session, and you have every reason to suspect that the current Registry has been damaged, you may want to exit Windows 95 to MS-DOS mode, rename the current Registry files with BAD extensions and then copy the DA0 backups to their equivalent DAT filenames. Doing so obviates depending on Windows 95 to take care of this the next time it opens. Although Windows 95 usually gets it right, there are times when a minor Registry problem can escape notice, in which case the slightly defective files would be copied to their DA0 backups. If you think this is a possibility, use the procedure given here to restore the Registry from the backup files. At the MS-DOS command prompt, type the following lines:

DOS Command	Comments
`attrib -s -h -r *.da?`	Clear attributes from Registry files
`rename SYSTEM.DAT SYSTEM.BAD`	Rename suspected bad SYSTEM.DAT
`rename USER.DAT USER.BAD`	Rename suspected bad USER.DAT
`copy SYSTEM.DA0 SYSTEM.DAT`	Create new SYSTEM.DAT from backup
`copy USER.DA0 USER.DAT`	Create new USER.DAT from backup
`attrib +s +h +r SYSTEM.DA?`	Reset SYSTEM.DAT, SYSTEM.DA0 attributes
`attrib +s +h +r USER.DA?`	Reset USER.DAT, USER.DA0 attributes

Reboot the system to reopen Windows 95 in the last known valid configuration. For convenience, these lines could be written into a batch file if they are needed with regularity.

Configuration Restore utility

The CFGBACK.EXE utility described in the preceding "Configuration Backup Utility" section is also used to restore the Registry from the compressed REGBACK*x*.RBK file created during the backup operation. Double-click on the file icon to open the Configuration Backup dialog box shown earlier in Figure 5-2. Then highlight one of the previous backups to enable the Restore and Delete buttons. Click the former to begin the restoration, during which the Working dialog boxes shown in Figure 5-10 are displayed, followed by this message at the conclusion of a successful operation:

> Your Configuration has been successfully restored. You need to shut down and restart the computer for your changes to take effect. Do you want to restart the computer now?

Despite the use of the "shut down" phrase, all you have to do is exit and restart Windows 95, which is exactly what happens when you click on the Yes button.

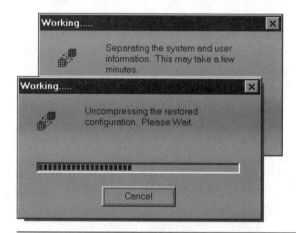

Figure 5-10 *During the Windows 95 Registry restoration process, the REGBACKx.RBK file is first uncompressed and then its system and file data are separated so that replacement SYSTEM.DAT and USER.DAT files can be created.*

Pay attention to the following message which appears before the restoration begins:

> WARNING: You have chosen to replace your current configuration with the backed-up one. Restore Selected Configuration?

As the message points out, the configuration restore operation is in fact a Registry *replacement* procedure. That is, the current Registry will be deleted and replaced by the backed-up version, and therefore key structures that exist in the current Registry but not in the backup copy will be gone forever. If you want to preserve a key structure, export it first, do the restore procedure, and then import the saved key structure back into the new Registry.

Emergency Recovery utility

If you used the ERU.EXE utility described previously to back up the SYS-TEM.DAT and USER.DAT files, then exit Windows 95, or reboot to a command prompt. Type **ERD** to begin the file restoration. Or if you've created an emergency recovery diskette, boot the system with it, and the ERD program (described below) is automatically executed. In either case, the Microsoft Emergency Recovery screen shown in Figure 5-11 should be displayed. Select the files to be restored, then scroll down to the Start Recovery option, and press the Enter key to begin the recovery. (If the screen shown in the figure is not displayed, refer to the "ERD File Variations" section later in this chapter, before continuing.)

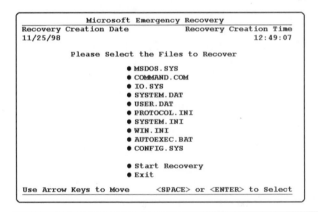

```
               Microsoft Emergency Recovery
Recovery Creation Date              Recovery Creation Time
11/25/98                                     12:49:07

          Please Select the Files to Recover

                      ● MSDOS.SYS
                      ● COMMAND.COM
                      ● IO.SYS
                      ● SYSTEM.DAT
                      ● USER.DAT
                      ● PROTOCOL.INI
                      ● SYSTEM.INI
                      ● WIN.INI
                      ● AUTOEXEC.BAT
                      ● CONFIG.SYS

                      ● Start Recovery
                      ● Exit

Use Arrow Keys to Move       <SPACE> or <ENTER> to Select
```

Figure 5-11 *The MS-DOS mode's Microsoft Emergency Recovery screen.*

If you've used ERU.EXE to back up just the SYSTEM.DAT and USER.DAT files, you may prefer to simply copy those files to the C:\Windows folder instead of running the ERD.EXE program. If so, note that the files are named SYSTEM.D_T and USER.D_T on the backup diskette or hard drive directory, and their system, hidden, and read-only attributes are not set. Copy the files into the C:\Windows folder, rename them with the correct DAT extension, reset the attributes, and then restart Windows 95.

The ERD.E_E file The file with this name in the *x:*\other\Misc\ Eru folder on the Windows 95 CD-ROM disc is transferred to the C:\Windows folder along with the ERU.EXE file if the accompanying ERU.INF file is installed. When the Recovery utility (ERU.EXE) is used for the first time to create an emergency recovery (backup) diskette, the ERD.E_E file is copied to that diskette (or to the C:\ERD folder) and renamed as ERD.EXE, so it's safe to assume that the three-letter filename stands for "Emergency Recovery Diskette." Execute this file in MS-DOS mode to begin the Registry (and other) file-recovery operation.

ERD file variations The screen shown in Figure 5-11 is not displayed in some later versions of the ERD utility. Instead, the following sequence begins if the user presses the Y key in response to the prompt. Boldface underlined type indicates user input:

```
A:\ERD
Control File = A:\ERD.INF
Emergency Recovery Utility. Press 'Y' to recover, or any
other key to exit


Y


Please wait...recovering files


Recovery Completed Successfully!
The configuration files have been restored. The
computer will need to be rebooted for the changes to take
effect.


To undo the recovery type: ERD.EXE /UNDO
Press any key to Continue
```

Be warned that the /UNDO switch in the preceding sequence does not work, as shown by the following sequence. Furthermore, the information displayed after typing **erd /?** is likewise invalid, as also shown here:

```
A:\>erd.exe /undo
Unknown or invalid switches
```

```
erd /?
```
Recovers old configuration files create [*sic*] by the
Emergency Recovery Utility.

```
EMRGRECV [/UNDO | /NOUNDO]
```

/UNDO   Specifies to undo changes made by a previous
            recovery.

/NOUNDO No "undo" information will be saved during
            recovery.

EMRGRECV /UNDO

```
Bad command or file name
```

Because no EMRGRECV file is on the diskette, it should come as no surprise that with or without the /UNDO switch, the "Bad command or file name" message is displayed.

Given these performance quirks, the ERD utility should be used with some caution. If the screen shown in Figure 5-11 is not displayed, you may prefer to abort the recovery if you don't want to restore all the files on the recovery diskette.

Windows 98 recovery procedures

To force a Registry restore operation, exit Windows to a DOS command prompt, and type the following command line:

SCANREG /RESTORE

This command displays a list of the four most recent CAB files, as shown in Figure 5-12. The fifth (oldest) set is not displayed and is erased if the Restore operation is initiated. The existing Registry—although not necessarily defective—is backed up in uncompressed format, as described in the "Backup of Corrupted Registry File" section earlier in this chapter. It is not however, labeled RBBAD.CAB unless Windows detects a problem with it. Otherwise, it simply takes the next available number in the RB00*x*.CAB filename series.

At the conclusion of the Registry restore operation, a "You Have Restored a Good Registry" message is displayed, and the only option is to restart the system, even if you wish to continue working in the DOS mode.

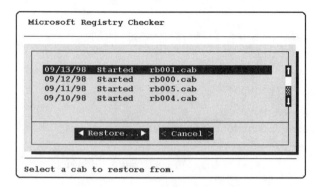

Figure 5-12 *The SCANREG /RESTORE command can be executed at a DOS command prompt to restore the Registry from one of the four most-recent CAB files, as shown in Figure 5-8.*

Real-mode Registry Editor

After exiting Windows 95 or 98 to the MS-DOS command mode, type one of the following command lines to restore all or part of the Registry, as shown here:

This command line:	Does this:
REGEDIT /C *filename*.REG	Creates a completely new Registry from *filename*.REG.
REGEDIT *filename*.REG	Imports *filename*.REG into the existing Registry.

Caution

Use the /C switch with extreme care because it replaces the entire current Registry with the backup version in the *filename*.REG file. If that file is indeed a valid version of the full Registry, then no harm is done. Otherwise, you're in big trouble.

If REGEDIT is followed by the name of a file and no command-line switches, then the subkeys specified in *filename*.REG are imported without affecting any other part of the Registry.

Registry Editor's Import option

To restore a previously backed up section of the Registry, open the Registry Editor's Registry menu, select the Import Registry File option, enter (or highlight) the filename to be imported, and click the Open button to complete the procedure.

Remember that the Import option does not necessarily execute a complete replacement of an existing key structure with a new one. Refer to the "Import Operations" section in Chapter 4 for details about the effect of the Import option on the existing key structure.

Third-Party Restore Utilities

As previously noted, third-party backup utilities are not discussed here. And neither, therefore, are the equivalent Restore utilities.

Registry Comparison Techniques

It's often useful to compare one version of a Registry file with another, either to discover the effect of a recent configuration change, as part of a troubleshooting session, to verify that an indirect edit (via Control Panel, for example) occurs where you think it does, or simply to get a better understanding of what's going on under the hood.

Of course, if you know (or think you know) exactly where a change will take place, then the simplest thing to do is open the Registry Editor and check the location before and after the edit takes place. In most cases, the Registry can remain open while the change is made elsewhere, then press function key F5 (Refresh), and the change should be noted. If not, exit the Registry and reopen it. If you need assistance tracking down the spot at which the action takes place, one or more of the following procedures may be of some assistance. To begin, follow these steps:

1. Export the suspected key structure as BEFORE.REG prior to making any change. If necessary, export an entire HKEY, but if possible export the smallest possible key structure to cut down the time it takes to make a post-change comparison.

2. Take whatever action whose effect you want to investigate.

3. Export the same key structure as AFTER.REG immediately after making the change.

Now compare the size of the two exported files. If they are not identical, then proceed to the "Word Processor File Comparison" section later in this chapter. Otherwise, keep reading here.

MS-DOS fc /b command

If you suspect some action makes a minor change to the Registry, such as changing a flag from 0 to 1, open an MS-DOS window and type the following line at the command prompt:

fc /B BEFORE.REG AFTER.REG

This command line executes a binary (byte-by-byte) comparison and displays a list of all differences, such as the following:

```
000005F0:  44 52
000005F1:  6F 65
000005F2:  20 41
000015AA:  59 64
000015AB:  6F 20
000015AC:  75 4D
000026F3:  20 65
```

If the list is short and the file size is 64 Kbytes or less, refer to the "MS-DOS Debug Utility" section which follows. Otherwise, refer to the "Norton Utilities Disk Editor" section later in this chapter.

MS-DOS debug utility

Load either of the files into the debug utility (C:\Windows\Command\DEBUG.EXE), type the following command at the debug prompt (a hyphen), and press the Enter key.

```
d cs:xxxx
```

In this command, *xxxx* is the last four digits of the eight-digit number cited above, plus hexadecimal 100. The addition is required because the debug utility begins at cs:0100, not CS:0000. Thus, to review the location at which byte 000005F0 changed from 44 to 52, type the following three lines in either column:

debug BEFORE.REG *or* debug AFTER.REG

d cs:06F0   d cs:06F0   (*to view byte 000005F0*)

q   q   (*to exit Debug*)

The ASCII text readout on the right side of the Debug screen should reveal enough of the actual Registry content to pin down the location at which the change took place. If necessary, press the D key one or more times to continue reviewing the Registry until you can make a positive identification. Once that's done, exit Debug, open the Registry, and proceed to the appropriate key\subkey to examine the area in context.

Norton Utilities Disk Editor

If the file is larger than 64 Kbytes, load it into the Norton Utilities Disk Editor (or similar), and scroll down to the eight-digit number cited above, but do not add 100 to it. Again, the right side of the screen displays the ASCII text of the Registry, making it possible to identify the location at which the change took place.

Word processor file comparison

If the BEFORE.REG and AFTER.REG files are quite large, or of different sizes, or contain many differences (or possibly, all of the above), load either file into any Windows word processor, and use that application's file-comparison option to find the places where it differs from the other one, as illustrated by this Microsoft Word example.

First, create the following two single-line files:

This is the file, before making a change.   Save as BEFORE.REG

This is the file, after making a change.   Save as AFTER.REG

While viewing either file, open the Tools menu and select the following menu options:

Word 97	Word 7.0 and Earlier
Track Changes	Revisions
Compare Documents	Compare Versions (button)

Type the name of the other file in the File name textbox at the bottom of the "Select File to Compare . . ." (Word 97) or "Compare Versions" (Word 7.0) window and click on the Open button. Depending on which file is onscreen, you will see "before" with a line through it (strikethrough font) and "after" underlined, or vice versa. In either case, the strikethrough font identifies text that does not actually appear in the present file. The underlined text is part of the present file but does not appear in the other file. Figure 5-13 illustrates both examples. Don't forget to erase these test files immediately after you're done because they are certainly not suitable for use in the Registry.

The description given here may vary from one word processor to another, but once you are familiar with specific file-comparison details, the Revisions option can be a powerful tool to help you review the differences between two versions of the same Registry key structure.

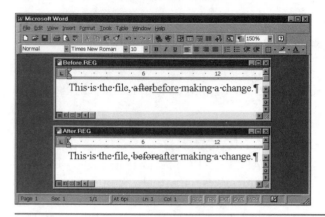

Figure 5-13 *In this much-simplified example of a Registry file comparison in Microsoft Word, the strikethrough font identifies text not actually present in the open file, while underlined text is present but does not appear in the other file.*

File-compare utilities

The File Compare applet can also be used to compare two versions of an exported Registry file, as shown by the Norton Utilities example in Figure 5-14. In most cases, the files are displayed in separate windows for side-by-side comparison, with differences highlighted in a distinctive color. An optional "Show Differences Only" mode may display only those lines that differ between files, and an additional option may summarize lines added, moved, and deleted and also identify the newest file.

Registry file comparison notes

Keep the following points in mind when comparing any two Registry files, regardless of the means used to make the comparison.

File size differences

If a Registry key structure is exported immediately before and after running a hardware or software setup procedure, there will be a significant difference in the before-and-after file size, due to the addition, revision, and possible deletion of various key structures. Although such a comparison is valuable to learn the precise effect of the setup procedure on the Registry, it takes a bit longer than a comparison made after a minor status change that does not effect the length of the exported sections.

Figure 5-14 *In Norton Utilities for Windows version 3.0, the File Compare applet displays side-by-side comparisons of Registry (or other) files. In this example, modified lines appear in a boldface font, while unchanged lines are gray. The "floating" Comparison Statistics window summarizes the differences between the compared files.*

Irrelevant revisions

Keep in mind that a file comparison may turn up revisions not directly related to the Registry action you are investigating. For example, when the same key is exported twice within a short interval of time, revisions are found in subkeys such as the two listed in the following table:

HKEY and Subkeys	Changed Subkey	Contents Pane
HKCU\Software\ ...	*RecentDocs*	MRUList=
HKLM\SOFTWARE\ ...	*UuidPersistentData*	"LastTimeAllocated"=

These revisions have nothing to do with a before-and-after Registry file comparison and should be ignored.

Word Processor Comparison Warnings

Keep the following points in mind before using a word processor to compare two Registry files.

Spell-Check

As far as any word processor is concerned, a Registry file is just another document file with one important distinction: just about every word is misspelled. So before comparing Registry files, make sure automatic spell-checking is disabled. Otherwise, the word processor spends much of its time pointing out all the errors and probably will be unable to complete the file comparison. Disable any other automatic "helpers" that may get in the way of the job at hand. And don't even think about a grammar check.

Comparison Time

If the Registry files are large, it may take several minutes to complete a comparison. Comparison time also increases if a fairly large key structure has been inserted in — or removed from — one of the files, because the routine must compensate for the significant content shift.

File Save

Don't do it. As you exit the word processor, it offers to save the compared files. If it does so, both may contain the strikethrough/underlined text, which renders the files useless for further Registry use. No harm is done if you plan to discard the files anyway, but otherwise, make sure you exit without saving.

Word processor versus file-compare utility

Because a good file-comparison utility is a single-purpose applet, it should be significantly faster than a word processor in making Registry file comparisons. However, if a word processor comparison reveals a difference between such files, it's reasonably easy to make a direct edit to the highlighted data, as required. In contrast, a file-comparison utility's Edit mode may load the file into Notepad or WordPad, and the user then has to scroll through the file to find once again the place that requires editing. It's not impossible to do that, but the word processor does make the job a bit easier. On the other hand, a differences-only display mode is usually unique to a file-comparison utility.

The serious Registry tweaker will probably want to use both methods of file comparison, due to their alternate manners of displaying the desired information.

Norton Utilities Registry Tracker

As a variation on the Registry file comparison techniques previously described, an applet such as the Norton Utilities Registry Tracker can display a detailed view of recent modifications to the Registry. For example, Figure 5-15 shows a Registry Editor view of a few subkeys under the *HKLM\Software\CLASSES\gopher* key. Because the *command* subkey cites IEXPLORE.EXE, it's obvious that Microsoft's Internet Explorer is currently the default browser. However, the Editor gives no indication of when the application took over this association. In contrast, the Norton Registry Tracker window in Figure 5-16 displays the recent history of the same key. Under various subkeys, a document icon with a plus sign indicates current data in that key's Contents pane, while an icon with a minus sign indicates data formerly in that location.

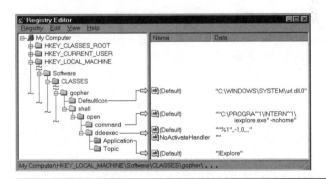

Figure 5-15 *This conventional view of a Registry subkey displays the current contents but gives no indication of the key's recent history.*

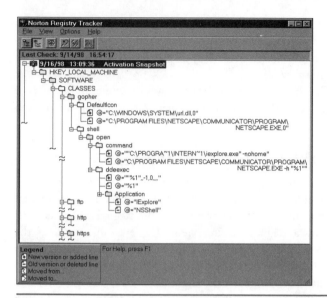

Figure 5-16 *In this Norton Registry Tracker applet window, the icons overlaid with plus and minus signs indicate current and past Registry content, respectively.*

Registry Cleanup Techniques

Although the Registry is not yet a completely self-healing animal, it does have the capability to repair (with a little help) some minor damage. This includes the deletion of leftover Registry entries (or "orphans") that should have been deleted by some application's uninstall procedure and trimming dead space that accumulates with the passage of time. Follow the procedures described in the next sections to help keep the Registry in reasonable health and, if not fashionably slim, then at least moderately unbloated.

Key structure deletion procedures

The first step in any Registry cleanup operation is to remove key structures no longer needed by Windows or its applications. To do so, follow the procedures listed here, in the order in which they appear.

Add/Remove Programs

Open Control Panel's Add/Remove Programs applet to uninstall any application no longer needed. This procedure deletes all files associated with the application and all keys that were written into the Registry when that application was installed.

So much for theory. Back in the real world, the uninstall procedure may not do a thorough cleanup job, and some leftovers can be found in the Registry. For example, Table 5-4 lists the keys written into the Registry if Netscape Communicator version 4.04 is installed. The "Netscape Uninstall" column indicates with a dot which keys were successfully removed by the uninstall procedure (not many) and indicates with a dash which were left in place (most). To clean up these post-uninstall orphan keys, continue reading here.

Table 5-4 *Netscape Communicator Registry Cleanup Summary*

Registry Key\Subkey	Contents Pane (partial listing)	Notes 1	2
HKCR\...			
.htm\ShellNew	"netscape.html"	–	–
.html\ShellNew	"netscape.html"	–	–
.shtml	"NetscapeMarkup"	–	–
.xbm	"NetscapeMarkup"	–	–
aimfile	C:\...Netscape\...	–	•
{0A522733-A626-11D0-8D60-00C04FD6202B}	CLSID_CNetscapeImport	–	–
{2D0A7D70-748C-11D0-9705-00805F8AA8B8}	(value not set)	–	•
{37B601C0-8AC8-11D0-83AF-00805F8A274D}	(value not set)	–	•
{481ED670-9D30-11CE-8F9B-0800091AC64E}	Netscape Hypertext Doc	–	•
{543EC0D0-6AB7-11D0-BF56-00A02468FAB6}	(value not set)	–	•
{543EC0D1-6AB7-11D0-BF56-00A02468FAB6}	(value not set)	–	•
{60403D81-872B-11CF-ACC8-0080C82BE3B6}	Netscape.Help.1	–	–
{61D8DE20-CA9A-11CE-9EA5-0080C82BE3B6}	Netscape Hypertext Doc	–	–
{7865A9A1-33A8-11D0-DEB9-00A02468FAB6}	(value not set)	–	•
{913A4A20-8EBF-11D0-BFAB-00A02468FAB6}	(value not set)	–	•
{C98D0190-7D81-11D0-BF8D-00A02468FAB6}	(value not set)	–	•
{CC3E2871-43CA-11D0-B6D8-00805F8ADDDE}	(value not set)	–	•
{CC3E2872-43CA-11D0-B6D8-00805F8ADDDE}	(value not set)	–	•
{DDF4AB60-8B84-11D0-9B63-00805F8ADDDE}	(value not set)	–	•
{E328732C-9DC9-11CF-92D0-004095E27A10}	Netscape.TalkNav.1	–	–

Continued

Table 5-4 *Continued*

Registry Key\Subkey	Contents Pane (partial listing)	Notes 1	2
{E67D6A10-4438-11CE-8CE4-0020AF18F905}	Netscape.Registry.1	–	–
{E8D6B4F0-8B58-11D0-9B63-00805F8ADDDE}	(value not set)	–	•
{EF5F7050-385A-11CE-8193-0020AF18F905}	Netscape.Network.1	–	•
giffile\shell\open\command	NETSCAPE.EXE	–	–
InternetShortcut\shell\...			
print\command	NETSCAPE.EXE	–	•
printto\command	NETSCAPE.EXE	–	•
Netscape.Help.1		–	–
Netscape.Network.1		–	–
Netscape.Registry.1		–	–
Netscape.Talk.Nav.1		–	–
Netscape Markup (and all its subkeys)		–	–
news\shell\open\command	NETSCAPE.EXE	–	•
snews\shell\open\command	NETSCAPE.EXE	–	•
Software\Progressive Networks\ RealAudio Player\4.0\Preferences\Browser1	NETSCAPE	–	–

HKCU\...

Software\Microsoft\Windows\CurrentVersion\...			
Explorer\MenuOrder\Start Menu\&Programs\Netscape Communicator		–	–
Run	AOL Instant Messenger	–	•
Software\Netscape (and all its subkeys)		–	–

HKLM\...

Software\Microsoft\Windows\CurrentVersion\Uninstall \Netscape Communicator	Netscape Communicator	•	†

Registry Key\Subkey	Contents Pane (partial listing)	Notes 1	2
Other (non-Registry items)			
Netscape-installed shortcut on desktop		•	†
C:\Program Files\Netscape\Communicator folder and subfolders		•	†
C:\Program Files\Netscape\Users folder and subfolders		–	N/A

1 Netscape Uninstall
2 Microsoft RegClean
– Not removed by indicated procedure.
• Successfully removed by Netscape Uninstall or Microsoft RegClean utility.
† Item successfully removed by Netscape Uninstall prior to running RegClean.

Registry Cleanup utility

It should be included with Windows, but it's not—perhaps because Microsoft's free Registry CleanUp utility (REGCLEAN.EXE) has the potential for causing damage and is best left in the hands of the experienced user only. You can, however, download the latest version from one of the following Web sites:

Web Site	Comments
`www.microsoft.com`	You may have to hunt for it. Microsoft frequently moves things around and isn't very good about helping you find what you're looking for.
`www.winmag.com`	*Windows Magazine* maintains a link to the latest version of the utility.
`www.woram.com`	The author's Web site maintains links to this and other Registry utilities.

The download filename is usually REGCLN*xx*.EXE, where *xx* is the current version number. Download the file, then double-click it to execute the Nico Mak WinZip Self-Extractor shown in Figure 5-17, which extracts the REGCLEAN.EXE utility and two others into the specified folder. The window shown in Figure 5-18 is displayed when the utility is executed, and at the conclusion of its Analysis and Correction phase, RegClean pauses to display one of the following messages:

RegClean has not found any registry entries that it can correct.

or

RegClean has finished checking the registry. It can now correct the errors it found, or you can cancel it.

Assuming errors are found and you elect to correct them, RegClean writes an undo file into the folder where it was installed with the following long filename:

Undo *computer name date time*.Reg

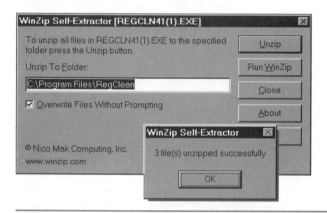

Figure 5-17 *The Microsoft RegClean utility can be extracted from the download file and placed in any convenient folder.*

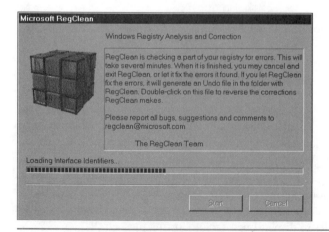

Figure 5-18 *The RegClean utility displays a progress report as it analyzes the current Registry.*

The file contains the keys that are no longer required, and RegClean deletes them from the Registry. To restore the deletions later on, simply double-click the undo file to import the keys back into the Registry. Refer to the utility's accompanying README.TXT file for additional details about using the utility.

In Table 5-4, the "Microsoft RegClean" column shows the effect of running the utility after Netscape Communicator's own uninstall procedure is executed. Note that RegClean found and removed many — but not all — the orphan keys left behind by Netscape's uninstall routine.

In this example, neither procedure resolves a potential problem in the *.htm\ShellNew* and *.html\ShellNew* keys. Both still cite a now nonexistent NETSCAPE.HTML file that was deleted from the C:\Windows \ShellNew folder by Netscape's uninstall routine. Therefore, if the cascading New menu is used to create a new HTML document, a "Problem creating object" error message is displayed. Refer to the "New Menu Option is Inoperative" section of Chapter 7 for assistance in resolving this problem.

Manual Registry cleanup

As noted previously, the Registry Cleanup utility usually does an excellent job removing orphan Registry keys but may leave a few stragglers behind, and these can be removed during a manual cleanup operation. Or if the utility is not available, then you'll have to remove all the Registry leftovers by hand. But before beginning the job, it's probably worthwhile to open the Windows Explorer and search for a C:\Program Files*application name* folder, or any other obvious traces of the "removed" application. With luck nothing will be there, but if something is found, try using the Delete key to remove it. If a message warns that doing so may have an impact on the Registry, refer to the "File or Folder Removal Problem" section of Chapter 7 for assistance in locating the Registry entries that cause the message to display.

But even if no warning message is displayed when a folder or file is deleted, some Registry orphans may still be left behind. To double-check, search the Registry's Data column for obvious clues such as a path formerly used by the application and also look for *filename*.EXE, where *filename* is of course the name of the application's executable file. If you find any such remnants, examine the Registry key structure under which they appear for references to a *CLSID* key that may also be deleted if no longer needed. If you're not sure of this, export any such key before deleting it, just in case you discover it's needed later on and have to reimport it.

Final CLSID key check

Keep in mind that although the first part of any *CLSID* key number is random, the final six bytes are derived from the network card installed on the PC where the software was created and remain constant. You can therefore expect to find multiple *CLSID* keys ending with the same six digits — for example, the ...00A02468FAB6} segment seen in five of the Netscape keys listed in Table 5-4. Assuming the previous procedures did a thorough Registry cleanup, a post-cleanup search for this string segment should be unsuccessful, unless some other software from the same source was created on the same system. Although a Registry key search is the obvious choice, you may want to search the Data column too, in case some other key makes a reference to a *CLSID* key that ends with the same string. With this in mind, any keys that are found can probably be deleted, but make sure each such key is exported first, just in case you need to recover it at a later date.

Refer to the "CLSID Generator Utility" section of Chapter 6 for details about how *CLSID* key numbers are generated.

Registry reconstruction procedure

Once all superfluous keys have been deleted, it's probably still possible to do a bit more Registry trimming. With data continuously moving into and out of the Registry during routine Windows operations, it's not unusual for a certain amount of empty space to accumulate over time. Although no harm is done, this does contribute to Registry bloat and may eventually affect performance if it becomes excessive. Use the following procedure from time to time to squeeze such dead air out of the Registry. Briefly stated, it exports the *HKLM* and *HKU* key structures into two temporary files, erases the existing Registry, then reconstructs it from the temporary files. As a result, the Registry file size may be reduced by 10 percent or more. To begin, exit Windows (or reboot) to a DOS command prompt, then perform the six steps listed in the following table:

Type This Command	To Do This
1. **Regedit /E C:\HKLM.REG HKEY_LOCAL_MACHINE**	Export the *HKEY_LOCAL_MACHINE* key structure to a file named HKLM.REG.
2. **Regedit /E C:\HKU.REG HKEY_USERS**	Export the *HKEY_USERS* key structure to a file named HKU.REG.

Type This Command	To Do This
3. **Rename SYSTEM.DAT SYSTEM.OLD**	Save present SYSTEM.DAT (just in case).
4. **Rename USER.DAT USER.OLD**	Save present USER.DAT (ditto)
5. **Regedit /L:C:\WINDOWS\SYSTEM.DAT /C C:\HKLM.REG**	Create a new Registry from the HKLM.REG file created in Step 1.
6. **Regedit /R:C:\WINDOWS\USER.DAT C:\HKU.REG**	Import the HKU.REG file created in Step 2 into the new Registry created in Step 5.

Note that the /C switch in Step 5 creates an apparently complete Registry — that is, one SYSTEM.DAT and one USER.DAT file. However, while the former file contains all the data imported from the HKLM.REG file, the latter is nothing more than a temporary "place marker" required by the next step. If it were missing, Step 6 would fail because Regedit would look for — but not find — the file into which it must import the contents of the HKU.REG file. To verify this (if you must), type the following command line:

REGEDIT /E C:\VERIFY.REG HKEY_USERS

This creates a 28-byte VERIFY.REG file that contains nothing but the required REGEDIT4 header, a blank line, and an [HKEY_USERS] header — sufficient evidence that the equivalent information is in the USER.DAT stub, where Regedit can find it and successfully import the contents of the HKU.REG file.

Because empty space is deleted as the export operation writes the two files (in Steps 1 and 2 above), the new Registry created from those files (Steps 5 and 6) will be somewhat smaller than it was, as shown by the following examples. The file sizes are from a typical system and will of course vary from one PC to another.

SYSTEM.DAT	2,204,176	USER.DAT	303,256	Original Registry files
HKLM.REG	2,285,993	HKU.REG	467,331	Temporary exported files
SYSTEM.DAT	1,912,864	USER.DAT	266,272	New Registry files

Part III

Customization

Chapter 6

Custom Registry Editing Techniques

Now that you've dutifully backed up the Registry using the procedures described in the previous chapter, this chapter resumes the discussion of Registry editing that began in Chapter 4, but with the emphasis here on how to customize the Registry to configure Windows according to your personal preferences. As already described, the Registry may be edited by simply executing the REGEDIT.EXE utility and having at it. But in addition to the basic editing techniques described in Chapter 4, other Registry editing techniques may prove helpful from time to time. Like just about everything else associated with the Registry, the procedures described in this chapter are for the most part undocumented. Until you are quite sure that a specific procedure works well on your system, make sure you back up the Registry before experimenting. When you are finally certain that a procedure will not harm the Registry, make a backup anyway. In many cases, the procedures described in the "Automated List Removal" section of Chapter 4 can be revised as appropriate to handle repetitive custom configuration projects. Refer to that section for further details.

The chapter begins with a look at a few custom editing techniques, then describes various menu and icon editing procedures, and concludes by describing a handful of other editing techniques to customize a specific aspect of the Windows desktop.

Registry Edits at Startup

In addition to the KillList.BAT file described in the "INF File as a Registry Editor" section of Chapter 4, other techniques may be employed to automatically edit the Registry, every time the system is powered on or every time the Windows GUI is loaded. In either case, begin by setting the desired Registry values, export the appropriate key structure to a *filename*.REG file, and then follow one of the procedures given here.

Real-mode edits

The procedures described in the "Registry Editor in Real Mode" section at the end of Chapter 4 can be applied to make routine Registry edits every time the system is powered on. For example, add the following line to your AUTOEXEC.BAT file to import a *filename*.REG file into the Registry as part of the startup procedure:

REGEDIT *filename*.REG

Revise this line to accomplish whatever editing task you would like to execute immediately before the Windows GUI opens. The technique might be useful if it becomes necessary to routinely clear restrictions set during a previous session, especially if those restrictions cannot be cleared once Windows fully opens.

Import from StartUp folder

As an alternative to the just-described real-mode procedure, place a *filename*.REG file (or a shortcut to it) in the C:\Windows\Start Menu\ Programs\StartUp folder. By doing so, the file will be imported into the Registry every time the Windows 95 GUI opens, which may be a convenient means to routinely reset various Registry values without rebooting the system.

Silent Mode Import

Note however, that this technique pauses the opening procedure to display an "Information . . . has been successfully entered into the Registry" message, which remains onscreen until the user clicks the OK button. To avoid the notification and pause, either use the real-mode edit method described above, or else write a shortcut command line as follows:

REGEDIT /S FILENAME.REG

The undocumented /S switch imports the specified file into the Registry but neither displays a message nor pauses until the OK button is clicked.

Export from StartUp folder

Although of limited usefulness, it's also possible to export a section of the Registry as part of the startup procedure by using the following command:

REGEDIT /E FILENAME.REG HKEY_CLASSES_ROOT\.bmp

In this example, the /E switch creates a FILENAME.REG file that contains the *HKEY_CLASSES_ROOT\.bmp* key structure. The silent mode /S switch described above is unnecessary because this action does not display a message or pause until the OK button is clicked.

Deletion from StartUp folder

The real-mode /D switch does not appear to be supported when the Registry Editor is run from within the Windows GUI. To automatically delete a Registry key structure, refer to the "Example of INF File use as Registry Editor" section of Chapter 4, and modify the file contents as necessary to delete the desired key structure.

Copy and Paste Operations

If it is ever necessary to create a new key based on the contents of an existing key, the latter key can be exported, revised as necessary, and then imported back into the Registry, as shown by this excerpt from an *exefile* key structure exported to an EXEFILE.REG file:

```
REGEDIT4

[HKEY_CLASSES_ROOT\exefile]
@="Application"
"EditFlags"=hex:d8,07,00,00

[HKEY_CLASSES_ROOT\exefile\shell\open]
@=""
"EditFlags"=hex:00,00,00,00

[HKEY_CLASSES_ROOT\exefile\shell\open\command]
@="\"%1\" %*"

[HKEY_CLASSES_ROOT\exefile\shellex]
```

```
[HKEY_CLASSES_ROOT\exefile\shellex\PropertySheetHandlers\
PifProps]
@="{86F19A00-42A0-1069-A2E9-08002B30309D}"


[HKEY_CLASSES_ROOT\exefile\shellex\PropertySheetHandlers\
{86F19A00-42A0-1069-A2E9-08002B30309D}]
@=""


[HKEY_CLASSES_ROOT\exefile\DefaultIcon]
@="%1"
```

To write a new *abcfile* key in the same section of the Registry, open the exported file for editing, change every occurrence of *exefile* (shown underlined above) to *abcfile*, save the edited file as ABCFILE.REG, and import it into the Registry. A new *abcfile* key should be seen with the same subkey structure and contents as the *exefile* key, which may now be edited to customize it as required.

If you use a word processor's search and replace feature to make more extensive changes, make sure to save the edited file as plain ASCII text, so that the word processor's own formatting code is not inserted into the file.

Command-Line Edits

In some cases it's possible to change the performance characteristics of a Windows application or applet by editing the Data entry in the appropriate *command* subkey. For example, the Media Player (*HKCR\mplayer*) applet's *shell\play\command* subkey shows the following Contents pane entry:

Name	Data
(Default)	"C:\WINDOWS\mplayer.exe /play /close %1"

As a result of the command-line switches shown here, if any file recognized by Media Player is double-clicked, the applet loads the file, plays it, and then exits. If you would prefer to have Media Player remain open after playing the selected file, simply delete the /close switch.

If you know the valid command-line switches for some other application's executable file, revise the appropriate Data column entry as desired to customize the way in which that application functions.

File Type Searches

The File Types tab — accessed via "Options" (in IE4, "Folder Options") on the Windows Explorer View menu — is often helpful in identifying details about a specific file type. It would be even more helpful if Microsoft weren't so infatuated with its own name. It's not unusual to find several dozen unrelated file types, from "Microsoft Access" to "Microsoft Word," which would be far easier to find if that repetitive first word were eliminated from the listings. Other listings are simply inconsistent, as shown by the following few examples:

Actual File Type	Listed As
Batch file	MS-DOS Batch File
Directory	File folder
Folder	Folder
INI file	Configuration Settings
Personal configuration info	Windows Explorer Command
Word document	Microsoft Word Document
WordPad document	Write Document

To put the File Types list into logical order, highlight any item on the list, click the Edit button, and rewrite the "Description of type" line as desired.

Hardware Profile Editing

This section describes how hardware profile data is written into the Registry as various hardware devices are added or removed. Although there should be little need to directly edit the keys described here, a quick review of the information presented may help to better understand the significance of some of the keys described here.

Consider a desktop system with only one hardware profile, typically identified as "Original Configuration." The Device Manager shows that the system components include a SCSI CD-ROM drive. The only two subkeys under the *Config* key's *0001* key are *Display* and *System* (both described in Chapter 4). In other words, this section of the Registry contains no information about the CD-ROM drive, nor is any required here for this single-profile system, as indicated by the tree structure labeled "A" in Figure 6-1.

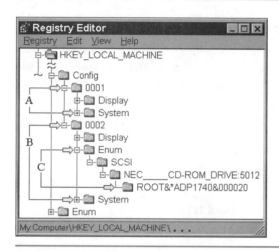

Figure 6-1 *The* Enum *subkey is displayed when certain hardware components are removed from a hardware configuration.*

If this hardware configuration is copied as, say, "Secondary Configuration," a new *0002* subkey appears under the *Config* key, and for the moment, its contents match those of the *Config\0001* key. Again, this key contains no CD-ROM information. But now, remove the CD-ROM drive from just this configuration by highlighting the CD-ROM drive, clicking the Remove button, and then selecting Secondary Configuration in the Confirm Device Removal dialog box shown in Figure 6-2.

In Figure 6-1, the secondary configuration (*0002*) key is labeled "B" and the subsection labeled "C" shows a new *Enum* (Enumerator) subkey, which in turn contains a *SCSI* subkey. Beneath that, a subkey gives the name of the removed CD-ROM drive, followed in turn by yet another subkey (*ROOT&...*) that specifies the SCSI adapter to which the CD-ROM drive was attached.

If the CD-ROM is now removed from the "Original Configuration," too, the contents of the *SCSI* subkey under the *Config\0002* key is flushed, and the CD-ROM configuration is lost to the entire system. But assuming the drive is in fact still physically attached to the system, Windows will detect its presence the next time the system is started, and the drive will be reinstalled to the Original Configuration (assuming that's the one specified when the system restarts). However, the drive will *not* be restored to the Secondary Configuration profile until such time as the system is restarted in that configuration. Nor will its absence be noted in the still-empty *SCSI* subkey under the *Config\0002* key.

Restore Hardware Previously Deleted from a Hardware Profile

The most reliable way to add hardware to any profile is simply to start the system in that configuration and leave it to Windows to detect, or redetect, its presence. Or double-click Control Panel's Add New Hardware applet and use the Add New Hardware Wizard.

As another alternative, open the System applet, select the Device Manager tab, and look for the desired device. If it is listed, that means it is currently installed in at least one hardware profile. That being so, highlight the device, click the Properties button, and examine the General tab. If the tab includes a Device Usage section near the bottom of the window, put a checkmark in the checkbox next to the configuration that currently lacks this device.

However, if the device is connected to a SCSI or other controller, then there is no System Usage section on the device's General tab, and the equivalent tab on the controller's General tab may already be enabled, especially if other devices remain in place. In this case, you can restore the disabled device by deleting its subkey under the *Enum* key, located under the appropriate *000x* key. For example, the section labeled "C" in Figure 6-1 showed the *0002* key's *Enum* subkey. Highlight the key name of the desired device (*NEC___CD-ROM_DRIVE:5012*, in this example) and delete it. Because the *Enum* key does not list any other devices, the entire *Enum* key could be deleted instead. Do *not* do this however, if a *BIOS* and/or other unrelated subkeys appear here. In that case, make sure you delete *only* the device that you want reenabled.

Once the CD-ROM drive is restored to both configurations, the *0002* key will still show the empty *SCSI* subkey. But if the drive is again removed from *Config\0002*, then again the *Enum* subkey will contain the information about the missing drive. In much the same manner, information about other devices removed from this secondary configuration will be written here.

Figure 6-2 *On a multiple configuration system, a hardware device can be removed from only one configuration by selecting the second radio button and the configuration to be edited.*

System Configuration Details

As noted in the "SR Version Check" section of Chapter 1, the currently-installed SR (Service Release) version of Windows may be verified via the "My Computer" icon's Context menu. If the Properties option is selected, the General tab displays System and Registration details, such as those shown in Figure 6-3. Some — but not all — of these details are recorded in the Registry, and the following sections briefly describe each item displayed by the General tab.

System

While Microsoft was busy persuading the world that Windows is an operating system, it apparently forgot to clarify this point here on the General tab, where it's simply "System." Immediately beneath it, the "Microsoft Windows 98" (or "Windows 95") line is taken from the SYSDM.CPL file, and the version number comes from the USER.EXE file, both of which are in the C:\Windows\System folder. If an original retail version of Windows 95 was subsequently upgraded by Service Release 1, a few of the original files are replaced (but not USER.EXE). Therefore, the SP1.INF file included in the upgrade writes the letter "a" into the Registry. Or if the computer was shipped with the SR2 version of Windows 95, an accompanying SETUP.INF file writes the letter " B" (note space before the letter) into the same Registry location, and this example is shown in Figure 6-4. In either case, the letter appears after the version number on the General tab. The INF files are found in the C:\Windows\Inf folder, and the SR version letter is in the [Strings] section of the file. Even though Windows 95 SR2 includes a newer version of USER.EXE, it retains the original version number, so only the letter " B" indicates this later version. If an installed application uses MSAA (Microsoft Active Accessibility), a still newer USER.EXE file may change the version number to 4.01.0970.

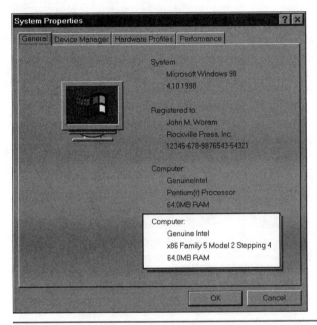

Figure 6-3 *If the "My Computer" object Context menu's Properties option is selected, the General tab displays system and configuration information. The inset shows revised CPU information that can be displayed by editing the Registry.*

Just to help keep things confusing, yet another version of Windows 95 closely resembles OSR2, although it's unofficially known as OSR2.1 — unofficially because there doesn't seem to be much public acknowledgment of its existence. Nevertheless, it was bundled with some new computers just prior to the introduction of Windows 98. The CD label reads "Microsoft Windows 95 ('& Microsoft Plus!' on some versions) With USB support," and the disc folder named \other\usb contains a USBSUPP.EXE file. If this file is executed on a computer that supports USB hardware, it replaces KERNEL32.DLL and a few other files with USB upgrades, but keeps the former versions on hand with an extension of o20 (letter "o" and the number "20"). For trivia buffs who remember when Windows 95 was code-named "Chicago," the OSR2.1 uninstall instructions are in a DETROIT.INF file.

Registered to

All information in this section really is taken from the Registry subkey shown in Figure 6-4 below, where you'll find the name of the current owner, organization, and one or more registration numbers that appear on the General tab. If you need to change the name of the registered owner and/or organization, your edits will show up the next time you look at the General tab. Although there's not much point in changing a product ID number, you might want to jot it down for future reference just in case you need to do a complete reinstall but don't recall what happened to that OEM certificate with the number on it.

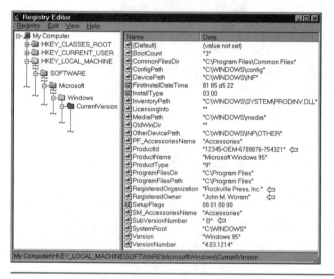

Figure 6-4 *This Registry key contains some of the information displayed by the General tab shown in the previous figure, as indicated by the four left arrows. Other information on that tab is taken from other sources.*

Computer

The CPU reported here is not always what it should be. Windows looks through its SYSDM.CPL file for the closest available match and then displays that information. For example, Windows 95 reports a Pentium-II CPU as a "Pentium Pro(r)," because the actual CPU type is not listed in the file. However, a borrowed SYSDM.CPL file from a Windows 98 system correctly lists the CPU as a "Pentium(r) II Processor" and adds another line reporting "Intel MMX(TM) Technology."

A temporary Registry edit may persuade Windows 98 to reveal a bit more information about the system CPU. On the "My Computer" desktop object's System Properties sheet, the Computer section usually reports information such as that shown in the first column of the following table:

Computer:	Computer:
GenuineIntel	Genuine Intel
Pentium(r) Processor	x86 Family 6 Model 3 Stepping 4
64.0MB RAM	64.0MB RAM

To display more detailed information, open the following Registry key and make the Contents pane edit shown here:

HKLM\Hardware\Description\System\CentralProcessor\0

Name	Data
VendorIdentifier	"Genuine Intel"

That is, insert a space in the VendorIdentifier data (or make any other minor edit). After doing so, the Properties Sheet report displays a revised report such as that shown in the second column of the preceding table. Note that this Registry edit is not permanent — the next time the system is rebooted, Windows 98 rechecks the CPU and rewrites the entry, thereby restoring the previous onscreen report.

As for the *xx.x*MB RAM report on the bottom line, the "MB RAM" is also picked up from SYSDM.CPL, but of course the number depends on what you have onboard your own system.

The CLSID Generator Utility

As noted in Chapter 2, each 16-byte class identifier subkey found under the *HKEY_CLASSES_ROOT\CLSID* key is a unique (one hopes!) character string that won't be duplicated by some other object. For programmers who must create a new CLSID number, various Microsoft Software Development Kit CD-ROM discs contain a CLSID generator utility (UUIDGEN.EXE) that can be executed from a command prompt, as shown here:

    E:\WIN32SDK\MSTOOLS\BIN\i386>uuidgen
    e1fd71e0-978d-11cf-aaee-444553540000

In this example, the utility generated the random CLSID shown on the second line above. For informational purposes, the CLSID number can be divided into three parts, as follows:

CLSID Component	Created From
e1fd71e0	Random number generator
978d-11cf-aaee	Current date and time
444553540000	Network address

The network address component is also found in one of several *HKLM* subkeys, as shown in Figure 6-5. If the system is not configured for network operation, the last six bytes are randomly generated, and a warning message is displayed. See the discussion of the message "Unable to determine your network address" in Chapter 8 for further details.

Registry Flags

A four-byte binary or DWORD entry in a Registry key's Contents pane usually represents a collection of "flags" that specify various characteristics of the associated object. For example, if the first byte in a hexadecimal D5 00 00 00 (which Microsoft calls a *binary value*) is converted to its actual binary value, each bit is a binary flag that is either set (1) or cleared (0). So if D5 (1101 0101) were edited to D4 (1101 0100), the change of the final flag from 1 to 0 would clear a certain attribute that was formerly set. This action might change the state of a Context menu option, a checkbox, a dialog box button, or some other attribute of an object. In examining these Registry flags, it's important to understand that a change from "1" to "0" does not necessarily mean that a checkbox has been cleared or a button disabled. Depending on the mood of the programmer-du-jour, it might just as well have the opposite effect.

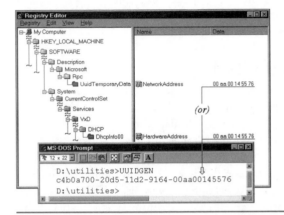

Figure 6-5 *If the UUIDGEN.EXE utility is executed from a DOS command prompt, the last six bytes are derived from the network card (if installed). These bytes are also written into an* HKLM *subkey Data entry, such as the NetworkAddress or HardwareAddress examples shown here.*

The following sections examine a few typical Contents pane entries in which various flags are specified. The bracketed entry in each heading indicates the entry that is displayed in the Contents pane's Name column, and the associated Data is often in four-byte binary format. However (this being Microsoft), you may occasionally encounter a longer binary string or a DWORD data entry instead. For example, the *CLSID* key for Internet Explorer 4 (*{871C5380...*) leads to a *ShellFolder* subkey whose Contents pane displays its data as follows:

Name	Data	Format and Operating System
Attributes	22 00 00 00	Binary in Windows 95
	22 00 10 00	Binary in Windows 95 if IE4 not yet set up
	0x00000022 (34)	DWORD in Windows 98
	0x00100022 (1048610)	DWORD in Windows 98 if IE4 not yet set up

Refer to "Data Format Comparisons" in Chapter 1 for the distinction between these two formats, and if you encounter other Attributes expressed as a DWORD, simply convert to binary format to follow the discussion below. Thus, read the 0x00000022 DWORD in the preceding table as 22 00 00 00 in binary format (note the reverse sequence, too).

In most cases, the flags represented by the third or fourth byte seem to have no present effect. Therefore in the interests of space, the binary equivalent of a "do nothing" byte is omitted.

Edit flags [EditFlags]

The Contents pane in many *HKCR* keys shows an EditFlags entry in the Name column, with a four-byte binary value in the Data column. Each of the 32 bits within those four bytes is an edit flag whose value (0 or 1) specifies the status of a specific aspect of the object in whose subkey the entry appears. To see the effect of these flags, select "Options" (in IE4, "Folder Options") on the Windows Explorer's View menu and then select the File Types tab. As each item in the Registered file types list is highlighted, various buttons and Edit options are disabled, according to the status of the associated bit in the EditFlags entry. A few examples are given in the following table along with their hex-to-binary conversions:

Registered File Type	EditFlags Data	In HKCR Subkeys
Application	d8 07 00 00	*exefile*
Application Extension *	00 01 00 00	*dllfile*
Device Driver	01 00 00 00	*drvfile*
File Folder, Folder	d2 01 00 00	*Directory, Folder*
MIDI Sequence	00 00 01 00	*midfile*
MS-DOS Application	d8 07 00 00	*comfile*
MS-DOS Batch File	d0 04 00 00	*batfile*
URL:File Protocol	02 00 00 00	*file*

* File type not seen, concealed by bit 24 flag (1).

Hex Data	Binary Equivalent *																							
D8 07 00 00	1	1	0	1	1	0	0	0	0	0	0	0	0	1	1	1	0	0	0	0	0	0	0	0
00 01 00 00	0	0	0	0	0	0	0	0	0	0	0	0	0	0	0	1	0	0	0	0	0	0	0	0
01 00 00 00	0	0	0	0	0	0	0	1	0	0	0	0	0	0	0	0	0	0	0	0	0	0	0	0
D2 01 00 00	1	1	0	1	0	0	1	0	0	0	0	0	0	0	0	1	0	0	0	0	0	0	0	0
00 00 01 00	0	0	0	0	0	0	0	0	0	0	0	0	0	0	0	0	0	0	0	0	0	0	0	1
D0 04 00 00	1	1	0	1	0	0	0	0	0	0	0	0	0	1	0	0	0	0	0	0	0	0	0	0
02 00 00 00	0	0	0	0	0	0	1	0	0	0	0	0	0	1	0	0	0	0	0	0	0	0	0	0
bit position	31	30	29	28	27	26	25	24	23	22	21	20	19	18	17	16	15	14	13	12	11	10	9	8

* Fourth Attributes byte (bits 7–0) not shown.

At present, one or more bits in the 31–16 range may be set, and in a few cases bit 8 may also be set. Because the final byte does not appear to be used (yet), the zeros in bits 7–0 are not shown in the above binary conversion.

High-bit (31–16) flags

Table 6-1 lists the effect of each bit that is set to 1. Thus, if "Application" is selected in the Registered file types list, the Remove (bit 28) and Edit (bit 27) buttons to the right of the list are disabled. The disabled Edit button prevents the status of other features from being verified, but if EditFlags is rewritten as D0 07 00 00 (to enable the Edit button), the following options on the Edit File Type sheet are indeed also disabled due to the indicated set bits:

Edit File Type Button	Set Bit
Change Icon	17
Edit	30
Remove	31
Set Default	18
Description of type line	16

Table 6-1 *Effect of EditFlags Settings*

Bit	Data *	To View Effect **	Effect
in *FileType* key's Contents pane			
31	80 00 00 00	Click Edit button	Remove button disabled †
30	40 00 00 00	Click Edit button	Edit button disabled †
29	20 00 00 00	Click Edit button	New button disabled
28	10 00 00 00	View File Types tab	Remove button disabled
27	08 00 00 00	View File Types tab	Edit button disabled
26	04 00 00 00	Reserved	None observed
25	02 00 00 00	Click Edit button	Item included in list ‡
24	01 00 00 00	View file types list	Item excluded from list
23	00 80 00 00	Click Edit button	Content Type (MIME) disabled
22	00 40 00 00	Reserved	None observed
21	00 20 00 00	Click two Edit buttons	Use DDE checkbox removed

Continued

Table 6-1 *Continued*

Bit	Data *	To View Effect **	Effect
in FileType *key's Contents pane*			
20	00 10 00 00	Click two Edit buttons	Application line disabled
19	00 08 00 00	Reserved	None observed
18	00 04 00 00	Click Edit button	Set Default button disabled
17	00 02 00 00	Click Edit button	Change Icon button disabled
16	00 01 00 00	Click Edit button	Description of type line disabled
8	00 00 01 00	Click Edit button	Confirm Open checkbox cleared
in any Shell\open *(or other action) key's Contents pane*			
8	01 00 00 00	Ignore bits 31 and 30 for this *Shell* subkey action only.	

* Data column entry, if only this bit is set.

** Open Explorer View menu, select Options (or Folder Options), select File Types tab, and take action specified here.

† Note *Shell\action* key at end of table.

‡ Required if no extension is associated with file type.

Confirm open after download (8) flag

As previously noted in the "MIME Contents Pane Modifications" section of Chapter 2, the File Types tab shows a MIME (Multipurpose Internet Mail Extension) content type on all SR versions of Windows 95 and also in Windows 98 (see Figure 2-4). In this case, the Edit File Type sheet shows three checkboxes, and the Confirm Open After Download checkbox is supported via the URL.DLL file. If the checkbox is cleared, the EditFlags setting described above changes to *xx xx* 01 00, where *xx xx* indicates that the first two EditFlags bytes remain as is. Thus, D8 07 00 00 becomes D8 07 01 00, and so on. The box is generally checked for most file types, although there are some exceptions where the bit-8 flag is set and thus a confirm-open message is *not* seen after downloading, as in the few examples shown here:

Registered File Type	HKCR Subkey	EditFlags Data
Channel File	*ChannelFile*	00 00 01 00
Internet Communication Settings	*x-internet-signup*	00 00 01 00
Internet Shortcut	*InternetShortcut*	02 00 01 00
Media Clip	*mplayer*	00 00 01 00

Registered File Type	HKCR Subkey	EditFlags Data
MIDI Instrument Definition	*idfile*	00 00 01 00
MIDI Sequence	*midfile*	00 00 01 00
Movie Clip (AVI)	*AVIFile*	00 00 01 00
RealAudio	*ramfile*	00 00 01 00
Sound Clip (Basic)	*Aufile*	00 00 01 00
Sound Clip (WAVE)	*SoundRec*	00 00 01 00

EditFlags override

In cases where the Edit File Type sheet shows several actions, an additional EditFlags entry in an Action subkey can override the flags that disable the Edit and/or Remove buttons. For example, Figure 6-6 shows the *HKCR\batfile* key structure. In the *batfile* Contents pane, the set bits (31, 30) have disabled the Remove and Edit buttons on the Edit File Type sheet. Therefore, if "MS-DOS Batch File" is selected, these buttons are disabled regardless of which action (edit, open, print) is selected. As a practical result, it is not possible to change the default editor (NOTEPAD.EXE) to some other text editor.

Special Case: The Change Icon Button

In this specific example, the Change Icon button remains disabled even if the bit-17 flag is cleared to zero. This is because Application File Type attributes are applied to all executable files with an EXE extension. Presumably, each such file has its own embedded icon (as, for example, MSPAINT.EXE, NOTEPAD.EXE, WORD.EXE, and so on), and a system-wide conversion of all these icons to a single icon cannot be accomplished via the Change Icon button. The presence of a *DefaultIcon* subkey beneath the *HKCR\exefile* key is what causes the button to remain disabled regardless of the flag setting. If there were some compelling reason (such as bad judgment) to force all executable files to display a common icon, this could be accomplished as described in the "Executable File Default Icons" section later in this chapter.

To remove this restriction, add a new binary EditFlags entry to the *batfile* key's *Edit* subkey, which is also shown in Figure 6-6, where the unique 01 00 00 00 flag serves as an override to the Remove and Edit flags prescribed in the *batfile* key by bits 31 and 30. Because the status of these bits is now ignored, the Edit button is enabled if the Edit action is highlighted, making it possible to specify some other application to use as a batch file editor. The *Open* subkey's own EditFlags entry remains at 00 00 00 00, so the *batfile* key's restrictions remain in effect if this action is selected. The *Print* subkey lacks an EditFlag entry, which is equivalent to a 00 00 00 00 setting.

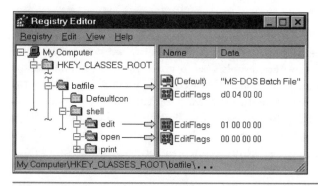

Figure 6-6 *The* batfile *key's EditFlags entry disables various buttons if "MS-DOS Batch File" is selected in the list of Registered file types. The* edit *subkey's 01 00 00 00 entry acts as an override that takes effect only if the Edit action is selected in the Edit File Type dialog box.*

Attribute flags [Attributes]

Under the *HKCR* key, the *CLSID* keys associated with several desktop objects lead to a *ShellFolder* subkey. That key's Contents pane contains an Attributes entry in the Name column, followed by a Data entry that functions in the same manner as the EditFlags entry described above. Despite the "Attributes" name, the entry has nothing to do with file attributes. Instead, the 32 flags enable or disable various options on each object's Context menu, as shown by the following examples. To verify these values, open the *HKCR\CLSID* key and search the Key column for *ShellFolder.* The Contents pane of each such key should display an Attributes entry, such as the entries that follow. The binary equivalents for these examples are also provided.

Object Name	Attributes	Object Name	Attributes
Briefcase	36 01 00 40	Microsoft Network	50 00 00 00
Dial-Up Networking	04 00 00 20	Recycle Bin	40 01 00 20

Attributes	Binary Equivalent *							
36 01 00 40	0 0 1 1	0 1 1 0	0 0 0 0	0 0 0 1	0 1 0 0	0 0 0 0
04 00 00 20	0 0 0 0	0 1 0 0	0 0 0 0	0 0 0 0	0 0 1 0	0 0 0 0
50 00 00 00	0 1 0 1	0 0 0 0	0 0 0 0	0 0 0 0	0 0 0 0	0 0 0 0
40 01 00 20	0 1 0 0	0 0 0 0	0 0 0 0	0 0 0 1	0 0 1 0	0 0 0 0
bit position	31 30 29 28	27 26 25 24	23 22 21 20	19 18 17 16	7 6 5 4	3 2 1 0

* Third Attributes byte (bits 15–8) not shown.

At present, several bits in the first byte may be set, and in a few cases, bit 16 plus others in byte 4 have also been observed to be set. No bits in the third byte (15–8) appear to be used, with one exception: If Internet Explorer 4 is installed but not yet configured, the third byte is 10 instead of the usual 00, as noted in the "Registry Flags" introduction earlier in this chapter. Table 6-2 lists the effect of each bit that is set to 1. Thus, if the Recycle Bin's Context menu is opened, it displays the following options because the associated bits (as indicated) are set:

Context Menu Option	Flag Byte	Set Bit
Properties	40	30
Paste	01	16
Open, Explore	20	05

Table 6-2 *Effect of Attributes Settings on Context Menu Options*

Bit	Data *	Enables This Context Menu Option
Byte 1 (bits 31–24)		
31	80 00 00 00	Unknown
30	40 00 00 00	Properties
29	20 00 00 00	Delete
28	10 00 00 00	Rename

Continued

Table 6-2 *Continued*

Bit	Data *	Enables This Context Menu Option
26	04 00 00 00	
Byte 1 (bits 31–24)		
25	02 00 00 00	Cut
24	01 00 00 00	Copy
Byte 2 (bits 23–16)		
16	00 01 00 00	Paste
Byte 3 (bits 15–8)		
15	00 00 10 00	†
Byte 4 (bits 7–0)		
07	00 00 00 80	Unknown
06	00 00 00 40	Unknown
05	00 00 00 20	ContextMenuHandler options (for example, Open, Explore)
02	00 00 00 04	Unknown
00	00 00 00 01	Unknown

* All four bytes in Data column, if only this bit is set.
† No effect on Context menu. Indicates Internet Explorer 4 is not set up yet.

Some care should be exercised if these flags are edited. You may want to disable an existing option (Delete or Rename, for example), in which case the associated bit can be changed from 1 to 0. However, if an inappropriate Context menu option is enabled, either an error message is displayed when that option is selected, or the selected option simply does nothing. There is also some variation in what the various attribute flags do from one object to another, so the preceding examples may not apply to other objects.

Other flags [ShellState, Settings, and so on]

These ShellState and Settings entries record the status of various configuration changes made via the Windows Explorer's View menu, as described subsequently, with data written into the Contents panes of the following Registry subkeys:

ShellState	HKCU\Software\Microsoft\Windows\CurrentVersion\Explorer
Settings	HKCU\Software\Microsoft\Windows\CurrentVersion\Explorer\CabinetState

If either entry is not currently present, open Explorer's View menu, select Options (Folder Options in IE4), make any change you like, and then click the Apply button. Now return to either Registry subkey, press F5 to refresh the window, and the appropriate entry is displayed in the Contents pane.

Windows 95 View tab data

The status of the "Hidden files" radio button and the "Hide MS-DOS file extensions" checkbox is written into the two least-significant bits in the fifth byte of the ShellState data string, as shown in Table 6-3. The status of the other two checkboxes is written into the fifth byte of a Settings data string in a *CabinetState* subkey, which is also shown in the table. If nothing else, this little table illustrates the extreme difficulty of trying to dope out some types of Registry trivia. For example, note that if one of the check boxes is checked, the associated bit is set (1); if the other is checked, its associated bit is *not* set (0).

Table 6-3 *Windows 95 View Tab Options and Associated Registry Entries*

View Tab Options		Name	Data *	Binary Equivalent **	
In HKCU\Software\Microsoft\Windows\CurrentVersion\Explorer					
Hide file types	Hide MS-DOS file extensions	ShellState	00	0000 0000	
Show all files	Hide MS-DOS file extensions	ShellState	01	0000 0001	
Hide file types	Show (checkbox cleared)	ShellState	02	0000 0010	
Show all files	Show (checkbox cleared)	ShellState	03	0000 0011	
Other checkboxes in HKCU\Software\Microsoft\Windows\CurrentVersion\Explorer\CabinetState					
Both cleared		Settings	3A	0011 1010	(10)
MS-DOS path checked		Settings	3B	0011 1011	(11)
Description box checked		Settings	2A	0010 1010	(00)
Both checked		Settings	2B	0010 1011	(01)

* Indicated Data is written into byte 5 of binary data string.

** (*xx*) shows status of the two bits (4 and 0) affected by these changes.

Windows 98 and IE4 General and View tab data

The View menu's Folder Options leads to a new General tab in Windows 98, and also in Windows 95 if IE4 is installed. Most changes made via the General tab's Web, Classic, and Custom style radio buttons, and the latter's Settings button, are written into the fifth byte of the ShellState entry as described above, although an IconUnderline entry in the same Contents pane is also used. These entries are not further described here.

The View tab offers considerably more options than its pre-IE4 counterpart, and most of these are written as individual DWORD entries in the Registry subkeys listed in Table 6-4.

View tab customization The presence of each option described above is determined by other subkeys under the *HKLM\\...\explorer* key, which is shown in Table 6-4, and any option can be removed from the list by deleting the appropriate subkey. Or, up to a point, the options can be customized. For example, of the six checkboxes in the Files and Folders section, five must be checked to enable an option (Show . . . , Allow . . . , Remember . . .) and one — the first — must be checked to *dis*able an option. To bring a little consistency to the list, open the *HideFileExt* key listed in Table 6-4 and make the following Contents pane edits:

Name	Change This:	To This:
Text	Hide file extensions for . . .	Show extensions for all . . .
CheckedValue	0x00000001 (1)	0x00000000 (0)
UncheckedValue	0x00000000 (0)	0x00000001 (1)
DefaultValue	0x00000001 (1)	0 or 1, as desired

Having done this, the box must now be checked to show all file extensions, which brings the option into agreement with those that follow. Because the former "Hide" option is now listed as "Show," the CheckedValue and UncheckedValue entries must be swapped so that the checkbox status agrees with the revised text. The DefaultValue entry simply indicates the checkbox status when the "Restore Defaults" button is clicked. Therefore, the user can set up a customized default set by editing the DefaultValue entry in this and in the other subkeys in this section.

The "Hidden files" section text might be revised by editing the Text entry in each of the following subkeys:

Subkey	Change This Text Entry	To This
Hidden\...	Hidden files	Show these file types:
NOHIDDEN	Do not show hidden files	All, except hidden
NOHIDORSYS	Do not show hidden	All, except hidden and system or system files
SHOWALL	Show all files	All

No further edits are required because these revisions don't change the status of any radio button — they simply describe in fewer words what each one actually does.

Similar edits might be made to other keys in this section to customize the entire list.

Table 6-4 *Windows 98 View Tab Options and Associated Registry Entries*

Advanced Settings Option	Subkey	Name	Data
Files and Folders			
in HKCU\Software\Microsoft\Windows\CurrentVersion\Explorer\...			
Remember each folder's view settings	Advanced	*ClassicViewState*	00000000 (0)
Display the full path in title bar	Cabinet State	*FullPath*	00000001 (1)
Hide file extensions for known file types	Advanced	*HideFileExt*	00000001 (1)
Show Map Network Drive button	Advanced	*MapNetDrvBtn*	00000001 (1)
Show file attributes in Detail view	Advanced	*ShowAttribCol*	00000001 (1)
Show popup description	Advanced	*ShowInfoTip*	00000001 (1)
Allow all uppercase names	Advanced	*DontPrettyPath*	00000001 (1)
Hidden Files (radio buttons)			
Do not show hidden/system files	Advanced	*Hidden*	00000000 (0)
Do not show hidden files	Advanced	*Hidden*	00000002 (2)
Show all files	Advanced	*Hidden*	00000001 (1)
Visual Settings			
Hide icons when desktop is viewed	Advanced	*HideIcons*	00000001 (1)
In HKCU\Control Panel\...			
Smooth edges of screen fonts	Desktop	*FontSmoothing*	"1"
Show window contents while dragging	Desktop	*DragFullWindows*	"1"

Continued

Table 6-4 *Continued*

Files and Folders: To Hide This Option . . .	Delete This Key
In HKLM\Software\Microsoft\Windows\CurrentVersion\Explorer\Advanced\Folder\...	
Remember each folder's view settings	*ClassicViewState*
Display the full path in title bar	*ShowFullPath*
Hide file extensions for known file types	*HideFileExt*
Show Map Network Drive button	*MapNetDrvBtn*
Show file attributes in Detail View	*ShowAttribCol*
Show popup description	*ShowInfoTip*
Allow all uppercase names	*DontPrettyPath*
Hidden Files (radio buttons)	*Hidden\...*
Do not show hidden/system files	*NOHIDORSYS*
Do not show hidden files	*NOHIDDEN*
Show all files	*SHOWALL*

Visual Settings: To Hide This Option . . .	Delete This Key
In HKLM\Software\Microsoft\Windows\CurrentVersion\Explorer\Advanced\Visual\...	
Hide icons when desktop is viewed	*HideIcons*
Smooth edges of screen fonts	*FontSmooth*
Show window contents while dragging	*DragFullWin*

Hidden Extensions and Files

By default, the Windows Explorer does not show extensions for known file types, nor does it shown hidden and system files. Therefore, system startup files (MSDOS.SYS and CONFIG.SYS) and hidden Registry files (SYSTEM.DAT and USER.DAT) won't be found in any Explorer window's Contents pane. Likewise, if Windows knows that it should open a document file in Word and a bitmap in MS Paint, then the DOC and BMP extensions won't appear either.

Fortunately, these dubious "enhancements" can be easily disabled so the knowledgeable user can have a better idea of what's on the system. To do so, open Explorer's View menu, select Options (Folder Options in IE4), and click the View tab. Then make your selection from the checkbox and radio buttons listed here:

IE4 Installed	IE4 Not Installed
Checkbox	**Checkbox**
Hide file extensions for known file types.	Hide MS-DOS file extensions for file types that are registered.
Radio button	**Radio button**
Do not show hidden or system files.	Hide files of these types (.DLL, .SYS, .VXD, .386, .DRV).
Do not show hidden files.	

Note that although the checkbox option does not change, the radio button options do: If IE4 is installed, files can be concealed according to their attributes; otherwise, files in a displayed list can be hidden without regard to their attributes. However, even if the above options are set so that all files and extensions are displayed, files with the following extensions (and possibly others) still do not display the extension:

Extension	HKCR*file type* Subkey
lnk	*lnkfile* (a Windows shortcut file)
mad	*Access.Shortcut.Module.1*
maf	*Access.ShortCut.Form.1*
mam	*Access.Shortcut.Macro.1*
MAPIMail	*{9E56BE60-C50F-11CF-9A2C-00A0C90A90CE}*
maq	*Access.Shortcut.Query.1*
mar	*Access.Shortcut.Report.1*
mat	*Access.Shortcut.Table.1*
pif	*piffile*
sfc	*SHCmdFile*
shb	*DocShortcut*
shs	*ShellScrap*
url	*InternetShortcut*
xnk	*xnkfile*

The reason these extensions don't appear is that the associated *HKCR\filetype* subkey's Contents pane contains the following entry:

Name	Data
NeverShowExt	""

The presence of this line disables the display of the associated extension, regardless of the Data entry. If it's important to see one of these extensions, simply delete the above line in the appropriate key's Contents pane.

If you make it a practice to save your document files in their own folders, you may find it convenient to hide the extensions for these file types. For example, if some folders are dedicated to word processor documents, while others store nothing but spreadsheets or bitmaps, you don't need to be reminded of the extension for each and every file in such folders. Add the NeverShowExt entry to the following *HKCR\filetype* subkeys to display the filename without the extension for files of the indicated type.

Extension	*filetype* Subkey
BMP	*Paint.Picture*
DOC	*Word.Document.8* (or similar)
XLS	*Excel.Sheet.8* (or similar)

Customizing the Desktop

By default, the My Computer, Network Neighborhood (if installed), Recycle Bin, and a few other objects are displayed on the desktop every time Windows starts. Some of these may be removed or relocated as described in the "Desktop Icons" section later in this chapter.

If you would prefer to simply remove all default desktop items and then set up your own custom desktop, try the following procedure:

1. Open the System Policy Editor and put a check in the "Hide all items on Desktop" checkbox shown in Figure 4-17 in the "System Policy Editor" section of Chapter 4.

2. Create one or more shortcut items in the following folder: C:\Windows\Start Menu\Programs\StartUp.

The next time Windows starts, the customary desktop icons are not displayed, but anything specified in the StartUp folder is. For example, to display an open Custom folder on the desktop, first use Explorer to create the folder as described in the following text. Then write the following shortcut in the StartUp folder:

C:\EXPLORER.EXE /root, C:\Custom

Rewrite the shortcut's Target line to open your own custom folder and repeat the procedure as required to open additional folders. Shortcuts to specific applications may of course also be placed in the StartUp folder, and they too will be displayed on the desktop in the usual manner.

The Explorer window

By default, every Explorer window opens in the single-pane Open mode, and every folder's Context menu shows Open as the default (boldface type) option. Follow the directions provided in the following sections to change this mode.

All Explorer windows

If you would prefer to have all folder windows open in the double-pane Explore mode, open the *HKCR\Folder\shell* key and change the (Default) entry's Data column from the empty string ("") shown in Figure 6-7 to "explore", which is also shown in the figure. This changes the Context menu default option from Open to Explore and affects all folders, including My Computer, Network Neighborhood, and Recycle Bin.

My Computer window

Unless the default mode has been changed from Open to Explore mode, as just described, double-clicking the desktop's My Computer icon (or any other folder icon) displays a single-pane Contents window such as that shown in Figure 6-8. Because the root of this window is, of course, My Computer, it does not display the icons for Network Neighborhood, Recycle Bin, and My Briefcase.

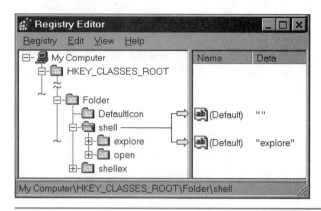

Figure 6-7 *By default, a desktop Explorer window opens in the single-pane Open mode because the Shell key's (Default) Data-column entry is empty. To open these windows in the two-pane Explorer mode, change the (Default) entry to "explore".*

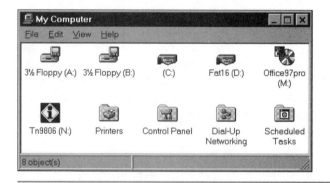

Figure 6-8 *The default single-pane Open mode for the My Computer window shows the available drives, plus Control Panel, Printers, and Dial-Up Networking folders. Windows 98 adds the Scheduled Tasks folder to the window.*

To open just the My Computer object in a two-pane Explorer view instead, open the *HKCR\CLSID\{20D04FE0...* key and add the subkeys shown within the boxed area in Figure 6-9. In the example shown in the figure, the new *open\command* subkey's command line ("explorer.exe /e,,/select,C:\") opens the My Computer window, which is also shown in the figure. Note that the Folders pane now shows the complete desktop tree, while the Contents pane duplicates that seen in the default mode shown in Figure 6-8, except that drive C is highlighted. Revise the command line as desired to create other opening formats, which will affect the appearance of the My Computer window only. Because this new key structure begins with a key named *open*, Windows assumes it to be the new default action for this object and adds it to the Context menu. To prevent confusion with the conventional Open option that remains on the same menu, give the new *open* key a distinctive name, such as the "Custom" entry seen in Figure 6-9.

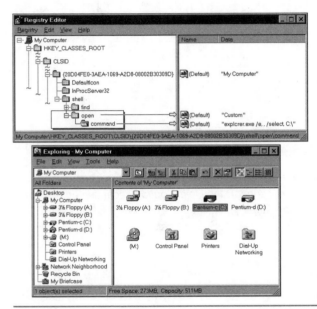

Figure 6-9 *To open the My Computer window in the two-pane mode, add the* open *and* command *keys indicated by the boxed area in the Registry Editor's Key pane.*

Desktop object removal

With a few notable exceptions, most desktop objects can be deleted via their Context menu's Delete option. However, Figure 6-10 shows a few desktop objects whose Context menus don't support that option. In most cases, the object can be removed by deleting one of the *HKLM\...\NameSpace* subkeys shown in the figure. As their names suggest, each subkey is a pointer to the *CLSID* key for the object specified in the Data column. By deleting the subkey, the object disappears from the desktop, yet the actual *CLSID* key remains intact under the *HKCR* key. The icon removal can be easily accomplished via the Tweak UI applet's

Desktop tab (see the Appendix for details); the procedure for removing an icon via a direct Registry edit is covered here.

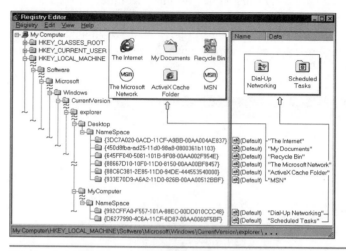

Figure 6-10 *Although the Context menus for some of the icons in the insets do not support the Delete option, most can be removed from the desktop by deleting the appropriate CLSID subkey under one of the NameSpace keys.*

My Computer

If the *HKCR\{20D04FE0...* subkey is deleted, the My Computer icon remains on the desktop but is inoperative and cannot be renamed. If it had been previously renamed, the name reverts to My Computer if the subkey is deleted, and it cannot be renamed again in the absence of the subkey. The icon and its default title seem to be hard-coded into the operating system, and there is no known Registry edit that can remove them from the desktop. If you must hide this object, rename it as " " and use an icon editing utility to create a transparent icon for it. Then move the now invisible icon to some desktop location where it will be safely out of the way. Or use the System Policy Editor to take everything off the desktop, as described in the "Customizing the Desktop" section earlier in this chapter.

Network Neighborhood

To remove this icon from the desktop, open the following subkey and add the indicated Name and Data (DWORD value) to its Contents pane:

HKEY_CURRENT_USER\Software\Microsoft\Windows\
CurrentVersion\Policies\Explorer

Name	Data
NoNetHood	0x00000001 (1)

If necessary, create the *Policies* and *Explorer* subkeys if they do not already exist. Erase this line to subsequently restore the Network Neighborhood to the desktop. In either case, the change takes effect the next time Windows is opened. Refer to "The System Policy Editor" section of Chapter 4 for additional information about the *Policies* subkey.

Dial-Up Networking

Figure 6-10 also shows the *NameSpace* subkey under the *HKLM\ ...\mycomputer* key. This icon appears in the My Computer window and, as described above, it can be removed by deleting the *{992CFFA0...* subkey shown at the bottom of the figure.

Menu Editing

This section describes ways to customize the appearance of various Windows menus by editing the Registry. After a brief review of general menu characteristics, detailed instructions pertaining to a few specific menus are given.

Cascading menus

Several characteristics of cascading menus can be customized via the Registry, as described in the following sections.

Delay time

If a menu option with a solid black right-pointing arrowhead is highlighted, a cascading menu appears to its immediate right. Under default conditions, the menu appears or disappears one-half second (500 milliseconds) after the highlight is applied or removed. This interval may be adjusted by adding a MenuShowDelay line to the Contents pane of the subkey listed here:

HKEY_CURRENT_USER\Control Panel\desktop

Name	Data	
MenuShowDelay	*"xxxx"*	*xxxx* = delay time in milliseconds

By setting the delay time to say, 2000, a cascading menu is not displayed until a menu option remains highlighted for 2 seconds. If the highlight is subsequently moved to another menu option after a cascading menu appears, the present menu continues to be displayed for another 2 seconds. Some users prefer a delay time of 1 second or more, to prevent cascading menus from popping up onscreen as the mouse pointer slowly moves across a menu. Also, the delay time permits the mouse pointer to move diagonally from a highlighted option to a cascading menu option without having the latter disappear if the pointer isn't moved fast enough. Or set the delay time to zero for instant menu access. Use the Menu Speed slider on TweakUI's Mouse tab to fine-tune this setting. To watch the effect of slider movement, open the key listed above and place the TweakUI applet's Mouse tab and the Registry Editor side by side. Note the current MenuShowDelay value and then slide the fader left or right. Now open the Registry Editor's View menu, click the Refresh option, and the value changes accordingly.

Menu option sequence

If Internet Explorer 4 is installed, the sequence of options listed on some cascading menus can be reordered. To do so, simply highlight any menu option, hold down the primary mouse button, and drag the option to the desired new position on the menu. This action writes (or rewrites) the desired sequence into a *Menu* subkey under one of the keys in the following Registry structure:

HKCU\Software\Microsoft\Windows\CurrentVersion\Explorer\ MenuOrder

In the *Menu* subkey illustrated in Figure 6-11, the Order entry's Data column lists the items on the menu in alphabetical order, along with the physical location for each item on the list. To automatically put the list itself in alphabetical order, simply delete the Order entry. With the sequencing instructions now missing, Windows sorts the list in alphabetical order the next time it opens.

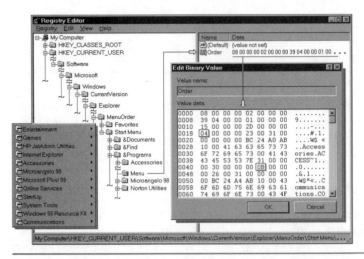

Figure 6-11 *A lengthy Order entry in each* Menu *key's Contents pane lists all menu options. In this example, the "Edit Binary Value" window inset shows that the Accessories and Communications options are currently located at positions 4 and 11 (hex 0B), as shown on the cascading Programs menu inset, where the Entertainment option is at position 0.*

Although the *HKLM\...\MenuOrder* key structure shows a *Menu* sub-key for each menu accessed via the Start menu, apparently not all of them are currently operational, as indicated by this list of menu items:

Order Option Supported	Not Supported
Documents	Find
Favorites	Settings
Programs	Start Menu

Menu alignment

The drop-down menus that appear within any Explorer window are by default aligned with the left edge of the selected menu name on the menu bar. To align these menus with the right edge instead, add the Registry entry shown here:

HKEY_CURRENT_USER\Control Panel\desktop

Name	Data	
MenuDropAlignment	"1"	*1* = right alignment

If the open window is positioned so that part of the menu would be off-screen to the left, the menu shifts to the right by whatever it takes to keep the entire menu onscreen. To restore the default alignment, either delete the line or reset the Data value to 0.

The Start menu

You can customize the Start menu in several ways, which may or may not require Registry editing. In several cases, a Start menu option opens a cascading menu of other options, most of which can be modified. The Start menu options are listed here in alphabetical order, as are the options on each of its cascading menus. The section concludes with a description of how to modify custom options at the top of the Start menu.

Table 6-5 summarizes the Registry keys and values that determine the appearance of both the Start menu and the various options that appear on its cascading menus. Refer to "Menu Option Sequence" above for details about resequencing the options on some of these menus. Most menus or menu options can be deleted by adding an entry into the Name column of the indicated key's Contents pane and writing a DWORD value of 00000001 in that entry's Data column, as shown in Figure 6-12. To reinstate the option, either delete the entry or change the DWORD value to 00000000. Most such changes take effect the next time Windows opens. In a few cases, these actions can be accomplished by checking/clearing the appropriate restriction box within the System Policy Editor, as indicated in Table 6-5. In other cases, however, the Policy Editor does not provide the necessary support, the edit described here appears to be undocumented, and the Registry must be directly edited to implement the change.

Table 6-5 *Start Menu Configuration Using the Registry Editor and/or Policy Editor*

Menu Option	Name *	Policy Editor Checkbox to Delete Option from Menu
Documents menu †		
To remove menu	NoRecentDocsMenu	Not available, use REGEDIT.
Favorites menu † *(this menu option present if IE4 is installed)*		
To remove menu	NoFavoritesMenu	Not available, use REGEDIT.

Menu Option	Name *	Policy Editor Checkbox to Delete Option from Menu
Find menu † §		
To remove menu	NoFind	Remove Find command.
Computer	*ShellFind* key	Not available, use REGEDIT.
Files or Folders	*ShellFind* key	Not available, use REGEDIT.
On the Internet	*Static\InetFind* key	Not available, use REGEDIT.
On the MS Network	*Static\MSNFind* key	Not available, use REGEDIT.
People	*Static\WabFind* key	Not available, use REGEDIT.
Help option *(deletion mechanism unknown)*		
Log Off *username*	NoLogOff	Not available, use REGEDIT.
Programs menu *(to sort cascading menus, see text)*		
Run option †	NoRun	Remove Run command.
Settings menu † *(menu does not appear if all options are deleted)*		
Active Desktop	NoSetActiveDesktop	Not available, use REGEDIT.
Control Panel	NoSetFolders	Remove folders.
Folder Options	NoFolderOptions	Not available, use REGEDIT.
Printers	NoSetFolders	Remove folders.
Taskbar and Start Menu	NoSetTaskbar	Remove Taskbar.
Windows Update	NoWindowsUpdate	Not available, use REGEDIT.
Settings menu ‡		
Windows Update	NoWindowsUpdate	Disable Windows Update.
Shut Down menu †	NoClose	Disable Shut Down command.
Other Windows 98 menus		
Hide all context menus	NoViewContextMenu	Not available, use REGEDIT.
Hide Taskbar (and Start menu) and Context menus	NoTrayContextMenu	Not available, use REGEDIT.

* DWORD Data entry of 0x00000001 (1) deletes option from menu.

† Name entry in ***Software\Microsoft\Windows\CurrentVersion\Policies\Explorer* key's Contents pane, Policy Editor checkbox in Local User\Windows 98 System\Shell\Restrictions section. Replace ** with the following: HKEY_CLASSES_USER to affect current user only, or HKEY_LOCAL_MACHINE to affect all users.

‡ Name entry in *HKLM\Software\Microsoft\Windows\CurrentVersion\Policies\ Explorer* key's Contents pane, Policy Editor checkbox in Local Machine\Windows 98 System\Shell\Restrictions section.

§ To delete option on cascading menu, delete indicated subkey located under *HKLM\Software\Microsoft\Window\CurrentVersion\Explorer\FindExtensions* key.

Note

Each edit described in the sections that follow may be applied to the current user only, or to all users, by making the edit in either of the following keys:

HKCU\...   Edit affects current user only.

HKLM\...   Edit affects all users.

Refer to Table 6-5 and its footnotes for details.

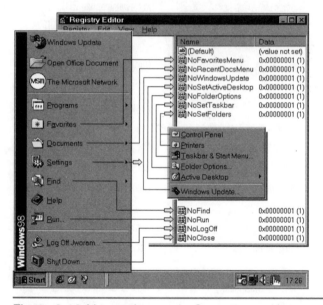

Figure 6-12 *Many options on the Start menu and its cascading Settings menu can be deleted by adding the appropriate entry to the HKCU\... or HKLM\...\Policies\Explorer key.*

Documents

The Start menu's cascading Documents menu lists the last 15 documents that were edited, as shown in Figure 6-13. Although the icon next to each document does not show the customary shortcut arrow, each item on the list is in fact a Shortcut file stored in the C:\Windows\Recent folder, and the same list is also maintained in the Registry.

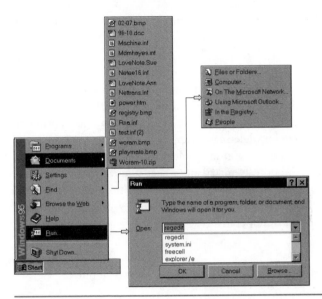

Figure 6-13 *The Start menu's Documents and Run options let you (or anyone else) review what you've done lately. The Find option also shows a list of files, folders, computers, and other items from your recent past.*

This document history list may be convenient on a single-user system because it permits the user to simply double-click on any list item to open the associated application and load the document for review or further editing. However, the list also lets snoopers know what the user has been doing lately, which may or may not be a diplomatic problem. If it is, refer to the INF File as a Registry Editor section in Chapter 4 for detailed instructions on how to erase this and other history lists whenever it becomes necessary (or advisable) to hide the evidence. The Tweak UI Paranoia tab also provides an option to clear this list, as described in the "Paranoia Tab" section of the Appendix. Or for greater peace of mind, refer to Table 6-5 for the Registry entry that completely removes the Documents option from the Start menu.

Favorites

This option is displayed on the Start menu if Internet Explorer 4 is installed and the three folders on its cascading menu (Channels, Links, Software Updates) are found under the C:\Windows\Favorites folder. If the Favorites folder is moved elsewhere, Windows tracks the move, and the folder is still accessible from the Start menu. However, if one of the folders on the cascading menu is moved, that folder is removed from the menu. Refer to Table 6-5 for the entry that deletes the Favorites menu from the Start menu.

Find

The options on this cascading menu are supported by subkeys under the *HKLM\...\FindExtensions* key, as described in the "FindExtensions" section of Chapter 3 and illustrated in Figure 3-15. Note that any option on this menu can be deleted by deleting the appropriate subkey, and the list of course varies depending on configuration details. A few typical subkeys are listed in Table 6-5, as is the Registry entry that removes the Find menu itself. Note, however, that if the Find menu is deleted from the Start menu, the Windows Explorer's Tools menu still shows a cascading Find menu option, but that option is inoperative.

Help

This menu option appears to be one of two that can't be removed.

Log Off *username*

Refer to Table 6-5 for the Registry entry that removes this option from the Start menu.

Programs

This option also appears to be a permanent fixture on the Start menu. The sequence of its folders and subfolders can be reordered as described in the "Menu Option Sequence" section earlier in this chapter.

Settings

Each of the six options on this cascading menu can be disabled by setting the Registry restrictions listed in Table 6-5 and shown in Figure 6-12.

The "Windows Update" option on the Settings menu looks to the following Registry keys for information on updating:

HKLM\Software\Microsoft\Windows\CurrentVersion\explorer \WindowsUpdate

HKLM\System\CurrentControlSet\Control\Update

If the *HKLM\...\WindowsUpdate* key is deleted, the Windows Update option remains on the menu, but selecting it has no effect. If the key is present, then information in the *HKLM\...\Update* key records the update history.

Shut Down

Refer to Table 6-5 for the entry that removes this option from the Start menu.

Suspend

This option may be displayed on a laptop computer's Start menu if enabled via a checkbox within a Power applet in the Windows Control Panel, and that applet provides the most direct method of controlling its appearance. The location of the Registry key where the Suspend status is recorded varies, with an example shown here:

HKLM\Enum\Root*PNP0C05\0000

Name	Data	Comments
APMMenuSuspend	01	01 = Suspend option appears on Start menu.
	00	00 = Suspend option removed from Start menu.

User-added options

The fastest way to add a custom option to the Start menu is to open Explorer, find the desired folder, application, or shortcut, and drag it to the Start menu button on the Taskbar. For example, if any icon in the Explorer's Folders pane is dragged to the Start button, it is displayed on the Start menu, as shown in Figure 6-14.

Custom cascading menus

There are two ways to create a cascading menu option at the top of the Start menu. To create a cascading Control Panel, Dial-Up Networking, or Printers menu, open the C:\Windows\Start Menu folder and create a new folder named *object name.{CLSID}* as shown here:

```
Control Panel.{21EC2020-3AEA-1069-A2DD-08002B30309D}
Dial-Up Networking.{992CFFA0-F557-101A-88EC-00DD010CCC48}
Printers.{2227A280-3AEA-1069-A2DE-08002B30309D}
```

In each case the name can be modified, but it must be followed by a period and the complete CLSID number enclosed in curly braces. This places the specified cascading menu option on the Start menu, as shown in Figure 6-14. Note however that if Internet Explorer 4 is installed, the Dial-Up Networking menu option displays an Empty menu, and the new folder is in fact empty. To insert the desired icons, open the regular Dial-Up Networking folder and drag/copy its contents into the new cascading-menu folder.

Figure 6-14 *This customized Start menu shows the effect of dragging various Explorer icons onto the Start button. In addition, the Control Panel option at the top of the list was installed by creating a new folder named Control Panel.{21EC2020 . . . as described in the text. If selected, it opens a cascading Control Panel menu, shown slightly to the right of the Start menu. The other (noncascading) Control Panel option on the menu opens a conventional Control Panel window.*

Creating your own cascading custom menu is far easier: Just create a new folder and move it to the Start menu. Make sure you don't create a shortcut, which will be displayed on the menu but not as a cascading menu.

The Context menu

The first few options on any Context menu are usually derived from the names of subkeys that appear directly under the selected object's *shell* sub-key. To revise the wording of any of these options, edit the appropriate

Contents pane. For example, Figure 6-15 shows the Context menu for a screen saver file, and the key structure for the Registry's *scrfile* subkey. The menu shows Configure and Test options because "C&onfigure" and "T&est" appear in the Data column of the *config* and *open* subkeys, respectively, where the ampersand specifies that the letter following it is to be underlined. If either text string were deleted from the Data column, the Context menu option would revert to the name of the subkey, with the first letter underlined by default, as for example the config and install options on the small Context menu excerpt in the same figure.

Sometimes the first letter on the menu is uppercase, although it may be lowercase in the actual subkey name. This is because, in the absence of a string in the appropriate Data column, the menu option name is taken from the SHELL32.DLL file, instead of from the subkey name. This is shown in Figure 6-15 by the menu's Test option, which becomes Open if "T&est" is deleted from the Content pane, even though the key itself is labeled "open."

The Print and Find . . . options are also read from SHELL32.DLL. For example, Figure 6-15 shows the *CLSID* key structure for the Network Neighborhood. By default, the Data column for the *find* (note lowercase *f*) subkey shows "&Find Computer . . .", and therefore the Context menu shows "Find Computer. . . ." However, if this Data column entry is deleted, the menu option becomes Find . . . (now it's an uppercase *F*) because this unique string is embedded in, and read from, the SHELL32.DLL file. The Open and Print menu options are likewise read from this file, which accounts for why they always appear with the first letter in uppercase and underlined.

Table 6-6 lists several subkeys in which a text string in the Contents pane Data column supersedes a menu option taken from a subkey name or from the SHELL32.DLL file. And, to summarize the use of an ampersand in the Data column, it specifies the underlined letter. If omitted, no letter is underlined, as shown by these edit subkey examples:

Contents Pane	Context Menu	Contents Pane	Context Menu
""	edit	e&Dit	eDit
&edit	edit	&Edit	Edit
edit	edit	Edit	Edit

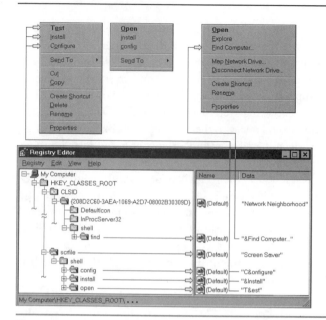

Figure 6-15 *The appearance of the first three options on the screen saver Context menu is determined by the Contents pane Data entries shown at the bottom of the window. The small menu to the immediate right shows the effect of deleting the "T&est" entry from the Data column. The "Find Computer . . ." option on the Network Neighborhood's Context menu is also specified in the* find *key's Data column. If erased, the option would revert to simply "Find."*

Table 6-6 *Use of Data Column to Specify a Context Menu Option*

HKCR Subkey	\shell Subkey	Contents Pane Data Column Shows	Context Menu Option Default	Other *
.pps	open	S&how	Show	Open ‡
{208D2C60... †	find	&Find Computer...	Find Computer...	Find... ‡
AVIFile	play	Play	Play	play
cplfile	cplopen	Open with Control Panel	(same)	cplopen
midfile, mplayer	play	Play	Play	play
Office.Binder.95	new	New	New	new
Power.Point.Show.7	show	S&how	Show	show
regfile	open	Mer&ge	Merge	Open ‡

HKCR Subkey	\shell Subkey	Contents Pane Data Column Shows	Context Menu Option Default	Other *
scrfile	config	C&onfigure	Configure	config
	install	&Install	Install	install
	open	T&est	Test	Open ‡
Unknown	openas	(value not set)	Open With...	Open With... ‡
(various)	print	(value not set)	Print	Print ‡

* Context menu option reverts to this string if string in Data column is deleted.
† CLSID number is for Network Neighborhood.
‡ Context menu shows this text string taken from SHELL32.DLL file *unless* an alternate phrase appears in Data column.

Add Context menu options

In addition to the options that are displayed on the Context menu by default, it's possible to add various custom options such as those described in this section.

Add to Zip This Context menu option is added via the *WinZip* subkey and its associated *CLSID* key, as illustrated in Figure 6-16. Since the *WinZip* subkey appears under the Asterisk key's *ContextMenuHandlers* subkey, it appears on the Context menu of any file that can be written into a compressed (zipped) archive file. In this example, the key was added by WinZip 6.0 from Nico Mak Computing, Inc.

DOS command Because the venerable command prompt substitutes speed for elegance, many users prefer to open a DOS box from time to time in order to perform an operation in far less time than required from within an Explorer window. As an example of what can be done, open the following Registry key and add the key structure shown here:

HKCR\folder\shell

Key and Subkey	Name	Data
DOS Prompt	(Default)	"Directory listing"
command	(Default)	"command.com /K DIR"

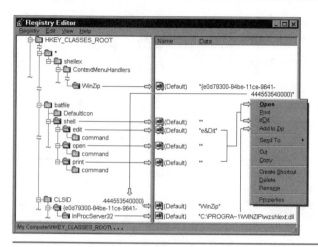

Figure 6-16 *This* batfile *key structure provides another example of how entries in the Contents pane Data column are displayed on the Context menu. The Add to Zip option is supported by the file specified in the* InProcServer32 *subkey seen at the bottom of the window.*

This places a Directory listing option on every folder's Context menu, and if selected, the *command* subkey displays a directory listing of the folder contents. The /K switch keeps the DOS window open until the user closes it. Simply replace the optional "Directory listing" text, the /K switch, and DIR command with your own choices, and the option executes whatever DOS command you need. Type **COMMAND** /? for a list of available command-line switches.

Merge If you decide to name potentially dangerous Registry files with an extension of, say, RE_ instead of the customary REG, you can add a Merge option to the file type's Context menu, as shown in Figure 6-17. With a new *.re_* subkey structure added beneath the *HKCR* key, the resultant Context menu shown in the figure is displayed for any file with that extension. The default action is Open, and the Context menu displays "Open in NotePad" as a reminder. Select the Merge option whenever you really do want to merge the file into the existing Registry. In either case, the *command* subkey executes either REGEDIT.EXE or NOTEPAD.EXE, as indicated in the Data column. This procedure prevents a critical file (with an RE_ extension) from being accidentally merged into the Registry by double-clicking it.

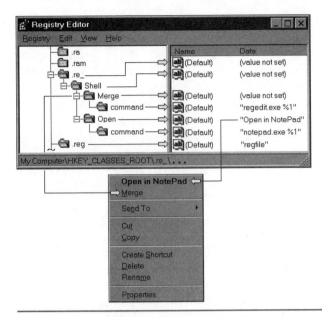

Figure 6-17 *The Merge and Open in NotePad options on this custom subkey's Context menu offer some protection against accidentally merging a critical Registry file with an extension of RE_ instead of the customary REG. The default option has been renamed Open in NotePad, and Merge is available as a nondefault option.*

Printto In at least one circumstance, an Action key located under a *FileType* key's *Shell* subkey does not appear on the Context menu. Using Printto as an example, this section shows how to force a missing action key to appear on the menu. For the purposes of this illustration, it is assumed that the *Printto* and *Printto\command* subkeys are present and in good working order. The same general procedure described here should be valid for any other action key that is missing from the Context menu.

If a document file icon is dragged to a printer icon and dropped there, the print job is handled by one of two subkeys in the Registry. If the appropriate *FileType* key contains a *Printto* subkey, then its *command* subkey handles the job. Otherwise, the regular *Print* subkey does the job. Assuming a *Printto* subkey exists for the file type, there's rarely a point to having a Printto option on the Context menu because by definition Printto is reserved for drag-and-drop operations. If the file is to be printed via the Context menu, then that menu's regular Print option is used, and the appearance of a Printto option would be redundant.

However, if you specify that a file is to be drag-and-drop printed using a different application than the default (see "Drag-and-Drop Print Editing," later in this section), then you may want Printto available on the Context menu for use when actual drag-and-drop printing is inconvenient.

To place the Printto option on the menu, open the *Printto* subkey and type **Printto** in the Contents pane's Data column, with an ampersand inserted immediately before the letter that is to be underlined — for example, **P&rintto**. This simple action places the option on the menu, with the letter *r* underlined. In fact, you may even enter **&Printto** to force the use of an underlined *P* for this option. However, because this letter is already used for the Print option, you may prefer to select some other letter instead.

Other missing options

If an unrecognized file type's Context menu is opened and its Open With... option selected, the user can specify the program to open the selected file. As noted in Chapter 2, if the "Always use this program to open this file" checkbox is checked, the next time a file with the same extension is selected, the Context menu displays the usual Open option instead of the Open With... option. However, other options appropriate to the same program may not be included on the Context menu.

To verify this, copy a short text file to the desktop and rename it as, say, TEXTFILE.XYZ. Then open its Context menu, select the Open With... option, put a check in "Always use this program . . ." checkbox, and associate the file with the Notepad applet. The next time you open the TEXTFILE.XYZ file's Context menu, the Open option is displayed, but the expected Print option is not. To find out why, open the *.xyz* subkey and note the entry in the Data column, which probably reads *xyz_auto_file*.

You'll also find a new *xyz_auto_file* subkey under the *HKCR* key, and its *Shell* subkey leads to an *open\command* subkey but not to an equivalent subkey for Print. To resolve the problem, simply erase the entire *xyz_auto_file* subkey structure (which won't be needed), then reopen the *.xyz* subkey, and change *xyz_auto_file* to *txtfile*. The next time you select any file with that extension, its Context menu will display the same options available to files with TXT and other extensions associated with Notepad.

Use the same general procedure to correct any other new file type whose Context menu does not list all the desired options.

Recycle Bin's missing Rename option

Note that the Rename option is missing from the Recycle Bin's Context menu. This is intentional because Windows requires this specific name to be present for proper operation. Accordingly, in the Recycle Bin's *ShellFolder* subkey, the Attributes flag is written to exclude the Rename option from the menu.

Change Context menu options

This section describes several modifications that can be made to any Context menu.

Change option name and/or underlined letter The first few menu options are the names of actions that are displayed under various *Shell* sub-keys under the *FileType* or *Program Identifier* key located under the *HKCR* key. For example, Figure 6-16 shows the *batfile* key and the three action subkeys that appear within its *Shell* key structure. The figure inset shows how these commands are displayed as Context menu options when any file with a BAT extension is selected. (The Add to Zip option is discussed separately, later in this chapter.)

Note that although the following three Registry subkey names are displayed on the Context menu, the menu's capitalization and sequence do not match that shown under the *Shell* key, as summarized here:

Subkey Name	Contents Pane	Context Menu	Actual Sequence
Edit	e&Dit	eDit	Default option
Open	""	Open	Other options, as described below
Print	""	Print	

In this example, the Edit option has been edited to display the unique capitalization shown on the Context menu, and the Open and Print options show an underlined uppercase first letter for the reasons described previously. On the menu, the action subkeys under the *Shell* key appear after the default option in the sequence in which they were added or edited in the Registry. These options are followed by other options added by the Asterisk key and by QuickView and other utilities. Thus, if an original Context menu sequence was Open, Print, edit, Add to Zip, and the *Print* subkey was subsequently edited, the new sequence would be Open, edit, Print, Add to Zip.

Change default option As just noted, the default action is always the first option listed on the Context menu, where it appears in boldface type (usually, as **Open**). The safest way to specify some other action as the default is to open Explorer's View menu, select Options, and click the File Types tab. Scroll down the list of Registered file types, highlight the desired file type, and then click the Edit button. Note the action listed in boldface type, which is the current default. To make some other action the default, highlight it and click on the Set default button.

It's often faster to accomplish the same task via the Registry, especially if the desired file type is not easy to find. For example, a batch file appears in the list of Registered file types under "M" for "MS-DOS Batch File." A Word document also appears under the same letter, but this time it's "Microsoft Word Document." If you haven't already resequenced this list (see "File Type Searches" near the beginning of this chapter), you can directly edit the Registry to save a bit of time searching an endless list of M-words. To do so, open a subkey such as *batfile,* then open the *Shell* subkey below it, and edit its Contents pane's (Default) Data column. Type in the name of any subkey action that appears below the *Shell* key (*edit* or *print,* for example) and then click the OK button. That action becomes the default action, and it is displayed at the top of the Context menu.

Delete Context menu options In certain cases, one or more options can be deleted from a Context menu for some default desktop objects. Refer to the "Attribute Flags [Attributes]" earlier in the chapter for instructions on how to delete Context menu options.

Hide Context menus In addition to the Start menu configuration options described earlier, two options that affect Context menus are listed in the "Other Windows 98 Menus" section of Table 6-5. The NoViewContextMenu entry prevents any Context menu from appearing when an object is highlighted and the right mouse button clicked. The NoTrayContextMenu entry prevents the Context menu from appearing for the Taskbar, Start button, and any minimized windows that are displayed on the Taskbar. At the right side of the Taskbar, the clock's Context menu is also unavailable, although the same restriction may not affect other items in the same (System Tray) area.

Delete or modify Send To option The Context menu's "Send To" option is supported by an *HKCR\{7BA4C740...* key structure in both versions of Windows, and if it is removed, the option no longer appears on any Context menu. Internet Explorer 4 adds a new *HKCR\ AllFilesystemObjects\Shellex\ContextMenuHandlers\SendTo* key structure in which the *SendTo* subkey cites the previously cited *{7BA4C740...* key. If the latter key is deleted, the Send To option is likewise removed from all Context menus. To place the Send To option on folder Context menus only, simply add the following subkey under the *Folder* key's own *ContextMenuHandlers* subkey:

Key Name	Name	Data
SendTo	(Default)	"{7BA4C740-9E81-11CF-99D3-00AA004AE837}"

As a result of this change, the Send To option no longer appears on Context menus for shortcuts or individual files.

Delete Recycle Bin options An Empty Recycle Bin option on the Recycle Bin's Context menu deletes the entire contents of the Bin, after an "Are you sure . . . ?" prompt verifies that you really want to do this. The Recycle Bin's *HKCR\CLSID\{645FF040...* key leads to a *Shellex\ ContextMenuHandlers* key structure, which in turn leads to a *{645FF040...* subkey. In other words, the Context menu is handled via the same key structure that supports the Bin itself. If the *{645FF040...* key immediately beneath the *ContextMenuHandlers* key is deleted, then the Empty Recycle Bin option is removed from the menu, which offers just a bit of extra added protection against accidental use. You can of course still empty the Recycle Bin by opening it and performing the operation from its File menu.

The Windows 98 Recycle Bin window offers a splendid opportunity for menu-related disasters, which can be removed by a Registry edit. If viewed as a Web page and no file in the Name column is highlighted, the Recycle Bin displays two Web-style links at the left side of the window. These links duplicate its File menu's Empty and Restore options, as shown in Figure 6-18. There is however a slight difference: If you click on either link, there's no "Are you sure?" prompt to verify that you really mean it. As a consequence, the entire contents of the Bin could be lost, or every file within it could be restored to its original location. To prevent either action, just open the following key structure:

HKCR\CLSID\{645FF040-5081-101B9F08-00AA002F954E}\shellex

If you delete the *shellex* key's *ExtShellFolderViews* subkey, the "helpful" options mentioned above will go away. The deletion has no effect on any of the other options to empty the Recycle Bin.

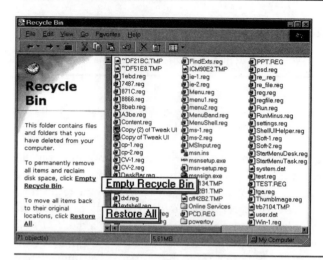

Figure 6-18 *If no file in the Recycle Bin's Contents pane is highlighted when either Web-style link (shown magnified in the insets) is selected, the action takes place without an "Are you sure?" prompt to verify that you're serious about this.*

The Desktop New menu

Two of the options on the desktop's New menu — Folder and Shortcut — are hard-coded into the SHELL32.DLL file in the C:\Windows\System folder and are therefore not functions of the Registry. During the Windows setup procedure, Registry entries for three other options — Bitmap Image, Text Document, Wave Sound — are taken from the SHELL.INF file, and the Briefcase option is taken from the NET.INF file (in each case, assuming the associated applet is installed during setup). Additional options may be placed on the New menu as various Windows applets and applications are installed. Options may be added to, or removed from, the New menu as described in the following sections.

Add menu option

In order to successfully add an option to the New menu, make sure a valid *Filename-extension* subkey exists and is associated with a Registered file type. For example, to add a "Custom Document" option to the New menu, open Explorer's View menu, select options, click the File Types tab and then the New Type button. Enter the following information:

Description of type:	Custom Document
Associated extension:	JMW (or any other new extension)
Actions:	Click New button, enter name of action and executable application name (for example, Open, and "C:\(*path here*)\ WINWORD.EXE" /n "%1"), then click OK and Close buttons.

Note: The quotation marks in the preceding text are needed to recognize a path or long filename containing spaces.

Once you do this, the *HKCR* key should show new *.jmw* and *jmwfile* subkeys. The latter contains a *Shell\open\command* subkey with the path and name of the executable file cited above. Now complete the following steps to add Custom Document to the New menu:

1. Highlight the *Filename-extension* subkey (*.jmw* in this example), open the Edit menu, and select the New Key option.

2. Type **ShellNew** in the NewKey #1 textbox and press the Enter key.

3. Open the Edit menu and select the New String Value option.

4. Create one (only) of the following String value entries in the Contents pane:

Name	Data
NullFile	""
FileName	WINWORD.JMW (or similar, assuming file exists)

Refer to the section "ShellNew Key" section of Chapter 2 for details about each of the entries listed above.

HTML document Although Netscape Navigator places a Netscape Hypertext Document option on the New menu, Internet Explorer does not provide a similar option. However, if both browsers are installed, then the New menu displays one of the following options, depending on which browser is the current default:

Default Browser	New Menu Option
Netscape Navigator 4.04	Netscape Hypertext Document
Internet Explorer 3 and Windows 95	Internet Document (HTML)

Continued

Default Browser	New Menu Option
Internet Explorer 4 and Windows 95	Internet Document (HTML)
Internet Explorer 4 and Windows 98	Microsoft HTML Document 4.0

If Netscape Navigator is subsequently uninstalled, the New menu continues to show the appropriate Microsoft browser option. This is because the Navigator setup procedure wrote a *ShellNew* subkey under the *HKCR\.html* key, and its Contents pane cites a NETSCAPE.HTML file that was written into the C:\Windows\ShellNew folder as part of the same procedure. As long as both items remain installed, then it doesn't matter which browser is specified by the *.html* key itself; either Microsoft's *htmlfile* or Netscape's *NetscapeMarkup* key will provide the appropriate option on the New menu.

If your current browser did not add its own option to the New menu, you may do so by editing the *HKCR\.htm* and/or *HKCR\.html* key. Add a *ShellNew* subkey under whichever one represents the extension you want to use. If a *ShellNew* subkey already exists beneath both keys, the *.htm* subkey takes precedence, and you may therefore wish to delete its *ShellNew* subkey if you want new HTML documents to use the HTML extension. After you've made your choice, edit the appropriate keys as follows:

Name	Data	Comment
(Default)	(value not set)	
Filename	"HTMLFILE.TXT"	Replace with filename and extension of your choice.
NullFile	""	If present, delete this line.

Now use Notepad or any ASCII text editor to write a file with the name and extension you used previously and save it in the C:\Windows\ShellNew folder. The file should contain at least the following two lines of HTML tags:

```
<HTML><BODY>
</BODY></HTML>
```

The cascading New menu should now display the appropriate new HTML document option, as was shown earlier in Figure 6-12.

MIDI file To put a MIDI sequence option on the New menu list, add a *ShellNew* subkey under the *HKCR\.mid* subkey with the following binary value in the Contents pane:

Name	Data
Data	4D 54 68 64 00 00 00 06 00 00 00 01 01 E0 4D 54 72 6B

This is the MIDI header data described in Chapter 2 and illustrated in Figure 2-14 and should exist only if a third-party MIDI recorder application is installed. It is shown here simply to illustrate how such an application might modify the Registry.

My Documents If the default "My Documents" object is removed from the desktop, a "My Documents Folder on Desktop" option is displayed on the New menu. If selected, the "My Documents" folder icon reappears, and the option is removed from the menu. Refer to ".mydocs" in Chapter 2 for details about this behavior.

Delete menu option

Deleting an option from the New menu is quite easy: Just delete the *ShellNew* subkey under the appropriate *Filename-extension* key, and the option disappears from the New menu.

Icons and the Registry

With the exception of the "Registry Icon Edits" section, this part of the chapter does not describe methods to alter the actual internal graphics content of an icon file, but rather it describes how to find an icon specified in the Registry and then looks at various ways in which some other icon may be selected. Some, but not all, such changes are recorded in the Registry, and of those that are, some may be easily changed without directly editing the Registry.

Registry icon edits

How many icons exist in the Windows galaxy? Perhaps not quite as many as stars in that other one, but certainly more than a few. And even the tiniest offers some opportunity for graphic creativity: At a depth of only 256 colors, a 16×16-pixel space allows $256^{16\times16}$ possibilities, which is not a small number. Yet despite the opportunity, the Registry's Key pane uses perhaps the only two stars in the GUI galaxy that can be confused for something else: the closed- and open-folder icons of the Windows Explorer.

On one hand, these icons should not cause a recognition problem: Survivors of the previous chapters know the difference between a Registry and an Explorer window, and they needn't be reminded that an open "folder" is not really an open folder, if one accepts Microsoft's definition of a Registry key. Yet there is a minor recognition problem — it's often rather difficult to spot the lone open yellow folder icon inconspicuously nestled in a long row of its closed yellow counterparts. The occasional Registry watcher won't be bothered by this, but for those who spend too much of their lives jangling Registry keys, something a bit more obvious would be nice.

Fortunately, the Registry Editor utility contains its own icon set, and it's quite easy to edit the open-folder icon so it stands out in the crowd. For example, Figure 6-19 shows the effect of changing the open folder into a large red arrow. The result of this edit in the Registry Editor window can be seen in Figure 6-21, and it is even more conspicuous in an actual Registry window on a color monitor. Before starting an editing session, make a backup copy of the Registry Editor utility as REGEDIT.BAK (or similar), then edit the original REGEDIT.EXE as desired. Discard the backup version only after you're satisfied with the use and appearance of the edited file.

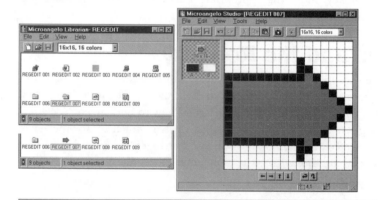

Figure 6-19 *This Microangelo Librarian applet window shows the REGEDIT.EXE file's open-folder icon before and after using the utility to change it to a prominent red arrow. The open Shell Icons key in Figure 6-21 shows the effect of the edit in the Registry Editor window.*

Desktop icons

Some or all of the object icons listed in this section are placed on the desktop during the Windows setup procedure. If an icon cited here is not displayed, it represents an object that was not installed, either because it is not supported (Network Neighborhood on a single-user system, for example) not available (My Documents requires Windows 98), or because the user elected not to install it (My Briefcase, for example). For future reference, the *CLSID* key for each object is provided in the following list, and that key appears as a subkey under the *HKCR\CLSID* key:

Object Name	HKEY_CLASSES_ROOT\CLSID Subkey
Inbox	{00020D75-0000-0000-C000- 000000000046}
Microsoft Network	{88667D10-10F0-11D0 -8150-00AA00BF8457}
My Briefcase	{85BBD920-42A0-1069-A2E4-08002B30309D}
My Computer	{20D04FE0-3AEA-1069-A2D8-08002B30309D}
My Documents	{450D8FBA-AD25- 11D0-98AB-0800361B1103}
Network Neighborhood	{208D2C60-3AEA-1069-A2D7-08002B30309D}
Recycle Bin	{645FF040-5081-101B-9F08-00AA002F954E}
The Internet	{FBF23B42-E3F0-101B-848-00AA003E56F8}
The Microsoft Network	{00028B00-0000-0000-C000-000000000046}

The ShellIconCache file

The hidden ShellIconCache file (note, no extension) in the C:\Windows folder contains copies of currently used icons, and this file restores desktop and Explorer icons every time Windows starts. During some routine icon-editing sessions (changing a shortcut icon, for example), the file is updated automatically. But when making some of the more complex edits described in the following sections, Windows often "forgets" to update the file, and so the change is not seen. In cases such as this, it becomes necessary to erase the file, which is described in one of the procedures that follows. After erasing the file, Windows needs a bit of extra time to restart as it rebuilds it. However, the icon edits will be written into the new file, subsequent restarts will not be delayed, and the changes will be permanent — at least until you decide to make further changes. Figure 6-20 provides a before-and-after view of the Start menu, to show the effect of some of the icon customization changes described in the following sections.

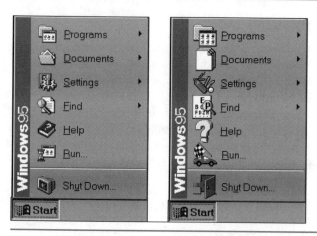

Figure 6-20 *A before-and-after look at the Start menu, to show how each of its icons can be customized to suit personal preference.*

Icon resource identifier

In most cases, the *DefaultIcon* subkey (described in the next section) specifies an icon source file and the number of an icon within that file, as for example in the "My Computer" *HKCR\CLSID{20D04FE0...* key structure. If its *DefaultIcon* subkey is opened, the Contents pane's (Default) line probably displays a Data entry such as those shown on the first two lines in the following list:

Name	Data
(Default)	"explorer.exe,0" [or, "C:\WINDOWS\Explorer.exe,0"]
	"C:\WINDOWS\System\shell32.dll,15"
	"C:\WINDOWS\SYSTEM\shell32.dll,-137"
	"C:\WINDOWS\SYSTEM\shell32.dll,-153"

Sometimes however, a negative number is given, as in the *DefaultIcon* key for Control Panel (-137), *batfile* (-153), and a few others, as shown by the last two lines above. Each such negative number is an icon resource identifier, which locates the icon without regard to its physical position in the file. Thus, if a new version of the file containing that icon were installed and the icon was now at a different position within that file, Windows would still find it — assuming, of course, that its resource identifier remained the same. The Windows 95 SHELL32.DLL file contains two versions of the Control Panel icon—a folder with a hammer (!) and screwdriver on it—at positions 35 and 46, while Windows 98 replaces the latter with a globe and flying Windows logo, and in both files the -137 resource identifier refers to icon 35. You may want to jot down any such negative value before changing it, just in case you need to return to the original value in the future, and more than one version of the icon is in the same file.

The DefaultIcon subkey

Many Windows icons are specified in a *DefaultIcon* subkey located under a *CLSID* or other Registry key. The key's Contents pane resembles the following entry:

Name	Data
(Default)	"C:\WINDOWS\SYSTEM\SHELL32.DLL, 12"

The actual path, filename, and icon number, of course, varies to indicate the actual source of the icon. To change that source, simply edit the Value data box to specify the desired icon source. If no effect is noted, then it's quite likely that a default icon specified under a *CLSID* key is superseded by another icon specified elsewhere. If this is the case, refer to the sections that follow for assistance in locating the currently active icon.

DefaultIcon search procedure

If you're not sure of the location of the appropriate *DefaultIcon* subkey, or even if such a subkey exists for the icon you want to change, make a note of the appropriate object type. Open Explorer's View menu, select Options (Folder Options in IE4) and then the File Types tab. Highlight the desired file type and note the extension listed in the "File type details" section of the tab. Then search *HKEY_CLASSES_ROOT* for a subkey with that extension name. Open the subkey, note the *Filetype* that appears in the (Default) entry's Data column, and then find the subkey with that name. Finally, open the *DefaultIcon* subkey underneath that key.

If the object is not a file type (Recycle Bin, The Microsoft Network, for example), follow the same procedure anyway, which will probably lead to a *CLSID* key. Open that subkey and then locate and open the *DefaultIcon* subkey beneath it.

If this general procedure does not locate the desired *DefaultIcon* subkey, then there's a good possibility that such a key does not exist for this object, as might be the case under either of the following conditions:

■ The default icon may be embedded in the executable file associated with that file type. To verify this, highlight the Registered file type (as above), click the Edit button and then the Change Icon button. (Refer to the "Edit Flags [EditFlags]," section earlier in this chapter, if one of these buttons is disabled.) Change the icon to anything else, then change it back again to the original icon and click the OK button. This action should force a *DefaultIcon* subkey to be written into the Registry.

■ Some icons are not specified in the Registry, or the Registry entry may not be immediately obvious. In this case, refer to the "Shell Icons Key" section below.

In a few cases, a partial icon change may be noted. For example, if the default icon for the Drive or the Folder icon is changed, the new icon is displayed only in the registered file types list: Drive and Folder icons elsewhere retain their original appearance. In cases such as this, refer to the "Drive Icons" or "Folder Icons" sections later in this chapter.

The Shell Icons Key In some cases, there is no *DefaultIcon* key for an object—for example, the default icons on the Start menu, various diskette and other drive icons, and the Share and Shortcut overlay icons. The fact that no *DefaultIcon* key exists for these objects may suggest that these icons are unchangeable, but in fact Windows does permit you to change most such icons via a *Shell Icons* subkey. Although not written into the Registry as part of the standard Windows setup procedure, the key is added to the Registry by the Windows 95 and 98 versions of Microsoft Plus! Or if MS Plus! is not installed, the subkey can be added by the user and then used to change various desktop and Explorer icons. Its location is given here:

HKLM\SOFTWARE\Microsoft\Windows\CurrentVersion\explorer \Shell Icons

Figure 6-21 shows the Contents pane for a typical *Shell Icons* subkey after MS Plus! has been installed. Each number in the Name column is associated with a specific object, and the information in the Data column identifies the icon that now supersedes the default icon for that object. Table 6-7 lists various Windows objects that can be specified by a number in the *Shell Icons* key's Name column. Each number listed in the table's "Icon Number" column corresponds to the icon position in the SHELL32.DLL file for that object, and the "COOL.DLL Equivalent" column lists the number of the equivalent icon in that file, which may be used as a replacement if MS Plus! is installed.

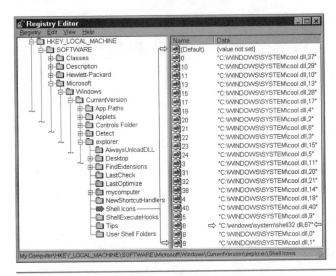

Figure 6-21 *The* Shell Icons *subkey displays a list of icons currently assigned to objects associated with the numbers in the Name column (as listed in Table 6-7). Note that object 6 (Drive, 3½" diskette) has been assigned icon 67 in the Windows 98 SHELL32.DLL file, which is a document page containing the letter* A. *The same icon is at position 62 in the Windows 95 version of this file. The Registry Editor lists Name column items in alphabetical order, which accounts for the 38, 4, 40, 5, 6 . . . sequence. Replacing the usual open-folder icon with a red arrow makes it easier to spot the open* Shell Icons *key near the bottom of the figure.*

Table 6-7 *HKLM\SOFTWARE\Microsoft\Windows\CurrentVersion\ Explorer\Shell Icons Subkey **

Object	Icon Number	COOL.DLL Equivalent	Note
Application (COM or DOS EXE file)	2	**	A
Audio CD	40	26	A
Drives			
3.5-inch diskette	6	8	A
5.25-inch diskette	5	9	A
CD-ROM	11	10	B
Hard	8	0	B
Network	9	1	B

Continued

Table 6-7 *Continued*

Object	Icon Number	COOL.DLL Equivalent	Note
Network, offline	10	29	A
RAM	12	**	A
Removable	7	**	B
Explorer Desktop (desktop/ pad and pencil)	34	**	A
Folders			
Closed	3	11	A
Open	4	18	A
Fonts folder	38	14	A
MSN, other document files	1	**	A
My Computer	15	28	C
Dial-Up Networking	33	27	D
Printers (see "Printers" entry below)			
Scheduled Tasks (uses icon in MSTASK.DLL)			
Network Neighborhood	17	17	C
Entire network	13	13	A
Each PC in network	15	28	A
Workgroup	18	**	A
Printers Folder	37	19	D
Add Printer	48/53	**	E
Generic (print to file)	50/55	**	E
Default	71/78	**	E
Network	49/54	**	E
Default	70/76	**	E
Parallel/serial/fax printer	16/16	23	E
Default	69/75	**	E
Program Group folder	36	24	A
Recycle Bin			
Empty	31	20	D
Full	32	21	D
Settings Menu			
Active Desktop	34	**	A
Control Panel (–137)	35	12	D

Folder Options	45	**	E
Printers (-138)	37	19	A
Taskbar and Start menu	39	**	E
Windows Update	46	**	E
Share (hand overlay)	28	34	A
Shortcut (boxed arrow overlay)	29	**	A
Shortcut (large arrow/white circle overlay)	30	**	
Start Menu			
Documents	20	2	A
Eject PC (undock)	26	32	A
Favorites	43	43	A
Find	22	3	A
Help	23	15	A
Log Off	44	**	A
Programs	19	4	A
Run	24	5	A
Settings	21	6	A
Shut Down	27	7	A
Suspend	25	33	A
Unregistered file type	0	37	A

* Icon number corresponds to icon position in SHELL32.DLL file and does not appear in the *Shell Icons* subkey if the device is not installed. If present, (A/B) format describes Windows 95/98 icons, and *xx/yy* numbers indicate Windows 95/98 icon positions.

** No icon in COOL.DLL file for this object.

A: *Shell Icons* entry supersedes default icon.

B: *Shell Icons* entry seen unless media AUTORUN.INF file specifies other icon.

C: Windows 98: if present, *DefaultIcon* subkey under *HKCU\Classes\CLSID* takes precedence.

D: *Shell Icons* entry has no effect. Use object's *DefaultIcon* subkey instead.

E: Icon change procedure is unknown.

(-*xxx*) Negative number indicates icon resource identifier (see text).

If the *Shell Icons* key entry for a Start menu icon or for any other object *not* also represented by a *DefaultIcon* subkey is removed, then the icon for that object reverts to the default icon resident in the SHELL32.DLL file. To select some other icon, refer to the beginning of the preceding "DefaultIcon Subkey" section if a key with that name exists. Otherwise, open the *Shell Icons* subkey or create a new subkey with this name if it does not already exist. Then use the following procedure to make the change:

1. Make a note of the path, source file, and icon number that you want to use as a replacement icon.

2. Using Table 6-7 as a reference, find the number that corresponds to the object whose icon you want to replace.

3. Open the *Shell Icons* subkey. If necessary, create a new key with this name.

4. Open the Edit menu, select the New\String value options, and type the number found in Step 2 over "New Value #1" (this is not necessary if that number already exists in the Name column).

5. Enter the information found in Step 1 into the Value data box, and click the OK button.

6. Exit Windows.

7. Erase the hidden ShellIconCache file (described below) in the C:\Windows\System folder.

8. Restart Windows.

Note

If the hard drive icon is changed by editing the *Shell Icons* subkey, that change is, of course, applied to all hard drives on the system. To change the icon for a single hard drive only, refer to the "Hard Drive Icons" section later in this chapter.

IE4 default icon modifications A further modification to the default icon specification occurs if Internet Explorer 4 is installed. If so, a new key structure is added to the Registry, and its effect may be demonstrated as follows. First, open the following Registry key:

HKCR\CLSID\{20D04FE0-3AEA-1069-A2D8-08002B30309D}

This is the *CLSID* key for the desktop's "My Computer" object, and its Contents pane shows "My Computer" or some other phrase in its Data column only if you edited this object name prior to installing Internet Explorer 4. Otherwise, the column displays a (value not set) entry. If so, you might want to change it to "My Computer" before continuing, just to see what happens later on. Leave the Registry Editor window open, but rename the Desktop object as "This Computer" by selecting the Rename option on its Context menu. After doing so, open the Registry Editor's View menu, select the Refresh option, and note that nothing happens — whatever was in the Data column before is still there.

Now open the *HKCU\Software\Classes\CLSID* key and note the presence of a *{20D04FE0...* subkey that may not have been there before. Its Contents pane lists the "This Computer" name and takes precedence over the "My Computer" that remains in the *HKCR\CLSID\{20D04FE0...* location cited above. If you highlight the new key and add a new *DefaultIcon* subkey beneath it, you can specify your own custom icon, which is now displayed on the desktop instead of the default icon for this object, as shown in Figure 6-22. Delete the *{20D04FE0...* key at this location (but *not* elsewhere), and the default "My Computer" name and icon reappear. Delete just the newly created *DefaultIcon* subkey, and the new name remains, but the icon reverts to the default. To see each such change after you make it, move the mouse pointer to any empty desktop area and press the F5 key to refresh the desktop.

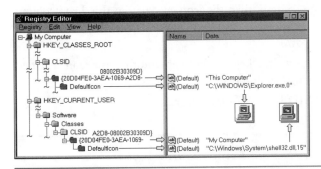

Figure 6-22 *The "My Computer" legend and icon specified in the* HKCU\... *subkeys at the bottom of the illustration take precedence over the same items specified in the* HKCR\... *subkeys.*

If you have an icon-editing utility that predates Internet Explorer 4, it may display the icon specified in this new Registry key structure, but if you use that editor to change the icon, the change may have no visible effect. That's because the utility changes the icon specification at the default location, but this information is superseded by the new key and therefore ignored. But delete the new *DefaultIcon* subkey, press F5, and the change is displayed.

Default icon precedence summary The following rules were tested by observing the icon displayed on the desktop for the "My Computer" object:

1. HKCU\Software\Classes\CLSID\{20D04FE0...\DefaultIcon

Requires IE4. If a *DefaultIcon* subkey exists at this location, the icon specified in its (Default) entry Data column is displayed on the desktop. If the subkey is present but the Data entry is invalid (" ", for example), a generic Windows document icon is displayed there instead.

2. HKLM\Software\Microsoft\Windows\CurrentVersion\Explorer \Shell Icons

Name	Data
15	"C:\Windows\System\SHELL32.DLL, *xx*

If an icon number specified in the Data column above appears here in the Name column, then the icon specified in this Data column (*xx*, in this example) is displayed instead. (See "Icon Precedence Example" below.)

3. If the previously cited keys are both absent, then the icon specified in the following location is seen:

HKCR\CLSID\{20D04FE0...\DefaultIcon

Name	Data
(Default)	"C:\Windows\System\SHELL32.DLL, 15"

If this key is absent, too, then the Windows default icon for the My Computer object is displayed.

Icon precedence example To see how this key relationship actually works, edit the following Registry key as shown here:

HKCU\Software\Classes\CLSID\{20D04FE0...\DefaultIcon

Name	Data
(Default)	"C:\Windows\System\SHELL32.DLL, 39"

This line assigns icon 39 (the flying Window logo) to the "My Computer" object, and that icon is now displayed on the desktop and next to "My Computer" in any open Explorer window. Now make the following additional edit:

HKLM\Software\Microsoft\Windows\CurrentVersion\explorer\Shell Icons

Name	Data
39	"C:\Windows\System\SHELL32.DLL, 41

Because this example assigns icon 39 to "My Computer" and then redirects all occurrences of that number to icon 41, the latter icon (a tree) is seen instead. Icon 39 happens to be the default icon for the Settings menu's "Taskbar and Start Menu" option, so the tree icon is displayed at that location, too.

Some superfluous *Shell Icons* key entries

Some *Shell Icons* listings are redundant and can be erased without having any effect. For example, both Recycle Bin icons are always written into the Recycle Bin's *DefaultIcon* subkey under the *{645FF040...* key. The MS Plus! setup procedure changes the *DefaultIcon* source file from SHELL32.DLL to COOL.DLL and the icon numbers from 31 and 32 to 20 and 21, and it inserts the following lines in the *Shell Icons* Contents pane to record the change:

Name	Data
31	C:\WINDOWS\SYSTEM\cool.dll, 20
32	C:\WINDOWS\SYSTEM\cool.dll, 21

In other words, object 31 (the empty Recycle Bin) is now represented by icon 20 in the COOL.DLL file, and object 32 (the full Bin) is icon 20. But now that MS Plus! has made this change, the inclusion of these entries in the *Shell Icons* Contents pane is not required. In fact, if either Data column entry were removed or changed, it would have no effect because the *DefaultIcon* listing takes precedence.

MS Plus! desktop themes

As a further consideration, if one of the MS Plus! desktop themes is selected, some *DefaultIcon* subkey entries will have been changed to specify the appropriate icons, as in this Recycle Bin example from the "Dangerous Creatures" theme:

Name	Data
(Default)	"C:\Program Files\Themes\Dangerous Creatures Recycle Full.ico,0"
empty	"C:\Program Files\Themes\Dangerous Creatures Recycle Empty.ico,0"
full	"C:\Program Files\Themes\Dangerous Creatures Recycle Full.ico,0"

Because these lines appear in the Recycle Bin's *DefaultIcon* subkey, they take precedence over the Recycle Bin icons (objects 31 and 32 in the *Shell Icons* subkey). If such a desktop theme is subsequently removed but MS Plus! itself is left in place, then the Recycle Bin's *Default Icon* subkey would once again refer to the COOL.DLL or SHELL32.DLL icons cited earlier.

Explorer window icons

The following Registry edits change the way bitmap and other graphics file icons are displayed within any Windows Explorer Contents pane.

Bitmap thumbnail icons

The *HKCR\Paint.Picture\DefaultIcon* subkey specifies the icon that appears next to every bitmap file (BMP extension), as shown in the first line that follows:

Name	Data
(Default)	"C:\Program Files\Accessories\MSPAINT.EXE,1"
(Default)	""%1"" (note two quotation marks on either side of the %1)

If the Data entry is rewritten as shown in the second line, each bitmap file displays its own distinctive icon, which is a thumbnail version of the actual bitmap image. In making the edit in the Value data box, include a quotation mark on either side of the %1 parameter so it will be enclosed in two sets, as shown in the preceding list. Doing this ensures that the replaceable parameter recognizes a long filename with a space in it.

Note, however, that this option considerably slows down an Explorer window with bitmaps in its Contents pane, because the distinctive thumbnail for each such file must be created separately as the window opens. If you like the feature enough to endure this slowness, you may want to make a point of keeping all bitmap files in a separate C:\BITMAPS (or similar) folder. That way Explorer won't be detained unless you specifically want to view your bitmap collection.

CPL and DLL icons

All CPL and many DLL files contain at least one embedded icon that can be displayed in an Explorer window by modifying the appropriate *DefaultIcon* key, as in the above bitmap example. Locate either or both of the following Registry keys and change the Data entry (which is usually the same for both file types), as shown in the first two lines in the following table. In either case, replace the data with the "%1" shown on the third line.

HKCR Subkey	Name	Data
cplfile\DefaultIcon	(Default)	"C:\Windows\System\shell32.dll,-154"
dllfile\DefaultIcon	(Default)	"C:\Windows\System\shell32.dll,-154"
(either of the above)	(Default)	"%1"

After making these edits, a search for all files with a CPL extension produces a display not unlike a Control Panel applet window, except that each icon title is the name of the file in which that icon is embedded, and there will, of course, be only one occurrence of each CPL file. The Control Panel itself may display two or more icons from the same CPL file. A similar search for DLL files displays the generic Windows document icon for each file that does not contain an embedded icon.

Internet Explorer thumbnail views

Two additional thumbnail view options are available if Internet Explorer 4 or greater is installed in Windows 95 or 98. If so, either may be selected by opening any Explorer window's View menu and choosing one of the following options.

View as Web Page If this option is selected, a single thumbnail view is displayed at the left of the Explorer window for any highlighted graphics file, as shown in Figure 6-23. Refer to "View Thumbnails" and the other sections that follow for information about the various file types that are capable of displaying a thumbnail image.

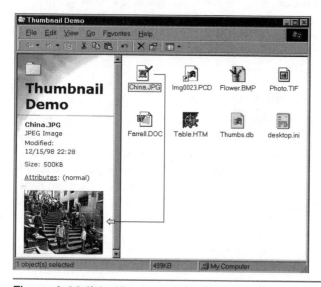

Figure 6-23 *If the View menu's "As Web Page" option is selected, a thumbnail image of the highlighted graphics file is displayed in the window.*

View Thumbnails If the Thumbnails option does not appear on the View menu, open the folder's Context menu, select the Properties option, and put a check in the "Enable thumbnail view" checkbox near the bottom of the General tab. In addition, the following conditions must be met to display a thumbnail view for a specific file type:

- The file type must be supported by Internet Explorer.
- A *ShellEx\{BB2E617C...* key structure (described below) must appear under the *HKCR\.ext* key for that file type.
- For some file types, a graphics filter file must also be installed.

To enable a thumbnail view for any file type, follow the instructions in the appropriate section that follows. To conceal a thumbnail view for any file type, simply delete the *{BB2E617C...* subkey under the appropriate *HKCR\.ext\ShellEx* key, where *.ext* is the *Filename-extension* key for the file type whose thumbnail view you wish to disable.

When the Thumbnails option is selected, Windows writes a hidden THUMBS.DB file into the folder, and this file contains the thumbnail images displayed whenever this option is selected, as shown by the example in Figure 6-24. The THUMBS.DB file is not required for the previously described View as Web Page option.

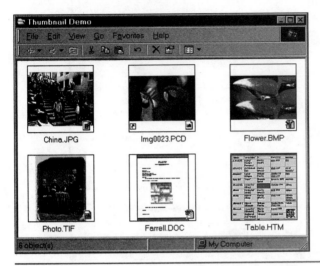

Figure 6-24 *If a folder's "Enable thumbnail view" option is selected, thumbnail images of all supported graphics files within that folder are displayed in the open folder window.*

Default graphics images On most systems, Windows displays a thumbnail view in either of the previously described options for each of the following file formats with no user intervention required:

File Type	Extension
Bitmap	BMP
Graphics Interchange Format	GIF
HyperText Markup Language	HTM, HTML
Joint Photographic Experts Group	JPE, JPG, JPEG
Portable Network Graphics	PNG
Shortcut	LNK
Windows MetaFile	WMF

The thumbnail shows up because these file types are supported by IE4, and the subkey structures shown in Figure 6-25 are installed by default as part of the browser's installation procedure. The "LNK file thumbnail interface extractor" seen at the bottom of the Figure's Contents pane provides a thumbnail view for a shortcut, only if the shortcut points to a supported graphics file.

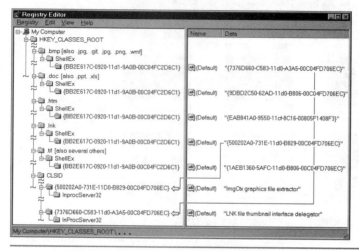

Figure 6-25 *An .ext subkey under the* HKCR *key may lead to a* Shellex\ {BB2E617C... *key whose Contents pane points to the* CLSID *key that supports thumbnail images for graphics files with that extension (BMP, JPG, and so on).*

Other graphics images Most other graphic file formats supported by IE4 require a similar key structure under the appropriate *HKCR\.ext* key, which is also shown in the figure. In addition, a graphics filter file must also be installed. Both requirements may be met as part of an application setup procedure, as shown in Figure 6-26 for Microsoft Office 97 Professional. However, it is not unusual for the required *{BB2E617C...* subkey to be omitted, and in this case, it must be added by editing the Registry. Table 6-8 lists some — but not necessarily all — file types that are capable of displaying a thumbnail view. In each case, the *CLSID* key cited in the table must be specified in the Data column for that file type, as was shown in Figure 6-24.

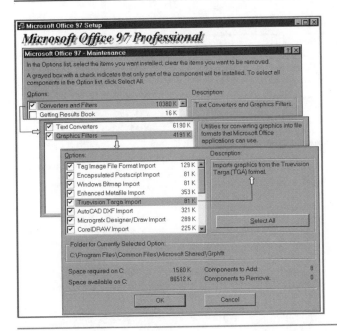

Figure 6-26 *Microsoft Office 97 is one of several Windows applications that provide filters to support thumbnail views of various graphics files.*

Table 6-8 *File Formats that Support Thumbnail View* *

File Format	Subkey †	Filter File ‡	Contents Pane Data §
Windows bitmap	*.bmp*	BMPIMP32.FLT	{7376D660-C583-11D0-A3A5-00C04FD706EC}
Corel Draw import	*.cdr*	CDRIMP32.FLT	{1AEB1360-5AFC-11D0-B806-00C04FD706EC}
Computer graphics metafile	*.cgm*	CGMIMP32.FLT	{1AEB1360-5AFC-11D0-B806-00C04FD706EC}
Word document file	*.doc*	None	{9DBD2C50-62AD-11D0-B806-00C04FD706EC}
Micrografx Designer/Draw	*.drw*	DRWIMP32.FLT	{1AEB1360-5AFC-11D0-B806-00C04FD706EC}
AutoCAD DXF import	*.dxf*	DXFIMP32.FLT	{1AEB1360-5AFC-11D0-B806-00C04FD706EC}
Enhanced metafile	*.emf*	EMFIMP32.FLT	{1AEB1360-5AFC-11D0-B806-00C04FD706EC}

Continued

Table 6-8 *Continued* *

File Format	Subkey †	Filter File ‡	Contents Pane Data §
Encapsulated Postscript	*.eps*	EPSIMP32.FLT	{1AEB1360-5AFC-11D0-B806-00C04FD706EC}
Graphics Interchange format	*.gif*	GIFIMP32.FLT	{7376D660-C583-11D0-A3A5-00C04FD706EC}
HyperText Markup Language	*.htm*	None	{EAB841A0-9550-11CF-8C16-00805F1408F3}
Joint Photographic Experts Group	*.jpg*	JPEGIM.FLT	{7376D660-C583-11D0-A3A5-00C04FD706EC}
Shortcut	*.lnk*	None	{500202A0-731E-11D0-B829-00C04FD706EC}
Kodak Photo CD	*.pcd*	PCDIMP.FLT	{1AEB1360-5AFC-11D0-B806-00C04FD706EC}
Macintosh picture	*.pct*	PICTIM.FLT	{1AEB1360-5AFC-11D0-B806-00C04FD706EC}
PC Paintbrush	*.pcx*	PCXIMP.FLT	{1AEB1360-5AFC-11D0-B806-00C04FD706EC}
Portable Network Graphics	*.png*	PNG32.FLT	{7376D660-C583-11D0-A3A5-00C04FD706EC}
PowerPoint Presentation	*.ppt*	None	{9DBD2C50-62AD-11D0-B806-00C04FD706EC}
Truevision Targa import	*.tga*	TGAIMP32.FLT	{1AEB1360-5AFC-11D0-B806-00C04FD706EC}
Tag Image File Format	*.tif*	TIFFIM32.FLT	{1AEB1360-5AFC-11D0-B806-00C04FD706EC}
Windows MetaFile	*.wmf*	WMFIMP32.FLT	{7376D660-C583-11D0-A3A5-00C04FD706EC}
Word Perfect Graphic import	*.wpg*	WPGIMP32.FLT	{1AEB1360-5AFC-11D0-B806-00C04FD706EC}
Excel spreadsheet	*.xls*	None	{9DBD2C50-62AD-11D0-B806-00C04FD706EC}

* Table is sorted by *Filename-extension* subkey name in column 2.

† Complete structure is HKCR\.ext\ShellEx\{BB2E617C..., where *.ext* is the subkey listed in this column.

‡ Default file location is the C:\Program Files\Common Files\Microsoft Shared\Grphflt folder. File names in italics are not required for thumbnail view support.

§ This data appears in the Contents pane of the specified subkey, enclosed in curly braces. See the following table for a description.

Contents Pane Description for CLSID Key	CLSID Key Cited Above
Office Graphics Filters Thumbnail Extractor	{1AEB1360-5AFC-11D0-B806-00C04FD706EC}
LNK file thumbnail interface delegator	{500202A0-731E-11D0-B829-00C04FD706EC}
ImgCtx graphics file extractor	{7376D660-C583-11D0-A3A5-00C04FD706EC}
Summary Info Thumbnail Handler (DOCFILES)	{9DBD2C50-62AD-11D0-B806-00C04FD706EC}
HTML Thumbnail Extractor	{EAB841A0-9550-11CF-8C16-00805F1408F3}

CD-ROM graphics files If the "Enable thumbnail view" checkbox is checked for a folder on a CD-ROM disc, an error message notes that "Windows cannot enable thumbnail view for *'folder name'* at this time." Or at any other time for that matter, but not because of a Registry problem. The required THUMBS.DB file cannot be written into the folder on the disc, and therefore the thumbnail view cannot be enabled. To create thumbnails for graphics files on a nonwritable CD-ROM disc, create a new folder on the hard drive and drag shortcuts into it from the graphics files on the disc. Then select "Enable thumbnail view" for the folder.

Microsoft Office files Some Microsoft Office document files (Excel, PowerPoint, or Word) display a thumbnail if you follow this procedure:

1. With the document opened in its associated application, open the File menu, select the Properties option, check the "Save preview picture" checkbox, and then save the file.

2. Make sure the associated *Filename-extension* key includes a *ShellEx\{BB2E617C...* subkey structure that cites a *CLSID* key for the appropriate graphics filter, as shown by the *.doc* key example in Figure 6-25.

Drive icons

Windows reads the CMOS configuration to determine the diskette drive configuration (A: = 3$\frac{1}{2}$, B: = 5$\frac{1}{4}$, and so on) and then uses the appropriate icon for each such drive, as was shown in Figure 2-12 in Chapter 2. To change either icon, refer to the "Shell Icons Key" section earlier in this chapter, and to Table 6-7. Refer to the same section and table for instructions on how to change the icon assigned to any other drive type (CD-ROM, hard drive, and so on).

In addition to these icon changes, a custom icon can be assigned to any removable medium or hard drive partition, as described in the next section.

Drive media icons

Most Windows CD-ROM discs contain an AUTORUN.INF file in the root directory, as described in the "AutoRun" section of Chapter 2. To briefly review here, the AUTORUN.INF file contains an `Icon=` line that specifies the icon to be displayed when that disc is inserted in the CD-ROM drive.

By default, Windows is configured to recognize an AUTORUN.INF file on various media and ignore it on others, based on the default Registry key data that follows and that can, of course, be revised as desired:

HKEY_CURRENT_USER\Software\Microsoft\Windows \CurrentVersion\Policies\Explorer

Name	Data	Binary Equivalent
NoDriveTypeAutoRun	95 00 00 00	1 0 0 1 0 1 0 1
		7 6 5 4 3 2 1 0

In the binary equivalent of the first byte (95) shown above, each bit set to 1 prevents a certain drive type from being recognized, according to the following list:

Bit	Drive Type	Bit	Drive Type
7	Reserved	3	Hard drive
6	RAM	2	Removable
5	CD-ROM	1	"NO_ROOT_DIR" *
4	Remote	0	Unknown

* Microsoft documentation gives no clue what this means.

Under default conditions therefore, the set bits prevent reserved (7), remote (4), removable (2), and unknown (0) drives from using the AutoPlay mode and the AUTORUN.INF file. Bit 7 is reserved for future drive types not yet defined.

To enable any diskette to display its own custom icon, change the Data entry above to clear removable drive bit 2 (91 = 1001 0001). Next, locate the icon you want to use to identify a removable media drive. If that icon is embedded in a larger file, such as SHELL32.DLL, you have two choices: make a note of its position within that file, or extract it to a small single icon file. For example, to display the colorful beachball icon found in the PIFMGR.DLL file, use Notepad to write one (not both) of the two-line files shown here:

```
[autorun]
icon=C:\Windows\System\PIFMGR.DLL,7
```

or . . .

```
[autorun]
icon=filename.ico
```

Name the file AUTORUN.INF and save it to the root directory of the appropriate removable media disc or cartridge. If you've extracted the icon to a separate icon file, give it a distinctive name and save it in the same root directory. From now on, Explorer will show the distinctive icon each time that disc or cartridge is inserted in the drive. You can even use a distinctive icon on each disc or cartridge, much like what you find on most new CD-ROM discs.

One side effect must be considered: With the NoDriveTypeAutoRun value changed as previously described, Explorer searches all removable media devices, including diskette drives, and this search takes extra time. If you get impatient with the wait, reset NoDriveTypeAutoRun back to 95. Otherwise, the delay may be a worthwhile tradeoff if you need to keep visual track of multiple devices.

Hard drive icon

Under default conditions, all hard drives are represented by the same icon (SHELL32.DLL, 9 or COOL.DLL, 0 if MS Plus! is installed). To use a different icon for one hard drive only, write the two-line AUTORUN.INF file shown above and place it in the root directory of that drive. Highlight the drive and press F5 to display the new icon, which takes precedence over any other icon change made via the *Shell Icons* subkey described previously. There is no need to edit the Registry to enable this feature because the hard drive bit (3, as shown previously) is cleared by default.

Executable file default icons

All files with a COM extension display the icon specified by the filename and icon number in the *HKCR\comfile\DefaultIcon* key's Data column, as shown in the following example. A different icon can be substituted by editing the Data column to specify some other icon source file and/or icon number.

HKCR Subkey	Name	Data
comfile\DefaultIcon	(Default)	"C:\Windows\System\SHELL32.DLL,2"
exefile\DefaultIcon	(Default)	"%1"

In contrast, the replaceable parameter ("%1") shown in the above *HKCR\exefile\DefaultIcon* key's Data column icon instructs Windows to display the distinctive icon embedded within most Windows-aware executable files (*filename*.EXE). If such a file lacks its own icon (as in many zipped EXE files), then Windows displays its own default icon, which is the same one seen for all COM files. To force Windows to display a common icon for all EXE files, replace the "%1" parameter seen above with the name of the icon source file and the icon number that you want to use. When you come to your senses later on, simply revert to the replaceable parameter and hope no one noticed what you'd done.

Folder icons

All folders display the same tired-yellow closed- and open-folder icons, and as with the Registry Editor's closed- and open-folder (= "key") icons, the one lone open-folder icon is sometimes difficult to spot. But it's not as difficult to change as the procedure described earlier in the "Registry Icon Edits" section. Instead, simply add or edit the following Registry entry to specify a more distinctive open-folder icon:

HKLM\SOFTWARE\Microsoft\Windows\CurrentVersion\explorer \Shell Icons

Name	Data
4	"C:\Windows\System\SHELL32.DLL,39"

Change the file and icon number shown above as desired and refer to the "Shell Icons Key" section earlier in this chapter for more details about this Registry key.

Folder Icons on the Desktop

Although not related to the Registry, the following suggestion may be useful for customizing a desktop with many folder icons on it. Move each folder off the desktop and into the C:\ (root) directory or elsewhere. Then drag a shortcut back to the desktop for each such folder. Each shortcut icon can be customized as desired, via the "Change Icon" button accessible from that shortcut's Properties option.

Shortcut icons

The small arrow overlay icon in the lower-left corner of an object icon serves as a visual cue that the icon represents a shortcut, and not the object's own executable file. Like many other desktop icons, it's possible to change the overlay icon by following the general directions in the "Shell Icons" section earlier in this chapter.

Table 6-7 (earlier in this chapter) indicates that the default shortcut overlay icon is object number 29. To change it to something else, open the *Shell Icons* subkey (as described earlier) and add a string value whose name is the number 29. Then enter the path, filename, and icon number for a replacement overlay icon in the Data column. In Windows 95, the example in the first line in the list that follows replaces the default arrow with a larger one that, due to its placement, is visible but not as obvious as the default arrow.

Name	Data
29	C:\Windows\System\SHELL32.DLL, 30
29	C:\Icons\Shortcut.ICO

In Windows 98, the location specified above is a small circle overlay icon, and the visual difference is not as great as the Windows 95 example. If you prefer the older large arrow overlay icon, use any icon editor to extract a copy of it from the Windows 95 SHELL32.DLL file and save it into a C:\Icons folder as Shortcut.ICO. Then edit the Contents pane as shown in the second line above. Revise the line to refer to the actual location and name of the icon file you want to use.

See also the "Explorer Tab" section of the Appendix for instructions that enable you to accomplish the same task without directly editing the Registry.

Delete shortcut icons

If you'd prefer to eliminate the shortcut overlay icon entirely, search the Registry's Name column for an IsShortcut entry, which should appear in the Contents pane of the following *HKCR* subkeys:

HKCR Subkeys	File Extension
ComicChatRoomShortcut	CCR
DocShortcut	SHB
InternetShortcut	URL
lnkfile	LNK
piffile	PIF

If an IsShortcut entry is deleted, all files with the associated extension no longer display the distinctive shortcut overlay icon. When you realize later on that the little arrow really was helpful after all, rewrite the IsShortcut line to restore it.

Other Editing Techniques

The concluding section of this chapter describes a few additional Registry edits that may be used to further customize the Windows configuration.

Animated window

When a window is minimized or restored, the transition in its size may take place in one of the two ways described in the following table. In either case, the effect is controlled by a MinAnimate entry in the Contents pane of the following key:

HKEY_CURRENT_USER\ControlPanel\desktop\WindowMetrics

Onscreen Effect of Window Transition	Name	Data
Gradually collapses/expands	MinAnimate	"1"
Disappears/reappears instantaneously	MinAnimate	"0"

Edit the Data column to change from one mode to the other. If a slow video system causes a problem with animated window performance, setting the Data entry to 0 may be desirable. The Window animation checkbox on TweakUI's General tab may also be used to handle this edit (see the Appendix).

Control Panel applet access

The usual method to access a Control Panel applet is to open the Start menu, select the Settings option, select the Control Panel folder icon, and then double-click the desired icon. For faster access, open the *HKCR\cplfile\shell* key and rename the *cplopen* key to simply *open*. To open a specific Control Panel applet, select the Start menu's Run option and type the name of its CPL file into the Open box. Table 6-9 lists various applets and their associated CPL files.

Table 6-9 *Control Panel Access via Start Menu's Run Command*

Control Panel Applet	Run Command †	Win98 Tweak UI Control Panel Tab
32bit ODBC	ODBCCP.CPL	Microsoft ODBC Control Panel
Accessibility Options	ACCESS.CPL	Windows Accessibility Control Panel
Add New Hardware, System	SYSDM.CPL	System Control Panel Applet
Add/Remove Programs	APPWIZ.CPL	Add/Remove Programs
Date/Time	TIMEDATE.CPL	Time/Date Settings
Desktop Themes	THEMES.CPL	Themes Control Panel
Display	DESK.CPL	Desktop Settings
Find Fast	FINDFAST.CPL	None
Fonts	MAIN.CPL	Mouse, Keyboard, and so on
Game Controllers	JOY.CPL	Game Controller CPL Main
Hewlett-Packard JetAdmin	JETADMIN.CPL	H-P JetAdmin C. Panel . . .
Internet, Users	INETCPL.CPL	Internet Control Panel
Joy Stick	JOY.CPL	Joystick Control Panel
Keyboard	MAIN.CPL	Mouse, Keyboard, and so on
LiveUpdate	S32LUPP1.CPL	LiveUpdate Manager
Messaging Settings	MLCFG32.CPL	Microsoft Mail Configuration Library
Modem	MODEM.CPL	Modem Control Panel
Mouse	MAIN.CPL	Mouse, Keyboard, and so on
Multimedia, Sounds	MMSYS.CPL	Multimedia Shell Extensions

Continued

Table 6-9 *Continued*

Control Panel Applet	Run Command †	Win98 Tweak UI Control Panel Tab
Network	NETCPL.CPL	Network Control Panel
Password	PASSWORD.CPL	Passwords Control Panel
Power Management	POWERCFG.CPL	Power Management Configuration Control Panel
Printers	MAIN.CPL	Mouse, Keyboard, and so on
Regional Settings	INTL.CPL	Regional Settings
Scanners and Cameras	STICPL.CPL	None
System, General tab ‡	SYSDM.CPL	System Control Panel Applet
Device Manager	,,1	
Hardware Profiles	,,2	
Performance	,,3	
Telephony	TELEPHON.CPL	Microsoft Windows Telephony Control . . .
Tweak UI	TWEAKUI.CPL	User Interface customization toy
Workgroup Post Office Admin	WGPOCPL.CPL	Control Panel Applet for MS Mail Workgroup . . .

† Indicated file must be present in C:\Windows\System folder. Type **CONTROL** *filename*.**CPL** to execute.

‡ Append ,,*x* to open indicated System tab.

Drag-and-Drop print editing

As noted in Chapter 2, drag-and-drop printing is handled by the *Printto* subkey or, in its absence, by the *Print* subkey, and under most circumstances, there would be little reason to change such settings. However, if you regularly use the Notepad applet to print TXT files, you may not care for its habit of printing the name of the file at the top of the page and the page number at the bottom. If so, try the following procedure to use the WordPad applet instead.

Open the *HKCR\txtfile\shell* subkey and create new *Printto* and *Printto\command* subkeys. In the latter's (Default) Data column, enter the command line copied from the *Printto\command* subkey found under the *Wrifile\Shell* subkey. After doing this, any TXT file dragged to a printer icon is opened and printed via the WordPad applet, thus eliminating Notepad's printed header and footer. When you do want Notepad's header and footer to be included on the printed page, use the Context menu's regular Print option instead of the drag-and-drop method.

Refer to "Other Missing Options" in the Context Menu section above for information about adding this option to the menu.

Fonts list

Certain differences will be noted if the C:\Windows\Fonts folder is examined in a DOS window and again in an Explorer window. For example, although a DOS listing of hidden screen font files (DIR *.FON /AH) usually shows 18 files, only 5 of these are listed in the Explorer window, because it shows *only* those files cited in the first Registry key that follows:

HKLM\SOFTWARE\Microsoft\Windows\CurrentVersion\Fonts

HKLM\SOFTWARE\Microsoft\Windows\CurrentVersion\fontsize\ *xxx*\User

The *HKLM\...\Fonts* key lists TrueType fonts and third-party FON files (if any), but only the five FON files also found in the second key listed above, where *xxx* is either *120* or *96*. The fonts cited in the *120* key are displayed if the system is configured for large fonts, while those in the *96* key are displayed if the system is configured for small fonts. Fonts listed in the other numbered key, and in both of the equivalent *System* subkeys, are not displayed in the Explorer window, even though present in the fonts folder.

If the name of any such "missing" file is added to the *HKLM\...\Fonts* list, it is displayed the next time the fonts folder is opened in an Explorer window. To do so, add one or more new lines such as the following:

Name	Data
8514-System	8514sys.fon
DOS applications	dosapps.fon

Make sure the Name entry is suitably descriptive and does not duplicate an existing entry. After restarting Windows, the font will be listed in the Explorer window. Or to see a complete list of all FON files in the C:\Windows\fonts folder without editing the Registry, simply use the Windows Find option to search for files named *.FON. In either case, double-click the file icon to display its contents.

Internet Explorer options

The Advanced tab on the IE4 Context menu's Properties sheet provides extensive custom-configuration options, with the current status of each one recorded under the following Registry key:

HKCU\Software\Microsoft\Internet Explorer

To prevent unauthorized users from changing these settings accidentally (or on purpose), the subkey that places each option on the Advanced tab can be deleted. To do so, open the following Registry key:

HKLM\Software\Microsoft\Internet Explorer\AdvancedOptions

Each Advanced tab section has its own subkey under this key, as listed here:

Advanced Tab Section	AdvancedOptions Subkey
Accessibility	*ACCESSIBILITY*
Browsing	*BROWSE*
HTTP 1.1 settings	*HTTP*
Java VM	*JAVA_VM*
Multimedia	*MULTIMEDIA*
Printing	*PRINT*
Searching	*SEARCHING*
Security	*CRYPTO*
Toolbar	*TB*

For each option listed under one of the tab sections, an associated subkey is under the *AdvancedOptions* subkey listed above. After verifying that the current status of an option is correct, simply delete the appropriate subkey to prevent it from being changed.

"My Computer" label in Registry Editor window

As shown in Figure 6-27 and in many other illustrations throughout the book, the six Registry HKEYs appear beneath a computer icon labeled "My Computer," and that phrase also is displayed in the Status bar at the bottom of the Registry Editor window.

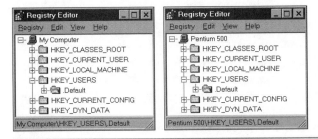

Figure 6-27 *The "My Computer" label at the top of the HKEY tree can be revised by editing the REGEDIT.EXE file.*

Because this label is embedded in the REGEDIT.EXE file, you'll need to edit that file if you want to change "My Computer" to something more descriptive of your own system. If so, make a copy of REGEDIT.EXE and then search for the phrase, which usually begins at one of the following locations:

0001A3BA   Windows 95, original retail version

00016C1A   Most Windows 95 SR versions

00019C26   Windows 98

In either case, it is written in Unicode format as shown here:

M.y. .C.o.m.p.u.t.e.r.   4D 00 79 00 20 00 43 00 6F 00 6D 00
                            70 00 75 00 74 00 65 00 72 00

Note that each letter is followed by a null character (ASCII 00), and that style must be preserved when changing "My Computer" to a new label.

Caution

Changing the "My Computer" serves no purpose other than a cosmetic one and should only be attempted by the user who is comfortable editing a binary file. The hexadecimal addresses cited above have been observed on several systems but are, of course, subject to change.

Network connections

If a network drive was mapped to a local drive letter and the "Reconnect at logon" checkbox checked when that letter was assigned, Windows expects to find that network drive every time it starts. If it is not available, a "connection not available" or "share name not found" message is displayed, along with a yes/no prompt to try again next time. If you click the No button, the connection record is deleted from the Registry. If this is a recurring problem because various network drives are frequently unavailable, yet the same set of drive mappings are regularly needed when they *are* available, set up the desired mappings and then export the *HKCU\Network\Persistent* key structure. Create a shortcut to it on the desktop, or in some other convenient location, and use that shortcut to restore lost drive mappings that become available again after Windows has opened.

Numeric tails

Although Windows supports long filenames, it always creates a conventional, or "8.3," filename for the sake of backward compatibility. The 8.3 name consists of the first six letters of the long filename, a tilde character, a number, the period separator, and the first three characters of the extension, as shown by these few examples:

Long Filename	8.3 Filename	"Friendly" 8.3 Filename
RatherLongLetter.Document	RATHER~1.DOC	RATHERLO.DOC
RatherEXTENDED.Doc	RATHER~2.DOC	RATHEREX.DOC
RatherLongmemo.txt1	RATHER~1.TXT	RATHERLO.TXT
RatherLongmemo.txt2	RATHER~2.TXT	RATHER~1.TXT
RatherLongmemo.txtfile	RATHER~3.TXT	RATHER~2.TXT

As the second column shows, a numeric tail (~1, ~2, and so on) is used to truncate a long filename to 8.3 format, even if the first eight characters of that name would be sufficient to distinguish one file from another.

An optional "friendly" naming convention may be used instead, in which the "~1" numeric tail is not used for the *first* occurrence of a long filename. Instead, the 8.3 name simply takes the first eight characters of the long filename, as shown by the examples in the third column. However, if the first eight characters are not sufficient to distinguish one name from another, then a "~1" tail is applied to the second file, a "~2" to the third, and so on.

To enable this feature, add the following entry as a binary value to the *control* subkey's Contents pane:

HKLM\System\CurrentControlSet\Control\FileSystem

Name	Data
NameNumericTail	0

Caution

Some Windows 95 documentation claims the NameNumericTail entry is not supported, and Windows 98 documentation makes no reference to it at all. However, the entry *is* supported in both Windows versions, in that the feature works as previously described. However, it's really more of a bug than a feature because some Windows applications do not recognize a long folder or filename created without the "~*x*" tail. Also, the numeric tail serves as an obvious visual clue that a long filename exists.

"Open With" dialog box

If you double-click on an unknown file type, the Open With dialog box lets you choose the program you want to use. It's easy to forget to clear the "Always use" checkbox if you don't want the association to be permanent. To permanently clear the default checkmark, open the following key:

HKCR\Unknown\shell\OpenAs\command

Double-click the (Default) entry in the Contents pane and then add a space and a %2 immediately after the %1 at the end of the Value data line. Exit the Registry, and the next time you double-click an unknown file type, the "Always use" checkbox will be clear.

Password length

By default a password must be three or more characters long. To require each user to create a longer password, edit the following Registry key to add the DWORD Data entry shown here:

HKLM\SOFTWARE\Microsoft\Windows\CurrentVersion\Policies\Network

Name	MinPwdLen
Data	*XX*

Replace *xx* with the new minimum length and remember the entered value is by default hexadecimal. So a minimum length of 10 means 16 decimal characters are required. To guard against hex/decimal accidents, click the Decimal radio button before entering the Value data.

Popup messages

As the mouse pointer hovers over various desktop objects or buttons, a popup box may describe the item under the pointer. If you find such distractions annoying, you can edit the Registry to disable the feature. Or you can add a popup messages to certain desktop objects that don't display one by default, or you can edit the message that does appear. Refer to one of the following sections for the appropriate instructions.

InfoTip

If an InfoTip entry is present in the Name column of a *CLSID* key's Contents pane, the Data column shows the text displayed in a popup box when the mouse hovers over the selected item on the desktop, or in an Explorer window's Contents pane. The following Registry edit disables the feature:

HKCU\Software\Microsoft\Windows\CurrentVersion\Explorer \Advanced

Name	Data
ShowInfoTip	0x00000000 (0)

Refer to the "Windows 98 and IE4 General and View Tab Data" section above and to Table 6-4 for details about this Registry key and how to make the edit from the Folder Options View tab.

To revise an existing InfoTip, search the Registry's Data column for a phrase from the existing tip and then edit the text in the Data column. To add a tip to an object that doesn't already have one, search the Data column for that object name and then add an InfoTip entry with the text you want to display.

ToolTip

Not unlike the InfoTip described previously, the ToolTip feature displays a popup explanation if the mouse hovers over a Minimize, Restore, or Close button, and this popup text can be disabled by editing a data flag in the *HKCU\Control Panel\Desktop* key's UserPreferenceMask entry. Although this feature is a mouse-related function, it may be edited via TweakUI's General (not Mouse) tab. Because the same entry affects many other user preferences, refer to the "General Tab" section of the Appendix and to Table A-4 for assistance in editing this key.

Part IV

Troubleshooting

Chapter 7

Troubleshooting Techniques

Anecdotal evidence suggests that the Windows Registry team may have included someone named Edsel Murphy, so it's safe to state that if anything can go wrong here, it will. And although all those anythings have not yet been uncovered, this chapter takes a look at a few that have turned up — some quite unexpectedly — while writing this opus.

Because Registry troubleshooting often requires access to Registry backup files, the chapter begins with a review of these files and the means to retrieve them independently of Windows' own automatic procedures, which are also briefly reviewed. This review is followed by a discussion of troubleshooting aids and general problem-solving suggestions, and then a look at some specific troubleshooting scenarios, both within and beyond the Registry itself.

If a suspected Registry problem announces itself with an error message, you may want to refer to Chapter 8 first, to see if that message is listed there. Otherwise, dig in here and look for either a specific solution or a technique that can be modified to resolve the problem.

Working with the Windows Registry Files

Because most of the general and specific troubleshooting procedures in this chapter have a direct impact on the Registry files, this section offers a review of those files and describes some basic techniques for working with them.

Registry file review

The Registry files were described in detail in Chapter 4 and listed in Table 4-1, while Registry backup files were covered in Chapter 5. For aid in surviving a Registry troubleshooting session, that information is briefly reviewed here. For more information, refer back to Chapters 4 or 5.

File	Location	Attributes	Contents
Windows 95			
SYSTEM.DAT	C:\Windows	S H R	HKEY_LOCAL_MACHINE key
SYSTEM.DA0	C:\Windows	S H R	Most recent valid backup of SYSTEM.DAT
USER.DAT	C:\Windows	S H R	HKEY_CURRENT_USER
USER.DA0	C:\Windows	S H R	Most recent valid backup of USER.DAT
Windows 98			
SYSTEM.DAT	C:\Windows	H R	HKEY_LOCAL_MACHINE key
USER.DAT †	C:\Windows	H R	HKEY_CURRENT_USER
Windows 95 and 98			
SYSTEM.1ST ‡	C:\	S H R	SYSTEM.DAT copy, created at successful conclusion of initial Windows setup procedure and not updated
USER.1ST	None	–	There is no USER.1ST equivalent to the SYSTEM.1ST file

† On a system configured for multiple users, each C:\Windows\Profiles*username* folder contains a USER.DAT and USER.DA0 for that user. See Chapter 4 for details.
‡ System attribute not set in Windows 98.

.DA0 files

These copies of the equivalent .DAT files were made the last time Windows 95 opened successfully and are therefore presumed to be replicas of the most recent valid Registry. Remember that Registry files with this extension appear in Windows 95 *only*. In Windows 98, Registry backups are stored in the five RB00*x*.CAB files, as described in Chapter 5.

Additional backup files

If a minor Registry file problem escapes detection the next time Windows opens, that problem will be copied into the newest set of backup files, and therefore will be transferred back to the Registry later on, if those backups are put to use. Because such minor problems did not cause trouble previously, with luck they won't cause trouble later either. However, there's always the possibility that a series of harmless little bugs will eventually merge into something big and unpleasant. Therefore, before doing any serious Registry troubleshooting, you may wish to make an additional set of backup files with, say, DA1 extensions for use in case the original DAT files and Windows' own backups become defective. If you follow the Windows 95 naming convention (.DA1, .DA2, and so on), then the file attributes will be set/reset automatically if the ATTRIBS.BAT batch file (described below) is used.

SYSTEM.1ST file

This file contains a copy of the *HKEY_LOCAL_MACHINE* key configuration only and is created as part of the initial Windows setup procedure. The file is a "baseline" reference of the initial hardware configuration, but it is not updated as subsequent changes are made to the system.

File attributes

Note that all these files have their hidden and read-only attributes set (plus the system attribute in Windows 95), and they are therefore not seen in a conventional MS-DOS mode directory listing.

In any Registry troubleshooting session, it often becomes necessary to copy, rename, or erase one or more of these files, and in order to do so, these attributes must first be cleared. The most convenient way to do this is in the MS-DOS mode for two reasons:

- After making any change, it will be necessary to restart Windows anyway, so there's no real point to working on the files from within the Windows GUI (graphical user interface).

- Although each file's attributes can be viewed via the file's Properties sheet, the system attribute cannot be cleared, as may be noted by the disabled System checkbox shown in Figure 7-1.

In the discussion that follows, whenever it is suggested that a certain Registry file be copied, renamed, or deleted, it is assumed that its attributes have first been cleared so that the operation can be performed and that the attributes will be reset later. To do so, follow the instructions given here.

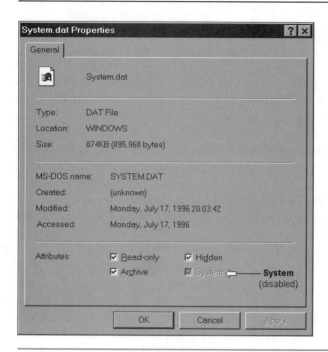

Figure 7-1 *The status of the system attribute can be verified but not changed via the General tab on a file's Properties sheet. To clear the attribute, type **ATTRIB** **filename.ext** **-s** at an MS-DOS command prompt.*

Clear file attributes At the MS-DOS command prompt, type one of the following lines, as appropriate. Windows 98 users should omit the system attribute (-s and later, +s).

Command Line	Clears Attributes For
attrib -s -h -r C:\Windows\SYSTEM.DAT	SYSTEM.DAT only
attrib -s -h -r C:\Windows\SYSTEM.DA?	SYSTEM.DAT and SYSTEM.DAO
attrib -s -h -r C:\Windows\USER.DAT	USER.DAT only
attrib -s -h -r C:\Windows\USER.DA?	USER.DAT and USER.DAO
attrib -s -h -r C:\Windows*.DA?	All files with any three-character extension (DAT, DAO, possibly others)
attrib -s -h -r C:\SYSTEM.1ST	SYSTEM.1ST (in C:\ directory)

Reset file attributes To restore the file attributes to their default state, retype the appropriate line, but replace each minus sign with a plus sign, as shown in these two examples:

Command Line	Resets Attributes For
attrib +s +h +r C:\Windows\SYSTEM.DA?	SYSTEM.DAT and SYSTEM.DAO
attrib +s +h +r C:\Windows*.DA?	All files with any three-character extension (DAT, DAO, possibly others)

Use the second line (*.DA?) with care, though, because it will set the attributes for all files with a DAT extension, such as C:\Windows\TTY.DAT and any other DAT file that resides in the same folder. It's unlikely that such files will function properly if their attributes are incorrectly set.

Attributes batch file If you frequently use the ATTRIB command to clear and set file attributes, the following batch file automates the process:

ATTRIBS.BAT File	Comments (not part of batch file)
goto %ATTRIBS%	Go to :SET or to :CLEAR, as appropriate.
:CLEAR	Attributes are currently cleared.
attrib +s +h +r C:\Windows\SYSTEM.DA?	Set SYSTEM.DA? attributes.
attrib +s +h +r C:\Windows\User.DA?	Set USER.DA? attributes.
set ATTRIBS=SET	Set ATTRIBS to indicate set attributes.
goto END	Bypass next section.
:SET	Attributes are currently set.
attrib -s -h -r C:\Windows\SYSTEM.DA?	Clear SYSTEM.DA? attributes.
attrib -s -h -r C:\Windows\User.DA?	Clear USER.DA? attributes
set ATTRIBS=CLEAR	Set ATTRIBS to indicate cleared attributes.
:END	End batch file.

Before running the batch file the first time, type **SET ATTRIBS=SET** at the command prompt, assuming the attributes are indeed set. When the batch file is run, the SET environment variable is detected, and program execution jumps to the :SET section, where the attributes are cleared and the environment variable is changed to CLEAR to indicate the new status.

The next time the file is run, the CLEAR variable is detected, and the attributes are again reset. At each subsequent run, the attributes toggle between set and clear. In Windows 98, omit the +s and -s attributes and use .DAT instead of .DA?, because there are no .DA0 files to be considered.

Windows 95 Registry file replacement

If there is a problem with the SYSTEM.DAT file, Windows 95 usually creates a new version by copying the backup SYSTEM.DA0 file that, as noted previously, was created at the conclusion of the most recent successful startup and should therefore be the best available recovery medium. There are times, however, when it copies the SYSTEM.1ST file instead, as, for example, if both SYSTEM.DAT *and* USER.DAT are corrupt. Although there is no explicit warning that SYSTEM.1ST has been used, the opening desktop reverts to its original appearance, and some shortcuts may not function.

The general appearance of the desktop should be sufficient warning that things are not quite the way they should be. But to verify the problem, exit Windows 95 and compare the size of the SYSTEM.DAT file with the SYSTEM.1ST file in the C:\ (root) directory.

On a typical system, the normal SYSTEM.DAT file is two to five times the size of the SYSTEM.1ST file. If however, SYSTEM.DAT is very close in size to SYSTEM.1ST, that's a definite clue that it was recently reconstructed from SYSTEM.1ST. If you have a recent valid backup copy of your previous SYSTEM.DAT file on hand, you may want to erase this newly created copy and replace it with the backup version.

Although there is no equivalent USER.1ST file, it's a pretty safe bet that the existing USER.DAT file is also not up to date. Many Windows applications write important configuration data into this file and will have to be reinstalled unless this information can be recovered from a valid backup version.

Windows 98 Registry file replacement

If SYSTEM.DAT and/or USER.DAT are corrupted or missing, Windows 98 retrieves a new set from the most recent RB00*x*.CAB file, as described in Chapter 5, and therefore does not make use of the SYSTEM.1ST file, as described in the *Windows 95* section immediately above.

Registry file comparison

If a Registry key structure is suspected of being incomplete, damaged, or otherwise invalid, it may be worthwhile to check the same key on another system known to be in good working order. Depending on the specific key, it may be possible to export the valid key from machine A, then erase the invalid key on machine B, and import the machine A version. Of course, this won't work if the key is associated with a specific hardware or software configuration that is not identical on both systems.

Other file replacement

If any non-Registry file cited in the Registry is damaged or missing, that file must, of course, be replaced with a valid copy. In the case of both versions of Window and many other applications distributed on CD-ROM disc, such files are compressed into CAB (cabinet) files similar to the ones used for Windows 98 backup sets. Therefore, the CAB file that contains the required file must first be found so that the file can be extracted, as briefly summarized here.

File finding

Because each CAB file also contains an uncompressed list of its contents, the Windows Explorer can be used to locate the desired CAB file. Select the Tool menu's Find Files or Folders option and enter the following information in the indicated boxes:

Tab	Box	Enter	Comments
Windows 95			
Name & Location	Named:	***.CAB**	Search all CAB files.
	Look in:	*x*:\Win95	CD-ROM drive letter, path
Advanced	Containing text:	*Filename.ext*	Name of desired file
Windows 98			
Name & Location	Named:	***.CAB**	Search all CAB files.
	Containing text:	*Filename.ext*	Name of desired file
	Look in:	*x*:\Win98	CD-ROM drive letter, path
Advanced	Not required for this search		

Note that although a conventional global file search (*.CAB = all files with the CAB extension) is valid, the Containing text: box does not support the use of the asterisk as a global filename (*.TXT = all files with TXT extension, for example). To find all files with a specific extension, omit the asterisk and enter the period and extension only.

File extraction

If the Windows 95 PowerToys CabView utility has been installed, a View option should appear on any CAB file's Context menu. The same option appears by default in Windows 98. If this option is selected, an Explorer window opens to display the compressed files within that CAB file. Highlight one or more files, open the Context menu, and select the single Extract option. Specify the location in which to expand the files and click the OK button to complete the process. If any selected file already exists in the specified location, it will be overwritten without a warning notice. You may therefore wish to expand the files into a C:\TEMP (or similar) location if you want to compare them with the existing version before making a final replacement.

To extract a file in a one-step find/extract operation, use the Extract utility (EXTRACT.EXE) in the C:\Windows\Command folder instead. Open an MS-DOS window, type **EXTRACT** for a list of command-line switches, and then type **EXTRACT** again, followed by the necessary switches. For example, type one of the following lines to extract SHELL32.DLL from an unknown CAB file:

Windows 95: **EXTRACT /A D:\WIN95\WIN95_02.CAB /E**
            SHELL32.DLL /L C:\TEMP

Windows 98: **EXTRACT /A D:\WIN98\WIN98_22.CAB /E**
            SHELL32.DLL /L C:\TEMP

The command lines shown here mean: sequentially search all (/A) CAB files, beginning with x:\WIN95\WIN95_02.CAB (Windows 95) or x:\WIN98\WIN98_22.CAB (Windows 98), and extract (/E) the SHELL32.DLL file into the location (/L) C:\TEMP. In this example, the CD-ROM is drive D, the desired file is eventually found (it's in WIN95_13.CAB or WIN98_38.CAB), and a copy is extracted into the C:\TEMP directory. If the file already exists in the specified location, an "Overwrite?" prompt is displayed.

Note

The many CAB filenames in the Windows 98 folder begin with Base . . . , Driver . . . , Net . . . , and of course, WIN98__ . . . , so a search that starts at WIN98_22.CAB (the first file in this series) may not turn up the desired file. If it doesn't, then use Explorer to search all CAB files (*.CAB) for the desired file, as described at the beginning of this section.

Safe mode and the CD-ROM drive

If a troubleshooting session requires you to open Windows in its Safe mode, remember that a minimal set of drivers are loaded and the CD-ROM drive won't be available. Therefore, if you need to run the Policy Editor utility (described in Chapter 4) or extract files from a CAB file on the Windows CD-ROM disc, you must boot with real-mode CD-ROM drive support in your CONFIG.SYS and AUTOEXEC.BAT files. To obviate the need to do this, copy POLEDIT.EXE and ADMIN.ADM to a diskette while the CD-ROM drive is available, for subsequent use when it is not.

The Windows 95 and 98 Resource Kits

The online versions of the resource kits are found in the following locations:

Version	Location	Files
Windows 95	\admin\Reskit\Helpfile	WIN95RK.HLP, WIN95RK.CNT
Windows 98	\tools\reskit\help	WIN98RK.HLP, WIN98RK.CNT, RK98BOOK.CHM

Either resource kit may be of some help in Registry troubleshooting sessions, and of course is also useful for problems not related to the Registry. For convenience, you may want to copy the WIN95RK.HLP and WIN95RK.CNT files into the C:\Windows\Help folder to make them available at all times. Because the *Windows 98 Resource Kit* is more extensive, refer to either of the identical README.DOC files in the \reskit and \reskit\help folders for further details. Note however, that the resource kit version on the Windows 98 CD is a sampler. You'll need to purchase the *Windows 98 Resource Kit* book (with accompanying CD) if you want the full-featured online version. However, both versions do include the same RK98BOOK.CHM (compiled HTML) file.

Figure 7-2 shows the Find Setup Wizard dialog box that is displayed the first time the Find tab is selected in Windows 95 or the Windows 98 sampler version. The Find option is not supported in the full version of the *Windows 98 Resource Kit*.

Figure 7-2 *The Find Setup Wizard proposes a minimum sized database. Accept or change the option, then click on the Next and Finish (not shown) buttons to complete the operations. The Creating Word List... status window shown in the inset appears while the STF file is being created.*

Note that "Minimize database size (recommended)" is enabled and — unless changed — will be applied when the Next and Finish buttons are clicked to create a WIN9xRK.FTS (Full-Text Search) file in the C:\Windows\Help (Windows 95) or the C:\Program Files\Win98RK (Windows 98) folder. If you subsequently need a more comprehensive search database, click the Rebuild button and select one of the other options shown in the figure. After clicking the "Customize" button, you can enable or disable each of the following options:

- Include untitled topics
- Include phrase searching
- Display matching phrases
- Support similarity searches

The new WIN9xRK.FTS file will be considerably larger, and searches will take longer but be more comprehensive. If you decide searches are too long and/or too comprehensive, click the Rebuild button once again and restore the minimal database.

The Find tab is not always the most reliable way to find something though, due to its case-sensitivity and Microsoft's erratic spelling practices. For example, a Windows 95 search for "HK" finds "HKEY_Current_User", "HKLM", "HKR", and seven topics only. In the Windows 98 sampler, the same search finds only "HKEY_USERS" and, as an added bonus, a definition of "hive" that doesn't apply to Windows 98.

General Troubleshooting Techniques

This section describes some procedures that may be useful during a troubleshooting session, regardless of the specific nature of the problem. If a Registry problem of uncertain origin occurs on a system configured for multiple users, it may be worthwhile to exit and ask some other user to log on and check for the same problem. If it no longer exists, then it is probably confined to the *HKEY_CURRENT_USER* section of the Registry, which is different for each user. However, if the problem is common to other users too, then it may be traced to *HKEY_LOCAL_MACHINE* instead.

Manual Registry recovery procedures

Windows is usually quite good about finding minor problems as it opens and, if necessary, restoring the Registry from one of the backup sets. However, sometimes a problem is so severe that the normal detection mechanisms don't function, and Windows tries to open despite severe Registry corruption. Even Windows 98 has problems here: Although it can detect the absence of the SYSTEM.DAT or USER.DAT file and retrieve a valid backup set, it has been found to ignore an accidental deletion of the complete *HKCR\CLSID* key structure — typically, some 500 Kbytes of data. In this case, startup gets as far as opening the Windows GUI, after which an "Illegal Operation" message is displayed, and the system halts.

Assuming the actual cause for such an opening message is unknown, exit Windows and reboot the system. Press F8 to display the StartUp menu, select the Command prompt option, and follow the appropriate steps described here.

Windows 95

Compare the SYSTEM.DA0 and USER.DA0 file sizes with the present SYSTEM.DAT and USER.DAT files. If the files are identical, then the DA0 backups are probably corrupted, too. But if not, there's a reasonable chance they're in good shape. If that's a possibility, rename the DAT files as SYSTEM.BAD and USER.BAD. Then make copies of the DA0 files as SYSTEM.DAT and USER.DAT and reboot the system. If all goes well, Windows 95 will open successfully. If not, you'll have to face up to reinstalling it.

Note

Before starting an extensive Windows 95 troubleshooting session, it may be worthwhile to copy the existing SYSTEM.DAT and USER.DAT files and then use the Nico Mak WinZip utility (or similar) to store them in compressed format, at about 25 percent of their uncompressed size. In fact, Windows 98 stores multiple compressed Registry backups, as described in the next section.

Windows 98

It's a reasonable assumption that the DAT files in the most recent RB00*x*.CAB file are also corrupt, because Windows failed to recognize the problem on its own and may therefore have saved the damaged Registry files as it attempted to open. However, if the recent problem occurred after the system had successfully started at least once on the same day, then this backup set may be good. If in doubt, note the file creation time. If it's quite recent, then the files within it are probably defective, too. Or to eliminate all guesswork, save the existing Registry files with BAD extensions, then extract the DAT files from the backup set that was made on the previous day, and restart Windows. Unless there's some very serious system malfunction, Windows 98 should once again open successfully.

Restriction recovery procedures

If a "Restrictions" message precludes a certain operation, one of the Registry's *Policies* subkeys probably contains an entry that must be removed in order to clear the restriction. If this restriction has been imposed by a system administrator, then, of course, that person should be consulted about lifting the restriction. Otherwise, try one of the following procedures, which are listed in order of difficulty (with the easiest first).

System Policy Editor

If no *Run* restrictions prevent its use, run the System Policy Editor utility (POLEDIT.EXE), which is in the following location on the Windows CD-ROM disc:

Windows 95   *x*:\admin\apptools\poledit

Windows 98   *x*:\tools\reskit\netadmin\poledit

Or use a diskette copy if one is available. In either case, open the Shell or System Restrictions book icon and clear the restrictions.

Refer to the "System Policy Editor" section of Chapter 4 for further details about this utility. Or if you can't run it to remove a restriction, try the following procedures in the order listed here.

RECOVER.INF file

Create the RECOVER.INF file as follows:

```
[version]
signature="$CHICAGO$"

[DefaultInstall]
DelReg=Recover

[Recover]
HKCU, Software\Microsoft\Windows\CurrentVersion\Policies,
HKCU, Software\Microsoft\Windows\CurrentVersion\Policies
      \System,
HKCU, Software\Microsoft\Windows\CurrentVersion\Policies
      \Explorer, NoRun,
```

The three lines shown in the [Recover] section do the following:

1. Delete the *Policies* key and all its subkeys, thereby lifting all restrictions.

2. Delete the *System* subkey under the *Policies* key to reenable the Registry Editor.

3. Delete the NoRun restriction only (remove Run command).

Write one of these lines (or similar) into the [Recover] section and then save the file as RECOVER.INF. Open its Context menu and select the Install option, which deletes the specified subkey or individual restriction.

If a restriction prevents you from following this procedure, continue reading here. Or refer to the "INF File as a Registry Editor" section of Chapter 4 for further details about using such a file to edit the Registry.

Real-mode recovery

Create the following Registry file, whose two-dword:00000000 lines remove the restriction on running applications and also reenable the Registry Editor (RestrictRun and DisableRegistryTools, respectively).

```
REGEDIT4

[HKEY_CURRENT_USER\Software\Microsoft\Windows
\CurrentVersion\Policies\Explorer]
"RestrictRun"=dword:00000000

[HKEY_CURRENT_USER\Software\Microsoft\Windows
\CurrentVersion\Policies\System]
"DisableRegistryTools"=dword:00000000
```

Save the file as RECOVER.REG, restart Windows in MS-DOS mode (reboot if necessary), log onto the C:\Windows directory, and type the following command line:

REGEDIT RECOVER.REG

This command imports the above Registry file and clears the restrictions cited previously. You can now open Windows and run the Policy Editor or the Registry Editor to clear any other restrictions that are still in place.

Alternative real-mode recovery

If your version of the real-mode Registry Editor supports the /D switch (see "REGEDIT Command Line Switches" in Chapter 4 and Figure 4-15), the following command line deletes the entire *Policies* key structure, thus removing all restrictions:

REGEDIT /d HKEY_CURRENT_USER\Software\Microsoft \Windows\CurrentVersion\Policies

To limit restriction removals to a narrower area, add the name of a subkey (*Explorer* or *Network*, for example) after the *Policies* key at the end of the line above.

Safe-mode recovery

As one more alternative, if the Registry Editor itself has not been restricted by a DisableRegistryTools line, open Windows in Safe mode and run the Registry Editor to clear some or all restrictions.

Recovery on multi-user system

On a system configured for multiple users, each user's custom USER.DAT file is located in the C:\Windows\Profiles*UserName* folder, as described in the "USER.DAT [HKEY_USERS]" section of Chapter 4. Therefore, if restrictions have been imposed on a specific user, those restrictions are written into that user's own USER.DAT file, *not* into the one residing in the C:\Windows folder. Although this file can be edited as described above, additional factors must be taken into consideration, as described here.

The System policy file On a multi-user system, user-specific restrictions are written into a system policy file, whose path and filename are probably similar to the following:

C:\Windows\CONFIG.POL

When the user logs on, the restrictions in CONFIG.POL are written into the Registry, thus resetting any restrictions that were lifted by editing the user's USER.DAT file during or after the previous Windows session. Therefore, restriction recovery is a three-step process, as summarized here:

1. Remove current restrictions from the USER.DAT file.

2. Disable CONFIG.POL, so restrictions are not reset when user logs on.

3. Reenable and edit CONFIG.POL to permanently remove restrictions.

The following sections give more details about each of these steps.

Step 1. Remove current restrictions Exit Windows to MS-DOS mode — by rebooting if necessary. Log on to the appropriate C:\Windows\Profiles*UserName* directory, clear the USER.DAT file's attributes, and copy it to the C:\ (root) directory (*not* into the C:\Windows directory). This is necessary so that the following command does not exceed the 128-character limit. Then type the following as one continuous line at the command prompt:

REGEDIT /R:C:\USER.DAT / EC:\FIXIT.REG HKEY_USERS\
Software\Microsoft\Windows\CurrentVersion\Policies

The command tells REGEDIT that (/R) the USER.DAT file is in the C:\ directory, that part of it is to be exported (/E) into a new file named FIXIT.REG, and the specific key to be exported is *HKEY_USERS\\ ...\Policies*. See the "REGEDIT Command-Line Switches" section near the end of Chapter 4, for more details on these switches and note that the *UserName,* which usually is displayed in the key path — HKEY_USERS\ John\Software\..., for example — is omitted here.

Having done that, open FIXIT.REG in any ASCII text editor to review the *Policies* key and the subkeys that contain the current restrictions. Find the restriction(s) you wish to lift and change the expression following the equal sign from dword:00000001 to dword:00000000 — or do a global search-and-replace if you want to clean the entire set of restrictions. Now type the following line at the command prompt to import the edited FIXIT.REG back into the USER.DAT file, thus clearing the restrictions:

REGEDIT /R:C:\USER.DAT C:\FIXIT.REG

The C:\USER.DAT file is now clear of restrictions and ready to be copied back into its original location. To do so, clear its attributes and copy it into your C:\Windows\Profiles*UserName* directory where it overwrites the original version. Then reset the attributes and erase the version in the C:\ directory (or don't erase it if you think you might need it again).

Step 2. Disable CONFIG.POL Temporarily rename the CONFIG. POL file as CONFIG.OLD to prevent the restrictions from being reimposed and log on with your user name and password. Ignore the "Unable to update configuration" message, and Windows should open without the previous restrictions.

Step 3. Reenable and edit CONFIG.POL Rename CONFIG. OLD back to its original CONFIG.POL name. Because the file still contains the old restrictions, run the System Policy Editor to remove them, and thus prevent history from repeating itself.

DLL file check

If you suspect a problem related to a DLL file, open the following Registry key and then check the subkeys listed here:

HKEY_LOCAL_MACHINE\System\CurrentControlSet\control \SessionManager

CheckVerDLLs	KnownDLLs
Known16DLLs	WarnVerDLLS

As noted in Chapter 3, a Windows application is *supposed* to check its own DLL files against those listed here, but it (or you) may have accidentally replaced a valid DLL file with another version, usually — but not always — older. If you find a suspect DLL file listed in one of the previously listed keys, check the version, date, and location of the file on your system against the same file in the appropriate Windows CAB file. If the latter is a later version, rename the current DLL file as *filename.*OLD and extract a fresh copy of the CAB file version into the same location, which is probably C:\Windows\System. Also review "Known16DLLs" in the "System and CurrentControlSet" section of in Chapter 3 for information about how Windows searches for 16-bit DLL files.

Registry key replacement

A problem caused by a missing or defective key may sometimes be resolved by importing a valid version of the same key, which is easy enough to do if that key had been saved prior to the problem. If not, use the Registry Editor in real mode to export the desired key structure from a backup copy of the Registry that is known (or at least, hoped) to be good. Then delete the suspected bad key, import the replacement version, and reopen Windows. Refer to the "Registry Editor in Real Mode" section of Chapter 4 for further details.

System restart procedures

If a troubleshooting procedure requires a Registry edit, the effect of that edit usually occurs immediately, although at times it is necessary to close and reopen Windows for it to be implemented. In such cases, it is often possible to save a bit of time by pressing the Ctrl+Alt+Delete keys instead of going through the usual Windows shutdown/restart routine. When the Close Program window is displayed, highlight the Explorer line, click the End Task button, and when the "Explorer . . . is not responding" dialog box is displayed, click the End Task button again. If the regular "Shut Down Windows" dialog box appears during this procedure, just click its No button. The desktop icons momentarily disappear and then reappear, and the recent Registry edit should now have taken effect. If not, it is necessary to go through an actual shutdown/restart procedure. In a few cases, it's even necessary to do an actual reboot, if a system hardware reset is required. If you're not sure about any of this, then the reboot procedure, of course, removes all doubt that the system has been given every opportunity to implement the edit.

Startup troubleshooting

In any troubleshooting session, the first order of business is to get Windows to open successfully on its own so that the effect of a Registry edit or other action can be evaluated and revised if necessary. But for those times when Windows can't get itself up and running without a little user assistance, this section describes a few procedures that may help get Windows underway.

MSDOS.SYS file problem

If multiple error messages are displayed as the Windows GUI opens and there is no logical explanation for them, it's possible that the MSDOS.SYS file is corrupted. Among the messages may be "Registry/configuration error," even though the Registry is not in fact damaged. If you suspect an MSDOS.SYS file problem, clear its hidden, system, and read-only attributes and then use the EDIT.COM utility in the C:\Windows\Command folder to examine it. The file should begin with the following section:

```
[Paths]
WinDir=C:\Windows
WinBootDir=C:\Windows
HostWinBootDrv=C
```

The first two lines must specify the folder where Windows is located (by default, C:\Windows), and the third line specifies the boot drive letter (note the absence of a colon following the drive letter). If any of these lines are missing or incorrect, Windows gets thoroughly confused as it attempts to open, which accounts for the misleading error messages. Make the necessary corrections, reset the file attributes, and reboot the system.

System shut down (or other problem) after displaying splash screen

After some configuration changes, a message advises that "You must restart your computer before the new settings will take effect. Do you want to restart your computer now?" The restart is required because Windows needs to execute a routine specified in the *HKLM\ ... \RunOnce* key (see the complete key structure later in this section) or make some other configuration adjustment. Windows may fail to reopen if a problem arises here, and it may even display the "It's now safe to turn off your computer" message — which is about all you can do at this point. On some systems with advanced power management, the computer may be powered off automatically, or some other unpredictable behavior may occur. If there's no obvious solution to the problem, try the following procedures in the sequence given here, until the problem is resolved:

1. **Boot from a startup diskette.** Just to rule out the slight possibility of a coincidental PC hardware problem, boot from a diskette to the DOS command prompt and try a few routine DOS commands, such as a directory listing, a file copy operation, and so on. It's unlikely, but a problem at this level must be resolved before continuing.

2. **Verify the VMM32.VXD file.** This file should be in the C:\Windows\System folder, and the startup problem may occur if it's missing or corrupted. If this is a possibility, extract a fresh replacement copy from the Windows CD-ROM.

3. Resolve WININIT file problems. A more likely culprit is a WININIT.INI file in the C:\Windows folder and a missing or damaged WININIT.EXE file. If you find the former, it probably contains one or more lines such as the following:

```
[rename]

C:\WINDOWS\SYSTEM\comctl32.BAK=C:\WINDOWS
\SYSTEM\comctl32.DLL

C:\WINDOWS\SYSTEM\comctl32.DLL=C:\WINDOWS
\SYSTEM\comctl32.001
```

In this example (and reading from right to left), line 1 renames the current COMCTL32.DLL file as COMCTL32.BAK, and line 2 renames the software supplier's replacement COMCTL32.001 as COMCTL32.DLL, so that it takes the place of the former file. The action takes place as the system restarts after a software installation, and the WININIT.INI file should be renamed as WININIT.BAK at the successful conclusion of the procedure. But if the file still exists with an INI extension, something went wrong during the startup procedure, and its presence is now the source of the failure. Rename the file as WININIT.BAK or give it some other extension if a previous WININIT.BAK is present. If necessary, rename all the files cited in the [rename] section back to their original extensions and review the section that follows before doing anything else.

4. Delete the Registry's *RunOnce* and *RunServicesOnce* keys. As part of the software reconfiguration procedure, Windows may have written one or more command lines in either key, which should have been executed once and then deleted. Chances are they were deleted even if the operation failed, but it's worth checking. Use the Registry Editor in real mode to export and then delete the *RunOnce* key, by typing the following two command lines at the DOS command prompt:

```
REGEDIT /E C:\TEMP\RUNONCE.REG
HKEY_LOCAL_MACHINE\SOFTWARE\Microsoft\Windows
\CurrentVersion\RunOnce
```

and . . .

```
REGEDIT /D
HKEY_LOCAL_MACHINE\SOFTWARE\Microsoft\Windows
\CurrentVersion\RunOnce
```

Type each command (from REGEDIT ... to ... \RunOnce) as one continuous line and press the Enter key at the end of each line. The first line saves the present *RunOnce* key into a file named RUNONCE.REG, and the second line removes the key from the Registry. Repeat the procedure for the *RunServicesOnce* key, too. After doing so, Windows should open properly if the problem was indeed a function of the *RunOnce* or *RunServicesOnce* keys or of the WININIT.EXE/WININIT.INI files described in the previous section. If so, import the keys back into the Registry and examine their contents. An executable file cited in the Contents pane may be corrupted or missing, so it's probably worth expanding a fresh copy from the distribution desk. Then delete the keys again.

5. **Examine the WIN.INI and SYSTEM.INI files.** Open WIN.INI in the EDIT.COM utility (in the C:\Windows\Command folder) and disable the Load= and Run= lines, but only if an unknown item is on either line. If possible, verify no problems are in the [386Enh] section of SYSTEM.INI. Because this check is apt to be inconclusive, use a backup SYSTEM.INI file if one is available.

6. **Uninstall the problem software.** If the above procedures resolved the startup problem, there's a very good chance that the software application that started this mess is improperly installed. Now's a good time to uninstall it and leave it uninstalled for a few days to see if any other problems surface. If not, reinstall it if you're feeling adventurous.

7. **Reinstall Windows.** If you're still reading this section, it's unfortunately time to reinstall Windows.

Post startup problem

If the Windows desktop opens successfully, yet a problem of unknown origin is immediately apparent, there's a very good chance it's caused by an application that automatically launches during startup. If no obvious clues identify the culprit, press the Ctrl+Alt+Del keys to display the Close Program window that lists all currently running programs, as shown in Figure 7-3. Although it's certainly possible to highlight an item on the list and click the Shut Down button to close it, that may or may not resolve the problem. If it does, so much the better: just repair — or get rid of — the offending item, and the problem is solved. But if this procedure doesn't yield results, the next step is to disable the StartUp and/or Run key groups described below. If deleting one of these groups resolves the problem, then use the following binary search technique to determine the specific item within that group that needs to be repaired.

Delete half the items in either list. If that resolves the problem, restore half of the deleted items. If it doesn't, then restore them all and delete half the items that weren't deleted on the first attempt. Keep attacking the list by halves until the single culprit is identified.

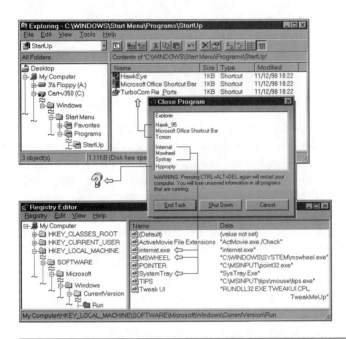

Figure 7-3 *The Close Program window in the middle of this composite illustration lists programs currently running. As indicated by the various lines and arrows, some are loaded via the StartUp group, others via the HKLM\...\Run key, and the origin of one (Hppropty) is uncertain.*

StartUp group It's quite easy to eliminate all these suspects. Just hold down the Shift key as Windows opens and the StartUp group is bypassed. If this resolves the problem, then open the StartUp folder and use the binary procedure described previously to find the problem application. But if the problem remains even when the entire StartUp group is disabled, then continue reading here.

The Run and RunServices key groups Most applications listed in the Close Program window that are not part of the StartUp group are listed in one of the following Registry keys:

HKCU\Software\Microsoft\Windows\CurrentVersion\Run

HKLM\SOFTWARE\Microsoft\Windows\CurrentVersion\Run

HKLM\SOFTWARE\Microsoft\Windows\CurrentVersion\RunServices

If necessary, export the *HKCU* key, then delete it and restart Windows. If this resolves the problem, reimport the key and again follow the binary procedure described previously. If it doesn't, export and delete either of the *HKLM* keys and repeat the procedure. Finally, export and delete the remaining *HKLM* key if the problem is still not resolved.

As an alternative to deleting one of these keys after exporting it, a semicolon may be placed at the head of any Data line entry to disable it.

Other startup applications If the Startup group is bypassed and the keys cited above are deleted, the Close Program window should show a single "Explorer" entry that is, of course, the Windows Explorer itself. However, it may show one or more other items such as the "Hppropty" item also seen in Figure 7-3. As is the case with this example, the item name may not be enough of a clue to determine the problem, and a Registry search may not turn up anything positive either. In this example, the search does reveal that a file named HPPROPTY.EXE is cited in the *HKLM\System\CurrentControlSet\control\InstalledFiles* key, but this information isn't much help. To identify the application associated with the file, use the Windows Explorer to search for it (often in the C:\Windows\System folder). Open its Context menu, select Properties, and then select the Version tab, which is shown in Figure 7-4. The information seen there should be sufficient to identify the application, which can now be uninstalled. If doing so resolves the problem, try reinstalling it. With luck the problem won't return, but if it does you may need to contact the manufacturer to see if a workaround or fix is available.

Shut down troubleshooting

Even if Windows opens successfully and actually works well, one of the following problems may be encountered at the end of the session.

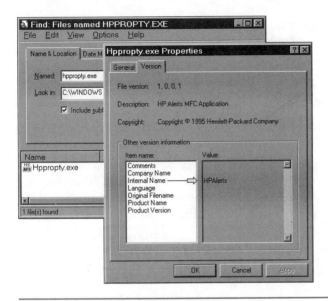

Figure 7-4 *The Properties sheet's Version tab reveals that the executable file listed in the Find dialog box is part of a Hewlett-Packard applet that can be uninstalled if necessary during a troubleshooting session.*

Restart in MS-DOS Mode is inoperative

An accompanying error message appears if this option on the "Shut Down Windows" menu won't work. Refer to that message in the next chapter, or review the "Restriction Recovery Procedures" section earlier in this chapter for assistance.

ShutDown button disabled in Close Program dialog box

If the ShutDown button in the Close Program dialog box is disabled, the "Disable ShutDown command" restriction is enabled. Refer to the "Restriction Recovery Procedure," section earlier in this chapter for assistance in removing this restriction.

System hang on shut down

Most such problems are not related to the Registry and will have to be analyzed and corrected by other means. But if all else fails, it may be worthwhile to review the "StartUp Group" and "Run and RunServices Key

Groups," sections earlier in this chapter. If one of the applications in these groups is causing the shutdown problem, follow the same procedures given earlier to isolate and then resolve the problem.

Troubleshooting within the Registry

This section describes various problems that may occur within the Registry itself and offers some suggestions for resolving them. If you can't find the exact source of the problem you've encountered, it's probably worth scanning the succeeding sections because the same general solution may be appropriate for a related problem within the Registry.

Connect Remote Registry option launches Microsoft Network Sign In window

As noted in Chapter 4, the Connect Remote Registry option requires an NT or NetWare server in order to function. If you nevertheless attempt to use it on a Windows 9x-only network system and Dial-Up Networking is enabled, the action may open the Microsoft Network's Sign In window (assuming it's installed, of course). When you click the Cancel button, an "Unable to connect" message is displayed. Click the OK button to clear the message and don't try this again.

Contents pane headings missing

If either the Name or Data heading is missing, it's probably offscreen to the left or right. If so, these headers can be quickly brought back into view by holding down the Ctrl key and pressing the plus sign (+) on the numeric key pad.

Or if the Name column is visible and a horizontal scroll bar is displayed at the bottom of the Contents pane, scroll to the right until the Data heading comes into view. Then drag that heading to the left, until both Name and Data can be seen. If neither the Name nor the Data heading is visible, place the mouse pointer in the blank Title bar and move it slowly to the left, until a double-arrow pointer appears. Drag the pointer to the right and release it. The Data heading should now appear. Repeat the procedure to bring the Name column back in view.

As an alternative, close and reopen the Registry Editor. This should display "N . . ." and "D . . ." in the Title bar. Drag the vertical lines next to each fragment to the right to display the complete heading.

HKEY_CLASSES_ROOT key is empty

If this key does not show a plus sign next to it, and the Contents pane displays a one-line (Default) and (value not set) entry, then the *HKLM\SOFTWARE\Classes* key is likewise empty, and therefore its contents do not appear under the *HKCR* key. This is probably due to an accidental erasure during the present Windows session, because if the key had been missing earlier, Windows would not have opened successfully. To resolve the problem, import a valid copy of the missing key structure, which should restore it at both locations. If only *HKLM\SOFTWARE\Classes* is restored, close and reopen Windows. Once both key structures are in place, press F5 (if necessary) to restore all desktop icons.

Key deletion problem

If an error message reports that a key cannot be deleted, it may be possible to export the key, edit its contents, and reimport it. The edits aren't important, but perhaps they will overwrite the corrupted data, making it possible to successfully delete the key.

If a subkey cannot be deleted, export the key at the next higher level, then erase that key and reimport it. The export/import action may be sufficient to clear the problem, and the subkey can now be deleted, or it will have disappeared on its own. But if this operation doesn't succeed, exit Windows and use the Registry Editor in real mode to delete the key. If all else fails, delete the Registry files and use one of the backup sets.

Key size problem

In Windows 95, the maximum size for stored information is about 64 Kbytes per Contents pane. Although a key with multiple subkeys can store data far in excess of this limit (as for example, any HKEY), no single Contents pane can exceed the limit. If a Registry import action would exceed this 64 Kbyte (approximate) limit, a misleading failure message citing Registry corruption or permission problems is displayed. If you suspect the real problem is related to size limitations, export a copy of the existing key and note its size. If the key contains subkeys, export each one separately, note its size, and deduct that from the size of the key in question (obviously impractical if there are very many subkeys). If the size of the key is near 64 Kbytes, then Microsoft documentation suggests examining the key's Contents pane and eliminating information no longer required. Because this is also impractical (or at least, very time consuming), a more viable workaround is to update to Windows 98, which does not have this limitation.

Missing data after importing Registry script file

The most likely culprit is an editing error in the file. For example, if a bracket is missing from any key specification, that key cannot be imported into the Registry. Despite the missing information, no error message is displayed, and the import operation concludes with a message that the operation was successful, even though it wasn't.

If you determine that a line is missing, either edit the appropriate line in the Registry script file to correct it or simply edit the Registry directly to fill in the missing information. Once that's done, reexport the corrected key if you think you might need it again in the future. Or at least make sure you erase the defective script file so that history doesn't repeat itself.

Missing data after export/import operation

If an ASCII character string entry in any Contents pane contains one or more low-order characters, such as a carriage return/line feed sequence (hexadecimal 0D 0A), the entire line containing that string will be missing if the key is reimported after deleting it. This can be easily verified in Windows 95 (but not Windows 98) by opening the following key:

HKLM\System\CurrentControlSet\control\PerfStats\Enum\VFAT\ DirtyData

In the Description entry, the Data column shows the following lengthy text string:

"The number of bytes waiting to be written to the disk. Note that ||dirty data is kept on a per cache block basis, and so a number ||higher than the actual number of bytes may be reported."

Each "||" indicates the presence of a carriage return/line feed sequence, and the string therefore appears as three lines in the Explanation dialog box shown in Figure 7-5. (Open the System Monitor applet, select "Dirty Data" and click the Explain button.) Now export this key, delete it, and reimport it. The Explain button no longer functions because the Description line is missing in the key's Contents pane.

Although the same character string also appears in the Windows 98 *DirtyData* subkey's Contents pane, the missing-line problem does not, and a comparison of each exported file reveals why. In the Windows Notepad applet, the exported Windows 95 file shows line breaks in the text at the locations of the "||" characters, thus indicating the invisible presence of the carriage return/linefeed characters, and these characters cannot be brought back into the Registry by REGEDIT's Import option.

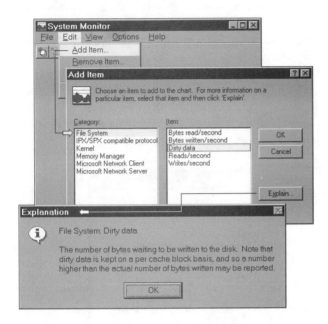

Figure 7-5 *Open the System Monitor's Edit menu and select the Add Item option. Highlight File System and Dirty Data, then click the Explain button to display the Explanation box seen at the bottom of this illustration. The break at the end of each line is due to carriage return/linefeed characters embedded in the Registry data.*

In contrast, the Windows 98 file's text appears as one long continuous line with ASCII printable characters \r and \n at the break points instead of the conventional carriage return/linefeed characters (hexadecimal 0D and 0A). Thus, the previous text string example appears like this:

Note that \r\ndirty data . . . and so a number \r\nhigher than. . . .

So although the Windows 98 Registry Editor can't import actual ASCII carriage return/linefeed characters either, it gets around the limitation via these substitutions. The Windows 95 Editor is not able to do this, however.

In the *DirtyData* key example the damage isn't permanent because the line is rewritten the next time Windows 95 opens. However, a system restart does not always recover all missing data; for example, Figure 7-6 shows the Contents pane for a *Local Modems* subkey immediately after installing the Windows 95 Microsoft Fax applet (not included with Windows 98). Five vertical arrows point to locations in various initialization strings where a nonprintable character (in this example, hexadecimal 0D or 0A) is displayed as a vertical bar. The figure also shows the key contents after exporting and viewing it in the Windows Notepad applet, where each single nonprintable character is displayed as a solid box, and the final byte in the three-character sequence (0D 0D 0A) at the end of the ModemId string produces a linefeed before the trailing quote. As in the previous example, each of these lines will be lost if the key is exported, deleted, and subsequently imported back into the Registry.

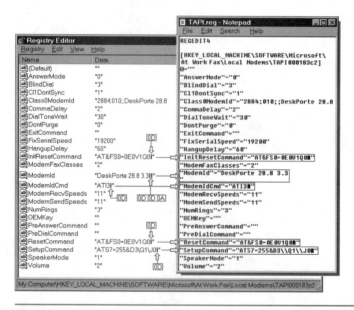

Figure 7-6 *Each vertical arrow points to a low-order ASCII character in a modem command string. Each horizontal arrow points to the equivalent line if the key is exported and viewed in Notepad. If the key is deleted and then reimported, each line containing a low-order character (shown boxed in the Notepad window) will be lost.*

If you suspect a key's Contents pane lacks string data entries that were formerly present, and the key contents are available in an exported REG file, it may be worthwhile to do a line-by-line comparison, looking for such anomalies as those shown in the Notepad segment of Figure 7-6. Depending on the nature of the missing line, it may or may not be essential to recover it: Missing explanatory text such as that shown in Figure 7-5 won't interfere with normal operations, but a modem initialization string that isn't quite right can certainly cause grief. There are two ways to correct the problem, both described here.

Reinstall software

To avoid the hassle of trying to figure out exactly what ASCII characters are causing the problem, simply uninstall the application and then reinstall it. Or in the case of a modem-related problem, turn the modem on and attempt to use it for the intended purpose. Chances are, Windows will query the modem and rewrite the lines as required.

Repair REG file

This solution works in Windows 98 only, and then only in text strings. Load the REG file into Notepad and make sure the Word Wrap option is enabled. While varying the horizontal size of the Notepad window, watch for text lines that break before the right edge of the window. There's no need to guess the identity of the characters causing the break—it's obviously a carriage return/linefeed sequence. Just place the mouse pointer at the end of each such line and press the Delete key to delete the invisible character sequence and bring the start of the next line up to the end of the present one. To restore the carriage return/linefeed sequence in a format that the Windows 98 Registry will accept, insert the ASCII replacement characters cited above.

Note that this technique is *not* valid for a modem initialization string: Although Windows 98 may know that the "\r" substitution is really a carriage return, the modem string still must be hexadecimal 0D.

Missing subkey or file specified by subkey

If a subkey and/or file specified in the Registry is missing, yet the function that one would associate with the missing element appears to be in good working order, that function is currently handled by some other means, and the "missing" element is simply a pointer to a file that may be installed in the future by an application or perhaps by a Windows upgrade. Refer to "{D3B1DE00...(Tools tab) and Disk Tools," in the "Other HKCR Subkeys" section of Chapter 2 for a specific example.

Recent edit lost when Windows restarts

As noted in Chapter 1 ("Contents Pane — INI File Comparisons"), some Registry configuration data may also be retained in an old INI file, which in most cases should be automatically rewritten to track a Registry change. However, this may not happen if the Registry is directly edited by the user, in which case the entry in WIN.INI (typically) may be rewritten into the Registry the next time Windows starts, thereby nullifying the recent edit. If you suspect this is happening, reedit the Registry and then look in WIN.INI for a line that specifies the same item. If one exists, edit it to agree with the Registry entry. If necessary, search other INI files if WIN.INI itself is not the problem.

Real mode problem

The next two problems may show up during a Registry editing session in real mode.

Import operation

If an error message indicates an unsuccessful import operation, there may not be enough conventional memory available for the Registry Editor to import a very large file into the existing Registry. If it's possible to do so, open Windows and retry the operation. If the nature of the problem prevents the GUI from opening, you may be able to edit the file you want to import in order to cut it into smaller segments that can be imported sequentially. Or in Windows 95, you can rename the existing SYSTEM.DA? and USER.DA? files so that Windows won't find them. This forces Windows to rebuild the Registry from the C:\SYSTEM.1ST file. In Windows 98, rename SYSTEM.DAT and USER.DAT, and Windows should extract a fresh set from the appropriate RB00x.CAB file. Once the Windows GUI successfully opens, use the Registry Editor's Import option to import the file into the Registry.

Incomplete command line

If a REGEDIT real-mode command followed by various switches, paths, and filenames exceeds 128 characters, it is not possible to write the entire command. This might happen if you try to edit a USER.DAT file in a location other than the C:\Windows folder, as shown in this example:

REGEDIT/R:C:\Windows\Profiles*username*\USER.DAT (and so on).

In this case, temporarily move USER.DAT into the C:\ (root) directory, and do the same for any file to be imported/exported, which should enable the command to be written in less than 128 characters. Move all files back to their proper locations after the operation is successfully completed.

The problem is also quite likely to occur if the system is booted from diskette. If so, REGEDIT looks to the diskette for the SYSTEM.DAT and USER.DAT files, unless the /L: and /R: switches explicitly direct it to the C:\Windows folder. But because these switches and the accompanying path\filename information take up so many characters, there won't be room within the 128-character limit to specify a lengthy key structure. If this becomes a problem, try to boot from the hard drive, press F8, and select the Command prompt option. Having done that, REGEDIT won't have to be told where the DAT files are, and the complete command can now be successfully written. However, if the key structure is still too long to fit, then you'll have to operate on a smaller key structure, even though this means the edit will affect a larger segment of the Registry.

Status bar is missing

The most likely reason for a missing Status bar is that is has been disabled. To restore it, either open the View menu and put a check next to the Status Bar checkbox or press the Alt+V, B keys. Hold down Alt+V and repeatedly press B to toggle the Status bar on and off.

Status bar shows incomplete key structure

The key structure displayed in the Status bar at the bottom of the Registry Editor window apparently has a 128-character limit (127 text characters, plus one unseen end-of-line marker), which is rarely a problem because most such structures fall well below that limit. There are however a few exceptions, such as the following:

Status Bar Shows:	Cumulative Character Count
My•Computer\HKEY_CURRENT_USER\So	32
ftware\Microsoft\Windows\Current	64
Version\Explorer\MenuOrder\Start	96
•Menu\&Programs\Windows•98•Reso¶ urce Kit\Menu	128

As a result of the length restriction, the "urce Kit\Menu" segment that ends line 5 does not appear in the Status bar, but there is no other consequence of this limitation.

Troubleshooting beyond the Registry

The problems described in this section may occur during a routine Windows session, as a result of an earlier Registry editing session, or perhaps because some application or action did something to the Registry all by itself.

Access denied problem

An "Access Denied" message usually occurs for a very good reason: A file is write-protected or in use by Windows, or some other condition prevents the user from gaining access. However, if the message shows up in a situation where such conditions are unlikely to be in effect, then its time to look to the Registry for the problem and, with luck, the solution, too.

For example, if Control Panel fails to open, this message is displayed if the {21EC2020... subkey is missing. Assuming the name of some other *CLSID* key associated with a problem applet is unknown, it might be worth searching the Registry's Data column for the name of the object that can't be accessed. If you find it, then this is not the problem. If you don't find it, then check another system on which the same problem does not exist. If you find a *CLSID* key whose Data column displays the object name, then export a copy of that key from the working PC and import it into the other one.

Device Usage section is not displayed on General tab

If a hardware device is highlighted in Device Manager and the Properties button clicked, the Device Usage section near the bottom of the General tab lists the available configurations. However, this section does not appear if the highlighted device is connected to a SCSI or other controller. If you want to edit a hardware profile to add or remove a device and its controller, highlight the controller and try again. Refer to the "Hardware Profile Editing" section of Chapter 6 if you need assistance doing so, or if you want to remove one device from a specific hardware profile, while leaving the controller itself enabled.

Desktop object won't open

If a desktop icon is present, but double-clicking it has no effect, it's possible that the associated *CLSID* key or in-process server file is either missing or damaged. To verify this, find the entry for the object in Table 7-1 and then check the *HKCR* key's *CLSID* key for the existence of the listed *CLSID* subkey. Assuming the key itself is present , open its *InProcServer32* subkey and verify the filename for the DLL file, which should agree with that given in the table. The file itself should be in the C:\Windows\System folder, unless otherwise specified.

Table 7-1 *Desktop Objects and Associated CLSID Subkeys*

Object	HKEY_CLASSES_ROOT\CLSID Subkey	InProcServer32
Briefcase, My	{85BBD920-42A0-1069-A2E4-08002B30309D}	SYNCUI.DLL
Computer, My †	{20D04FE0-3AEA-1069-A2D8-08002B30309D}	SHELL32.DLL
Control Panel	{21EC2020-3AEA-1069-A2DD-08002B30309D}	SHELL32.DLL
Dial-Up Networking	{992CFFA0-F557-101A-88EC-00DD010CCC48}	RNAUI.DLL
Printers ‡	{2227A280-3AEA-1069-A2DE-08002B30309D}	SHELL32.DLL
Inbox	{00020D75-0000-0000-C000-000000000046}	MLSHEXT.DLL
Internet Explorer, version 1	{0002DF01-0000-0000-C000-000000000046}	EXPLORER.EXE

Continued

Table 7-1 *Continued*

Object	HKEY_CLASSES_ROOT\CLSID Subkey	InProcServer32
version 3	{3DC7A020-0ACD-11CF-A9BB-00AA004AE837}	SHDOCVW.DLL
version 4	{871C5380-42A0-1069-A2EA-08002B30309D}	SHELL32.DLL
MS Network, Windows 95	{00028B00-0000-0000-C000-000000000046}	MOSSTUB.DLL
Windows 98	{88667D10-10F0-11D0-8150-00AA00BF8457}	None §
Network Neighborhood	{208D2C60-3AEA-1069-A2D7-08002B30309D}	SHELL32.DLL
Recycle Bin	{645FF040-5081-101B-9F08-00AA002F954E}	SHELL32.DLL

† Indented objects are in My Computer window.

‡ If CLSID key is damaged or missing, object may be accessible via Start menu, Settings option.

§ Launched via MSNDC.EXE.

Expand a fresh copy of the same file from the Windows CD-ROM disc into that folder, overwriting the current file if it is present. Then double-click the object again. If it still doesn't open, and no other solution is apparent, then you may have to uninstall and reinstall the object, or else rerun the Windows setup procedure.

Another possibility is that the object icon may have been placed on the desktop via the Tweak UI applet's Desktop tab, even though Windows does not support this usage. If that's a possibility, refer to the "Desktop Tab: Desktop Object Problems" section later in this chapter, for additional details.

Desktop object opens, then closes

This problem may occur if an inappropriate application is associated with the default action for an object. For example, consider a system with extensive multimedia support. If a new Wave Sound icon is double-clicked, the Registry's *.wav* key cites the *SoundRec* key, and that key's *Shell\open\command* subkey attempts to play the file; the player window opens, and the applet finds nothing to play and closes immediately. Under the circumstances, the action is normal because the new object contains nothing but unplayable header data for a waveform file.

In this case, the solution is simple: *don't* double-click a New Wave Sound.wav icon. Instead, open its Context menu and select the Record option. Record what you like and then save and exit. The next time you double-click the object, you'll hear your masterpiece. Apply the same general procedure to troubleshoot other objects that don't behave as expected; that is, open the Context menu and select one of the nondefault options.

Diskette drives accessed when Windows Explorer opens

Under default conditions, the Windows Explorer makes no attempt to read diskette drives when it opens. If however, it does attempt to read the diskette drives, the NoDriveTypeAutoRun entry in the *HKCU\ Software\...\Explorer* subkey's Contents pane has probably been set to some value other than its default (binary 95 00 00 00), which seems to be a fairly common Windows problem. Refer to the "Drive Media Icons" section of Chapter 6 for more details about this subkey entry and how to set it so that Explorer ignores diskette drives when it opens.

Drive letter missing

If a drive letter for a valid drive does not appear in any Explorer window (including My Computer), open a DOS window and log onto the missing drive. If necessary, put a diskette or removable media cartridge in the drive, as appropriate. If the drive is available and seems to be functioning properly, then a set Registry flag is probably the reason it does not appear in the Windows Explorer. Refer to the "My Computer Tab" section of the Appendix for information about the NoDrives entry, which can be quickly edited via the Tweak UI applet, as described there.

E-mail-with-attachment transmission failure

If there's a chronic problem sending e-mail messages that include a file attachment in a specific format, it's possible that the MIME (Multipurpose Internet Mail Extension) information for that file type is missing or corrupted. To verify this, open the *HKCR\.ext* subkey for that file format and look in the Contents pane's Name column for a Content Type entry. For example, the *.bmp* key's Content Type entry should show "Image/bmp" in its Data column. Next, check the *HKCR\ MIME\Database\Content Type* key structure for a subkey with that name. If that key's Contents pane cites a *CLSID* key, make sure the key exists, and that any files cited in its own subkeys are present, and so on. If none of these steps turns up a missing key or file, then the problem may exist at the receiving end of the chain. If possible, try sending the same file to another location served by a different ISP (Internet Service Provider). Or send a smaller file of the same type to the same location. If that transmission succeeds, then your ISP may restrict files that exceed a certain size. Knowing that won't resolve the problem, but at least it removes your own Registry from the list of suspects.

File association troubleshooting

During normal operations, double-clicking a document — or document shortcut — icon opens the appropriate application, and the document is loaded into its application window. Thus, a document file opens in the default word processor, a bitmap is seen in the Paint applet, and so on. When a new application is installed, its custom setup (if there is one) should ask if it can take over an association, although some applications just do it without permission, while others leave existing associations as is and don't offer to change them. Therefore, sooner or later, everyone encounters a situation in which the "wrong" application is launched when an icon is double-clicked. To troubleshoot and resolve such problems, first open the application and load the desired file into it, just to make sure this procedure works. If not, then that problem will have to be resolved before continuing.

Assuming the application successfully loads the document for editing or viewing, the next step is to examine the existing associations, as shown in the composite *HKCR* key structure in Figure 7-7. If Internet Explorer were installed, the *.gif* and *.jpg* keys near the top of the Key pane would cite *giffile* and *jpegfile* keys, respectively, as indicated by the boxed Data entries labeled 1 in the figure. Under the *giffile* and *jpegfile* key structures, the *open\command* subkey specifies the path and filename for Internet Explorer, and so this application opens whenever a GIF or JPG file icon is double-clicked. In contrast, if HiJaak Pro had been installed first, the *.gif* and *.jpg* keys would cite a *HiJaak.Image* key structure, which is also shown in the figure by the boxed Data entries labeled 2. In this example, both applications leave existing associations undisturbed, so the one installed first would retain these associations.

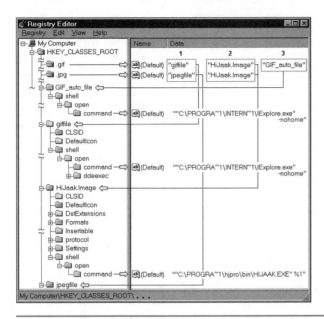

Figure 7-7 *If Microsoft's Internet Explorer is installed, the .gif and .jpg keys cite* giffile *and* jpgfile *keys, as indicated by the boxed data entries (1) at the top of the Contents pane. At the bottom of the window, the* jpgfile *key structure, not shown here, is identical to that shown for the* giffile *key. But if HiJaak Pro had been installed first, both keys would cite a* HiJaak.Image *key instead (2). Later on, if the "Open With" option were used to associate .gif files with Internet Explorer, a new* GIF_auto_file *key may be written into the Registry, and its subkey structure lacks the* CLSID *and* DefaultIcon *subkeys seen under the regular* giffile *key.*

To change these or any other associations from one application to another, simply edit the appropriate *.ext* key and edit the (Default) Data entry to cite the desired file type. Microsoft provides an alternate method to accomplish the same thing—almost. In this example, in order to open a GIF or JPG file in HiJaak Pro instead of Internet Explorer, open any such file's Context menu, select the "Open With" option, and highlight the new application in the program list. Next, put a checkmark in the checkbox next to Always use this program . . . , and click the OK button to conclude the operation. The argument against using this method is that it leaves the *.gif* key pointing to the *giffile* subkey but then changes that key's command subkey so that HIJAAK.EXE is executed instead of IEXPLORE.EXE. In other words, it ignores the entire *HiJaak.Image* subkey structure in favor of this newly modified *giffile* structure. As a potentially-troublesome side-effect, if an *.xyz* key (where *xyz* is some other extension — perhaps one not yet familiar to the user) also points to the *giffile* subkey, then a double-click on a *filename.xyz* icon will also launch HiJaak Pro, which may not be desirable. By manually editing the Registry as previously described, all key structures remain intact, and a file that opens in HiJaak Pro is directed to the correct structure, where subkeys appropriate to that application are presumably available, too.

Lost association recovery

Although the above procedure can restore an old association, the user must know what that association was in order to restore it. For example, if some new application took over an existing *HiJaak.Image* key's association, but the user did not remember the name of that key, it could be found via the following search technique:

1. Open the *HKEY_CLASSES_ROOT* key and scroll down beyond the last subkey whose name begins with a period. This saves a bit of time — none of these *File-extension* keys has the required information, so there's no point in searching them.

2. Highlight the next subkey (to begin the search at that location), then open the Registry Editor's Edit menu, select the Find option, put a checkmark in the Data checkbox only, and search for HIJAAK.EXE. Ignore all successful finds until you reach one where the Contents pane shows a highlighted open "command" subkey. The Status bar at the bottom of the Registry Editor window will read as follows:

    MyComputer\HKEY_CLASSES_ROOT*xxx*\shell\open\command

    The *xxx* segment is the desired key name, which in this case is *HiJaak.Image*.

3. Now that the desired key name is known, change the *.gif* and/or *.jpg* key's (Default) entry from whatever it is to read "HiJaak.Image", and the desired association is restored.

Association recovery after uninstall operation

If an application is uninstalled, it may leave one or more empty *File-extension* subkeys under the *HKCR* key. For example, if HiJaak Pro is uninstalled, the *.gif* subkey's Contents pane looks like this:

Name	Data
(Default)	""
Content Type	"image/gif"

This example shows that the uninstall procedure removed the citation in the (Default) line but left the subkey itself in place. If the application is subsequently reinstalled, or some other application is installed that is supposed to pick up the *.gif* file association, it may not do so. The reason is because its setup procedure sees the existing line — even though it has a null ("") value — and leaves it alone.

To illustrate this, temporarily rename the existing *.gif* subkey as, say, *.gifx*, and then write the following little TEST.INF file:

```
[version]
signature="$Chicago$"


[DefaultInstall]
AddReg=TestKey


[TestKey]
HKCR,".gif",,2,"giffile"
HKCR,".gif","Content Type",2,"image/gif"
```

Save the file, open its Context menu, and select the Install option. This creates a new *.gif* subkey whose Contents pane displays the two lines in the [TestKey] section above, as would happen if these lines were part of an application's setup procedure. Next, delete the "giffile" entry in the *.gif* key's Contents pane, which would happen if the same application were subsequently uninstalled.

Now select the Install option once again to simulate the effect of reinstalling the same application, or of installing a new one. This time, the install procedure has no effect, and the nulled (Default) line is left as is. As a result, the desired association is incomplete, and a double-click on a GIF file icon now prompts you to choose the program you want to use. For example, assuming you've just reinstalled HiJaak Pro, selected it from the program list, and checked the "Always use this program . . ." checkbox, the GIF file now opens in HiJaak Pro. However, the Registry entry is not what might be expected. The *.gif* subkey cites neither the restored *HiJaak.Image* key nor the former *giffile* key. Instead, it shows a unique *gif_auto_file* citation, shown in Figure 7-7 by the boxed Data entry labeled 3. A new key structure with that name contains a simple *shell\open\command* key structure, but there's no *DefaultIcon* or *Shellex* key structure. As a result, a GIF file shows one of the Windows generic icons, and its Context menu lacks all the options appropriate to a GIF file. To fix things, simply edit the *.gif* subkey to cite the *HiJaak.Image* key. Then delete the *gif_auto_file* key, which is no longer needed.

Default application detection

Sometimes as an application opens, it detects it is currently not the default for this kind of operation, and asks (pleads?) if you'd like to make it so. You can then click on a Yes or No button as desired. For the benefit of the user who doesn't want to be bothered repeatedly by this extra step, such messages usually include a checkbox to disable it, as shown in Figure 7-8 for Internet Explorer and Netscape Navigator browsers. Note that to repeat the message next time, the Internet Explorer checkbox must be checked and the Netscape Navigator checkbox *not* checked — an inconsistency that makes it just that much easier to permanently lose one of these messages by accident.

To reenable the Internet Explorer message, open Control Panel's Internet applet, select the Programs tab, and put a check in the checkbox next to "Internet Explorer should check to see whether it is the default browser." Doing so edits the following Registry key's Contents pane:

HKCU\Software\Microsoft\Internet Explorer\Main

Name	Data
Check_Associations	"yes"

Although Netscape Navigator has a similar key (*HKCU \Software\Netscape\Netscape Navigator\Main*), it does not support the Check_Associations entry. Instead, your preference is written into a text file, as follows:

File path and filename: `C:\ProgramFiles\Netscape\`
                                  `Users\username\PREFS.JS`

Add or edit this line: `user_pref("browser.wfe.ignore_`
                                  `def_ check", true)`

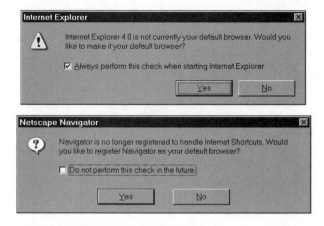

Figure 7-8 *If Internet Explorer is not the default browser, it repeats the default check the next time it is launched if the checkbox in this opening message (top) is checked. If Netscape Navigator is not the default (bottom), it too repeats the default check if its opening message checkbox is* not *checked.*

To reinstate the message box, either delete the entire user_pref line or change the last word to *false* to indicate that the user preference to ignore the default browser check is now false. And that being so, the message reappears. In other words, tell Internet Explorer "yes, *do* check for default status," and tell Netscape Navigator "no, *don't* ignore default status." In either case, the result is the same.

If some other application presented a similar message, but that message no longer appears and there's no obvious way to reinstate it, it's worth looking in the appropriate Registry key structure for a *Main* subkey and a Check_Associations (or similar) entry. If you find it, you're lucky. Otherwise, check the application's own folder for a text file, which may have a misleading extension (as in Netscape's PREFS.JS file). Or look for an INI file dedicated to that application. For example, Nico Mak's popular WinZip 6.3 utility adds a WINZIP32.INI file to the C:\Windows folder, and a line in its [fm] section reads assoc=0 if the inquiry message has been disabled.

Nag screen troubleshooting

Not unlike the "Don't ask" choices of the applications described in the previous section, some applications open with a welcoming message, a tip of the day, a registration screen, or a series of introductory windows. When you grow tired of one of these virtual introductions or warnings (it doesn't take long), the message area usually contains a checkbox to disable it. The following sections list the Registry (and other) locations where such information is stored for a few representative applications. If you want to reinstate such a message later, a variation on one of the following techniques may do it.

Free software offer

A typical (and annoying) nag screen example is America Online's "Instant Messenger," shown in Figure 7-9, which entices you with a free software offer at frequent intervals and offers three choices: "Yes! Sign Me Up," "Tell Me More," and "No." The nag screen does not offer to kill itself, but you can do the job by checking the Registry keys listed here and taking the action described in the text that follows.

HKCU\Software\America Online\AOL Instant Messenger (TM)

HKCU\Software\Microsoft\Windows\CurrentVersion\Run

Name	Data
AOL Instant Messenger (TM)	"C:\Program Files\ ... (*more*)"

If the *HKCU\...\AOL...* key structure is present, delete it. In the *HKCU\...\Run* key, delete *only* the entry shown in the Name and Data columns.

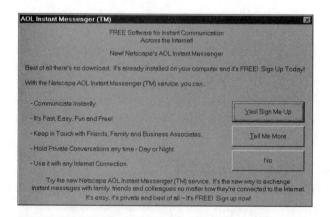

Figure 7-9 *A typical nag screen that can be killed by editing the Registry*

Microsoft Office 97

To disable the opening Tip of the Day screen, select the Office Assistant's Options button and clear the checkbox next to "Show the Tip of the Day at Startup." To reinstate the tip feature later, simply check the box again. In either case, the current status is written into the following key (note that the Registry's *8.0* key refers to Office 97):

HKCU\Software\Microsoft\Office\8.0\Common\Assistant

Name	Data	Tip of the Day Is:
AsstShowTipofDay	0x00000001 (1)	Enabled
	0x00000000 (0)	Disabled

The tips themselves are embedded in the following file:

C:\Program Files\Microsoft Office\Office\WWINTL32.DLL

Windows 95

The opening Tip of the Day feature may be disabled via the checkbox in the area beneath the tip, and if Tweak UI is installed (see the Appendix), its Explorer tab offers a Tip of the Day checkbox to toggle the screen on and off, as desired. Otherwise, edit the following Registry key:

HKCU\Software\Microsoft\Windows\CurrentVersion\Explorer\Tips

Name	Data	Tip of the Day Is
Show	01 00 00 00	Enabled
	00 00 00 00	Disabled

The tips are located in the following Registry key:

HKLM\SOFTWARE\Microsoft\Windows\CurrentVersion\explorer \Tips

Note that although both Office 97 and Windows 95 store their data as four bytes, Office 97 uses a DWORD, while Windows 95 does it in binary format. Both formats were explained in the "Data" section of Chapter 1.

Windows 98

Although the just-cited *HKCU\...\Tips* key and the Show entry in its Contents pane are both also present in the Windows 98 Registry, the *HKLM\...\Tips* key is not. Furthermore if it is added and tips are written into its Contents pane, they are not displayed, regardless of the status of the Show entry's Data column. It would therefore appear that this feature has been disabled (perhaps in response to popular demand).

Configuration Backup utility

This utility opens with several introductory screens, whose future appearance is determined by a REGBACK.INI file. See the "Configuration Backup Utility" section and Figure 5-1 in Chapter 5 for details. Note however that the Registry plays no part in the status of these introductory screens.

File missing problem

If a folder or file has been renamed or relocated, various "cannot find" messages may be displayed when an application requiring the renamed/relocated item is executed. Depending on specific circumstances, Windows may be able to find the missing item, or it may find the closest (but incorrect) match. If you recall the previous location and or name of the missing item, search the Registry for occurrences of that string and make the necessary replacement edits. For example, if a new drive or partition shifts the CD-ROM drive from drive D: to drive E:, search the Registry for all occurrences of "D:\" and change them to "E:\".

Mouse buttons reversed during startup but correct during Windows session

Left-handed users may find it necessary to click the "wrong" mouse button to dismiss a message seen as the Windows GUI opens. This is normal though — the message is displayed before the startup procedure has reached the point where the mouse buttons are swapped.

"Open With" dialog boxes appear during startup

If an "Open With" dialog box, or a cascading series of them, appears as the Windows GUI opens, there are that many Shortcuts in the StartUp group that Windows doesn't recognize. Chances are, the *HKCR/lnkfile* key structure is either missing or incomplete. If so, all desktop Shortcut icons have been replaced with the Microsoft generic document icon too. To resolve the problem, compare the *lnkfile* key structure with one on a system where the problem does not exist. If necessary, edit the existing key structure or import a new version from the other PC. While you're at it, check for the existence of the *{00021401...* key cited beneath the *lnkfile* key.

Setup procedures look for CD-ROM in wrong location

If an application (or even Windows itself) was installed from a disc in CD-ROM drive *x*, and the drive was later assigned to a different (usually, higher) letter, subsequent updates will try without success to find the installation disc at the location specified by the original drive letter. Although it's usually possible to redirect the upgrade routine to the new drive letter, it's probably easier in the long term to search the Registry's Data column and change all references to the drive from "*x:*" to "*y:*", where *x* and *y* are the old and new drive letters for the CD-ROM drive.

Post-installation problem

If any problem occurs immediately after installing some new software or hardware and can't be resolved by non-Registry troubleshooting, it may be worthwhile to find the new device's INF file, which should be in the C:\Windows\Inf folder. If you're not sure of its name, the same file may be on the distribution diskette(s) or CD-ROM disc. Open the file for editing, find the [Install] or [DefaultInstall] section, and look for a DelReg= line (if necessary, look for DelReg= in other sections, too). Note the name of the sections listed on every DelReg= line, and then review those sections to see what Registry keys were removed when the device was installed.

Recycle Bin icons are reversed

Windows sometimes gets confused when a desktop theme is changed. For example, if an MS Plus! theme is removed in favor of the Windows default, you may see an empty icon when the Recycle Bin is not empty, and vice versa. To correct this reversal, open the Registry Editor's Edit menu, select the Find option, check the Data box, and then search for "Recycle Bin". In the Key pane, click the plus sign next to the *{645FF040...* key and then open the *DefaultIcon* subkey that appears beneath it. Note the *empty* and *full* data entries and swap the icon numbers at the end of each line. Or if a different file is used for each icon (. . . *Empty.ico, 0* and . . . *Full.ico, 0* for example), then swap the filenames, too.

ScanDisk bad-cluster check

If a cluster has been marked as bad, ScanDisk for Windows makes no attempt to repair it. The procedure described in this section forces ScanDisk to test and attempt to repair such a cluster, although there is some risk in doing so. For example, some applications mark a cluster as bad even if it is not, in order to prevent other applications from accessing those clusters. Or a marginal cluster may have been marked as bad by some other utility, yet a ScanDisk test might not detect the same problem. In these or similar cases, if ScanDisk reset the bad-cluster mark, there could be subsequent problems with data corruption. However, if you have a valid reason for forcing ScanDisk to retest bad clusters, you can force it to do so by opening the following Registry key to display the listed Contents pane entry:

HKEY_CURRENT_USER\Software\Microsoft\Windows
\CurrentVersion\Applets\Check Drive

	Name	Data
Change:	Settings	*aa bb cc* 00
To read:	Settings	*aa bb cc* 04

Leave the first three bytes (*aa bb cc*) as is and change the fourth byte's hexadecimal value from 00 to 04 to force ScanDisk to retest all clusters formerly marked as bad. If an apparently good cluster is discovered, ScanDisk offers three options: leave it as is, mark it as good, or retest it. In case of doubt, choose the latter option. If the retest passes, the cluster probably is good.

Thumbnail problem

As noted in Chapter 6, two thumbnail view options are available if Internet Explorer 4 or greater is installed in Windows 95 or 98. Because not all file types support this option, you may want to refer to the "Internet

Explorer Thumbnail Views" section in that chapter for details on what to expect, and then you can refer to one of the following sections if what you see is not what you expect. To avoid repeating the same suggestions several times, they're offered once here: If part of a key structure is missing, refer to Table 6-8 in the previous chapter for assistance in reconstructing it. If a DLL file is missing or suspected of being defective on a Windows 95 system, simply uninstall and reinstall Internet Explorer 4.0. Because IE4 is apparently welded into Windows 98, it is easier to extract a replacement file from one of the following Windows 98 CAB files:

Filename	Location
SHDOCVW.DLL	WIN98_38.CAB
SHELL32.DLL	WIN98_38.CAB & WIN98_39.CAB (it's in two parts)
THUMBVW.DLL	WIN98_39.CAB

Extract the file into the C:\Temp folder or some other convenient location, then exit Windows, and replace the suspect file with the newly extracted version. If this doesn't resolve the problem, it may be necessary to reinstall Windows 98.

Thumbnails option troubleshooting

If this View menu option is selected and the expected graphics thumbnails are not displayed, follow the appropriate procedure below to resolve the problem.

Thumbnails option missing from View menu If the option is not yet displayed on the View menu, open the folder's Properties sheet and place a check in the "Enable thumbnail view" checkbox near the bottom of the General tab. Because this feature is embedded in the SHELL32.DLL file, its absence would indicate that IE4 is not installed, or there's a problem with the installation.

All files do not display Thumbnail view If the Thumbnails option is present but selecting it has no effect, then the Registry key and/or the file cited in the *InprocServer32* Contents pane below might be missing or defective. If the View menu's "as Web Page" option described below is also inoperative, then the prime suspect is the THUMBVW.DLL file.

CLSID\{8BEBB290-52D0-11D0-B7F4-00C04FD706EC}

InprocServer32   (Default)   "C:\Windows\System\
                                                    THUMBVW.DLL"

Some files do not display Thumbnail view Although most systems display thumbnail views for BMP, GIF, HTM, HTML, JPG, and JPEG files by default, a third-party application may delete one or more Registry subkeys that support this feature if the application is uninstalled. In other cases, the Thumbnail view depends on two elements—the appropriate Registry subkey *and* one of the following:

File Type	Thumbnail View Requires
Graphics image	A graphics filter for that file type
Text document	A preview image embedded in the document

If either is missing, then files of that type do not display a thumbnail view, either in the Explorer Contents pane or if the View menu's "as Web Page" option (described below) is selected. The first step is to look for the subkey structure that supports the Thumbnail view, as shown by this *HKCR\.bmp* key example:

```
.bmp
  ShellEx
    {BB2E617C-0920-11D1-9A0B-00C04FC2D6C1}
```

If any part of this structure is missing, it would account for the lack of a Thumbnail view for the file type.

View menu's "as Web Page" option troubleshooting

If the View menu's "as Web Page" option is selected, a single thumbnail of the selected file is displayed in the left margin of the Contents pane. If the expected thumbnail does not appear, refer to one of the following sections for assistance.

View menu's "as Web Page" option missing If the option does not appear on the View menu, open the *HKLM\...\CurrentVersion* key (complete path below) and make sure the *ExtShellViews* and *{5984FFE0...* sub-keys are present, as shown here.

Key and Subkeys	Name	Data
HKLM\Software\Microsoft\Windows\CurrentVersion\...		
ExtShellViews\...	(Default)	(value not set)
{5984FFE0-28D4-11CF-AE66-08002B2E1262}		
	(Default)	(value not set)
	HelpText	"Displays items in Web View"
	MenuName	"as &Web Page"
	TooltipText	"Web"

Note that although the *{5984FFE0...* key cited above appears as a subkey under various other Registry keys, no subkey with this name appears under the *HKCR\CLSID* key itself.

All files do not display Thumbnail view If the View menu's "as Web Page" option is selected but no file displays a thumbnail, then the following Registry key may be missing or defective:

CLSID\{7487CD30-F71A-11D0-9EA7-00805F714772}

InprocServer32   (Default)   "C:\Windows\System \SHDOCVW.DLL"

Although the *CLSID\8BEBB290...* subkey has no effect on this option, the THUMBVW.DLL file does, and its absence might also account for a problem. However, it's unlikely that the SHDOCVW.DLL file is missing because its absence would have prevented Windows from opening successfully.

Some files do not display Thumbnail view Refer to the previous "Some files do not display Thumbnail view," section which describes how to resolve this problem within both the Thumbnails option and the "as Web Page" Option.

Volume-tracking problem

Occasionally an application diskette functions properly at first, but later an error message warns that the diskette is invalid. Or a prompt is displayed telling you to insert the correct diskette, even though that diskette is in fact in the drive and appears to be in good order. The problem may be caused by the Windows volume-tracking system, which is briefly reviewed here.

When Windows first accesses a diskette, it writes data into the 8-byte OEM field within the boot sector, at hexadecimal offsets 03-0A. This space customarily identifies the OEM supplier of the diskette software, but the volume-tracking system overwrites it with a unique volume identification number, which is subsequently used to verify that the current diskette is the correct one. Although this may prevent accidental disk writes to the wrong diskette, some applications may no longer recognize the diskette after the OEM field has been changed, even though the diskette itself is in fact neither invalid nor damaged.

Several workarounds to this problem are given here, although none are satisfactory for all situations.

Write-protect the diskette

If Windows can't write to the boot sector, the volume-tracking system caches the diskette's label and serial number instead. Obviously this is not an appropriate solution if it is necessary to write to the diskette during normal operations. However, it is generally good operating procedure to write-protect any new application diskette, especially before running an install or setup procedure from that diskette. If it turns out to be necessary to write to that disk, a message lets you know about it. In that case, you may want to review the rest of this section before continuing.

Edit the NoVolTrack subkey

Figure 7-10 shows the Contents pane for the *HKLM\System\CurrentControlSet\control\FileSystem\NoVolTrack* key, in which each entry shows a 10-byte hexadecimal string in the Data column. The first two bytes (underlined in the figure) are the offset at which the OEM field begins, which is usually at byte 3, or 03 00 in the reverse notation shown in the figure. The final eight bytes are the OEM field itself.

When a diskette is first accessed, its OEM field is compared with those listed in the *NoVolTrack* key's Contents pane. If a match is found, the field won't be overwritten by the volume-tracking system. Therefore, a diskette can be protected against a volume-tracking overwrite by writing its OEM field into the Registry *before* Windows gets the chance to write to that diskette. If this is a consideration, use the following procedure to accomplish this.

1. Temporarily write-protect the diskette.

2. Use the Debug utility to view its boot sector. Assuming the diskette is in drive A, open a DOS window and type the boldface portions of the following lines:

C:\WINDOWS>**debug**   (to run the Debug utility in the
                              C:\Windows\Command folder)

-L CS:0100 0 0 1   (to load the boot sector from the
                              diskette in drive A)

-D CS:0100 010F   (to display the first 16 bytes)

```
0F64:0100  EB 3C 90 4D 53 44 4F 53-34 2E 30 00 02 01 01 00   .<.MSDOS4.0.....
```

-Q   (to exit the Debug utility)

3. Make a note of the OEM field, which is indicated here by the underlined 8-byte hexadecimal string. Then use the Registry Editor to create a new binary-value entry in the *NoVolTrack* key. Use any convenient name, then enter **03 00** in the Data column, followed by the eight bytes from the OEM field. If the OEM field does not begin at offset 3, revise the first two hexadecimal characters as appropriate.

4. Close and reopen Windows.

5. Remove the diskette's write protection.

From now on, the diskette can be used for normal read/write operations, and the volume-tracking system won't overwrite the OEM field.

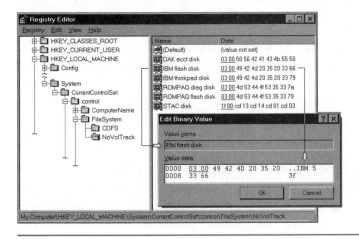

Figure 7-10 *The Windows volume-tracking system will not overwrite a diskette's OEM field if that field is listed in the* NoVolTrack *key's Contents pane. The underlined bytes indicate the file offset where the OEM field is located.*

Get a new diskette

The edit procedure just described obviously won't work if the volume-tracking system has already overwritten the OEM field. Assuming you know what that field was, you could always restore it and then edit the Registry, but who reads OEM fields before the fact? The more likely resolution is to contact the software supplier and get a new diskette. Or, depending on how alert their technical support is, you might try asking for the OEM field over the phone.

Shortcut Troubleshooting

There are several possibilities to consider if double-clicking a shortcut icon doesn't produce the expected result. First, try a few other shortcuts and see what happens. Then refer to whichever explanation below best describes the problem.

DOS shortcuts don't work

If every MS-DOS shortcut opens an "Open with" dialog box, but other shortcuts continue to function properly, then the problem is probably related to the *piffile* subkey. To verify this, select the Start menu's Shut Down option and select "Restart the computer in MS-DOS mode." If the "Open with" dialog box is displayed, then the *piffile* subkey is either missing or corrupt, and a valid version will have to be imported into the Registry, as described in the "Windows 95 Registry File Replacement" and "Windows 98 Registry File Replacement," sections earlier in this chapter.

All Windows shortcuts don't work

If DOS shortcuts continue to work, but all Windows shortcuts don't, then refer to one of the following procedures.

Shortcut icon opens an Open With dialog box

The most likely culprit is a missing or corrupt HKCR*lnkfile* subkey. If in doubt, exit and restart Windows. If there is a *lnkfile* problem, several Open with dialog boxes may be on the desktop — one dialog box for each Windows shortcut in the StartUp group. In addition, each such shortcut in that group is displayed with a generic Microsoft document icon, and Shortcut icon titles on the desktop may show an *lnk* extension.

To resolve the problem, import a valid copy of the *lnkfile* key back into the Registry. Then place the mouse pointer on any clear desktop area and press F5 to refresh the desktop and restore the Shortcut icons to their previous condition. See also the problem described in the section immediately following.

All Windows Shortcut icons have no effect

If nothing at all happens when any Windows shortcut is double-clicked, the problem is probably with the shortcut *CLSID* key, which is `{00021401-0000-0000-C000-000000000046}`. Or there's a missing *CLSID* subkey with this name beneath the *HKCR\lnkfile\ shellex\ContextMenuHandlers* key. In either case, Shortcut icons remain correct though still inoperative. To determine which key is missing, open any shortcut's Context menu. If the Open option is present and operational, the *{0021401...* key is probably missing. But if the option is not present on the menu, the *CLSID* subkey with the same name (mentioned above) is missing. In either case, import a valid copy of the missing key into the Registry.

DOS and Windows shortcuts inoperative

If all shortcuts are inoperative, press F5 to refresh the desktop. Chances are, *all* document icons will change to the generic Windows document icon, and the Recycle Bin and Network objects may display unlabeled folder icons. This indicates larger problems within the entire *HKCR* key structure, and if a valid backup is not available, it's probably necessary to reinstall Windows.

Shortcut icon titles display LNK extension

Even if the Windows Explorer is not configured to hide extensions of registered files (via an option on the View tab), a few such extensions remain hidden anyway, due to a NeverShowExt entry in the Contents pane of the appropriate *FileType* key. If the NeverShowExt line is missing from the *lnkfile* key's Contents pane, then any Shortcut icon title that does not show the LNK extension will not be recognized as a shortcut and therefore won't work. This should be an issue only if an inexperienced user sees a Shortcut icon title's LNK extension, deletes it, and then wonders why the shortcut has become disabled. So even if there's some point to displaying other extensions that Windows wants to conceal, it's probably better to leave this one hidden. Refer to the "Hidden Extensions and Files" section of Chapter 6 for a complete list of hidden file extensions and the means to show or rehide one or more of them.

Context Menu Troubleshooting

Problems related to various Windows menus are described in this section.

Duplicate or erroneous options

Although not impossible, it's unlikely that a Windows menu will display options that aren't supposed to be there, and if such options do show up, the most likely cause is an experiment that didn't work out as expected. For example, the source of an Empty Recycle Bin option on a bitmap Context menu can be traced to a *ContextMenuHandlers* subkey under the *Paint.Picture* key, as described in the "Context Menu" section of Chapter 6 and illustrated in Figure 6-12. In problems such as this, the solution is obvious: just delete the erroneous key structure, and the menu option disappears.

Figure 7-11 illustrates an even more unlikely condition, which at first may not be traceable to a recent customization session. Here, the menu shows duplicate action options (Open, Explore) as well as a Context menu option (Sharing) not appropriate to the object, which in this example is the Microsoft Network.

This problem showed up sometime after a new Microsoft Network icon was placed in a custom folder, as described in Chapter 6, and its *{00028B00...* subkey was deleted under the *NameSpace* key shown in Figure 6-20. Later, the icon was dragged back to the desktop, where it now displays its own Context menu options plus others associated with any folder, hence the duplicate and erroneous options seen in Figure 7-11.

To verify and resolve a problem such as this, export the *HKCR\folder* key, then delete it from the Registry, and recheck the Context menu. If the options are gone, reimport the deleted key, and delete the object on the desktop. Then reinstate the *{00028B00...* subkey under the *NameSpace* key and restart Windows. The object should again appear on the desktop — this time with the correct Context menu.

Disabled Context menu options

Both versions of Windows permit the user to hide one or more drive letters, as described in the "My Computer Tab" section of the Appendix. It has been noted that if drive letter B is cleared on Windows 98 systems only, two options on the Start button's Context menu become disabled. The only known workaround at this time is to recheck the drive B checkbox, or edit the Registry as described in the same section of the Appendix.

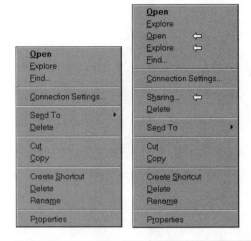

Figure 7-11 *The correct Context menu for the Microsoft Network is shown on the left, while the menu on the right shows duplicate Open and Explore options and an erroneous Sharing option. Such entries may be displayed if an object normally associated with the desktop is recreated in a folder.*

Missing Context menu options

Figure 7-12 shows a few Context menus on which various options are missing, usually because of a missing Registry key. A few examples are reviewed in the following sections.

Open

If this option is missing, along with others (Explore or Find, for example) found on folder menus, the *HKCR\lnkfile* key's *ContextMenuHandlers* sub-key is missing, as shown by the third menu at the top of Figure 7-12. In this case, shortcut icons won't function either. Refer to the "Shortcut Troubleshooting" section earlier in this chapter for assistance in resolving the problem.

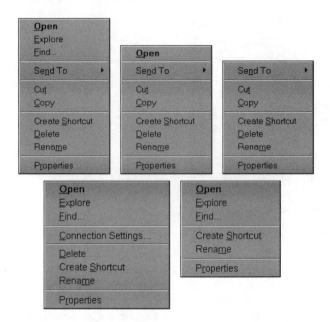

Figure 7-12 *The Context menu options for folder (Open, Explore, Find) and application (Open only) shortcuts don't appear if the* lnkfile *key's* ContextMenuHandlers *subkey is missing, as shown by the third menu at the top. The examples in this section show the effect of a missing* ContextMenuHandlers *subkey under the Microsoft Network's* CLSID *key.*

Send to

If this Context menu option is missing, the most likely reason is that the *CLSID* key for this service is missing. Check for the presence of the *HKCR\CLSID\{7BA4C740...* key listed in the following table, and if it is indeed missing, either import a copy of this key structure from another system, or add the following *SendTo* key and *SendTo* subkey beneath the *HKCR\CLSID* key.

SendTo Key	Name	Data
{7BA4C740-9E81-11CF-99D3-00AA004AE837}		
	(Default)	"Microsoft SendTo Service"
SendTo Subkey	***Name***	***Data***
InprocServer32	(Default)	C:\WINDOWS\SYSTEM\ SHDOCVW.DLL"
	ThreadingModel	"Apartment"
IE4 Key	***Name***	***Data***
HKCR\AllFilesystemObjects\shellex\ContextMenuHandlers\Send To		
	(Default)	{7BA4C740-9E81-11CF-99D3-00AA004AE837}

If Internet Explorer 4 (or greater) is installed, check for the existence of the IE4 key structure listed in the preceding table and make sure the *Send To* subkey's Contents pane contains the entry shown in the table. The Contents panes of all other keys in this structure are empty. This key structure places the Send To option on the Context menu of all file system objects — that is, shortcuts, folders, and files.

Other missing options

Figure 7-12 also shows the effect of a missing *ContextMenuHandlers* subkey under the Microsoft Network's *CLSID* key.

New menu option is inoperative

If an option on the cascading New menu fails to create a new file of the specified type, there's a problem with the *ShellNew* subkey under the *HKCR\filename-extension* key for that file type. For example, a NETSCAPE.HTML file is written into the C:\Windows\ShellNew folder if Netscape Communicator is installed and it is cited by the *HKCR* key's *.htm\ShellNew* and *.html\ShellNew* subkeys. If the application is subsequently uninstalled, the file is deleted from the ShellNew folder but the *ShellNew* subkeys continue to refer to it. Therefore, if the New menu is used to create a new HTML document, a "Problem creating object" message is displayed because Windows can no longer find the specified file. The immediate fix is to open each *ShellNew* key and make the following revisions:

Name	Data	Comments
FileName	"netscape.html"	Delete this line.
NullFile	""	Add this line.

Or refer to the "HTML Document" section of Chapter 6 if you need assistance rewriting these *ShellNew* subkeys to specify some other file.

Properties sheet troubleshooting

If there is a problem with a Context menu's Properties option, you may see an error message when that option is selected, or the Properties sheet may open but be missing some tabs. In either case, the problem can usually be traced to either a missing subkey or a missing file. Follow the procedures described in this section to identify the missing element, and once you know what it is, either edit the Registry to restore the key structure or expand a fresh copy of the missing file.

Error message

If a "Properties not available" message appears when you select the Properties option, the culprits are a missing subkey related to the object or a DLL or CPL file cited in a *PropertySheetHandlers* key. To verify this, make a note of the object whose properties are not available, then find the *CLSID* key for that object.

For example, if the message appears when you attempt to view the properties for any file with a certain extension, search the *HKCR* key for the subkey with that extension name, open it, and note the *FileType* key listed in the (Default) entry's Data column. Now search for that key. Or if you already know the *FileType*, proceed directly to that key instead. Open the key and then the *shellex* key beneath it. This should lead in turn to a *PropertySheetHandlers* subkey. If that key's Contents pane shows a text string in the (Default) entry's Data column, a subkey with that name should be displayed immediately below the *PropertySheetHandlers* subkey, and its Contents pane should specify a *CLSID* subkey. Or if the Data column shows a (value not set) or an empty ("") string, the subkey itself should be labeled with the *CLSID* subkey name instead. (See Figure 2-7 for examples of both subkey formats.)

Once you know the correct *CLSID* number, find the subkey under the *HKCR\CLSID* key whose name is that number. That key's own *InProcServer32* (or similar) subkey indicates the DLL or CPL file that supports the missing Properties sheet.

Missing Properties tab

If only a General tab is displayed when a Context menu's Properties option is selected and no error message is displayed, then there are two possibilities: There are no other properties for the selected object or a *PropertySheetHandlers* key or subkey is missing. When in doubt, try to verify that a Properties tab is indeed missing. If it is, search for the *CLSID* key associated with the object and then for the *PropertySheetHandlers* subkey. If that key's Contents pane shows a text string in the (Default) entry's Data column, then a subkey with that name should appear immediately below the *PropertySheetHandlers* subkey, and its Contents pane should specify a *CLSID* subkey. Or if the Data column shows either (value not set) or an empty ("") string, then the subkey itself should be labeled with the *CLSID* subkey name instead. (See Figure 2-7 for examples of both subkey formats.)

Once you know the correct *CLSID* number, find the subkey whose name is that number, under the *HKCR\CLSID* key. That key's own *InProcServer32* (or similar) subkey indicates the DLL or CPL file that supports the missing Properties sheet.

Erroneous tab

Figure 7-13 shows a valid Properties sheet and the same sheet with erroneous General and Sharing tabs. The problem and its solution are described in "Duplicate or Erroneous Options" in the "Context Menu Troubleshooting," section earlier in this chapter; refer to that discussion for help resolving the problem.

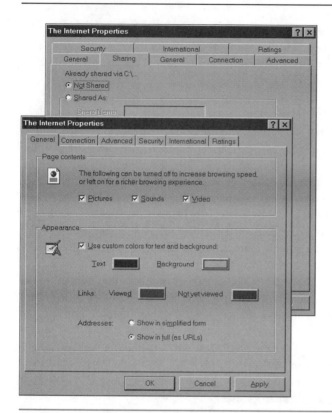

Figure 7-13 *The correct Internet Properties sheet is in the foreground, while the sheet behind it includes a duplicate (and erroneous) General tab and a Sharing tab that does not belong on this sheet. Note that the Sharing tab displays conflicting information: that the Internet object is already shared (correct) and that it is not shared (incorrect).*

Troubleshooting Other Menus

A few problems with other Windows menus are briefly reviewed in this section.

Expected option does not appear on desktop's cascading New menu

If an option that should be displayed on the menu is missing, refer to "Add Menu Option" in the Desktop New Menu section of Chapter 6 for assistance in placing that option on the New menu.

Disabled or missing Start menu option

Various menu options may be missing or disabled if certain restrictions have been set by the System Policy Editor. Refer to the "System Policy Editor" section of Chapter 4 if you need assistance verifying, or lifting, such restrictions.

System Policy Editor: Some File, all Edit menu options are disabled

This condition occurs if the System Policy Editor can't find the ADMIN.ADM file, which should be written into the C:\Windows\Inf folder if the utility is installed from the Windows CD-ROM disc. If the Open Template File dialog box is displayed and ADMIN.ADM is listed in the filename area, click the Open button. Otherwise, click the down arrow next to the Look In bar immediately below the Title bar. Select the C:\Windows\Inf folder and highlight the ADMIN.ADM file if it is present. Otherwise, copy the file from the CD-ROM disc and try again. Or if you want to run the Policy Editor from a diskette, make sure ADMIN.ADM is also copied to that diskette.

Tweak UI Troubleshooting

A few problems that may occur when using the Tweak UI applet are described in this section. Because most of these are related to Tweak UI command lines in the *HKLM\ ... \RunServices* or ... *Run* keys, refer to the "Tweak UI at Startup" section near the end of the Appendix for more details, or if the solutions suggested in this chapter don't work.

Desktop tab: "Create as File" button has no effect

This problem has been noted with the original Windows 98 version of Tweak UI. If you have the Windows 95 version, temporarily rename the Windows 98 TWEAKUI.CPL file as TWEAKUI.BAK and then copy the Windows 95 TWEAKUP.CPL file into the C:\Windows\System folder. Use it to take advantage of the Create as File feature and then return to the Windows 98 version of Tweak UI when you're finished.

Desktop tab: Desktop object problems

If an object icon has been placed on the desktop by checking one of the boxes in the Special desktop icons list, that icon can't be removed by highlighting it and pressing the Delete key. Or in some cases, double-clicking the icon has no effect. If so, the Context menu displays only a Create Shortcut option if the object was placed there via the just-described checkbox. A full Context menu is displayed if it was created via the Create as File button. If any of these problems occur, Windows probably does not support this usage, as hinted at by the "Not all icons can successfully be placed on the desktop . . ." message at the top of the Desktop tab.

If the Delete key action has no effect, open Tweak UI again, select the Desktop tab, and clear the checkbox next to that icon to remove it. If Tweak UI is no longer installed, open the following Registry key and delete the *CLSID* subkey associated with that object:

HKLM\SOFTWARE\Microsoft\Windows\CurrentVersion\Explorer \Desktop\NameSpace

General tab: "Restore Factory Settings" button has no effect on Special Folders section

The Restore Factory Settings button restores settings only in the other two sections of this Windows 95 tab. If you want to return to the default folder but don't recall its location, review the information in the following Registry keys:

HKCU\Software\Microsoft\Windows\CurrentVersion\Explorer\Shell Folders

HKCU\Software\Microsoft\Windows\CurrentVersion\Explorer\User Shell Folders

The *Shell Folders* key lists the default locations, which are superceded by any entries in the *User Shell Folders* key. So, to return to the default location, simply delete the appropriate line in the latter key. Tweak UI now shows the original default folder location.

IE4 tab: Erroneous help (via What's This? button)

The help feature appears to be out-of-sync on the Internet Explorer 4 tab. Select any Settings item, and the What's This? button brings up an explanation of some other item on the list, which may indicate a communication problem between TWEAKUI.CPL and the accompanying TWEAKUI.HLP file, but it's nothing that can be resolved via the Registry.

Network tab: Logon prompt is displayed at startup

If the Log on automatically at system startup option is checked, but the system still pauses at the startup logon prompt, the TweakLogOn command line is probably missing from the *HKLM\...\RunServices* key. Clear the checkbox, click the Apply button, then check the box, and again click the Apply button. This action writes the required entry into the Registry, and the logon pause should no longer take place.

Paranoia tab: Various Clear . . . at logon options don't work

The problem is similar to that described in the section immediately above, except that it applies to the *HKLM\...\Run* key. But as described in the previous section, it can probably be quickly resolved by clearing and resetting any checkbox.

Troubleshooting Uninstall Procedures

This section describes problems that may show up on two occasions. Either the Control Panel's Add/Remove Programs applet is opened and an application listed on the Install/Uninstall tab is selected, or a folder in a Windows Explorer window is selected. In either case, the selected item cannot be deleted due to one of the symptoms described in this section.

File or folder removal problem

If a message warns that the removal of a file or folder may have an impact on the Registry, the application within the folder should be removed via the Add/Remove Programs applet, as previously described. However, if the solutions offered there have no effect, or can't be used because the application does not appear on that list, it's usually worthwhile to delete all Registry entries pertaining to the folder before deleting the folder itself. To do so, click on the No button and then use REGEDIT to search the Data column for the appropriate path. For example, if the message appeared as you tried to delete a C:\Program Files\Accessories\Whatever folder, search for C:\Program Files\Accessories\Whatever, which will probably show up in a *Command* subkey's Data column. Once you find it, work your way up the immediate tree structure, which typically comprises a *Whateverfile\Shell\open\command* (or similar) structure. Export the entire

Whateverfile key (for safekeeping) and then delete it. Repeat this procedure until you have found all references to the same item. If any such key is a *FileType* key, then also search the *HKCR* section's Data columns for any references to that file type. For example, a *.wha* subkey may refer to the *Whateverfile* key. If so, and you're deleting the *Whateverfile* key, then you don't need the *.wha* key either.

Once you've done all this, exit, restart Windows, and then try the same delete operation that originally generated the message. If the message is displayed again, that's your clue that you haven't found all the Registry entries. In this case, make a search for "C:\PROGRA~1 \ACCESS~1\WHATEVER", or simply for "\WHATEVER".

Refer to the "Registry Cleanup Techniques" section of Chapter 5 for information about deleting Registry keys whose presence may not be detected when you try to delete a folder from within the Windows Explorer.

WIN.INI and removal problem

If the Registry search-and-destroy operations previously described don't work, it's possible the folder selected for deletion is cited on a LOAD= or RUN= line in the WIN.INI file, and — despite a warning about an impact on the Registry — the folder is *not* in fact cited in the Registry. Or the folder may have been cited in both locations, and although the Registry entries have been deleted, the INI citation remains. To verify this, simply check the WIN.INI file. Delete the citation to the folder and its executable file, then restart Windows, and try the folder deletion again.

Install/uninstall tab troubleshooting

The list of Windows software displayed on the Install/Uninstall tab is maintained in the Registry as shown in Figure 7-14. In most cases, the *Uninstall* subkey name bears a close resemblance to the name on the list. If not, though, a DisplayName entry in the subkey's Contents pane shows the list name, as shown by the inset in the figure.

If a well-behaved (and listed) application is uninstalled, it should remove all folders associated with itself and all Registry entries, and it should finally remove its own name from the list. But if it doesn't, there's a good possibility that the application's folder has already been deleted — or possibly, renamed. As a result, the uninstall routine can't find the specified application and therefore cancels. In most cases, the problem can be traced, and perhaps resolved, by finding the application's uninstall routine, which appears in a subkey beneath the following Registry key structure:

HKLM\SOFTWARE\Microsoft\Windows\CurrentVersion\Uninstall

Beneath that key, the application subkey's Contents pane shows an entry in one of the following formats:

Name	Data
UninstallString	C:*path**filename.exe*
UninstallString	C:\Windows\UNINST.EXE ...\DELSL*x*.ISU
UninstallString	RUNDLL32.EXE ... *filename*.INF
UninstallString	RUNDLL SETUPX.DLL ... *filename*.INF
Nothing is listed	The UninstallString entry is missing.

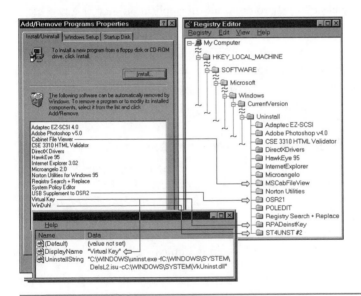

Figure 7-14 *The Install/Uninstall tab's list of software that can be uninstalled is maintained in the Registry, where there is an* Uninstall *subkey for each item on the list. Despite the occasional minor variation between an application name and its Registry key, the resemblance is usually close enough to identify the appropriate key – but not always. The inset at the bottom shows the Contents pane for the uninformative* RPADeinstKey *key, which reveals its true identity.*

Depending on the specific uninstall procedure (as executed by one of the lines above), there may or may not be an error message, and if there is one, it may or may not be informative. Therefore, follow one of the procedures described in the following sections whose titles may correspond to the message (or lack of one).

Path and filename cited in message

Open the Windows Explorer and verify that the path is in fact missing. If it is, then the application has already been removed, probably by simply deleting its folder from with Explorer. In this case, the Registry subkey that still displays the application in the Add/Remove list can be deleted, either by directly editing the Registry or via the Tweak UI applet's Add/Remove tab, which is described in the Appendix.

However, if Explorer shows that the path is still there, but the cited file isn't, then the cleanest way to uninstall the application may be a two-step procedure:

1. Reinstall the application, which should write a fresh copy of the missing file into the appropriate location.

2. Repeat the uninstall operation, which should now find the desired file and successfully conclude the procedure.

Path and filename not cited in message

Although the message may unhelpfully list the name of the application that failed the uninstall procedure (which you knew anyway), it's up to you to guess why the operation failed. In this case, open the *HKLM* key structure cited previously and find the appropriate subkey. The UninstallString entry should identify the path for that application. Armed with that information, follow the instructions given in the section immediately above this one.

Uninstall button has no effect

If an application on the Add/Remove applet's Install/Uninstall tab is selected and clicking the Add/Remove button has no effect, the uninstall routine probably cites an INF file that is missing. If so, the uninstall procedure terminates, but no message is displayed. To verify this, open the Registry key cited previously and find the subkey for the specified application. In that subkey's Contents pane, the UninstallString entry's Data column shows a lengthy string that terminates with the name of an INF file. That file should be in the C:\Windows\Inf folder but probably isn't. If you can locate a copy of the required INF file elsewhere (on the installation diskettes or CD, if you're lucky), copy it into the C:\Windows\Inf folder and then try the uninstall operation again. Otherwise, try the reinstall/ uninstall operation described earlier in this section.

Chapter 8

Registry Error Messages

This chapter lists some of the error messages that may be encountered as a result of problems related to the Registry, the Registry Editor, and the System Policies Editor. Each message is accompanied by information to help verify the source of the problem and resolve it. Reference is frequently made to a troubleshooting section in Chapter 7, which may be consulted if additional information is needed to resolve the problem. If no reference to a section in Chapter 7 is given, it's still worth checking the chapter for assistance.

The error messages in the present chapter are organized into the following sections:

Section	Error Message Seen
Registry Editing Session	When opening or using the Registry Editor
Real Mode Editing Session	When using the Registry Editor in real mode
System Startup	As Windows opens after a Registry editing session
System Shutdown	As Windows closes
Backup and Restore	When using the Configuration Backup/Restore utility
Uninstall Procedure	When uninstalling an application or deleting a folder
Other Error Messages	During session not related to the Registry but nevertheless traceable to a Registry problem

To avoid wading through irrelevant messages, refer to the appropriate section for assistance in resolving the problem. However, if a message can't be found where you would expect it to be, try looking through the other sections before abandoning hope.

Because many messages begin with the magic word "Windows" followed by a rambling phrase, some messages have been edited to focus on the subject of the error, and not the perpetrator, as shown by these examples:

Original Error Message	Revised Message
Windows cannot find . . .	Cannot find . . .
Windows encountered an error accessing . . .	Error accessing . . .
Windows has detected a registry/configuration error.	Registry/configuration error

Many messages cite the name of a specific key or other item, which varies according to the nature of the problem. Such citations are given here in italics — cannot find *filename,* for example. In the actual message, *filename* is of course replaced by the name of the missing file. A parenthetical explanatory phrase (*like this*) is also inserted occasionally, if needed to clarify some aspect of the message. Despite protests from the Microsoft Word spelling-checker, Microsoft's own spelling variations (*cancelled, canceled, unaccessible,* for example) have been left as they appear in the actual messages.

In troubleshooting some of the error messages given here, don't forget to backup (export) a key before deleting it, unless you are certain it is indeed no longer needed. By so doing, the key can be imported back into the Registry if required. Keep this suggestion in mind before reaching for the Delete option.

Remember that the SYSTEM.DAT and USER.DAT files, and the Windows 95 .DA0 backups, have their hidden, read-only, and system attributes set. In Windows 98, the two DAT files have their hidden and read-only attributes set. In order to copy, rename, or erase these files, the attributes must first be cleared. Refer to Chapter 7 if you need assistance in doing so. Windows 98 backup files are in the five RB00*x*.CAB files in the C:\Windows\Sysbckup folder, as described in Chapter 5.

Registry Editing Session

The messages in this section are seen as the Registry Editor opens or while you are using it to edit the Registry. Refer to one of the other sections of this chapter for assistance if a Registry-related message is displayed at any other time.

Access code is invalid. The most likely reason for this message is that the computer is configured for user profiles, and the current user does not have access to the Registry. If necessary, refer to the "Restriction Recovery Procedure" section in the previous chapter for assistance in gaining access to the Registry.

A far less likely cause for this message is an ancient copy of REGEDIT.EXE that predates the 7/11/95 file creation date of the first commercial release of Windows 95. In the unlikely event that your copy has an earlier date, expand a copy of the REGEDIT.EXE file from your own Windows CD, and get rid of the older version.

Cannot create key: Error while opening the key My Computer. This message indicates that attempting to create a new key immediately beneath "My Computer" at the top of the Registry Editor window is illegal.

Cannot delete *keyname*. Error while deleting key. Chances are the key has already been deleted. Open the View menu, select the Refresh option, and the key should disappear. If it doesn't, then close any application that may be preventing the deletion and try again. But first, make sure the key has been exported (because apparently it's needed). Refer to the "Key Deletion Problem" section in Chapter 7 for additional assistance.

Cannot edit *Name entry* (in any Contents pane): Error reading the value's contents. If the Device Manager and Registry Editor are both open, this message may be displayed if you double-click an item whose Resources tab is currently displayed by the Device Manager. To resolve the problem, toggle to a higher level subkey and then back again. If necessary, select the View menu's Refresh option and then try again. To avoid the problem in the future, close the Device Manager before trying to edit the Registry. If this message is displayed while you're editing Contents pane data within the HKDD section, remember that this data is maintained dynamically and cannot be edited via the Registry Editor.

Cannot import *path\filename*.REG: . . .

Note the rest of the message and refer to the following appropriate message continuation:

. . . Error accessing the registry. The most likely problem is the specific HKEY into which the specified file should be imported. In the specific case of the *HKEY_DYN_DATA* key, the message shown in Figure 8-1 serves as a reminder that its data is maintained dynamically by the system and cannot be imported by the user. For any other key, you might want to delete the existing key and then try the import procedure again.

Figure 8-1 *This message serves as warning that data cannot be imported into the* HKEY_DYN_DATA *key, which is maintained dynamically by Windows.*

. . . **Error opening the file. There may be a disk or file system error.** The first step is to verify that the cited file actually exists. If not, then the error is that someone may have accidentally deleted or moved it. But if the file is in the location specified by the message, then it's probably corrupt. If possible, open it in a text editor and see if it can be repaired.

. . . **Error writing to the registry.** The message gives no indication of the nature of the error, so it's difficult to impossible to guess the cause of the problem. However, the message has been seen on Windows 95 systems when trying to import a file into a key that would cause the size of that key to exceed approximately 64 Kbytes. Refer to the "Key Size Problem" section of Chapter 7 for further details.

. . . **The specified file is not a registry script. You can import only registry files.** If you accidentally tried to import an invalid Registry file, that's the reason for the message. However, if the file is believed to be a valid Registry script file (*filename.*REG), then perhaps it's damaged. Refer to the "Creating a Registry Script File for Importing" and "REGEDIT4 File Header" sections of Chapter 4, then open the file in an ASCII text editor, and make sure the file header is correctly written and that the general file format is correct. Edit the file as required (the most likely culprit is the file header) and then try again.

Cannot open . . . messages.

Note the rest of the message and refer to the following appropriate message continuation:

. . . **DefaultIcon: Error while opening key.** If this message is displayed during an attempt to view a *DefaultIcon* subkey under any *HKCR\AutoRun\x* key (where *x* is a number corresponding to a drive letter), there is probably no icon specified in the AUTORUN.INF file on the CD-ROM disc currently in the drive. To verify this, open the Registry Editor's View menu and select the Refresh option. The *DefaultIcon* subkey should no longer appear under the numbered key.

. . . **HKEY_CLASSES_ROOT: Error while opening key.** Open the View menu and select the Refresh option. If the plus sign next to the *HKCR* key disappears, then the *Classes* subkey under *HKEY_LOCAL_MACHINE\SOFTWARE* is probably missing or corrupt. To verify this, open *HKLM\SOFTWARE* and check for the existence of the *Classes* subkey. If it exists and appears to be in good order, then exit Windows via the Shut Down menu's Restart the Computer option. The Restart the computer in MS-DOS mode option probably won't work.

If the *HKLM\SOFTWARE\Classes* key structure does not exist, then import a valid copy of this key into the Registry before restarting. In either case, the *HKCR* key should be rebuilt from the valid *HKLM\SOFT-WARE\Classes* key when Windows restarts.

. . . *keyname*: **Error while opening key.** You may encounter this message if you attempt to open a key that was just deleted at a different location. For example, if you delete a certain *HKCU\Software\keyname* key during a clean-up operation, and then proceed directly to the *HKU\.Default\Software\keyname* key, that key might still be displayed, even though it was in fact just deleted. If you click the minus sign (if any) next to the key, the subkey structure beneath it may likewise be displayed, even though it too is in fact gone. To verify this, Open the View menu and select the Refresh option. The entire key structure should vanish.

If it is in fact important to export this missing key, then reimport the subkey under the *HKCU* key that was recently deleted (assuming you exported it prior to the deletion, of course). Having done that, this *HKU* version of the same key can now be exported.

Cannot rename *keyname*: Error while renaming key (*or* value). If this message is displayed while editing a subkey in the *HKEY_DYN_DATA* section, it is because these keys cannot be edited via the Registry Editor.

Cannot rename *keyname*: The specified key name . . . Note the rest of the message and refer to the following appropriate message continuation:

. . . **already exists. Type another name and try again.** This one should be self-explanatory. If not, it's time for a break.

. . . **contains illegal characters.** The only illegal ASCII character seems to be the backslash (\). Try some other character. Although most characters in the extended character set are not illegal, their use should be avoided if only for the sake of clarity.

. . . **is too long. Type a shorter name and try again.** The maximum length for a key name is 255 characters. If you need more space to express yourself, you should think about writing a book.

Export Registry File. The selected branch does not exist. Make sure that the correct path is given. Just disregard the last sentence, which makes no sense at all. If you highlight a key and select the Export option, then both the key and its path are obviously correct. The real problem is stated in the previous sentence: Although the selected branch no longer exists, apparently the Registry Editor window needs updating. Open the View menu, select the Refresh option, and the selected key structure should vanish. Because it wasn't there in the first place, it can't be exported.

Failure writing to the system registry. The registry may be corrupt, or you may not have the required permissions to write to the registry. If you're not sure about this, try to import a small subkey known to be good to some other location in the Registry. If the message repeats, then a data corruption or permissions problem will have to be resolved. Another possibility that is not apparent from the message is that the attempted import causes the key to exceed an approximate 64 Kbyte limit imposed in Windows 95. If this is a possibility, refer to the "Key Size Problem" section in Chapter 7 for assistance.

HKEY_DYN_DATA Error Messages. If any message is displayed while editing this HKEY, the problem is related to memory—yours. That is, you forgot that this key should not be edited. The *HKDD* key information is dynamically written and continuously refreshed by the system, and it cannot be changed via editing.

REGEDIT.EXE is not a valid Win32 application. This unlikely news is probably the result of damage to the application's file header. Rename the file as REGEDIT.OLD and expand a fresh copy into the C:\Windows folder. Once the Registry Editor is back in operation, discard the damaged REGEDIT.OLD file.

Registry Editor: Registry editing has been disabled by your administrator. The message indicates that the "Disable Registry editing tools" restriction is enabled. Refer to the "Restriction Recovery Procedure" section of Chapter 7 if you need to reenable this feature.

Unable to delete all specified values. This message, shown in Figure 8-2, is displayed if you attempt to delete the (Default) entry on the first line of any Contents pane. If this is the sole remaining entry in a subkey that is no longer needed, then delete the subkey itself.

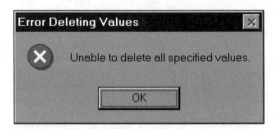

Figure 8-2 *The usual cause of this message is an attempt to delete a (Default) line in the Contents pane or another item that cannot be removed.*

The message is also displayed if you try to delete any Contents Pane entry in an *HKDD\Config Manager\Enum* subkey. These entries cannot be deleted or edited by the user.

Real-Mode Editing Session

As described in Chapter 4, the Registry Editor can also be run in real mode — that is, from an MS-DOS command prompt before opening, or after closing, the Windows GUI. Real-mode operations cannot function in a DOS window within Windows itself.

Cannot export path\filename.ext: ...

The message should be interpreted to mean "Cannot export the specified Registry key *to* the file indicated by *path\filename.ext.*" Note the rest of the message and refer to the following appropriate message continuation:

. . . Error creating the file. Most likely, the *path\filename.ext* format was not typed correctly. Make sure the specified path exists and that *filename.ext* does not. If it does, it will be erased without warning.

. . . The specified key name does not exist. The message is displayed if you try to export a nonexistent key to a file named *path\filename.ext.* If the message is displayed when attempting to export one of the six HKEYs, refer to the "Real Mode Export Notes" section of Chapter 4 for an explanation.

Error accessing the registry: The file may not be complete. This message may be displayed if you try to import a very large file into the Registry, because not enough conventional memory is available to handle the operation. You may want to try rebooting in a configuration that frees up as much conventional memory as possible. Or refer to the "Real Mode Problems" section of Chapter 7.

Invalid switch. Type **REGEDIT** (or **REGEDIT /?**) to review the list of valid switches. The /D switch is not listed or supported in the original version of Windows 95. The undocumented /S switch is invalid in real mode.

Parameter format not correct. Probably some switch-related information typed on the REGEDIT command line is in error. If necessary, type **REGEDIT** and review the correct syntax. Or refer to the "Registry Editor in Real Mode" section of Chapter 4 for assistance.

Too many parameters. Either that, or information that must follow a parameter (actually, a switch) was accidentally omitted.

Unable to open registry (14) — System.dat. See "Error accessing the registry" earlier in this chapter, which describes the same problem.

Unable to open registry (1,016) — *path\filename.ext.* The message really means that REGEDIT could not find the specified Registry file, and therefore no action was taken. The number 1,016 may be significant, but then on the other hand, it may not.

System Startup

Some messages listed in this section are probably erroneous if displayed during a system restart after you edit the Registry or after you use the System Policy Editor utility. Such messages are often part of a sequence of error messages, including one or more pertaining to the Registry itself. For example, a message reporting insufficient memory or an incorrect display is clearly erroneous if the memory and/or display functioned properly before editing the Registry. As a general rule, just ignore any message that seems to have nothing to do with the Registry and resolve the immediate Registry problem first. Once the Registry itself is in good shape, the non-Registry message may no longer be displayed. If a message does persist though, then there is a problem not related to the Registry, which will have to be resolved.

If several erroneous error messages are displayed at startup, there's also a possibility that the MSDOS.SYS file is corrupted. Refer to the "MSDOS.SYS File Problem" section of Chapter 7 for help in verifying this possibility.

If a command-line message is displayed and is immediately replaced by the Windows opening splash screen, press the Escape and Pause keys. This clears the splash screen and halts the startup procedure so that you can read the message. Once you've seen it, press any key to resume the startup.

Cannot find a device file that may be needed to run Windows. The windows registry or SYSTEM.INI file refers to this device file, but the device no longer exists. If you deleted . . . (etc.)

This message may conclude as shown by the following two examples. Follow the directions given here, as appropriate.

. . . filename.vxd (*followed by*) **Press any key to continue.** If you're not sure why this message is displayed, check the [386Enh] section of SYS-TEM.INI for a device=filename.vxd line. If that line exists, then the cited file was probably erased from the C:\Windows\System folder, either by accident or on purpose. If in doubt, place a semicolon at the beginning of the line to disable it. If some application subsequently displays a "cannot find *filename*.vxd" message, you can probably find a copy of the missing file in that application's distribution diskettes. If so, expand the file into the folder and reenable the SYSTEM.INI line.

If the previously cited device line is not in SYSTEM.INI, then open the Registry and highlight the *HKLM\System\CurrentControlSet\ Services\VxD* key. Open the View menu, select the Find option, and search the Data column for *filename*.vxd. If you know the open subkey under the *VxD* key is no longer needed, then highlight it and delete it. If you're not sure, export the key first and then delete it. As stated previously, an error message informs you if any application needs the missing file. If so, restore it to the C:\Windows\System folder and import the key back into the Registry.

. . . **Press any key to continue.** (No device file is listed, and Windows opens properly when any key is pressed.) Because no file is specified, the problem is in the Registry, not in SYSTEM.INI. Highlight the *HKLM* key cited previously, but this time search the "Values" column for *StaticVxD,* which can be found in practically every subkey. As each one is highlighted by the search process, watch the Data column for an empty ("") entry. If one is found, then delete the open subkey.

Cannot import *path\filename*.**REG: . . . (further explanation here).** If this message is displayed as the Windows GUI opens, there's a REGEDIT shortcut in the StartUp group that specifies a file that can't be imported, perhaps because it no longer exists. If so, remove the shortcut from the StartUp group to prevent the message from repeating. Refer to this message in the "Registry Editing Session" section if further assistance is needed to resolve the problem.

Cannot open *filename.ext:* **Error opening the file. The previous registry has been restored.** There may in fact be a problem with the cited file, or that file may not exist. In any case, REGEDIT has copied the backup Registry files to create a new Registry.

Connecting X: to \\(computer name)\(folder or filename). In most cases, this is simply an informational message displayed briefly as Windows opens. If the connection fails, however, it is followed by an error message. Refer to that message here for assistance.

Display: There is a problem with your display settings. The adapter type is incorrect, or the current settings do not work with your hardware. If this message is displayed after you edit the Registry and reopen Windows, just ignore it and resolve any Registry error messages that follow. If the message persists, then there is indeed a display problem that will have to be resolved.

Display: Your display adapter is not configured properly. To correct the problem, click OK to start the Hardware Installation wizard. Due to a Registry corruption problem, Windows probably created a new SYS-TEM.DAT file based on the contents of the SYSTEM.1ST file. Although you can correct the immediate problem by clicking OK, this does not resolve any other issues related to the original problem. Refer to the discussion of file recovery in the "General Troubleshooting Techniques" section of Chapter 7 for additional information.

Error accessing the system registry. You should restore the registry now and restart your computer. (See Figure 8-3 for the complete message.) Note that the button at the bottom of the message window is labeled Restore From Backup and Restart, and no other alternative is available. Furthermore, the Close button in the upper-right corner of the window has no effect. Just click on the Restore button and restart the computer when prompted to do so. If Windows is able to restore the Registry from its backup files, no further messages are displayed.

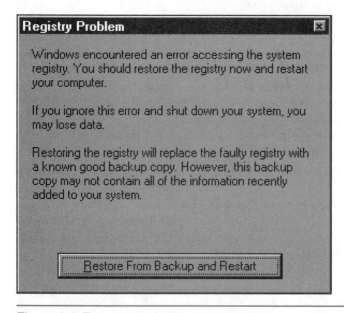

Figure 8-3 *The message implies you actually have a choice. Just click on the Restore button and hope for the best.*

Error encountered while backing up the system registry. Make sure you have enough space on the drive for three copies of the file C:\WINDOWS\SYSTEM.DAT [*or,* USER.DAT]. This error should not cause any loss of information, but if space is not made on the drive you may experience additional problems. Please fix the problem, and then restart your computer. Assuming "the problem" is indeed limited space, then you'll have to free some space by moving or deleting some files. However, the message may also be related to a defective driver loaded by the CONFIG.SYS or AUTOEXEC.BAT file. If this is a possibility, reboot the system and bypass any such drivers. If that resolves the problem, then determine which driver is causing the problem and replace it.

When you press the OK button, if the desktop reverts to its initial appearance when Windows was first installed, then the current SYSTEM.DAT file was probably just copied from the early SYSTEM.1ST file in the C:\ (root) directory. In that case, this message will probably reappear every time you open Windows. If so, refer to the "Windows 95 Registry File Replacement" or "Windows 98 Registry File Replacement" section of Chapter 7 for assistance.

Error in filename.ext. Missing entry: (or similar explanation). If the message context is unclear (after all, this *is* Windows), and the filename does not suggest anything that loads via the StartUp folder or WIN.INI's `load=` or `run=` lines, open the following Registry key:

HKEY_LOCAL_MACHINE\SOFTWARE\Microsoft\
Windows\CurrentVersion\Run

Search the Data column for an entry in which the cited filename appears. Chances are, a switch or parameter on that line is invalid. If necessary, uninstall the application and then reinstall it.

Error loading *filename.ext*. The system cannot find the file specified. Although the message is self-explanatory, the reason for its appearance may not be. In case of doubt, open the *HKLM\...\Run* key cited in the previous message and search the Data column for a line that lists the cited file. If you can't account for why the file is missing, uninstall the application and then reinstall it.

Explorer: This program has performed an illegal operation and will be shut down. If the problem persists, contact the program vendor. If you click the Close button, an empty desktop is displayed, and on pressing the Ctrl+Alt+Del keys, the Close Program window is completely empty. This indicates a serious Registry corruption problem that was nevertheless undetected by Windows during startup. Do *not* let Windows try to start again, or it may backup the corrupted Registry and thereby destroy a good backup set (if it has not done so already). Instead, go directly to the "Manual Registry Recovery Procedures" section of Chapter 7 for assistance in resolving this problem.

"Nag" screen messages on startup. They're not exactly error messages, but you may be bombarded with a variety of welcomes or tips as part of the Windows opening festivities. In most cases, a checkbox can be cleared (or checked) to permanently delete the message screen. Others, however, are displayed at regular intervals until you either do what they want you to do or figure out how to kill them. If you need help disabling (or possibly, reenabling) such messages, refer to the "Nag Screen Troubleshooting" section of Chapter 7.

Networking: The following error occurred while reconnecting *X:* **to** *(network computer name)\(share name).* **The share name was not found. Be sure you typed it correctly. Do you want to restore this connection the next time you log on?** A subkey under the *HKCU\Network\Persistent* key refers to a network share name (network drive, folder, or file) that is not presently available. If you click the Yes button, the contents of the subkey are deleted, and the message won't be displayed again the next time Windows opens. Click the No button if you believe the problem is temporary and want to reattempt the same connection the next time Windows opens. See the "Network Connections" section of Chapter 6 if this is a recurring problem.

New Hardware Found. Various erroneous new hardware messages may be displayed during startup if there is a Registry problem. Just click the Cancel button as often as required. Click the Yes button when prompted to restart the computer. If the message repeats, then Windows probably has redetected some hardware device that needs to be installed again. If all else appears to be well, then follow the prompts to complete the hardware detection procedure.

Registry/configuration error . . .

Refer to the appropriate message continuation seen here for assistance:

. . . Choose Safe mode, to start Windows with a minimal set of drivers. Windows may choose the Safe mode for you and continue to load itself without giving you the option to intervene. If a Registry Problem message such as that seen in Figure 8-3 is displayed, then refer to that message in this section. Or if Windows eventually opens in its Safe mode, exit Windows and restart the system. If the same message sequence repeats and backup Registry files are not available, then you'll have to reinstall Windows.

Note that this message is also seen if there is an error in the MSDOS.SYS file. If so, choosing safe mode will usually display one or more errors messages and Windows will not open. If necessary, refer to the "MSDOS.SYS File Problem" section of Chapter 7 for assistance.

. . . Choose,[*sic*] Command prompt only, and run SCANREG. This message is displayed when Windows 98 detects a corrupted Registry file on startup and the system halts at the command prompt. When the ScanReg utility is run, Windows retrieves the most recent good backup set, then prompts you to restart the system. Although the nature of the error is not revealed, the four startup files are saved into an RBBAD.CAB file in the C:\Windows\Sysbckup folder, as described in the "Backup of Corrupted Registry File" section of Chapter 5.

Registry File was not found. Registry services may be inoperative for this session. (Message may be followed by a full-screen MS-DOS command prompt.) This message is usually attributable to a SYSTEM.DAT problem that Windows did not resolve by using a backup file. Rename the existing SYSTEM.DAT as SYSTEM.OLD (or similar). In Windows 95, make a copy of SYSTEM.DA0 as SYSTEM.DAT. In Windows 98, expand a fresh copy of SYSTEM.DAT from the most recent RB00x.CAB file or from successively older backups in the other RB00x.CAB files. If the problem persists, then rerun the Windows setup procedure.

Registry Problem. If this phrase is displayed in the message window's title bar, the accompanying text provides specific details, as shown by the examples in Figures 8-3 and 8-4. Refer to those messages here for further assistance.

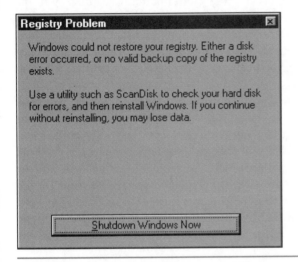

Figure 8-4 *Another no-choice message. Like the message seen in Figure 8-3, the close button in the upper-right corner does nothing but provide a nice decorative touch.*

Restrictions: This operation has been cancelled due to restrictions in effect on this computer. Please contact your system administrator. If the message is displayed as Windows opens, count the number of times the OK button must be clicked to get rid of it. That's the number of programs (unidentified, of course) in the StartUp folder that can't be executed due to Registry restrictions. If you need to verify this, restart Windows and hold down the Shift key to bypass these programs. If this resolves the problem, then either remove the items from the Startup folder, or refer to the "Restriction Recovery Procedures" section of Chapter 7 for assistance in removing the restrictions.

Shortcut, Problem with: (followed by explanatory message). If some shortcuts don't work after restarting Windows 95, it's possible that the SYSTEM.DAT file was corrupted, and Windows created a new version based on the SYSTEM.1ST file in the C:\ (root) folder, rather than using the SYSTEM.DA0 file. To verify this, refer to the "Windows 95 Registry File Replacement" section of Chapter 7.

System Error: Windows cannot read from drive A: If this is a network drive, make sure the network is working. If it is a local drive, check the disk. And if it's neither of the previously described problems, the message doesn't make much sense. Yet it may be displayed if the Registry files are severely damaged. If so, clicking the Cancel button leads directly to the Windows Setup wizard's User Information screen. If valid backup Registry files are available, exit the Setup procedure, replace the current SYSTEM.DAT and USER.DAT files with valid backup versions, and restart the system. Otherwise, you may have to complete the Setup procedure to restore the Registry.

System Settings Change: To finish restoring your registry, you must restart your computer. Do you want to restart your computer now? This is usually the final message after one or more other messages about a Registry problem are displayed. If you click the Yes button, the system should restart with no further problems noted. It should, but if it doesn't, it may return to a previously-seen Registry Problem message. If valid backup Registry files are available, replace the current SYSTEM.DAT and USER.DAT files with the valid backup versions and restart the system. Otherwise, you may have to complete the Setup procedure to restore the Registry.

If you click the No button in the System Settings Change box, the message loop may repeat, display a "Windows is running in safe mode" message, and then repeat the message cycle.

There is not enough memory to load the registry, or the registry is corrupted. Some devices may not function properly (DOS screen). If this message is displayed when Windows starts or restarts after you edit the Registry, then it's quite likely the problem has nothing to do with memory. If a password prompt appears shortly after the message is displayed, it will probably be followed by an erroneous "You have not logged on at this computer before" message. If so, click the No button to continue and resolve any other error messages that are displayed.

Unable to open VxD. Error code: 2 If this message is the last of several puzzling error messages seen as the Windows GUI opens, the problem may be caused by a corrupted MSDOS.SYS file. If so, refer to the "MSDOS.SYS File Problem" section in the previous chapter if you need assistance verifying this.

Unable to update configuration from *location*. **Error** *xx: (explanation here).* **You may need to contact your administrator.** Or maybe not: the location specified in the message may be listed in the *HKLM\System\CurrentControlSet\control\Update* key, and for one reason or another, that location is now unavailable. The explanation following the error number may provide additional information, as shown in the following few examples:

Error 2: The system cannot find the file specified.

Error 3: The system cannot find the path specified.

Error 5: Access is denied.

Error 21: The device is not ready.

Error 161: The specified path is invalid.

If you're not sure how to resolve the problem, delete the Verbose entry in the *Update* subkey's Contents pane. This does not resolve the problem, but it does prevent the message from repeating each time Windows opens. Refer to "Settings" in the "Start menu" section of Chapter 6 for information about this key.

Windows could not restore your registry. Either a disk error occurred, or no valid backup copy of the registry exists. Use a utility such as ScanDisk to check your hard disk for errors, and then reinstall Windows. If you continue without reinstalling, you may lose data. If there is indeed a problem with the hard disk, follow the advice given in this message. However, if the message is displayed after you edit the Registry and restart the system, then the more likely problem is that a valid copy of the Windows 95 backup SYSTEM.DA0 and/or USER.DA0 files could not be found in the C:\WINDOWS folder, or the Windows 98 backup sets are not in the C:\Windows\Sysbckup folder. If you have backup copies located elsewhere, move them into the correct location and try again.

Or if you previously used the Registry Editor's Export option to save a full copy of the Registry into a *filename*.REG file, reboot the system to a command prompt and then use the REGEDIT utility in its real mode to restore the Registry. If you need assistance with this, refer to the "Registry Restore Procedures" section of Chapter 5 for detailed instructions. However, if you do not have a full backup file available, you'll have to reinstall Windows.

In Figure 8-4, the button at the bottom of the message window is labeled "Shutdown Windows Now"; no other choice is available, and the

Close button in the upper-right corner has no effect. Press the Shutdown button, and the System Settings Change window is displayed. Refer to the discussion of that message, earlier in this chapter, for additional details.

Windows was not properly shut down. One or more of your disk drives may have errors on it. Press any key to Run ScanDisk on these drives.... Believe it or not, it's not a Registry issue and is mentioned here simply to save the curious user endless search hours looking for a Registry entry that isn't there. Instead, Windows (SR2 and Windows 98) clears a "Clean Shutdown" bit as it starts and then resets it during a proper (that is, a *clean*) shutdown. If the system is improperly shut down (powered off during a Windows session, for example), the bit remains cleared, and so Windows knows there was a problem during the previous session. Make it happy: Let it run ScanDisk and remember to do a clean shutdown next time.

If Norton Disk Doctor is installed, this message is not displayed, and the Norton diagnostic/repair procedure begins automatically.

You have not logged on at this computer before. Would you like this computer to retain your individual settings for use when you log on here in the future? If this message is displayed after you edit the Registry, it is probably erroneous. Assuming you *have* logged on previously, click the No button to continue. In fact, do so even if you have not logged on here before and resolve the Registry problem first.

System Shutdown

The following messages are typical of those that may appear as the system is shut down.

Access to the specified device, path, or file is denied. If the message is displayed when the Shut Down menu's Restart in MS-DOS mode option is selected, refer to the same message in the "Other Error Messages," section later in this chapter.

MS-DOS Prompt. One or more programs did not close. Quit your other programs, and then try again. If no MS-DOS programs are in fact open, the message is probably erroneous, as sometimes happens when shutting down Windows after using the Registry Editor or the System Policies Editor. Just ignore the message and try the Shutdown procedure again. If the problem persists, open the C:\Windows\Start Menu\Programs\StartUp folder and examine various MS-DOS shortcut icons. Make sure each one is set to Close on exit.

Sharing. There are *x* user(s) connected to your computer. Shutting down your computer will disconnect them. Do you want to continue? If this message is displayed when you attempt a shutdown after using the Policy Editor, it may be erroneous. If you're sure no users are connected, then click the Yes button to continue. Otherwise, click No and use the Net Watcher applet to verify connections. If there are none, then ignore the message and shut down the system. The message may be followed by an erroneous MS-DOS prompt or other message.

This program cannot be run due to restrictions in effect on this computer. Please contact your system administrator. The message may be displayed if the Shut Down menu's Restart the computer in MS-DOS mode option is selected (in Windows 98, the option is simply Restart in MS-DOS mode). Or it may show up if any MS-DOS prompt is selected or if "Command" is typed in the Start menu's Run box. If so, a "Disable MS-DOS prompt" restriction has disabled the desired action. Refer to the "Restriction Recovery Procedure" section in the previous chapter if you need assistance resolving this problem.

Backup and Restore

Messages such as these may show up during a Registry backup or restore operation.

Backup cannot find this file (during a file comparison after backup). Refer to the "Errors occurred during this operation" message that follows.

Errors occurred during this operation. Do you want to view them now? (Error log reports "Microsoft Backup cannot find this file" for files named HKLMBACK and HKUBACK.) If the Microsoft Backup utility is configured for full backup, these two temporary files are created in the C:\Windows folder, backed up along with everything else, then used during a Restore procedure to rebuild the Registry. Because the files have no other purpose, they are erased from the C:\Windows folder when the Backup utility is exited. Therefore, the error message is displayed if the utility is subsequently reopened for file comparison, because the files are no longer available for comparison. This is part of the normal backup/restore operation, and if no other "cannot find" message is seen, the backup set can be presumed to be good.

Registry 'Replace' function failed internally. Look for any hidden files. The Configuration Backup utility creates hidden files and subsequently erases them at the conclusion of the backup procedure. This message may occur during a Restore operation, if the files were not erased at the conclusion of the last backup. If so, use Explorer's Find option to seat the C:\Windows folder for all "*.~~R" files and erase them. Or open an MS-DOS window and type the following commands:

attrib -h *.~~R   To unhide the hidden temporary files

erase *.~~R   To erase them

Now try the Restore operation again.

System restore operation failed. This ominous message is displayed in Windows 98 if the user selects the Cancel option (seen in Figure 5-12) before a Registry restore action begins. Just ignore it. If however the message is displayed during a restore operation, then try to restore the Registry from a different RB00x.CAB file instead.

Topic does not exist. Contact your application vendor for an updated Help file (129). On some SR versions of Windows 95, the Configuration Backup utility's Help Topics window displays a Contents tab that leads to a Troubleshooting book icon. The message is displayed if the "Registry restore fails with an error" document icon is selected. To access the topic (which is *not* missing), select the Find tab and type **Registry** in the textbox at the top of the window. Then check the "Registry restore fails with an error" topic below and click the Display button. Or refer to the previous "Registry 'Replace' function failed," message which covers the same ground.

Uninstall Procedure

One of the messages listed here may be displayed during a Windows uninstall procedure or when you attempt to delete a folder in an Explorer window. If so, follow the instructions given here and then repeat the operation that caused the message to be displayed. In all cases, refer to the "Troubleshooting Uninstall Procedures" section of Chapter 7 if you need further assistance in resolving the problem.

Once you've completed the uninstall or folder-removal operation without bumping into an error message, you may want to consult the "Registry Cleanup Techniques" section of Chapter 5 for assistance in cleaning up additional Registry entries that may remain in place.

Error occurred while trying to remove *application name*. Uninstallation has been canceled. If the message is displayed when you try to use Control Panel's Add/Remove Programs applet to remove an application, then that application may have already been removed manually. However, its presence on the Install/Uninstall list indicates that remnants remain in the Registry.

Setup cannot find the files on '*X:*\' from which you originally installed the product. If this is a network server, make sure that the server is still available. This message may be displayed if you try to uninstall a Windows application via Control Panel's Add/Remove Programs applet. If the problem is not related to a server, the most likely explanation is a recent drive letter change, as might occur if a newly installed drive pushed the CD-ROM drive letter from, say, D to E, and the application had been installed from a CD-ROM disc prior to the change. If possible, temporarily uninstall the new drive so that the CD-ROM can fall back to its original drive letter, then try again. Or locate the Registry references to the former drive letter, change them to the new letter, and then retry the uninstall procedure.

Setup Error 544: Setup is unable to open the data file *path\filename.*STF; run Setup again from where you originally ran it. This is another uninstall error message. The cited path and filename are listed in a Registry *Uninstall* subkey, and the file containing the information needed to complete the procedure may be missing or corrupted. When you click the OK button, the following messages may be displayed in succession:

Setup Error 723: The processing of top-level information has failed.

Setup was not completed successfully.

Just ignore them, don't waste time speculating about the other 722 setup errors, and refer to the "Troubleshooting Uninstall Procedures" section of Chapter 7 for further assistance.

This change may impact one or more registered programs. Do you want to continue? This message is displayed if you try to delete a file or folder from within Explorer and a Registry entry refers to that item. It also shows up if the delete action would remove an executable file cited in a Load= or Run= line in WIN.INI, even if there is no reference to that file in the Registry. In either case, click the No button, resolve the Registry or WIN.INI conflict, and then try again. Refer to the "File or Folder Removal Problem" section of Chapter 7 if you need assistance doing so.

Unable to locate the installation log file (*path and file name here***).** **Uninstallation will not continue.** This message indicates the uninstall routine uses the C:\Windows\UNINST.EXE utility, and that utility can't find what it needs to do the uninstallation procedure. The cited file may be missing, but it's more likely that the contents of the entire path are gone.

Other Error Messages

Although a few messages discussed in this section make direct reference to the Registry, most don't and may not even seem directly related to a Registry problem. In either case though, the suggested action or edit may resolve the problem that caused the message to be displayed.

Access to the specified device, path, or file is denied. A restriction is in effect that prevents the desired operation from occurring. If the message is displayed when the Shut Down menu's Restart in MS-DOS mode option is selected, try to run any DOS application. If a "Program cannot be run due to restrictions . . ." message is displayed, that confirms the existence of an MS-DOS restriction.

In other cases, if there is no obvious explanation for this message, the Registry's *CLSID* key for the specified object may be among the missing. If that's a possibility, then refer to the "Access Denied Problems" section in the previous chapter for assistance in resolving the problem.

Fatal exception 0E has occurred at 0028:*xxxxxxxx* in VxD VMM(06) + *xxxxxxxx*. Fatal exception messages may be generated by a variety of causes, but this one is usually the result of a damaged Registry file. If a fatal exception message repeats after restoring the Registry from valid backup files, then try to isolate it to the specific application event the causes it. In this case however, the solution may not be related to the Registry.

Device Status: . . .

When using Device Manager to view system configuration, a small exclamation mark or other icon overlay indicates a device problem, as shown in Figure 8-5. Select that device, click the Properties button, and note the message in the General tab's Device status section. Two of the many messages that may be displayed are also shown in the figure and listed here:

. . . Invalid data in registry (Code 9.)

. . . Registry returned unknown result (Code 19.)

Each code number is simply a cross-reference to the message itself, and neither gives sufficient information to deduce the specific problem. However, if any such message is displayed in this area, the general problem is that some item in the current Registry database does not agree with an actual device setting, probably due to a hardware/software configuration conflict. Because the Registry has, in effect, "got it wrong," the best solution is to click the OK button and then the Device Manager tab's Remove button for the cited device. Exit Device Manager, open Control Panel's Add/Remove Hardware applet, and follow the prompts to reinstall the device. If this does not clear up the configuration problem, then you may need to contact the device manufacturer for further assistance.

Invalid (*or* damaged, unrecognizable, etc.) diskette. Windows over-writes the OEM name field on a diskette as part of its volume tracking system. As a result, some applications may no longer recognize the diskette, and therefore an error message is displayed the next time it is accessed, even though it is in fact neither invalid nor damaged. Unfortunately, the only workaround is to use the Debug utility (or a similar utility) to restore

Figure 8-5 *An exclamation mark or other overlay icon (see inset) indicates a problem with the device on which it is displayed. Click the Properties button and check the General tab's Device Status section for a clue, such as the Registry problems seen in this composite illustration.*

Refer to the "Volume Tracking Problem" section of Chapter 7 for more information about this "feature" and for ways to protect yourself against it.

Modem is Busy or Not Responding. If this problem cannot be resolved by other means, open the following Registry key and look for the Contents pane entries listed here:

HKLM\System\CurrentControlSet\Services\Class\Modem\0000\ Settings

Name	Data (original)	Data (revised)
FlowControl_Hard	"\Q3"	""
InactivityTimeout	"\T<#>"	""
SpeedNegotiationOn	"N1"	""

Double-click each Name entry and delete the highlighted string in the Value Data box. Each data string varies from those shown here, depending on the specific hardware configuration, but in any case, it should be deleted. However, do not delete the Name entry itself. When in doubt, open the *0000* key one level above *Settings* and make sure the DriverDesc entry agrees with the modem that is actually installed. If all else fails, open Device Manager, highlight the modem, and click the Remove button. Then exit, reopen Windows, and reinstall it. If necessary, restart the system once with the modem physically removed or, if external, powered off.

Problem creating object: The system cannot find the file specified. If the message is displayed when the cascading New menu is used to create a new file or a certain type, there is a problem with that file's *HKCR\.ext\ShellNew* subkey. Refer to the "New Menu Option is Inoperative" section of Chapter 7 for assistance, or refer to the "HTML Document" section of Chapter 6 if the problem involves a new HTML document.

Program Not Found: Windows cannot find *filename*.EXE. This program is needed for opening files of type '(*type description*).' If this message box is displayed after double-clicking a document file with a certain extension, then the executable program required to open that file is either missing, or the record of its location in the Registry is incorrect. The several methods of resolving the problem are described here.

1. **Find the *filename*.EXE file.** If necessary, use Explorer to find, or verify, the location of the *filename*.EXE file. If the file cannot be found, then you'll need to expand a fresh copy into the appropriate folder. Refer to "File Finding" in the "Other File Replacement" section of Chapter 7 if you need assistance locating a missing file.

2. **Enter path to the *filename*.EXE file.** If you enter the correct path to the specified file, Windows writes that information into the [programs] section of WIN.INI, and it takes precedence over the Registry entry that is presumably obsolete. Although this is the fastest resolution to the immediate problem, it works by bypassing the Registry instead of fixing it. If you need to resume operations quickly, you may want to use this method now and then repair the Registry later when you have more time, by following the procedure given immediately below.

3. **Repair the Registry Data.** Open the Registry's *HKCR* key and highlight the *.ext* subkey, where EXT is the extension of the document file. In the (Default) row, make a note of the string in the Data column, search HKCR for the subkey with that name, and open its *Shell\Open\command* subkey. The (Default) Data string indicates the path where the executable file should be located. If necessary, change the path to indicate the correct location. Or if the path is correct, then note the name of the executable file and expand a fresh copy of that file into the indicated location.

Note

If you enter a new path in response to the "Cannot find" message, that path is written into the [programs] section of WIN.INI, and the information in the Registry remains unchanged.

Properties for this item are not available. If this message is displayed when a Context menu's Properties option is selected, the most likely culprits are a missing subkey related to the object or a DLL or CPL file that supports the Properties sheet. If you need help locating the missing element, refer to the "Properties Sheet Troubleshooting" section of Chapter 7.

A less likely suspect is an erroneous Attributes entry in a *ShellFolder* subkey. If this key exists and bit 30 is set, then the Properties option is listed on the Context menu where, presumably, it belongs. However, if the bit is set to 1 when it should be 0, then the option is erroneous, and this error message is displayed when it is selected. Refer to the "Attribute Flags [Attributes]" section and Table 6-2 in Chapter 6 for additional details.

Restrictions: This operation cannot be run [*or*, has been cancelled] due to restrictions in effect on this computer. Please contact your system administrator. Assuming the message is valid, contact your administrator if you want to remove the restriction. If the restriction is accidental, then refer to the "Restriction Recovery Procedures" section of Chapter 7 for assistance in removing it.

SDMErr (80000003): Registry access failed. The message indicates that Registry damage prevents Windows from successfully completing a hardware detection operation. Refer to the "Registry Reconstruction Procedure" section of Chapter 5 for instructions on reconstructing the Registry; then retry the operation that produced the message.

The object that '(*path here*)\MS-DOS Prompt.pif' refers to has been removed or is unaccessible. If this message follows an "Operation has been cancelled" message, it indicates a "Disable MS-DOS prompt" restriction is in effect. Just ignore it, resolve the problem that caused the previous message, and this one will go away, too. Refer to the "Restriction Recovery Procedures" section of Chapter 7 for assistance in removing it.

Unable to determine your network address. The UUID generated is unique to this computer only. It should not be used on another computer. This message is displayed if the CLSID Generator utility (described in Chapter 6) is run on a machine that lacks a network card. If the device is temporarily unavailable (a removed PC card network adapter, for example), reinstall it and try again. Otherwise, the last six bytes of the CLSID number are randomly generated, and apparently the odds are not as favorable that the entire number will be unique within the universe as we know it.

You must restart your computer before the new settings will take effect. Do you want to restart your computer now? It's not an error message, of course — it's just to let you know that a recently-completed configuration procedure will not take effect until the system is restarted. If a problem occurs after doing so, and the solution is not obvious, refer to the "System Startup" and "System Shutdown" sections of the previous chapter for assistance.

Appendix

Tweak UI and the Registry

The Tweak UI (tweak the User Interface) applet began life as one of several applets included in the free Power Toys download on the Microsoft Web site. It offers many Windows customization features and — perhaps due to its popularity — is now included on the Windows 98 CD-ROM disc. Because Tweak UI is such a convenient means to demonstrate the Windows Registry in action, the following sections describe the edits made as each of its features is enabled or disabled by the user. Although most such edits could be made by directly editing the Registry, it is certainly easier to let Tweak UI do the work instead. These edits are examples of the relationship that exists between almost any Windows application and the Windows Registry, and by following along with the descriptions given here, the user may get a better idea of general Registry editing procedures. To do so, open the Registry Editor and locate the key cited in the descriptions that follow. Note the current value of the appropriate item in the Contents pane, leave the Registry Editor window open, and make a change from within Tweak UI. Click the applet's Apply button, then open the Registry Editor's View menu, and select the Refresh option (or simply press F5). The change should be immediately noted in the Contents pane. In a few cases it may be necessary to close and reopen the Registry Editor for the change to take effect.

Tweak UI Installation

Installing Tweak UI is one of life's simpler chores. In fact it probably takes longer to describe the task than to actually do it. The first step is to locate the required files, as described here for both versions of Windows.

Windows 95 files

Windows 95 users can download the complete PowerToys suite — or just Tweak UI — from the Microsoft Web site. Those who lack the patience to penetrate Microsoft's electronic labyrinth may find it much faster to get there via the *Windows Magazine* Web site (`http://www.winmag.com`), which tries its best to maintain unbroken links to this and other free downloads. Download the file (current name is W95TWEAKUI.EXE), move it into a C:\TEMP folder or another convenient location, double-click it to extract the TWEAK UI files and then refer to the "Installation Procedure" section below to continue.

Windows 98 files

The Tweak UI files are conveniently located on the Windows 98 CD-ROM disc, in the \tools\reskit\powertoy folder that, despite its name, does not contain any other applets from the original PowerToys suite. Presumably these applets will continue to be available at the Microsoft Web site, but they are not discussed in this appendix.

Installation procedure

The following files can be found in one of the locations cited above.

Filename	Contents	Destination
TWEAKUI.CNT	Tweak UI help contents	C:\Windows\Help
TWEAKUI.CPL	Tweak UI applet	C:\Windows\System
TWEAKUI.HLP	Help file	C:\Windows\Help
TWEAKUI.INF	Installation instructions	C:\Windows\Inf
README.TXT	General information	None (not copied)

To install the applet, open the TWEAKUI.INF file's Context menu and select the Install option to copy the files into the destination folders previously listed. The installation procedure places a Tweak UI icon in the Control Panel window; the icon can be dragged to the Windows desktop to create a shortcut to it. It also adds a Registry entry that permits Tweak UI to perform various user-specified actions on startup. Additional details are provided in the "Tweak UI at Startup" section at the end of this appendix, after the actions themselves have been introduced and described.

The Windows 98 Install procedure pauses at the "Introducing Tweak UI" step to display the "About Tweak UI" window shown in Figure A-1, and you must close the window to proceed. Although this is no major problem for a one-time installation, it might be worthwhile to copy the \powertoy folder to a diskette if you want to do multiple unattended installations. Then clear the TWEAKUI.INF file's read-only attribute, open it in Notepad, find the [TweakUI.Add.Reg] section header, and put a semicolon in front of the last line in that section, as follows:

```
[TweakUI.Add.Reg]
; HKLM, %SMWCV%\RunOnce ... Main %18%\TWEAKUI.HLP"

...

[Strings]
SMWCV="Software\Microsoft\Windows\CurrentVersion"
```

The %SMWCV% segment in the HKLM line (abbreviated above) is a pointer to an entry in the [Strings] section shown by the last two lines above. In other words, the complete Registry key structure is *HKLM\Software\ Microsoft\Windows\CurrentVersion\RunOnce.* By disabling this line, the help screen pause during the Install procedure is eliminated.

Tweak UI Applet Tabs

The following sections describe the relationship between the Windows Registry and the various options available via Tweak UI's tabs. Because their purpose is to show how a typical application or applet writes data into the Registry, tab option descriptions are limited to whatever is needed to follow along. Although most options are self-explanatory, some additional information is available via the Tips button on the Mouse tab, and the help (question mark) button and "What's This?" popup help. Note however that the quality of this help varies from reasonably-informative to worse than useless.

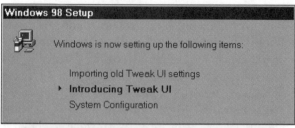

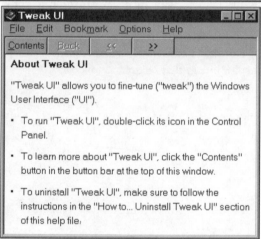

Figure A-1 *The Windows 98 Tweak UI setup procedure pauses at this screen until the user closes the "About Tweak UI" window. A simple Registry edit can eliminate this step, which may be helpful when installing the applet on multiple systems.*

The tabs are listed here in alphabetical order, although they don't appear that way in either of the Tweak UI applets. In Windows 95, they appear in two horizontal rows, while Windows 98 contains a single horizontal row with a pair of arrow buttons at the end. Click the appropriate button to scroll the tabs in either direction. The figures in the sections that follow illustrate both styles. Unless otherwise noted, entries in the Data column in the accompanying tables indicate the default value for that item, or the value if that item alone is enabled. Note that the manner in which data is recorded varies from one Tweak UI tab to another, and even within a single tab. For example, the status of seven options in the Windows 98 General tab's Effects section is determined by seven binary flags within a single UserPreferenceMask entry (see Table A-4). In contrast, the status of the nine options in the IE4 tab's Settings section is written into nine different entries of four bytes each (see Table A-5), even though only one bit is required to record each option's current status. In many cases a lengthy key structure abbreviated in the text (*HKCU\...\CurrentVersion,* for example) is listed in full within the appropriate table.

Add/Remove tab

The text at the top of this tab notes that "The following software can be automatically removed by Windows," and although the statement is certainly true, it does not apply to this tab. Instead, if a listed application is highlighted and the Remove button clicked, that application disappears from the list in Control Panel's Add/Remove Programs applet, which was shown in Chapter 7 in Figure 7-14. Tweak UI accomplishes this by removing the associated Registry entry (shown in the same figure) while leaving the application itself and its other Registry entries undisturbed. As a result, the application continues to function normally but can no longer be uninstalled via the Add/Remove Programs applet.

This feature can be convenient for preventing unauthorized "helpers" from removing applications by accident or on purpose, but it does make things difficult if you eventually decide the application should indeed be removed. Therefore, you may want to export a copy of the associated Registry key to diskette before clicking the Remove button. By so doing, you can import it back into the Registry later on if it becomes necessary to do a full uninstall. The feature is also helpful if an application has been removed, but its listing on the Add/Remove list remains. In this case, Tweak UI's Remove button is the fastest way to delete the listing, too.

Although the Edit button can be used to edit any *Uninstall* subkey, note that the nomenclature differs from that seen in the Registry Editor window, as follows:

Edit Button	Registry Editor
Uninstall Command dialog box	**Name column in Contents pane**
Description:	DisplayName
Command:	UninstallString

Boot tab

Although this tab has no effect on the Registry, its functions are briefly listed for the sake of completeness. As each option is modified, the Windows MSDOS.SYS startup file is edited (see Table A-1). The edit takes effect when the Apply button is clicked. To restore the MSDOS.SYS file to its original post-setup configuration, click on the "Restore Factory Settings" button.

Table A-1 *Boot Tab: Startup File Modifications*

Tab Options	MSDOS.SYS Line	Factory Settings
General		
Function keys available	BootKeys=1	1
For *xx* seconds (Windows 95 only) †	BootDelay=xx	2
Start GUI automatically	BootGUI=1	1
Display splash screen while booting	Logo=1	1
Allow F4 to boot previous operating system †	BootMulti=1	0
Autorun Scandisk	AutoScan=	1
Never		0
After prompting		1
Without prompting		2
Boot Menu		
Always show boot menu †	BootMenu=1	0
Continue booting after *xx* seconds †	BootMenuDelay=xx	30

† Enabled only if BootKeys=1.

In the Windows 98 Tweak UI, the former "Function keys available for x seconds" (with x adjustable by the user) is replaced by just "Function keys available" because the option to vary the BootDelay time is no longer supported. Although a `BootDelay=2` line still appears in the Windows 98 MSDOS.SYS file, changing the delay from 2 (seconds) to some other value has no effect.

Restore Factory Settings

This button restores the MSDOS.SYS file lines to the original factory settings listed in Table A-1. It does not however affect default settings not shown on the Boot tab.

Control Panel tab (Windows 98 only)

The Control Panel tab is yet more proof that the INI file is still with us. For example, if you use the Windows System Policy Editor (see Chapter 4) to restrict access to Control Panel's Network applet, the Network icon remains in place, but if you double-click it, a message advises that "Your system administrator disabled the Network control panel." But if the Tweak UI Control Panel tab's NETCPL.CPL checkbox is cleared, then the Network icon itself disappears from Control Panel. The Policy Editor writes its instructions into the Registry; Tweak UI doesn't (at least, not in this case). Instead, it adds a "netcpl.cpl=no" line in the [don't load] section of CONTROL.INI. But whether it's the Registry or the INI file, neither restriction will permanently stop the knowledgeable hacker from defeating it. However, the complete absence of the Network icon may deter the casual visitor from accidentally messing up your system.

Desktop tab

This tab displays a list of "Special desktop icons," even though a few of them are conventional object icons that appear by default on most Windows desktops. A typical list is given in Table A-2, along with the associated CLSID number for each object.

Table A-2 *Desktop Tab*

Tab Options	Registry Key Structure and Subkey Name
Special desktop icons	HKLM\SOFTWARE\Microsoft\Windows\ CurrentVersion\explorer\Desktop\ NameSpace\...
ActiveX Cache Folder	{88C6C381-2E85-11D0-98A8-0800361B1103}
Control Panel	(see "Create as File" section following this table)
Dial-Up Networking	{992CFFA0-F557-101A-88EC-00DD010CCC48}
Inbox	{00020D75-0000-0000-C000-000000000046}
Internet, The	{FBF23B42-E3F0-101B-8488-00AA003E56F8}
Internet Cache Folder	{7BD29E00-76C1-11CF-9DD0-00A0C9034933}
Internet Explorer	{871C5380-42A0-1069-A2Ea-08002B30309D}
Internet Mail	{89292102-4755-11CF-9DC2-00AA006C2B84}
Internet News	{89292103-4755-11CF-9DC2-00AA006C2B84}
Microsoft Network, The	{00028B00-0000-0000-C000-000000000046}
MSN (Microsoft Network)	{933E70D9-A6A2-11D0-826B-00AA00512BBF}

Continued

Table A-2 *Continued*

Tab Options	Registry Key Structure and Subkey Name
My Documents	{450D8FBA-AD25-11D0-98A8-0800361B1103}
Network Neighborhood	(see "Network Neighborhood Icon" section following this table) ‡
Printers	(see "Create as File" section following this table) †
Recycle Bin	{645Ff040-5081-101B-9F08-00AA002F954E}
Scheduled Tasks	{D6277990-E3F0-101B-8488-00AA003E56F8}
Shell Favorite Folder	{1A9BA3A0-143A-11CF-8350-444553540000}
Subscription Folder	{F5175861-E3F0-101B-8488-00AA00A45957}
URL History Folder	{FF393560-C2A7-11CF-BFF4-444553540000}

† Show on Desktop option disabled.
‡ Create as File option disabled.

Create as File Button DOS Filename	Long Filename	Extension
INBOX-1 .{00 0	Inbox.	{00020D75-0000-0000-C000-000000000046}
THEINT~1.{FB 0	The Internet.	{FBF23B42-E3F0-101B-8488-00AA003E56F8}
CONTRO~1.{21 <DIR>	Control Panel.	{21EC2020-3AEA-1069-A2DD-08002B30309D}
PRINTE~1.{22 <DIR>	Printers.	{2227A280-3AEA-1069-A2DE-09002B30309D}

Context menu options

If any object on the Desktop tab's Special desktop icons list is highlighted, its Context menu displays the options described in the following sections. If an option is disabled (see Table A-2), it is not supported by that object.

Show on Desktop If a checkmark appears next to this option, the box to the left of the object is also checked (and vice versa), the *CLSID* key name shown in Table A-2 is displayed as a subkey under the *HKLM\...\NameSpace* key structure, and the object's icon appears on the desktop. If the checkbox is cleared, the associated *CLSID* subkey under the *NameSpace* key is deleted, and the icon is removed from the desktop.

Create as File This Context menu option duplicates the action of clicking the "Create As File" button near the bottom of the Desktop tab. In either case, a zero-byte file is created at the location specified by the user — usually C:\Windows\Desktop — and its name takes the format shown by the first two examples under the "DOS Filename" section in Table A-2. Note that the extension is the CLSID number associated with the object, and that this extension does not appear under the object icon at the specified location.

An exception to the previously described file-creation examples is if the "Create As File" option is selected for either the Control Panel or printers, then a folder with that name is created instead, as shown by the last two examples under the "DOS Filename" section in Table A-2.

Once a file or folder has been created, it may be dragged to any convenient location, such as the Windows desktop or elsewhere. To remove the object icon later on, simply highlight it in Explorer and delete it.

As a convenient means of finding all such items, open Explorer's View menu, select Options (Folder Options in IE4), and then review the View tab options to make sure no file extensions are hidden. Now open any folder in Explorer view and click the Size button so that zero-byte files appear immediately below the list of folders. Any filename that still does not display an extension was probably created as previously described and may be deleted if no longer needed.

Rename If this option requires an explanation, it's time to turn the computer off and take a break.

Network Neighborhood icon

As one exception to the Desktop tab list described above, the Network Neighborhood checkbox does not place a *CLSID* subkey under the *NameSpace* key. Instead, if this checkbox is cleared, Tweak UI edits the Registry as described in the "Desktop Object Removal" section of Chapter 6. But first, the following message is displayed when the Apply button is clicked after clearing the checkbox:

> Removing the Network Neighborhood from the desktop has additional consequences which are not obvious. Would you like to see additional information about this?

The additional information points out that "hiding the Network Neighborhood icon will prevent Explorer from accessing resources via UNCs." The unexplained UNC (Universal Naming Convention) format identifies a network resource in the following manner:

\\network computer name\sharename\path\filename

However, anyone who takes the trouble to hide the Network Neighborhood should not be surprised to find that network resources are hidden. The additional information screen also notes that "In order to access network resources from Explorer, you need to map them to a drive letter." A Network folder may of course be mapped to a local drive letter, but this step is often unnecessary. In case of doubt, simply select Explorer's Network Neighborhood folder, search for the desired resource, and attempt to use it. If there's a problem, then try the drive mapping. If the problem persists, then the resource is not designed for network use.

Explorer tab

This tab displays the selection of radio buttons and checkboxes shown in Figure A-2 and described in the following sections.

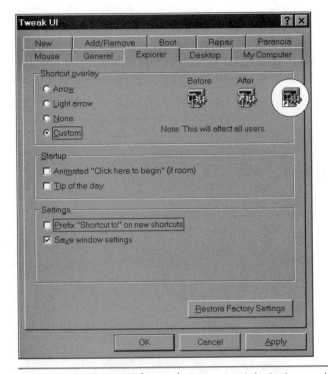

Figure A-2 *The inset (circled) shows the default shortcut icon, which has been replaced by a larger yet less obtrusive arrow (SHELL32.DLL, 30 in Windows 95 only). Clear the Prefix "Shortcut to" checkbox to eliminate the "Shortcut to" that by default precedes every shortcut icon title.*

Shortcut overlay

Under default conditions, a shortcut icon is identified by a small boxed arrow overlay in the lower left corner of the icon, and the Arrow radio button in the Explorer tab's Shortcut overlay section is enabled. If some other radio button in this section is clicked, that information is written into a subkey beneath the *HKLM\...\CurrentVersion* key, as shown in the "Shortcut Overlay" section in Table A-3. The number (29) in the Name column is associated with the Shortcut icon overlay, and the Data column identifies the new icon that now takes the place of the default overlay icon. The None icon is transparent and therefore invisible. When the Custom radio button is selected, a Change Icon window allows the user to select the desired icon, such as the large arrow overlay that was available in the Windows 95 SHELL32.DLL file (but not present in the Windows 98 SHELL32.DLL file). Because this change takes place in the *HKLM* section of the Registry, it affects all users, as indicated by a note in the Shortcut overlay section of the Explorer tab.

For more details on the Shell Icons Registry key, refer to the "Shell Icons Key" section and to Table 6-7 in Chapter 6.

Startup

When the Windows GUI opens, a welcome screen displays a "Did you know" tip, and a moving "Click here to begin" banner slides across the Taskbar toward the Start button. Each of these features is controlled by a subkey entry under the *HKCU\...\CurrentVersion* Registry key structure shown in the "Startup" section in Table A-3. In both examples, the default data entry is shown, and when the associated checkbox is cleared, the first byte (default state shown underlined) changes from 00 to 01, or vice versa. Note the inconsistency between the two settings: in the first example, the animated banner is not disabled (00 00 00 00), which might have been better written as StartBanner 01 00 00 00 to follow the style (and common sense logic) of the second example.

Settings

The checkboxes in this section write entries into the various subkeys listed in the "Settings" section in Table A-3. The Link entry is written into the *Explorer* subkey if the Prefix checkbox is cleared; if the checkbox is checked, the entire entry is deleted. The NoSaveSettings example is another of those Microsoft double-negatives; if Save window settings is enabled (checked), then NoSaveSettings is *not* enabled, as indicated by the Data string of zeros. As in the Startup examples in the "Startup" section of

Table A-3, the underlined byte changes from 00 to 01 if the checkbox is cleared.

Table A-3 *Explorer Tab*

Tab Options *	Subkey	Name	Data
Shortcut Overlay	HKLM\SOFTWARE\Microsoft\Windows\CurrentVersion\...		
Arrow (default)	*explorer\Shell Icons*	–	–
Light arrow	*explorer\Shell Icons*	29	TWEAKUI.CPL,2
None	*explorer\Shell Icons*	29	TWEAKUI.CPL,3
Custom	*explorer\Shell Icons*	29	User specified
Startup	HKCU\Software\Microsoft\Windows\CurrentVersion\...		
Animated "Click here to begin"	*Policies\Explorer*	NoStartBanner	<u>00</u> 00 00 00
Tip of the day	*Explorer\Tips*	Show	<u>01</u> 00 00 00
Settings	HKCU\Software\Microsoft\Windows\CurrentVersion\...		
Prefix "Shortcut to" on new shortcuts	*Explorer*	Link	<u>00</u> 00 00 00
Save window settings (Win95), or	*Policies\Explorer*	NoSaveSettings	<u>00</u> 00 00 00
Save Explorer window settings (Win98)	*Policies\Explorer*	NoSaveSettings	<u>00</u> 00 00 00
Adjust case of 8.3 filenames (Win98)	*Explorer\Cabinet State*	Settings (checked) Settings (cleared)	...<u>3A</u>... † ...<u>BA</u>... †
Color of compressed files (Win98)	*Explorer*	AltColor	00 00 ff 00 ‡

* Windows 95 and 98 versions of Tweak UI, unless otherwise noted.

† Indicates fifth of 12 bytes of binary data in Data column.

‡ Bytes 1–3 are RGB components of specified color. Byte 4 is zero.

Restore Factory Settings

This button restores the Shortcut overlay to the default small arrow icon, puts a check in each box, and rewrites the Registry entries as required.

General tab

This tab displays the checkboxes and other features illustrated in Figure A-3 and described in the following sections.

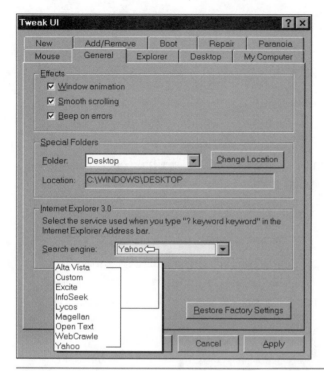

Figure A-3 *Click on the Search engine's down arrow to display a list of available search engines supported by Internet Explorer 3.0. In Windows 98, the "3.0" is not displayed.*

Effects

The checkboxes in this section write entries into the Registry under the subkeys listed in Table A-4, all of which appear under various *HKCU\...* key structures, as listed in that table.

Table A-4 *General Tab*

Tab Options	Subkey	Name	Data	Binary Equivalent *	
Effects	**HKCU\Control Panel\...**				
Beep on errors †	*Sound*	Beep	"Yes"	–	
Activation follows mouse ‡	*Desktop*	UserPreferenceMask	11	0001	0001
Menu animation	*Desktop*	UserPreferenceMask	12	0001	0010

Continued

Table A-4 *Continued*

Tab Options	Subkey	Name	Data	Binary Equivalent *	
Combo box animation	*Desktop*	UserPreferenceMask	14	0001	0100
List box animation	*Desktop*	UserPreferenceMask	18	0001	1000
Menu underlines	*Desktop*	UserPreferenceMask	30	0011	0000
X-Mouse AutoRaise	*Desktop*	UserPreferenceMask	50	0101	0000
Mouse hot tracking effects	*Desktop*	UserPreferenceMask	90	1001	0000
Show Win version on desktop	*Desktop*	PaintDesktopVersion	"1"	–	
Smooth scrolling †	*Desktop*	SmoothScroll	01	0000	0001
Window animation †	*Desktop\ WindowMetrics*	MinAnimate	"1"	–	
Special Folders	HKCU\Software\Microsoft\Windows\CurrentVersion\Explorer\...				
Windows default location is:	*Shell Folders*	Desktop	"C:\Windows\Desktop"		
Location (of Desktop folder)	*User Shell Folders*	Desktop	"(user-specified path)"		
Internet Explorer	HKCU\Software\Microsoft\Internet Explorer\...				
Search engine	*SearchURL*	(Default)	"http://av.yahoo.com..."		

* If binary equivalent is given, Data column shows byte 1 (of 4) only.
† Windows 95 and 98. All others are Windows 98 only.
‡ This option is on Mouse tab. Included here to show effect on Data.

Effects help   Refer to the "Animated Window" section of Chapter 6 for details about window animation, and use the popup help feature for information on Smooth scrolling and Beep on errors in Windows 95. In Windows 98, the help button reports that help is not available for any item in the Effects section, but that's not correct. Left-click any item to display the "What's This?" popup and then click on it to display a reasonably detailed help screen.

Special folders

The popup help text states that the location of certain "special folders" can be changed, which may suggest this option moves a folder from one location to another. But that's not quite what happens. Instead, the Folder box lists one of these special folders, and the grayed Location box beneath it indicates the source of the objects currently associated with that folder. The following examples show how this feature works.

By default, Windows displays various objects on the desktop, including those found in Explorer's C:\Windows\Desktop folder, such as Briefcase, Online Services, and the user's own desktop shortcuts and other objects. The default location of this Desktop folder appears in the *HKCU\...\Shell Folders* subkey, as shown by the first line in the "Special Folders" section in Table A-4. However, if the Desktop folder is selected in the General tab's Special Folders section and the Change Location button is clicked, then some other folder can be selected instead. This information is written into the *HKCU\...\User Shell Folders* key shown by the second line in the "Special Folders" section in Table A-4, and all objects (folders and files) in the new user-specified location are displayed on the desktop in place of those in the C:\Windows\Desktop folder. In other words, information written into the *User Shell Folders* key takes precedence over similar information in the *Shell Folders* key.

As one more example, a new C:\Windows\Start Menu\Programs\ StartUp2 folder might be created, with an alternate group of Startup shortcuts in it. Now select the Startup folder and change its location to the new StartUp2 folder. The next time Windows starts, the applications specified in that folder will be executed instead of those in the default StartUp folder. As in the previous example, the new Startup entry is written into the *HKCU\...\User Shell Folders* key.

Internet Explorer 3.0 (Windows 95), Internet Explorer (Windows 98)

If you type "? *keyword*" in the Internet Explorer's Address bar, the search engine specified here is used to search for the keyword you typed. The Registry records the appropriate information, as shown by the example in the "Internet Explorer" section in Table A-4.

Restore Factory Settings (Windows 95 only)

This button, which does not appear in the Windows 98 Tweak UI, restores the Effects and Internet Explorer sections to their original settings but has no effect on any changes made within the Special Folders section. If you need assistance restoring a default folder location, refer to the "Tweak UI Troubleshooting" section of Chapter 7.

IE4 tab (Windows 98 only)

This tab contains the single section described here.

Settings

In keeping with current events, most of the tweaks listed in this section have nothing to do with you-know-what. To cite one example, there's a checkbox for "Show Documents on Start Menu" which really means "Show Documents *option* on Start Menu." The documents themselves show up on a cascading menu if this option is selected, but there is no known connection between this tweak and Internet Explorer.

The checkboxes in this section write entries into the Registry under the *HKCU\...\CurrentVersion* subkeys listed in Table A-5.

Table A-5 *IE4 Tab**

Tab Options	Subkey	Name	Data †
Settings	HKCU\Software\Microsoft\Windows\CurrentVersion\...		
Active Desktop enabled	*Policies\Explorer*	NoActiveDesktop	00 00 00 00
Add new docs to Docs on Start Menu	*Policies\Explorer*	NoRecentDocsHistory	00 00 00 00
Allow Changes to Active Desktop	*Policies\Explorer*	NoActiveDesktopChanges	00 00 00 00
Allow Logoff	*Policies\Explorer*	NoLogoff	00 00 00 00
Clear document, run typed-URL history	*Policies\Explorer*	ClearRecentDocsOnExit	01 00 00 00
Detect accidental double-clicks	*Explorer\Advanced*	UseDoubleClickTimer	01 00 00 00
IE4 enabled	*Policies\Explorer*	ClassicShell	00 00 00 00
Show Documents on Start Menu	*Policies\Explorer*	NoRecentDocsMenu	00 00 00 00
Show Favorites on Start Menu	*Policies\Explorer*	NoFavoritesMenu	00 00 00 00

* Windows 98 only.

† Data value if indicated option is enabled (checked).

Mouse tab

The controls on this tab do not duplicate those available via Control Panel's Mouse applet, but instead add a few supplementary features that are briefly described in the following sections and listed in Table A-6.

The Windows 98 version of Tweak UI displays a mouse wheel section that is disabled (grayed) unless a Microsoft Intellimouse (or similar) is installed. For comparison purposes, the Mouse tab in the Windows 95 and Windows 98 Tweak UI applets are shown in Figures A-4 and A-5.

Table A-6 *Mouse Tab: HKCU\Control Panel\Desktop Entries*

Tab Options	Name	Data
Menu Speed		
Menu speed (Fast = 0, Slow = -2)	MenuShowDelay	400
Mouse Sensitivity		
Tab Options	**Name**	**Data**
Double-click	DoubleClickHeight	"4" †
	DoubleClickWidth	"4" †
Drag	DragHeight	"2"
	DragWidth	"2"
Use Mouse Wheel for Scrolling		
Use mouse wheel for scrolling (checkbox)	WheelScrollLines	"3" ‡
Scroll a page at a time (radio button), or	WheelScrollLines	"-1"
Scroll by x lines at a time (x is user-specified)	WheelScrollLines	"x"
Activation Follows Mouse		
Activation follows mouse	UserPreferenceMask	11 §

† Specified in half-pixel increments.
‡ Default value indicates checkbox enabled, three-line scroll set.
§ Byte 1 (of 4). See Table A-4 for other changes to this Data entry.

Menu Speed

This slider varies the Registry's MenuShowDelay setting, which is described in the "Cascading Menus" section of Chapter 6.

Mouse sensitivity

The two options listed here affect mouse movement.

Double-click The setting determines how far the mouse pointer may move between two clicks, which will still be considered a double-click action. Although the displayed Double-click range is 1–32 pixels, in one-pixel increments, Table A-6 shows that this data is written in half-pixel increments (x = 2-64).

Drag If an object is selected and the primary mouse button held down, the mouse pointer must be moved the specified distance before the selected object is dragged. You may want to increase the value if an object is dragged accidentally when you click on it. Unlike the Double-click option previously described, Drag data is written in one-pixel increments.

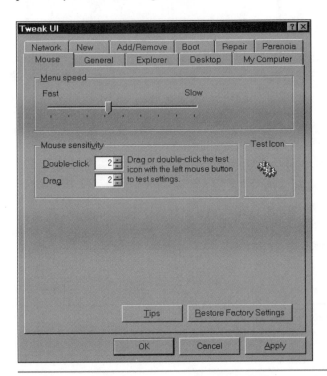

Figure A-4 *Tweak UI's Windows 95 Mouse tab adds a few features not found on Control Panel's Mouse applet but does not support additional features found in the Windows 98 version seen in Figure A-5.*

Use mouse wheel for scrolling (Windows 98 with mouse wheel device only)

The effect of these settings on the Registry is shown in Table A-6. Refer to the What's This? popup help for further details.

Check Box: Activation follows mouse (X-Mouse)

If you wonder what this means, the What's This? help offers the following unhelpful information:

The "Activation follows mouse" check-box enables X-Mouse style window activation.

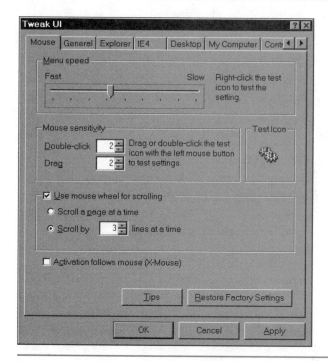

Figure A-5 *In Windows 98, the "Use mouse wheel for scrolling" section of the Mouse tab is enabled if the installed mouse supports this feature. This section is disabled (grayed) if a conventional mouse or trackball is installed.*

Or to put it another way, if you enable X-Mouse activation, then X-Mouse activation is enabled. If that's not sufficiently informative, just think of it as a "Mouse pointer activates window" option. If this is enabled (checked) and the mouse is moved across several open windows, the window under its pointer becomes active until the pointer moves beyond its boundaries. Note that this option shares the UserPreferenceMask entry line with the Effects options described in Table A-4 earlier in this appendix. And remember to disable it again when it gets to be a nuisance.

Tips

In lieu of the conventional help menu found on most Windows applications, Tweak UI's help is accessible via a Tips button that appears on the Mouse tab only. When the button is clicked, it leads to the expected Contents, Index, and Find tabs found on most other help screens. There may be a good reason for making help available via the Mouse tab only and for calling it "Tips" instead of "Help." But then again, there may not.

Other help is available via the help (question mark) button in the upper right corner of the Tweak UI window and also from the What's This? button, subject to the quirks cited in some of the other sections of this appendix.

Restore Factory Settings

The options are reset to the factory values shown in Table A-6.

My Computer tab

This tab displays a list of drives A–Z, with a checkbox next to each one, as shown in Figure A-6. If a checkbox is cleared, that drive letter (if present on the system) is not shown in the My Computer or Explorer windows, with the exception of drive C:, which continues to be displayed in any Explorer window. The list of disabled drive letters is written into the following Registry key:

HKCU\Software\Microsoft\Windows\CurrentVersion\Policies\Explorer

If selected drive letters are disabled via the My Computer tab, the data is written into the subkey's Contents pane as shown by the first line that follows:

Name	Data	Data Type	Comments
NoDrives	02 09 F3 00	Binary	Via Tweak UI
NoDrives	0x03ffffff (67108863)	DWORD	Via System Policy Editor

To verify the removed drive letters, reverse the data bytes (*only* in the Tweak UI example), convert them to their binary equivalents, and label each bit with a drive letter, in the reverse sequence shown here:

Hex Data	Binary Equivalent *					
00 F3 09 02	1 1 1 1	0 0 1 1	0 0 0 0	1 0 0 1	0 0 0 0	0 0 1 0
03 FF FF FF	1 1 1 1	1 1 1 1	1 1 1 1	1 1 1 1	1 1 1 1	1 1 1 1
Bit Number:	23 22 21 20	19 18 17 16	15 14 13 12	11 10 9 8	7 6 5 4	3 2 1 0
Drive letter:	X W V U	T S R Q	P O N M	L K J I	H G F E	D C B A

* Underlined byte (bits 31–24) not shown.

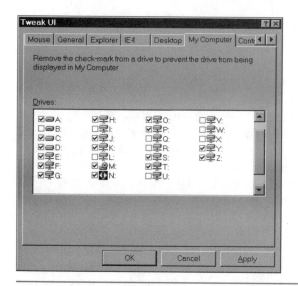

Figure A-6 *Clear any checkbox to remove that drive letter from My
Computer and Explorer windows. This four-column checklist is
actually a single column in the My Computer tab's Drive window.*

In the first example, the checkboxes next to drives B:, I:, L:, Q:, R:, and
U:–X: were cleared via Tweak UI's My Computer tab. For comparison purposes, the second line shows the effect of using the System Policy Editor's
Hide Drives option to restrict access to all drives, as previously described in
the System Policy Editor section of Chapter 4. If that option were in fact
used, then Tweak UI's My Computer tab would show that all drive letter
checkboxes were cleared.

As one more bit of Windows trivia, note that Tweak UI writes its data
in binary format, while the System Policy Editor does it as a DWORD.
The data is converted from one format to the other according to the most
recent means of access.

Note

The previously described NoDrives entry is the only Registry
edit that Tweak UI (or the user) makes when removing a drive
letter. However, there appears to be a side effect if the drive
B: checkbox on a Windows 98 system is cleared. As
expected, that drive letter is no longer seen in an Explorer
window. As *not* expected, the Start button Context menu's
first two options (usually, Open and Explore) are disabled
(grayed). The options are re-enabled when the drive B: box is
again checked.

Network Tab

This tab contains a single section: Logon.

Logon

This feature may be convenient on a PC configured for a password prompt at startup, but only if one person uses the system in a low-security environment. If so, put a check in the "Log on automatically at system startup" checkbox, enter the user name and password, and click the Apply button. The next time the opening password prompt window appears, Tweak UI automatically enters this information, and the Windows GUI opens without a pause for user input. In Windows 98, the "Clear last user" option (see "Paranoia Tab" below) must be cleared in order for the automatic logon to function.

Note that if this feature is enabled, the user's password is written into the Registry in unencrypted format, as shown in Figure A-7, where it can be viewed by anyone who has just finished reading this sentence. You may therefore want to delete this key if the system is to be left unattended and snoopers are in the neighborhood.

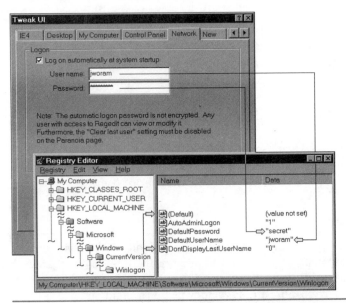

Figure A-7 *If the Network tab's "Log on automatically at system startup" box is checked, user name and password data is written into the Registry in an unencrypted format, which can be read by anyone who knows it's there.*

New tab

This tab can be used to create or remove a *ShellNew* subkey under one of the *HKCR* key's *Filename-Extension* subkeys. For example, if an HTM file residing on the desktop (or elsewhere) is dragged into the New tab's checkbox area, a *ShellNew* subkey is created under the *HKCR\.htm* key, and its Contents pane displays a FileName entry that cites the name of that HTM file. In addition, an "Internet Document (HTML)" or "Netscape Hyptertext Document" (or similar) entry is displayed in the checkbox list and also as an option on the desktop Context menu's cascading New option, as shown in Figure A-8.

If a checkbox is cleared, a minus sign is appended to the associated *ShellNew* subkey name (for example, *HKCR\.htm\ShellNew*), thus disabling that key until the checkbox is subsequently rechecked. If instead the object is highlighted and the Remove button is clicked, the associated *ShellNew* key is deleted from the Registry. However, the Remove button is disabled if that key's Contents pane contains a Command entry. Refer to the "ShellNew Key" section of Chapter 2 for details about this key.

Paranoia tab

If everyone picks on you, then this is definitely your tab, and you'll find it shown in Figure A-9.

Covering Your Tracks

In Chapter 4, the "INF File as a Registry Editor" and "Automated List Removal" sections described how to delete various history lists (and why you'd want to). The checkboxes in this section of Tweak UI make the task a bit easier by writing data into one of the Registry keys listed in Table A-7. Depending on which box is checked, the Contents pane entry with the uninformative Name of "1" shows one of the Data entries listed in Table A-7, where the "Binary Equivalent" column indicates the flag that is set for that Data entry. If more than one box is checked — and thus more than one flag is set — then the Data entry changes accordingly.

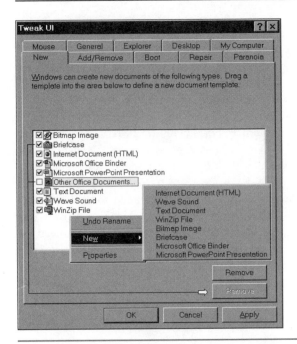

Figure A-8 *The New tab's document list shows items that may appear on the Desktop's New menu. Note that the cleared item (Other Office Documents) is missing from the cascading New menu shown in the inset. The Remove button is disabled if the selected item's ShellNew key contains a Command entry in its Contents pane, as in the Briefcase and Other Office Documents . . . objects shown here.*

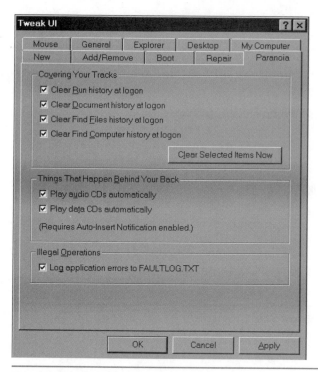

Figure A-9 *Windows now offers support to the suspicious user, as shown by this fully-utilized Paranoia tab.*

Table A-7 *Paranoia Tab*

Tab Options	Name	Data †	Binary Equivalent
Covering Your Tracks *			
HKCU\Software\Microsoft\Windows\CurrentVersion\Applets\TweakUI			
All boxes cleared	1	"0"	0000 0000
Run history	1	"1"	0000 0001
Find Files history	1	"2"	0000 0010
Find Computer history	1	"4"	0000 0100
Document history	1	"8"	0000 1000
Internet Explorer history	1	"16"	0001 0000
Network connection history ‡	1	"32"	0010 0000
Telnet history ‡	1	"64"	0100 0000

Continued

Table A-7 *Continued*

Tab Options	Name	Data †	Binary Equivalent
Windows 98: all boxes checked	1	"127"	0 1 1 1 1 1 1 1
HKLM\SOFTWARE\Microsoft\Windows\CurrentVersion\Winlogon			
Last User	DontDisplayLastUserName	"1"	
Things That Happen Behind Your Back	**HKCR\Audio\shell**		
Play audio CDs automatically	(Default)	"play" (or "" if disabled)	
Play data CDs automatically	See "Drive Media Icons" in Chapter 6.		
Illegal Operations			
HKLM\SOFTWARE\Microsoft\Windows\CurrentVersion\Fault			
Log applications errors . . .	LogFile	"C:\Windows\FAULTLOG.TXT"	

* All listed items are actually "Clear . . . at logon."
† Data value if only this option is enabled (checked).
‡ Windows 98 only.

Clear Selected Items Now Click the button with this name at any time to perform the desired Clear operations, which otherwise take place only at logon.

Things that happen behind your back

Perhaps so-named in keeping with the Paranoia theme, the features within this section require that Auto-Insert notification is enabled for your CD-ROM drive. To verify this, open Device Manager, select the specific drive, click on the Properties button, and select the Settings tab. Place a check in the "Auto insert notification" checkbox.

Play audio CDs automatically If this box is checked, the CD-audio applet (CDPLAYER.EXE) automatically plays an audio compact disc when it is inserted in the CD-ROM drive. The *HKCR\Audio\shell* Registry subkey determines the status of this function by editing the Contents pane data, as also shown in Table A-7.

Play data CDs automatically If this box is checked, a data CD-ROM disc will be recognized when it is inserted in the CD-ROM drive, provided it has an AUTORUN.INF file in its root directory. For further details, including a description of the associated Registry key and its Contents pane, refer to the "Drive Media Icons" section of Chapter 6.

The action of checking the checkbox clears the CD-ROM bit (bit 5) described in that section.

Illegal operations

Application errors should be illegal even for those who don't suffer from paranoia. But until the appropriate laws are passed, it's possible to log these errors as they occur.

Log application errors to FAULTLOG.TXT The *HKLM\...\ Fault* subkey is written into the Registry the first time this checkbox is checked. If the checkbox is subsequently cleared, the key remains in place, but the LogFile entry shown in Table A-7 is deleted.

Repair tab

Figure A-10 shows the five repair buttons that appear on this tab in Windows 95, while Windows 98 presents a drop-down menu with seven options on it. Each of these is briefly described here, although only the Repair Regedit button has much significance to the Registry.

Repair Associations

The Windows 95 popup and Windows 98 Description section both advise that this button/option returns Explorer icons to their factory settings and restores the default associations for standard file types. But in fact, it seems to have no effect on desktop icons. However, associations are restored to their default settings, and the opening welcome screen reappears the next time Windows opens.

Repair Font Folder

In order to function properly, the C:\Windows\fonts folder must contain a valid DESKTOP.INI file, and the folder must have its system attribute set. If a font-related problem occurs, click this button to repair any damage that may have affected this folder.

Rebuild Icons

Every now and then Windows gets a bit confused about the icons it's supposed to display, especially if the hidden ShellIconCache file contains erroneous data. Depending on the nature of the problem, clicking on this button may resolve it. Refer to the "ShellIconCache File" section of Chapter 6 for details about the purpose of this file.

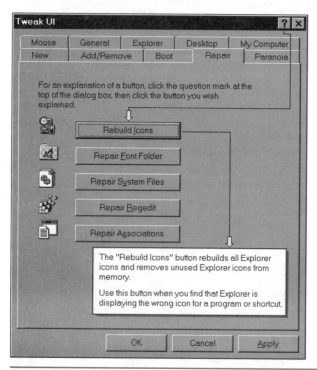

Figure A-10 *Click the question mark icon and then one of the five rebuild buttons to get an idea what that button offers. The inset at the bottom explains the function of the Rebuild Icons button on this Windows 95 Repair tab. In Windows 98, the same information is displayed in the Description section of the tab.*

Repair Regedit

Under normal conditions, the Registry Editor's vertical Split bar should be aligned so the Key pane is clearly visible, and the Contents Pane Name and Data columns should likewise be visible. To fix a problem with any of these items, close the Registry Editor, open Tweak UI, select the Repair tab, click the Repair Regedit button, close Tweak UI, and reopen the Registry Editor. Better yet, forget what you just read and make the adjustments manually. See the "Contents Pane Headings Missing" section in Chapter 7 for details.

Repair System Files

Some applications may replace a critical DLL or other file with another version, which could create a startup problem. Click this button to copy the correct versions of such files from the hidden C:\Windows\Sysbckup folder back to the C:\Windows\System folder.

Repair Temporary Internet Files (Windows 98 only)

This option is similar to the one described in the "Repair URL History" below, but it acts on the C:\Windows\Temporary Internet Files folder and the subfolders beneath it.

Repair URL History (Windows 98 only)

The Description section invites you to use this option ". . . when you find the URL History folder has lost its magic and is acting like a normal folder." The trained magician will know that there is no folder named "URL History" — the Description section is really referring to the C:\Windows\History folder (however, the properties for this folder do describe it as a "URL History" folder). This option may resolve minor problems with this folder, but it won't repair serious damage such as a missing *CLSID* key associated with the folder.

Tweak UI at Startup

Several Tweak UI options take effect as Windows opens, and if any of these are selected, the RUNDLL32.EXE file must execute the applet segment that tweaks the system into shape as specified by the selected options. To do so, Tweak UI writes an entry into one or both subkeys listed in Table A-8.

Table A-8 *Startup Features Supported by Tweak UI*

Tab Options	Subkey	Name	Data
Network	HKLM\SOFTWARE\Microsoft\Windows\CurrentVersion\...		
Log on automatically . . .	*RunServices*	Tweak UI	"RUNDLL32.EXE TWEAKUI.CPL, TweakLogon"
Paranoia tab	HKLM\SOFTWARE\Microsoft\Windows\CurrentVersion\...		
"Clear . . . at logon" (any)	*Run*	Tweak UI	"RUNDLL32.EXE TWEAKUI.CPL, TweakMeUp"

Index

Numbers

000x subkey, Config, 81

A

About Registry Editor option, Help menu, 15
Access code is invalid error message, 381
Access Denied message, troubleshooting, 342
Access subkey, Security, 94
Access to specified path, device, or file is denied
    error message, 394, 397
Accessibility subkeys, Status Indicator, 73
Action keys, 37–40
Add to Zip option, Context menu addition, 263
Add/Remove Programs applet, key structure
    deletion procedure, 210–213
Add/Remove tab, Tweak UI, 407
AddrArb subkey, address arbitrator, 100
Addresses subkey, RemoteAccess, 78
AFTER.REG file, file comparisons, 203–206
alignment, menu editing, 253–254
alternative real-mode recovery, troubleshooting,
    324
animated windows, creating, 298–299
AOL free software offer, nag screen, 352
AppEvent subkey, 69–73
Applets subkeys
    CurrentVersion, HKCU, 105–108
    CurrentVersion, HKLM, 109–114
applications
    current user software configuration, 78–80
    CurVer (current version) subkeys, 54–55
    Data subkey entries, 48–49
    dot-three (.xxx) file extension conventions, 24
    running only allowed, 175–176
AppPatches subkey, application patches, 98–99
Apps subkey, AppEvent, 71–72
Arbitrators subkey, Windows resource
    allocations, 100
ASCII file, INI files, 4
asterisk (*) subkey, 27–30
Attribute flags, described, 238–240
AudioCD subkeys, 51–52
AUTOEXEC.BAT file
    importing a file on startup, 222
    Registry elimination, 3
automated list, INF file removal procedure,
    168–169
automatic backups, Windows 95, 184–185
automatic imports, disabling, 152–154
AUTORUN.EXE file, 52–53
    drive media icons, 294–295
AVI files, single properties sheet pointer, 43

B

Backup (LastBackup) subkey, CurrentVersion,
    HKLM, 109
backup and restore e433rror message, 395–396
Backup cannot find this file error message, 395
backup files, Registry, 312
Backup.DA0 file, Registry backup recovery, 197
backups
    automatic, Windows 95, 184–185
    Backup (LastBackup) subkey, HKLM, 109
    Configuration Restore utility, Windows 95,
        198–199
    Content pane entry prior to editing, 143
    corrupted Registry files, Windows 98, 194
    Emergency Recovery utility, Windows 95,
        186–189, 199–201
    forcing, Windows 98, 192
    hard copy (print), 195–196
    real-mode, Windows 98, 194–195
    restore procedures, 196–203
    SCANREG.INI file, Windows 98, 192–193
    SYSTEM.1ST file, Windows 98, 194
    TAPECONTROLLER subkey, 91
    third-party restore utilities, 203
    third-party utilities, 195
    Windows 95 procedures, 183–189, 312
    Windows 98 procedures, 190–196, 312
    Windows 98 restore procedures, 201–203
BEFORE.REG file, file comparisons, 204–205
binary data, described, 17–18
binary searches, described, 147
binary value, described, 232
binary-DWORD data conversion, described, 18
BIOS subkey, plug-and-play BIOS, 85
bitmap thumbnail icons, Explorer window
    display, 286–287
BitsPerPixel (color depth), Settings subkey,
    HKCC\Display, 118
Boot tab, Tweak UI, 407–408
brackets [and] characters, HKEY naming
    convention, 22
Briefcase, ContextMenuHandler subkey
    installation, 27–28
briefcase (.bfc) subkey, ShellNew, 47
BriefcaseMenu subkey, 27–28, 63–64
BriefcasePage subkey, 30, 63–64

C

CAB files, 317
calling card accounts, Cards subkey, HKCU, 108
Cannot create key: Error while opening key
    My Computer error message, 381
Cannot delete keyname error message, 381
Cannot edit Name entry: Error reading the
    value's contents error message, 381
Cannot export path\filename.ext error message, 385

Continued